THE WAR
OF
THE RAVEN

THE WAR OF THE RAVEN

The career of
Kapitänleutnant Georg Gerth
1888-1970

CHRIS HEAL

Published by Chattaway and Spottiswood
Four Marks, Hampshire

candspublishing.org.uk
chrisheal@candspublishing.org.uk

All rights reserved. No part of this publication may be reproduced, stored in a retrieval system or transmitted, in any form or by any means, electronic, mechanical, photocopying, recording or otherwise, without prior permission in writing from the publisher.

© Chris Heal, 2023

The moral right of Chris Heal to be identified as the author of this work has been asserted.

This is a historical work of non-fiction. It is a much abridged version of *Sound of Hunger*, published in hardback by Uniform in 2018, ISBN: 978-1-911604-41-9, 754 pages, RRP: £30. The names, characters and quotes of the principal characters, events and incidents are taken from contemporary archives, except where stated otherwise.
Opinions about characters, events and incidents are the views of the author.

A catalogue record for this book is available from
the British Library.

ISBN 978-1-9161944-7-2

Design and typeset: Mary Woolley, www.battlefield-design.co.uk
Cover design, maps and advertisements: Paul Hewitt, www.battlefield-design.co.uk
Print liaison and website: Andy Severn, www.oxford-ebooks.com

Printed on demand: www.ingramspark.com

CONTENTS

Author's note		7
Introduction: Famine		9
List of maps		13
1	A passing view of extermination	21
2	War in the Baltic	28
3	*UB 12* and the attack on Sunderland	37
4	The execution of Charles Fryatt	48
5	Nightmare patrol	59
6	The loss of *Little Mystery*	64
7	A hectic day	81
8	Balance sheet	84
9	A visit to France	86
10	Lucky mine and a mishit	95
11	Gerth's sea war	102
12	On the beach	103
13	Coastguard Serin and the Belgian cavalry	120
14	Intelligence gift	150
15	Prisoners of War	192
16	Gerth's call for help	223
17	Amidst the ruins	248
18	Long arm of the war	269
Appendix 1: Crew of *UC 61* (26 July 1917)		285
Appendix 2: Abbreviations & common German words		291
Bibliography		293

Author's note

In 2016, I was asked by the Maritime Archaeology Trust, based in Southampton, to assist in a small way with a five-year Heritage Lottery-funded project as part of the Centenary of the First World War. The project was called *Forgotten Wrecks*, intended to chart and record some 700 South Coast sites that resulted from the conflict. My short-term assignment became a multi-year investigation that led to the u-boat war, famine as a weapon by both sides in the conflict and a close view of many of the characters involved in either plotting against or supporting the rise of Adolf Hitler.

At the heart of the story were two brothers from Berlin, both u-boat captains, Erich and Georg Gerth. The two men had very different wars. Erich began as a naval spy in South America and managed only one operational u-boat patrol in 1918 in the Mediterranean which was responsible eventually for many deaths. Georg fought through much of 1917 in the North Sea and the English Channel and became a prisoner of war.

The brothers' inter-war years could not have contrasted more: Erich caught up in society, the Freikorps and their murderous escapades and religious conflict between Lutherans, Jews and Catholics; Georg seeking the life of a hermit philosopher when his home city was fire-bombed by the British in a raid more devastating than Dresden.

At each new shocking and unexpected revelation, my co-researcher, Jacqui Squire, used to say, 'This is the story that keeps on giving.'

I wrote a book, *Sound of Hunger*, published in 2018, over 750 pages, a true doorstop, which told of all that we had found. Erich and Georg's careers allowed the inclusion of many of the awful things that that occurred before, during and after the war and as much context as I found useful. I wanted to explore events that were integral to the Gerth brothers, to see how they were altered by what they were taught and experienced. The part of *Sound of Hunger* that concerned *UC 61* was later translated into French (with additional material) by Lt Col Henri Lesoin in a book titled *La dernière patrouille de l'UC 61*.

This year, I was asked to extract the lives of Erich and Georg into two conventional paperbacks starting from the time when they finished their naval training and ending with their deaths: this book, *The War of the Raven*, is about Georg; its companion, S*aints & Sinners*, is about Erich.

They are fascinating and independent stories of how war, beliefs and the search for power and peace changes everything.

Introduction
FAMINE

Starving local populations to death was no new idea. The first recorded instance was during the Peloponnesian War in the fifth century BC. Whenever men fought, armies would surround unrepentant or fearful cities, cut off food and water supplies and wait. Citizens held out because of uncertainty as to their fate after a forced surrender.

Britain was probably the first power to implement a systematic, modern, naval blockade when, from 1756, the Royal Navy sealed off the major ports of Brest and Toulon with the goal of forcing the French fleet to fight the blockading force.[1] In 1793 and 1795, 1812-1814, and in the Crimean and Boer Wars, Britain stopped food shipments to its enemies.[2]

In 1899, the Polish military strategist Ivan Bloch argued that the future of war 'is not fighting, but famine, not the slaying of men, but the bankruptcy of nations and the break up of the whole social organisation'.[3]

At the beginning of the Great War, much emotive language was used to support the British blockade of Germany and its allies. Increasingly during the war, and during the blockade's continuance as a vital part of pressure brought to bear in the Versailles peace negotiations, the voices in opposition became strident. Its consequences in human terms were long-lasting and devastating. The blockade was not a 'starvation policy' for a town or localised area, but

---

1   Osborne, *Blockade*, p. 6. Mahan, *Influence of Sea Power upon the French Revolution*.
2   Hull, *Scrap of Paper*, p. 164.
3   Lambert, *Armageddon*, p. 2.

a preparedness to embrace 'untargeted mayhem'.[4] Almost a million civilians died and many more had their mental capacities blighted.

According to Winston Churchill, the intent was to treat 'the whole of Germany as if it were a beleaguered fortress', and avowedly sought to 'starve the whole population – men, women, and children, old and young, wounded and sound – into submission'.[5]

Sir Charles Ottley, secretary to the Director of Naval Intelligence, prophesised that British sea power would slowly grind the German people 'exceedingly small' and that 'grass would sooner grow in the streets of Hamburg'. He confidently predicted that 'wide-spread dearth and ruin would be inflicted' upon Germany.[6]

In the beginnings of a response, in November 1914, Admiral Tirpitz told an American journalist that Germany had the means in the form of u-boats to intercept the bulk of Britain's food imports. The German Press began to agitate for 'employing the new weapon'.[7] The call became a *mêlée* of prominent financiers, shipping and industrial magnates, politicians, and scientists.[8]

Two distinguished German professors from the University of Berlin added that Britain 'with brutal frankness has established the starvation of our population as a war aim'.[9] If German proposals were going to violate international law, Britain had set the precedent. The scholars explained how much Britain depended on imports and recommended a 'combined air and undersea attack with u-boats to destroy shipping and Zeppelins to attack food warehouses in the ports'.

Trade means exchange of goods. If Germany lived by selling her products to Britain, Britain lived equally by selling her products to Germany. Germany was beaten because she was dependent for her very existence on trade with her enemies. But Britain cut Germany off from all alternative sources, and so starved her out; but there were moments during the war 'when Germany, by her submarine campaign, came so near to cutting us off,' said George Bernard Shaw, 'that for some months we read the lists of sunken ships with our hearts

---

4 Devlin, *Too Proud to Fight*, pp. 158-67, 191-200.
5 Churchill, *World Crisis*, 1915, p. 215.
6 Offer, *Agrarian Interpretation*, p. 232.
7 Offer, *Agrarian Interpretation*, p. 354.
8 Tarrant, *U-Boat Offensive*, p. 14.
9 Offer, 'Bounded Rationality', p. 183.

in our mouths. It was a frightful starving match, and for nearly a year we were racing neck to neck, or at least seemed to be; for we did not know how impossible it was for Germany to keep up her submarine fleet'.[10]

One can understand if the British blockade was viewed retrospectively for many years as nationally awkward and not greatly discussed.

'The very existence of the struggle is probably unsuspected by the majority of Englishmen.'[11] What began in 1914 was of a different scale and scope from anything before attempted using the economy of, initially, one nation to beggar another. At the time, the strategy of stopping the flow of food and raw materials, of communication and finance, into an enemy state was presented not as an innovation, but as an 'age-old' weapon of war.[12]

Much of the blockade's detail and its effects were kept secret until after the Second World War. The British later admitted looking 'to the use of every possible weapon, legal and illegal, by which the Central Powers could be starved out'.[13] In 1937, the First Lord of the Admiralty, Alfred Duff Cooper, stated '… we did everything in our power to starve the women and children in Germany.'[14]

There is now considerable material available at British, French, American and German archives and the blockade has been slowly but increasingly subject to serious academic review. However, even today, it is more the property of historians than the man-in-the-street.

This book concerns the small part played by one minor German u-boat captain and his crew as his nation responded to a threat to their very existence. The research centres on long hours studying original American, Belgian, British, French, German and Swiss archives.

---

10   Shaw, 'Preface', in Richter, *Family Life*, pp. 7-8.
11   Consett, *Triumph of Unarmed Forces*, p. ix.
12   Weinreb, *Modern Hungers*, p. 16.
13   Peterson, *Propaganda*, p. 83.
14   *Time*, 2/8/1937, p. 17.

List of maps   Page

Journey to South West Africa, 1912
(Chapter 1)   15

Naval action against Sunderland, *UB 12*, 1916
(Chapter 3)   16

Second, third and fourth patrols with *UC 61*, 1917
(Chapters 6-11)   17

Third Battle of Ypres and the failure to capture the u-boat canals, 1917
(Chapter 12)   18

Final patrol in *UC 61*, 25-26 July 1917
(Chapters 12-13)   19

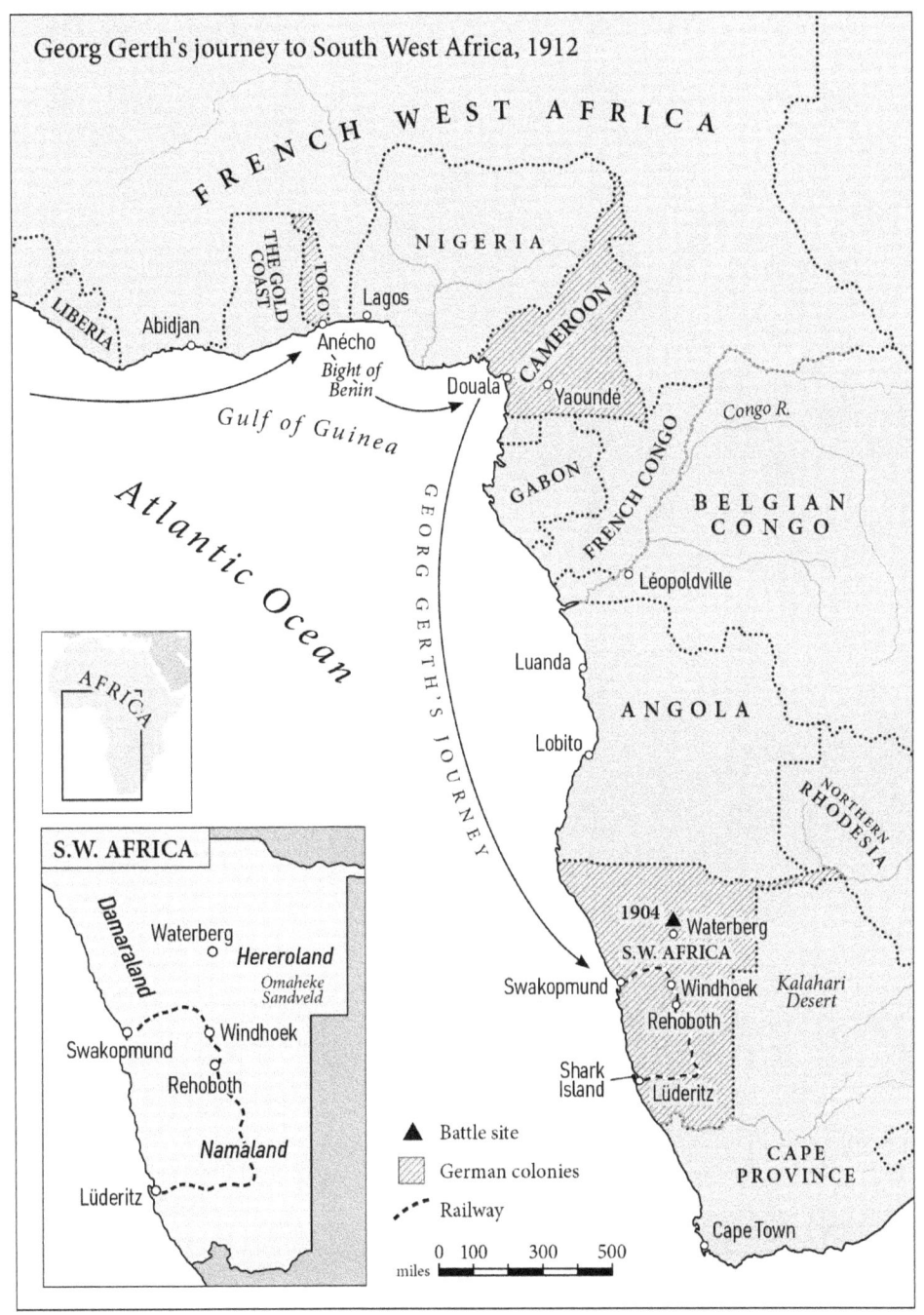

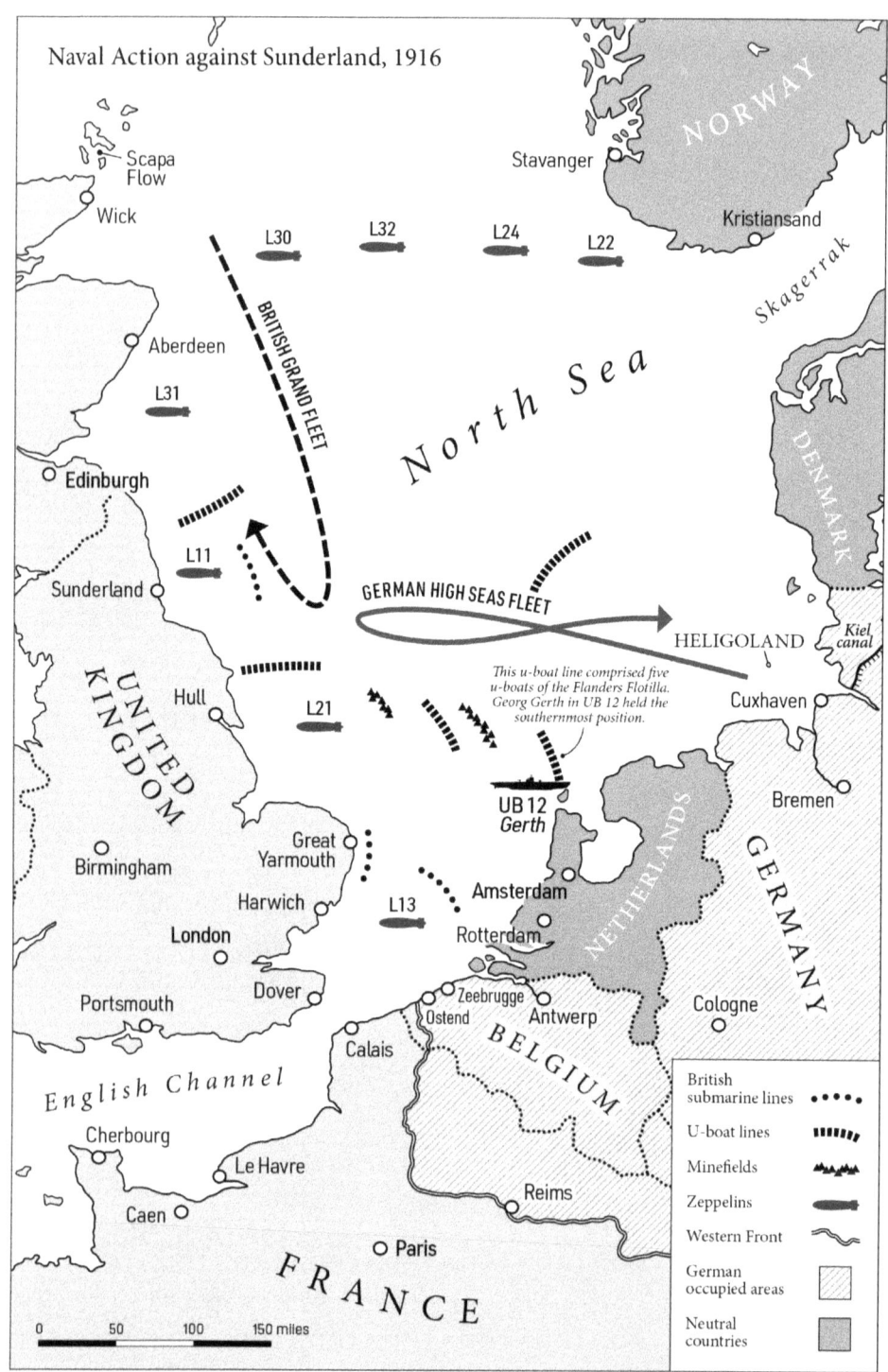

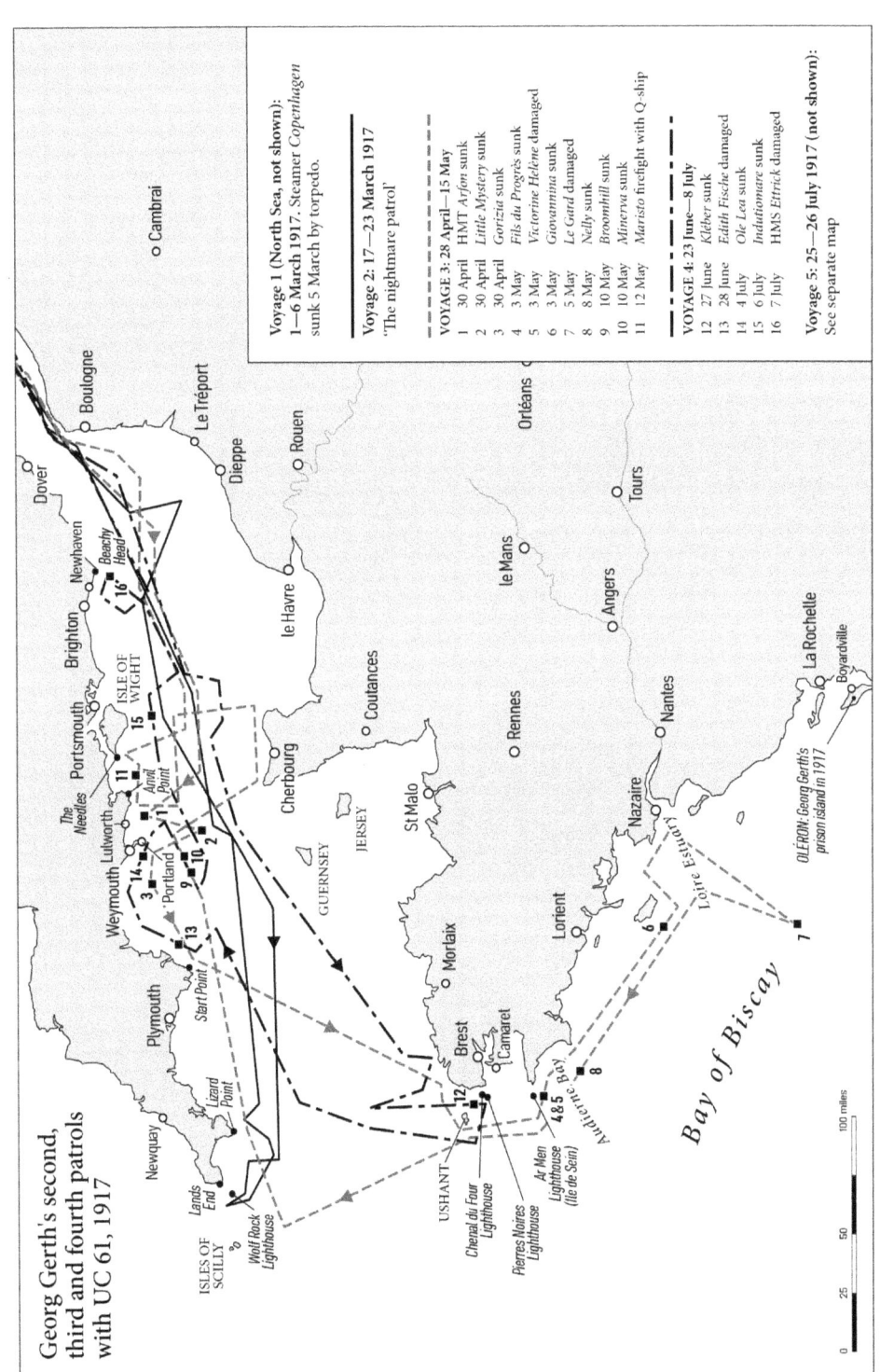

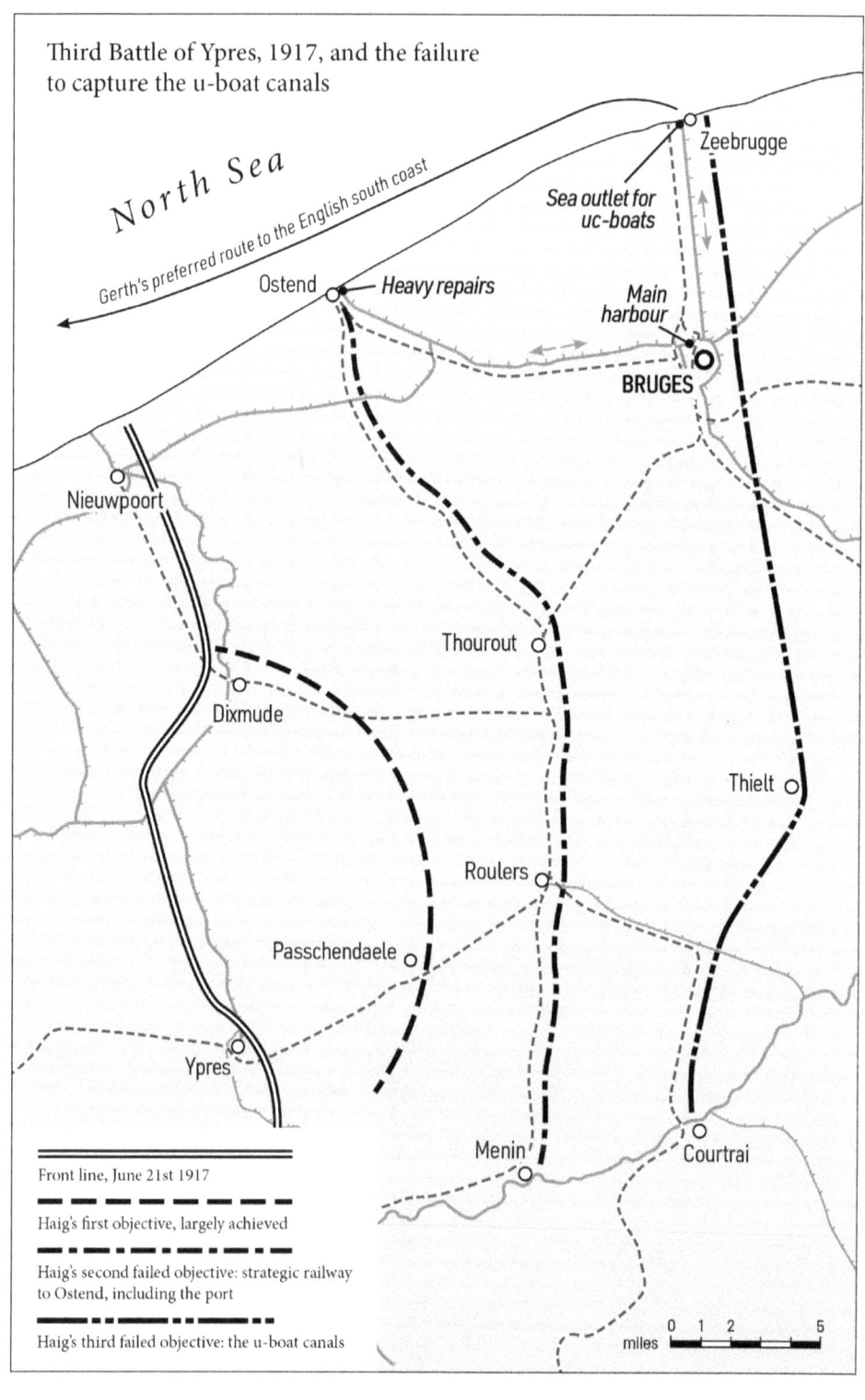

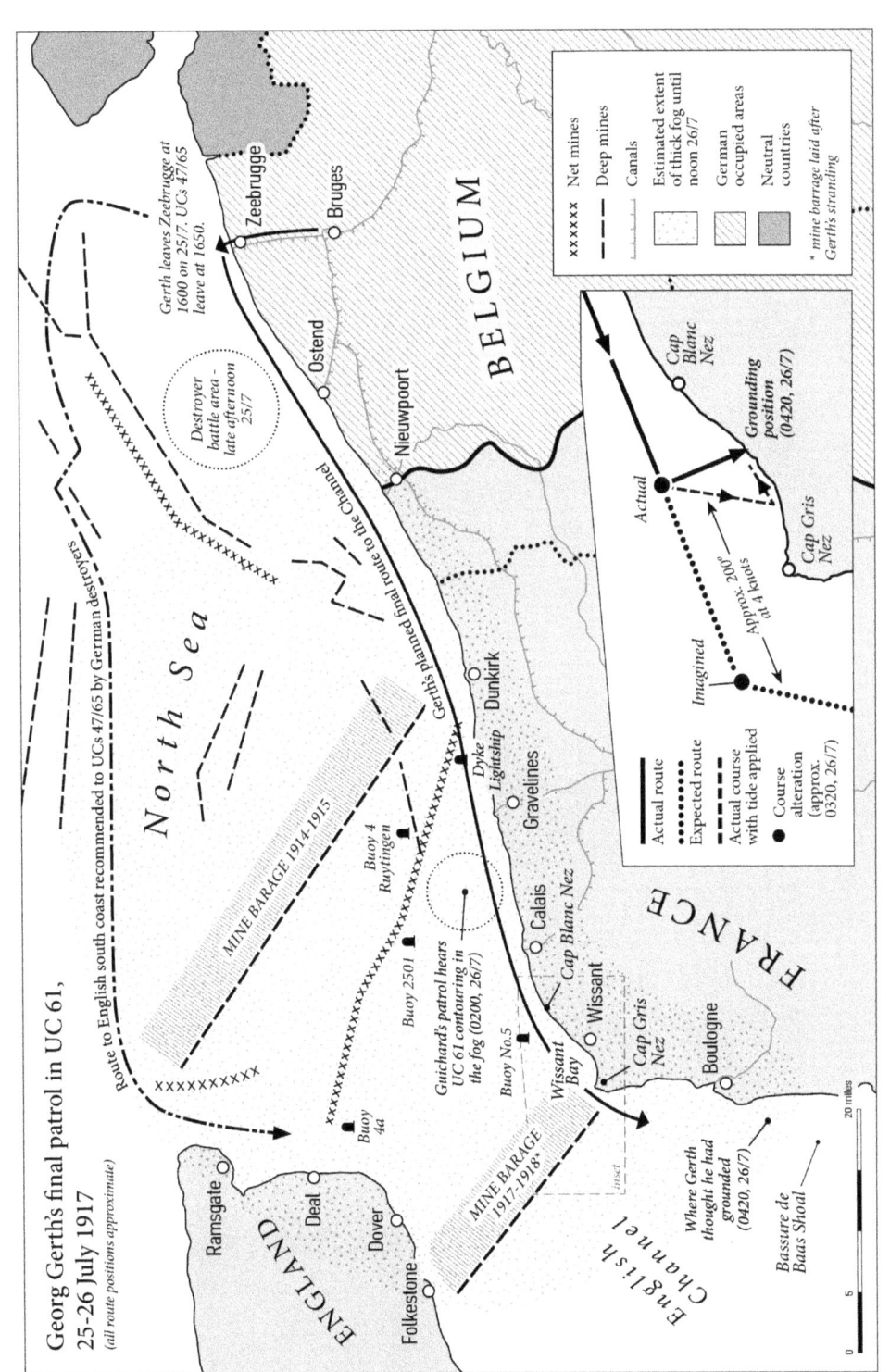

1
A PASSING VIEW OF EXTERMINATION

Georg Gerth's first seagoing appointment was for just over two years, until the end of 1911, on the *Preussen*, a pre-dreadnought battleship and 'good sea boat'. *Preussen* was a result of Tirpitz's 1898 Naval Law furthering the race to supremacy at sea against the British. During Gerth's service she was stationed in Wilhelmshaven and Kiel as part of the Second Battle Squadron.[1]

Gerth then spent the whole of 1912 in a coveted posting as a junior officer aboard the *Panther* on the West African station. *Panther* was one of six Iltis-class gunboats built for service in Germany's colonies with a range of just under 4,000 miles and a complement of nine officers and 121 crew.

Panther had an interesting early career in a number of trouble spots. The year of her commissioning, 1902, she sank a rebel ship which had hijacked a German steamer carrying weapons to the Haitian government. A few months later, she took part in the naval blockade of Venezuela where later she bombarded Fort San Carlos near Maracaibo. *Panther* received considerable damage in return fire from, ironically, the Krupp gun within the fort and was forced to retire. In 1905, *Panther* sent men ashore to search for a German deserter at the Brazilian port of Itajahy, where, somewhat farcically, they kidnapped the wrong man. The incident became known as the 'Panther Affair'.

---

1   Gröner, *German Warships*, Vol. I, pp. 14-16, 104-5, 105-6.

In 1911, *Panther* became notorious when she was sent to Agadir during the Second Moroccan Crisis. The ship's mission was to apply pressure on the French as they attempted to colonise Morocco, and also to extract compensation in French Equatorial Africa for Germany's loss of influence in North Africa. By the time of Gerth's service, the boat's duties took her to Togo, the Cameroons and to South-West Africa, all seized by the Germans in 1884, where she paraded as a statement of naval might.

Georg Gerth travelled to join *Panther*, probably, aboard a steamer of the Woermann Line, one of the largest German shipping companies trading into Africa. Woermann made their early money by supplying cheap potato spirit to African natives and the company used its knowledge of West African ports to advise and assist the German government on colonial acquisitions. The firm was also complicit in the South-West African death camps during the Herero and Nama wars.[2]

This was Georg's first trip outside Europe and might have been a tug on his emotions and political ideas had he known what he was looking at as his transport steamed by.

The Republic of Liberia began in 1822 as a settlement of the American Colonization Society which believed black people would face better chances for freedom in Africa than in America. Almost 20,000 freed and free-born black people returned to Africa. Liberia declared its independence in 1847, but was not recognised by the USA until 1862 during the American Civil War.

Gerth then passed the recently-acquired German colonies of Togo and Cameroon and traversed the Bight of Benin and the Guinea coast from where Europeans had bought upwards of ten million slaves. Next came the Belgian Congo, Leopold's previous fiefdom, with atrocities still underway in its interior and, finally, to German South-West Africa which was in the dying days of its own particular genocide. In one of the few memories of this time, Christa-Maria, Georg's daughter, remembers her father describing African huts and the general living conditions of the natives.

One might expect a large detachment of the crew of the *Panther*, the symbol of German naval power in the region, to be at Windhoek on 27 January 1912, having travelled by the new slave-built railway from the coast at Swakopmund. It was the Kaiser's birthday, an event 'always celebrated with a degree of

---

2   Olusoga & Erichsen, *Kaiser's Holocaust*, pp. 40, 167.

patriotic fervour in South-West Africa'. However, this was a special occasion centred on the unveiling of the 'Rider Statue', a *Schutztruppe*, a colonial trooper, in uniform.

Around seven o'clock in the morning, before the summer heat, citizens passed along Kaiser-Wilhelmstraße with window displays of imported luxuries, Gartenstraße where hot water springs fed the new swimming pool, and through the Memorial Gardens with its manicured lawns and duck ponds. The main speaker was the new governor, Theodore Seitz, who explained that the statue was to honour the dead and to encourage the living to build on what had been a hard war, 'fought selflessly for the love of the Fatherland' against the native population. The venerated soldier announced to the world that 'we are masters of this place, now and for ever'.[3]

> *What had once been the home of the Herero was now a European city in miniature ... The Germans were masters not only of South-West Africa's future, but of its past. Their version of the war had been set in stone and was now cast in bronze. The inauguration of the Rider Statue was the culmination of the process of historical denial and distortion. The brutality of the settlers in the years leading up to the war, General von Trotha's Extermination Order and the concentration camp system were expunged from official history.*[4]

The Herero were cattle herders in the area known as Damaraland; their southern neighbours and traditional enemies were the pastoral Nama, related to the Hottentot. In 1883, Franz Lüderitz fraudulently bought a stretch of coast from the local chieftain. Twenty years of inter-tribal fighting, skirmishes with German settlers and various broken treaties resulted in some of the Nama under Henrik Witbooi rising against the Germans in 1903, mainly over land rights.

By this time, the Herero were seen by many Germans as cattle thieves and a source of slave labour while others called for their extermination.[5] The Herero rebellion, under paramount chief Samuel Maharero, began in January 1904 along the railway line from the coast to Windhoek.[6] There is good evidence

---

3   *Kolonial-Post*, 1937, p. 6.
4   Olusoga & Erichsen, *Kaiser's Holocaust*, pp. 231-32.
5   Bridgman, *Revolt of the Hereros*, p. 130.
6   Pakenham, *Scramble*, Chapter 33, 'Kaiser's First War'; Olusoga & Erichsen, *Kaiser's Holocaust*, Chapters 8-9, 'Rivers of Blood and Money', 'Death Through Exhaustion'.

that the bitter fighting which followed was sparked by a Lieutenant Ralph Zürn, the local station commander, who was renowned for his 'utter contempt for the Herero'. Herero fighters pursued unpunished German rapists, killed settlers in their beds, burned farms, and the German garrisons were 'desperately assailed'. *Panther*'s predecessor, the gunboat *Habicht*, landed eighty-five marines; 500 marine volunteers followed in February and twenty-seven of these were killed in the fighting.

Kaiser Wilhelm sent General Lothar von Trotha, 'man enough not to let moral or political qualms cloud his judgement', to crush the revolt 'by fair means or foul'. When the civilian governor Hermann von Wissmann learned that Trotha was being considered as commander, he tried to prevent the appointment. He called Trotha 'a bad leader, a bad African, and a bad comrade'.[7] After murderous service in East Africa, Trotha was in China as part of the international force to quell the Boxer Uprising. He was present at the public execution of the assassins of German ambassador Baron Wilhelm von Ketteler in Peking and led the punitive expedition to the Ming graves to punish Boxers for killing Chinese Christians.

By August, most of the Herero had concentrated in a strategic dead end, the Waterberg plateau, a stony upland on the western edge of the Omaheke sandveld, leading to the great Kalahari desert. The Battle of Waterberg was deliberately indecisive and the Herero escaped through a gap carefully left in Trotha's net. When the Herero had been hustled into the desert, Trotha sealed off the last waterhole to ensure they died of thirst.

> *A great number, especially the old, ill and women and children, died of starvation and thirst as they ran for their lives through the desert. But a great many were also shot to death, for the conduct of the war changed with the Battle of Waterberg. The brutal potential of colonial war, sporadically evident now burgeoned into methodical regularity ... Trotha issued orders that no quarter was to be given to the enemy. No prisoners were to be taken, but all, regardless of age or sex, were to be killed.*
>
> *Trotha said, 'We must exterminate them, so that we won't be bothered with rebellions in the future' ... 'The Germans killed thousands and thousands of women*

---

7   Hull, *Absolute Destruction*, pp. 26-27.

and children along the roadsides ... I saw this every day.' After the battle, Trotha assembled the few prisoners and hanged the men.⁸

In October, Trotha issued his infamous Extermination Order 'of which there are few parallels in modern European history outside of the Third Reich':

> *I, the Great General of the Mighty Kaiser, von Trotha, address this letter to the Herero people. The Herero are no longer considered German subjects. They have murdered, stolen, cut off ears and other parts from wounded soldiers, and now refuse to fight on, out of cowardice. I have this to say to them ... the Herero people will have to leave the country. Otherwise I shall force them to do so by means of guns ... Every Herero whether found armed or unarmed, with or without cattle, will be shot. I shall not accept any more women or children. I shall drive them back.*

The Germans then turned their attention to a short war with the Nama. Late in 1906, after three days in the fetid hold of a Woermann Line steamer, two thousand Nama prisoners were offloaded at Lüderitz and marched in single file along the narrow causeway to Shark Island to join the thousand existing Herero inmates. It was a concentration camp, but rather an extermination camp, one of six across the country, of the utmost brutality, without facilities, a place where the captive local population was taken to be worked and starved to death and which they did at a daily body count of over twenty.

The camp was plainly visible to the white inhabitants of Lüderitz. An industry developed around the supply of body parts.

'In the Swakopmund concentration camp in 1905, female prisoners were forced to boil the severed heads of their own people and scrape the flesh off the skulls with shards of broken glass'.⁹ The camp physician at Shark Island, Dr Hugo Bofinger, used the inmates for his studies into scurvy which was endemic in the camp.¹⁰ He injected his living subjects with a range of substances,

---

8   Hull, *Absolute Destruction*, pp. 46-49, 56-57.
9   Olusoga & Erichsen, *Kaiser's Holocaust*, Chapter 12, 'The Island of Death'.
10 In 1914, Bofinger was the garrison physician in Stuttgart (Frowde, *History of Medicine*). See also, from 1913, the work of Eugen Fischer, *Die Rehobother Bastards*, the first successful application of modern Mendelian genetics to human anthropology. Rehoboth was a town fifty miles south of Windhoek which contained a mixed-race tribe, the Bastars, pushed out of the Cape by the Boers. Fischer was a German professor of medicine, anthropology and eugenics and, later, a member of the Nazi Party. He was director of the Kaiser Wilhelm Institute of Anthropology, Human

including arsenic and opium, and then performed autopsies to gauge the results. Bofinger also sealed skulls preserved in alcohol in tins for export to the Institute of Pathology at the University of Berlin where they were used by racial scientist Christian Fetzer in experiments designed to demonstrate the anatomical similarities between the Nama and the anthropoid ape.

Shark Island can certainly be placed in the same sentence as Auschwitz and Buchenwald.

Georg Gerth would have known some of the horror of his South-West African destination from spirited public debate in Germany. In 1906, Georg Lebedour, a deputy of the Social Democratic party, raised the issue of the Shark Island death camp in the Reichstag.[11] Debates in 1906 and 1907 'about the annihilation of some of the natives and the total slavery of others' led to a bitter impasse and the defeat of the colonial budget.

There was genuine horror at the activities of the government and the army in South-West Africa. The Reichstag elections of 1907 were fought on a single issue, South-West Africa.[12] It became known as the 'Hottentot election', so called because of the nationalist atmosphere whipped up by the Pan-Germans during the campaign. The Social Democrats gained half a million votes and yet lost half of their seats.

The remainder of the Herero population was reduced by 1907 to about 20 per cent of its size and was living out of sight in desert camps when Gerth arrived in 1912; they were 'discovered' in 1915 by 'shocked' South African troops when they invaded the colony.[13]

From Zurich, Christian philosopher and pacifist, F W Förster, warned that the world was entering a new era of wars; the new conflicts were radically different from the old type of war. 'They arose in the midst of industrial and power and science. Their political doctrine was imperialism, the doctrine of the

---

Heredity, and Eugenics, and was appointed rector of the Frederick William University of Berlin, now Humboldt University, by Adolf Hitler. Fischer's ideas informed the Nuremberg Laws of 1935 which served to justify the Nazi Party's belief in German racial superiority. Hitler read Fischer's work while he was imprisoned in 1923 and used it to support the ideal of a pure Aryan society.

11 Olusoga & Erichsen, *Kaiser's Holocaust*, pp. 221-22.
12 Hobson, *Imperialism at Sea*, p. 316.
13 *Whitaker Report*, United Nations Economic and Social Council Commission on Human Rights, 2/7/1985. Nuhn, *Sturm über Südwest: Der Hereroaufstand von 1904*, stated that because in 1904 there were 40,000 Herero living in German South-West Africa and therefore, 'only 24,000' could have been killed. Sarkin-Hughes, *Colonial Genocide and Reparations Claims in the 21st Century*, puts the number at 100,000.

military conquest and economic exploitation of weaker races. The American war against Spain and the British war against the Boers were mere preludes of the new imperialist era and its devastating conflicts.'[14]

After a year on the West Africa Station, Gerth left at the beginning of 1913 for the Baltic and a tour aboard the torpedo training ship, *Württemberg*. His return, presumably, included some time on leave in Berlin to see his mother and to give her some African gifts.

In 2021, Germany agreed to pay Namibia €1.1bn as it finally officially recognised the Herero-Nama genocide in what Angela Merkel's government said amounted to a 'gesture of reconciliation but not legally binding reparations'.[15]

---

14 Koebner, *Imperialism*, p. 247.
15 *The Guardian*, 28/5/2021.

2
WAR IN THE BALTIC

We junior sub-lieutenants dreamed of flying and submarines, of destroyers and airships, as it seemed such hard lines to waste one's life as a watchkeeper in a sword belt on the quarter-deck of a moored ship of 23,000 tons whilst one's comrades-in-arms and friends waged the war which drained the life blood of all young Germany.[1]

On Saturday, 1 August 1914, the German ambassador at St Petersburg delivered his country's declaration of war to Russia in its first formal act of 'defensive aggression'.

The day before, Georg Gerth, an oberleutnant with less than one year's seniority, reported as watch officer to his latest ship, *SMS Amazone*. This was a ship in decline and surely not the prestige posting of Georg's dreams. *Amazone* was launched in 1900 in Kiel at a cost of just under five million German Reichsmark, one of ten members of the *Gazelle* class, the first modern light cruisers for Tirpitz's Imperial Navy.[2] Her days in the overseas reconnaissance force of the High Seas Fleet with a full complement of thirteen other officers and 243 enlisted men, had just ended. *Amazone* was to start the war as a coastal defence ship; too worn out, too slow at a reducing twenty-one knots, too lightly

---

1   Niemöller, *From U-boat*, p. 18.
2   Herwig, *'Luxury' Fleet*, p. 28.

armed with ten 10.5cm guns and two torpedo tubes, and too thinly-armoured with a deck less than an inch thick to withstand dreadnought weaponry.[3]

In another two years, even this limited coastal assignment was too onerous for *Amazone*. She was stripped of her guns and designated a u-boat training ship. The following year, in 1917, she no longer went to sea and sat out the war as a barracks for navy regiments.[4]

Gerth's previous ship, *SMS Württemberg*, another aged lady, a twenty-three-year-old armoured frigate, was based in Kiel.[5] His new posting meant a move about 500 miles along the Baltic coast to Danzig, modern day Gdańsk in Poland. *Württemberg*, in use as a torpedo and test ship since 1906, was the last of the four Sachsen class boats, the others all taken out of active service in 1910 and used as target hulks for the fleet. Here, on the south-eastern shore of the Baltic Sea, Gerth spent eight months honing and passing on his newly-gained torpedo skills to naval ratings and sea cadets. Altogether, Gerth was to spend over two-and-a-half years based in the Baltic, with just four eventful months on the *Amazone*.

The Baltic, despite its surface area being equivalent to almost 75 per cent of the North Sea, is one of the lesser known seas of Europe to those who do not live nearby. It connects to the North Sea through the Kattegat, controlled by Denmark, and the Belt Seas, with their dangerous rocks and narrow and shallow channels. Because there is little tidal flow into the Atlantic, Baltic water is brackish and, as a result, almost half of its surface can ice over in winter. Its major cities include Copenhagen, Stockholm, Helsinki and St Petersburg.

The significance of the Baltic area in 1914 was both military and commercial. It was a maritime and land front between Germany, which since reunification in 1871 occupied much of the southern coast including modern-day Poland, Lithuania, Latvia and Estonia, and with Russia, which controlled Finland. There were many German ports: Danzig, Eckernförde, Kiel, Königsberg, Memel (modern day Klaipėda), Libau (from 7 May 1915, modern day Liepāja), Lübeck, Riga (from 3 September 1917) and Stettin, connected to Berlin by canal.

---

3   Gröner, *German Warships*, Vol. 1, pp. 91-102.
4   *SMS Amazone* may have been old, but she was long-lived. One of six cruisers permitted to the Reichsmarine after Versailles, she went back to active duty during the 1920s and served again as a barracks ship in the 1950s and was finally broken for scrap in 1954.
5   Gröner, *German Warships*, Vol. 1, pp. 7-8.

All of these were of strategic significance for safe military shipbuilding, including the u-boat fleet, for relatively secure open water for naval training, and for protected commerce. Being nearest to the Baltic's exit allowed Germany to bottle up Russia's capital ships in the Gulf of Finland. The Germans used their Baltic navy to bombard Russian-controlled cities, like Riga and Reval, modern day Tallinn, to support military advances.

Russia was forced to find alternative supply routes: by railway through Sweden and Finland; in ice-free months, around the top of Norway to Archangel; lengthy journeys from the Crimea if the Bosphorus could be passed; and from Russia's eastern seaboard on the Pacific Ocean.

The Kaiser Wilhelm Canal, sixty-one miles long, from Kiel to Brunsbüttel was opened by the Emperor in 1895 and provided Germany with a direct route within its own territory from the Baltic to the North Sea. By 1914, the canal had been widened to take dreadnought battleships. Neutral Sweden and, for different political reasons, Russian-occupied Finland, had significant pro-German elements in their populations.[6] The Baltic provided Germany with the easiest route to trade with Scandinavia. Through neutral Norway and Denmark, Germany received vital food and war supplies which often originated in Allied countries or the United States. Pro-German Sweden underpinned the German war effort by, particularly, swopping iron ore from Lulea for coal. The main danger to these sea transfers came from Russian and British submarines.

It was in this Baltic maelstrom of politics and weather that Gerth and the *Amazone* were to guard the Baltic against Allied submarine attacks. The British declined to send surface ships through the Skagerrak and the heavily-mined Kattegat and instead decided in October 1914 to send three submarines to operate alongside the Russians at their base at Lapvik.[7] Only two, *E 1* and *E 9*, made it; the third *E 11* found the defences of the Belt too alert and aborted.

On 18 October, the first day of entering the Baltic, *E 1* fired two torpedoes at the armoured-deck cruiser, *Victoria Louise*, like *Amazone* reduced through age to coastal defence; both missed, one narrowly astern and the second ran down

---

6 One of Georg Gerth's sea cadet classmates in the Crew of 1907 Horst von Pflugk-Harttung was evicted one after the other from Sweden, Norway and Denmark for organising and arming pro-Nazi factions in the early 1930s.

7 Submarines *E 1*, *E 9* and *E 11* (McCartney, *British Submarines*), pp. 20-28.

the side of the vessel after it was spotted and the vessel swung to starboard under full helm.[8]

German coastal defences therefore knew immediately of the British submarine intrusion. News reached the Baltic Sea commander-in-chief, Grand Admiral Prince Heinrich of Prussia, the Kaiser's younger brother, later that morning. Increased patrols were ordered. On 20 October, *E 1* entered Danzig Bay and its captain saw through his periscope three cruisers lying in the inner basin. They were Gerth's ship, the *Amazone*, and the *Lübeck* and *Augsburg*.[9] All three had recently returned from a raid towards the Gulf of Finland in company with *U 26*, commander Kapitänleutnant Egewolf Freiherr von Berckheim, who successfully torpedoed the Russian cruiser *Pallada*.[10] All 597 men on the *Pallada* died.[11] *E 1* was unable to attack *Amazone* and her two sister ships and turned for the Russian base at Libau.

In 1916, in a covert interview in Copenhagen, ambassador Sir Henry Lowther at the British Legation reported his informant explaining that 'nothing would hasten the end of the war more quickly' than the sinking of ships trading between Sweden and Germany in the Baltic.[12] 'A bold game in these waters during the next two months is the one thing dreaded by both Germany and Sweden.' When the German naval attaché visited a few weeks before, he 'showed great uneasiness' because he had to deal with eleven English and Russian submarines.

Early in December, Gerth was transferred from *Amazone* to a shore position as third Admiral staff officer in the Baltic Sea's Coastal Defence Cruiser Division, the *Küstenschultz-Division der Ostee*, where he stayed until October 1915.[13] The division was commanded at that time by Vice-Admiral Robert Mischke who

---

8   Wilson, *Baltic Assignment*, pp. 30-31.
9   *Lübeck* and *Augsburg* were two more ageing light cruisers, both survived the war and were handed over in 1920 as part of the Versailles peace treaty, *Lübeck* to the British and *Augsburg* to the Japanese.
10 Wilson, *Baltic Assignment*, p. 38. Von Berckheim was killed with all of his crew when *U 26* hit a mine off Hanko in the Gulf of Finland the following August. Its wreck has been found by Finnish divers (uboat.net; press release 2/6/2014, Helsinki: hbadewanne.fi).
11 uboat.net.
12 *TNA*, FO/371/2679, p. 20.
13 Curriculum vitae, Dissertation, University of Würzburg, 5/1923. For background on the British submarine fleet in the Baltic, a main preoccupation of German Coastal Command (Wilson, *Baltic Assignment*), Chapters 4, '1914: The First Campaign' and 5, '1915: The Opening Moves', pp. 40-77.

reported to Prince Heinrich. The Prince's main family residence was at Kiel Castle, burned to the ground during the second world war, from where the Prince conducted his command's business with his admiral's flag flying from one of the towers.

It may be here that one of the few comments ever made by Georg Gerth to his family about his time in the Imperial Navy has its roots. His work as a flag officer might well have taken him into respectful contact with Prince Heinrich. Gerth's family, in the 1960s, expressed surprise when they learned that the Kaiser had a wizened arm. Gerth, sitting in the corner with a book and his customary glass of red wine, rarely spoke, but at the mention of the Kaiser's arm he said, 'I knew that. I played tennis with him once while he was on an inspection tour.'[14] Tirpitz, meeting the prince aboard *Blitz* in 1872, commented that William's 'crippled arm is somewhat noticeable, especially because of his various manoeuvres to try to make the bodily characteristic not noticeable'.[15]

> *[The Kaiser's] breech delivery by forceps required over ten hours and resulted in nerve damage that irretrievably affected his left arm.*[16] *A breach baby, he had been pulled from the womb with such force that his left arm was wrenched from his socket, severing some ligaments ... Doctors wrapped his arm in the carcases of freshly slaughtered rabbits, administered electric shock treatments, and made him wear a kind of straitjacket designed to prevent him turning his head to the left.*[17]

A further four British E-class submarines were sent out in August 1915; *E 8*, *E 18* and *E 19* got through to the Baltic while *E 13* ran aground in Danish waters between Malmö and Copenhagen. *E 13* was scuttled after two German torpedo boats under direct orders from Vice-Admiral Mischke, Gerth's superior, opened fire on her with torpedoes, machine-guns and shell fire from a range of 300 yards. Firing continued after the men abandoned ship and took to the shallow water. The engagement ended when the Danish torpedo

---

14 Interview by the author with Georg Gerth's daughter, Christa-Maria Gerth, at her home in Germany, 16/11/2016.
15 Kelly, *Tirpitz*, p. 38. *Blitz* was one of two steel-hulled ships, the first of any kind in by the German Navy, built in the 1880s, and which led to the later *Gazelle* light cruisers.
16 Asprey, *German High Command*, p. 141.
17 Large, *Berlin*, pp. 52-53.

boat *Søulven* placed herself between the submarine and the two German ships. Fifteen *E 13* crew members were killed.[18]

> *Such a monstrous outrage on international law and neutral rights is in keeping with the methods Germany has consistently pursued. She has transformed war into wholesale murder, regardless of the dictates of humanity and of the restrictions imposed by civilisation. The unjustifiable slaughter of the men of E 13 is one more notch on the long score we have to settle with the homicidal brood of Prussia.*[19]

Four older British C-class submarines were then stripped down and towed to Archangel in the summer of 1915 from where they were barged by canal and river to St Petersburg, reassembled and, in the spring of 1916, joined the flotilla. There were now two attempted blockades in place, that of the Germans on the Russian fleet, and that of the British and Russian submarine flotillas on the Swedish iron ore trade. A great deal of merchant shipping was sunk including, in one day, 22,000 tons by *E 19*. The Germans were quickly forced to employ a convoy system, a regime rejected in the Atlantic by the British Admiralty for several years at great cost in merchant shipping to Great Britain and the Allies.

In July 1915, the Germans began a land offensive which included an amphibious operation on the Baltic flank. To support the landing, they brought in battlecruisers from the High Seas Fleet.[20] This must have been a major preoccupation for the Baltic naval staff while Gerth was in post at the Coastal Defence Division. The armoured cruiser *Prinz Adalbert* was seriously damaged by an *E 9* torpedo, *E 19* sank the light cruiser *Udine* and, the next month, August 1915, *E 1* torpedoed and damaged *Moltke*, one of four battle cruisers travelling in line abreast with a close escort of destroyers.[21] *Moltke* was able to continue under her own power, but the attack so disconcerted flotilla commander Admiral Franz von Hipper that he signalled a return to harbour. The action, much lauded by the Russians, 'in no small part contributed to the cancellation of the German landings at Riga'.[22] The repaired *Prinz Adalbert* was torpedoed and sunk by *E 8* in October. Gerth's ship, *Amazone*, had two near misses by torpedo, the first failure

---

18 'Stricken E13 Shelled', *The Times*, 23/8/1915, p. 6.
19 'The Situation in Russia', *The Times*, 23/8/1915, p. 7.
20 Hezlet, *Submarine and Sea Power*, p. 35.
21 Gray, *British Submarines*, p. 84.
22 McCartney, *British Submarines*, p. 23.

was off Cape Arkona in May when *E 1* missed from a thousand yards, the second was at the Battle of the Gulf of Riga when *E 18* was unsuccessful.

Somewhere in the middle of all of this British submarine activity, Gerth made the decision for a serious career change. He applied to become a u-boat captain and was accepted to undergo training. It is likely that, with the u-boat school based in the Baltic, Gerth mixed with other potential officer applicants. The constant requests for volunteers to become u-boat commanders would have crossed his staff desk. They would have been regularly discussed in the officers' mess where he may also have met von Berckheim, the Baltic u-boat ace, and his fellow commanders.

The 'most experienced and venturesome executive officers and non-commissioned officers' volunteered for submarine service to overcome the boredom of fleet life.[23] In contrast to Britain's navy, where officers specialised in torpedoes, gunnery, navigation or signalling, their German counterparts received intensive training in all these fields, but did not commit to a particular branch. This facilitated, say, the ability to move a gunnery officer from a cruiser to command a u-boat.[24]

Perhaps also it was the lure of command at a junior rank; dissatisfaction, even, with an outlook of more big ship life; but, certainly, a desire to swap his shore job for another involving action and an ability to hit back. The discontent of executive officers was reflected by the popular slogan scrawled up on the walls on Wilhelmshaven, *'Lieb' Vaterland, magst ruhig sein, die Flotte schläft im Hafen ein*, 'Dear Fatherland, Rest assured. The fleet lies in harbour – moored'.[25]

Historian Bouton takes a different view about the crews that manned the u-boats. No continuous extensive use of submarines had been made to the middle of the winter of 1916, but by March 1916 many u-boats were being sent out. At first, they were manned by volunteers, and there had been a surplus of volunteers, for the men of the submarine crews received special food, more pay, liberal furloughs and the Iron Cross after the third trip.[26]

'Within a year, however, conditions changed decidedly.' The men of the fleet reckoned that a submarine rarely survived its tenth trip. The view of Seaman Richard Stumpf aboard the battleship *Helgoland* was that the 'best and most

---

23   Herwig, *Naval Officer Corps*, p. 194.
24   Mulligan, *Sharks Not Wolves*, pp. 33-34.
25   Herwig, *Naval Officer Corps*, p. 180.
26   Bouton, *Abdicates*, pp. 89-90. Gibson, *Submarine War*, pp. 182-83.

intelligent of our officers have been transferred to cruisers, torpedo boats and submarines ... With a few exceptions those who have remained behind don't have much on the ball'.[27]

By 1918, official 'qualification reports' declared submarine lieutenants as 'proven, enthusiastic, and energetic officers of whom we can be proud' while the reports on lieutenants in the fleet were 'very unfavourable'.

> *The Admiralty naturally published no accounts of u-boats that failed to come back, and this added a new terror to this branch of the service. Volunteers were no longer to be had. The result was that drafts were resorted to, at the first from men of the High Seas fleet, and later from the land forces. Such a draft came to be considered as equivalent to a death sentence.*[28]

The submarine offensive 'greatly strained the internal cohesion of the naval officer corps'. The two arms of the navy grew apart: battleships and cruisers fretted in harbour to the frustration of their battle-hungry junior officers.[29] With the German fleet bottled up in Wilhelmshaven and Kiel, the answer was *Kleinkrieg*, 'small operations to erode the Royal Navy's superiority through the use of mines, coastal batteries and submarines'.[30]

When the British had 'lost a few battleships, the strengths of the two sides would be more equal and the High Seas Fleet would be able to risk a [Tirpitzian] battle'.

Small ship commands meant prospects were only available to younger people and not in sufficient numbers to 'persons in higher stations in life'.[31]

---

27   Horn, *War, Munity and Revolution*, p. 75, cited in Mulligan, *Sharks Not Wolves*, p. 34.
28   Herwig, *Naval Officer Corps*, p. 251. The heavy losses among army aviators had brought about a similar state of affairs at the same time in the army. Volunteers for the fighting planes ceased offering themselves and forced service became necessary.
29   Herwig, *Dynamics*, p. 99. 'This "war of lieutenants" troubled senior officers as submarines required few flag-rank officers. [In February 1917,] when Germany decided to risk all on the u-boat gamble, Admiral Eduard von Capelle, Tirpitz's successor at the navy office, warned that emphasis on submarine building would endanger the long-term capital-ship program and called for the creation of a special "submarine cemetery" after the war.'
30   Strachan, *First World War*, p. 197.
31   Herwig, *Luxury Fleet*, p. 224. 'Personnel considerations weighed heavily in the controversy between the competing schools of thought ... u-boats and cruisers do not require admirals.' Rear-Admiral Karl Hollweg: 'You must take into consideration how organisation and promotion will function in a navy which has replaced its capital ships with dirigibles and submarines. This is a problem which has not been solved yet.'

Many of the best junior officers transferred to the u-boats, often replaced on the capital ships by cadets or reservists. For returning u-boat skippers, mostly lowly lieutenants and junior captains, the fleet's problems were a world away: dog-tired after two or three weeks at sea cramped in a noisy, smelly, uncomfortable and tense tin their immediate needs were a lengthy wash, fitful sleep and relentless alcohol.[32] The pressure never lifted; their boat had to be repaired, re-provisioned, and got back to sea.

---

[32] Bouton, *Abdicates*, pp. 89-90.

3
UB 12 AND THE ATTACK ON SUNDERLAND

Gerth's u-boat training lasted for nine months from October 1915. It was sometime in this period that he gathered the nickname Die Rabe, 'The Raven', which was used openly by officers and crew and stuck with him for the rest of his naval career and was even recorded by the British Admiralty.[1]

Gerth arrived in Bruges in June 1916 to take command of *UB 12*. Commanders were cloistered from the general run of military strategy, seldom mixed with the traditional officers of the Grand Fleet, and serviced their boats in remote parts of Bruges and Ostend.

> *Since the u-boats operating from the Flanders base slipped in and out on short forays, an especial kind of under-sea craft was developed. This craft was dubbed the ub-boat. These ub-boats were small and stumpy and had a far shorter radius of action than ocean-going u-boats. Some were so tiny that they were nicknamed sewing machines. Their crews numbered only about twenty and, even then, were frightfully crowded in the narrow space.*[2]

UB 12 was a 'Type 1' submarine, the smallest of Germany's u-boats, which, while variously useful, were not going to win the war for Germany. Designed

---

1   *TNA*, ADM 137/4161, 'German Submarine Officers'.
2   Thomas, *Raiders*, pp. 226-27.

in most part before the start of war and built until 1915 at the Germania and Weser yards in Hamburg and Bremen, they cost about 700,000 Reichsmark.[3] *UB 12* left Bremen in sections carried by railway for final assembly at the Imperial Dockyard at Hoboken, Antwerp. Between Antwerp and its Flanders base there was a careful practice of 'breaking-in' when deficiencies in material and construction were discovered. 'The responsible flotilla commander worked continually to stop leaks so as to remove treacherous oil and petroleum tracks.'[4]

Less than twenty-eight meters overall and weighing 141 tons submerged, *UB 12* had a single diesel engine driving a three-bladed propeller, supported for submerged running by two sixty-one cell batteries. Accounted poor sea-boats with limited manoeuvrability, Type 1 ub-boats could travel a maximum of 1,650 nautical miles at a leisurely five knots on the surface, perhaps forty-five miles at four knots underwater before recharging, and were, therefore, constrained to the North Sea. Only a few hardy commanders ventured as far south as Dover. Their single skin hulls were increasingly vulnerable to improving Allied mines, depth charges and bombs.

> *UB-1 boats received much criticism as being too slow, too small and not powerful enough with their single propulsion. On the surface, they could not catch up with fleeing merchantmen and they did not have enough endurance to remain submerged for long periods. After an hour under water the batteries usually ended up depleted … Heavy swell and stormy circumstances made it impossible to keep at periscope depth. The constant vibrations, pitching and rolling made the compass deviate and put delicate instruments out of action.*[5]

It is important to understand that these early submarines were essentially surface vessels that could dive rather than modern boats designed to stay underwater for weeks on end. U-boat historian John Terraine was 'surprised how tightly the u-boats were locked to the surface' which in many cases was their downfall as enforced diving used limited battery power and soon required vulnerable time on the surface recharging.[6]

---

3   Gröner, *German Warships*, pp. 22-23.
4   Gayer, *Submarine Warfare*, p. 5.
5   Termote, *Krieg unter Wasser*, p. 36.
6   Terraine, *Business in Great Waters*, p. xv. Terraine's book, with *U-Boat Offensive*, by Tarrant, lead the field. Both also cover the u-boats in WW2.

Fighting power was limited, 'almost laughable – feeble instruments of war', consisting of two 45cm torpedo tubes below the waterline at the bow and only one torpedo for each.[7] If a ub-boat on the surface tried to stop a ship, it had only personal weapons and one Maxim machine gun with 1,600 rounds to enforce its will. To prevent sea water damage, the machine gun had to be hauled up with every surfacing and fixed to the conning tower on a detachable pedestal.[8] The gun was little use against aircraft because it could not be angled high enough. If there was any aggressive response from a target ship, *UB 12* carried no deck gun and had to beat a hasty retreat. It took thirty-three seconds to dive from a standing start, twenty seconds if trimmed ready and underway, and the normal depth limit was fifty metres.

The longitudinal stability of these ub-boats was delicate; when diving at more than four to six degrees inclination the deck area tended to act as a sheer plane forcing the boats to a deeper angle and, unless vigorous action was taken, they eventually stood on their heads.[9]

When a torpedo was fired, compensation tanks were designed to flood and therefore compensate for the sudden loss of the 770-kilogram weight. With too little water, the bow shot to the surface; with too much water, the u-boat would almost immediately sink to the bottom. Oberleutnant Otto von Heimburg, commander of *UB 14* and *UB 15*, was one of the first to disparage the early 'sewing machine' motion of his u-boat after an 'iron tadpole' had been fired.[10]

> *I was knocked sprawling as the boat made a wild leap. It took me bewildered moments to figure what had happened. I had never fired a torpedo from a sewing machine before and had not anticipated what would happen. The boat was so small that when relieved of the weight of the torpedo at the bow she popped up like a jack-in-the-box. 'To the bow,' I yelled. 'To the bow.' And every man who could leave his station scrambled to the bow, the combined weight bringing it down level.*[11]

---

7   Terraine, *Business in Great Waters*, p. 20.
8   Termote, *Krieg unter Wasser*, p. 88.
9   Padfield, *Dönitz*, p. 83.
10   Gibson and Prendergast, *German Submarine War*, p. 38. Heimburg was awarded the 'Pour le Mérite' in 1917 having sunk 62,000 tons of enemy shipping, including the British submarine *E 20* and the British troop transport *HMS Royal Edward* in the Mediterranean. At the end of WWII, Soviet forces abducted him, then a fifty-five-year-old retired naval officer, and transported him to a POW camp near Stalingrad where he died in late 1945 (uboat.net).
11   Thomas, *Raiders*, pp. 133-34.

UB 12 had nine commanders over its life of three-and-a-half years and accounted for only twenty-four enemy and neutral vessels which carried contraband. Thirteen of these were small fishing boats of the Lowestoft fleet, most much less than half the size of *UB 12*, which were all threatened by machine gun, stopped, boarded, and scuttled with explosives. After the end of Gerth's captaincy in November 1916, *UB 12* was the first of its class to be rebuilt at the bow end when the torpedo tubes were removed and the forward of its four watertight compartments was adapted to take four external mine chutes, each containing two mines.[12] As a consequence, *UB 12*'s last eight victims were all indiscriminate minings.

> *'Mystery' Q-ships went on bravely tackling the enemy. The Lowestoft armed smacks, for instance, during 1916 had some pretty stiff tussles, and we know now that they thoroughly infuriated the Germans, who threatened to have their revenge. Looked at from the enemy's aspect, it certainly was annoying to see a number of sailing smacks spread off the coast, each obviously trawling, but not to know which of them in a moment could cut her gear and sink the submarine with a gun. It was just that element of suspense which made a cautious German officer very chary of going near these craft, whereas he might have sunk the whole fishing fleet if he dared.*[13]

Primary evidence on individual u-boat activity comes from flotilla records held at the military archives in Freiburg; from Gerth's own daily war diary - Kriegstagebuch (KTB) - handwritten in old German and, for this book, acquired from the u-boat museum at Cuxhaven; and admiralty records held mostly at Kew near London, particularly reports of sightings, actions and sinkings which include official interviews with the captains of lost ships.[14] An excellent and quick overview of a u-boat's and a commander's activities can be found at the voluntary website uboat.net.

---

12 BA-MA, RM 120/40 U-Boote, Vol. 2: Marinekorps report 12/1916, dated 18/1/1917, to the chief of the admiralty staff. Suggestions made by the Siemens company for this conversion of the oldest ub-boats (*UB 1-17*) were twice turned down the previous summer ('Inspection of U-boat fleet', 24711, Kiel, 5/8/1916). *TNA*, ADM 137/3899, p. 22. Gröner, *German Warships*, p. 23. Compton-Hall, *Submarines at War*, p. 85.
13 Chatterton, *Q-ships*, p. 52.
14 www.uboot-recherche.de from where scans of the KTBs of individual u-boats for given periods may be bought as cds. See also for *UB 12*, Spindler, *Krieg zur See*, pp. 6, 82, 121, 232.

Georg Gerth was in charge of *UB 12* for just over four months of routine, short-range voyages and little obvious success. Gerth took over the u-boat from Oberleutnant zur See Wilhelm Kiel on 26 June 1916 while it was undergoing repairs and maintenance in the Bruges shipyard. Kiel's most recent victim, a 4,777-ton British steamer in ballast from Hull for Philadelphia, was *UB 12*'s single torpedo success.[15] Gerth was now the sole officer commanding a thirteen-man crew.

Events moved even more quickly than I anticipated. Before we had fully mastered the rudiments of the innumerable novelties and intricacies of a submarine and with heads still buzzing from things as yet unknown to us, eg automatic vents, crash dives, blowers and trimming pumps, ballast and diving tanks.[16]

In many respects, *UB 12* was a lucky boat, making ninety-eight patrols. Gerth's flotilla leader, Karl Bartenbach, used his ub-boats for training his new leaders. Within a few months, usually only three or four, the slightly experienced and briefly blooded commanders were transferred as quickly as possible to the new more powerful and more dangerous uc-boats coming off the production lines in 1917 and 1918. Of these new uc-boats for *UB 12* commanders, Kiel's *UC 18* was sunk by gunfire from a stricken British Q-ship *Lady Olive* off St Malo; two were rammed; depth charges and mines claimed two more.[17] Only three of *UB 12*'s nine captains survived the war. *UB 12*'s last commander, Oberleutnant Ernst Schöller, was lost with all hands without trace, probably mined, in August 1918 in the North Sea, one the few unfound u-boat wrecks of the Great War.[18]

---

15 uboat.net.
16 Niemöller, *From U-boat*, p. 19.
17 After receiving cannon fire which wrecked her engine room, *Lady Olive* was ordered 'abandon ship' by *UC 18*. Seaman William Dumaresq sighted the u-boat directly in line with his gun and chanced eight shots which hit the hull. *UC 18* sank with all hands. *Lady Olive* sank later, but its crew in three boats and two rafts were stalked by a second u-boat. The French destroyer *Dunois* rescued her crew the following afternoon after a cat and mouse game and ramming of the second u-boat 'the port propeller guard crashing against the boat so that it ripped out the latter's starboard side'. Dumaresq was awarded the DSM (Chatterton, *Q-Ships*), pp. 104-8. This last claim is rejected by the log of the *Dunois* which mentions only sighting a conning tower and firing at it while continuing to pick up crew (www.memoiredeshommes.sga.defense.gouv.fr), p. 746.
18 U-boat diver Jan Lettens assumes a mining and reports several probable contacts from 1976, most recently on 15/12/2009 at 51°20, 099'N, 01°29, 978'E, using a Trisponder Positioning System: a small object has been located protruding from the edge of a sandbank at a depth between 5.5 and 9.5 metres (wrecksite.eu, accessed 11/3/2017). *Royal Navy Submarines Museum (National Museum of the Royal Navy)*, Gosport, 'U-boat Activities and Losses', Vol. 1, p. 153.

Bartenbach gave his commanders hand-written orders, usually instructing three uc-boats to sea at the same time, but with different destinations. Gerth was out in *UB 12*, his new command, the day after the handover so it can be assumed he took on most if not all of the existing crew.

Smaller German submarines were usually stationed as 'outposts' at the entrances to the German Bight, as it was believed, especially after the Battle of Jutland, that England would 'endeavour to recover lost prestige by attempting an advance. But this did not occur.'[19] German submarine officers bridled under their restricted role as 'mobile sentry boxes'.[20]

Gerth was to take up standard three-day sentry duty - the 'outpost' - off the Flanders coast and to have care of big torpedo boats and larger submarines as they sailed into and back from the North Sea. Radio messages were sent from 1100 to 1110 and from 1200 to 1210. He was to take carrier pigeons for emergency messages back to Bruges. It was a training exercise.

> *The coast was in a constant state of alert for surprise landings by the British. Belgian Flanders was protected by countless artillery emplacements, but it was still considered a worthwhile precaution always to have a couple of small U-boats on station just off the coast. This sentry duty was much deprecated as there was rarely, if ever, any contact with the enemy, yet we were obliged to remain in the state of the highest alertness at all times ... Our Flotilla Chief began to edge us farther and farther offshore until his bagful of u-boats went across the North Sea: finally, we were operating off the English coast itself. Now at last we felt we were real u-boatmen: now we could get busy in the murderous manner we had dreamed of all these weeks and months!* [21]

Throughout the 131 days of his *UB 12* career, Gerth seized chances in slack times while on patrol or on sentinel duty to practise his diving, navigation and torpedo attack procedures. He was trained to keep his records simple and direct with no emotional language. The records include the hand-annotated charts of his voyages with a key: one line with arrow - journey above water, two lines with arrow – journey under water, dotted line with arrow – drifted above water, circle with a cross in middle – resting on the sea bed.

---

19   Gayer, *Submarine Warfare*, p. 21.
20   Hezlet, *Submarine and Sea Power*, p. 25.
21   Fürbringer, *Legendary*, p. 14.

When the expected attack by the British fleet did not materialise, the Flanders Flotilla was allowed a more offensive role. There is no doubt that *UB 12* and its crew was driven hard. If the boat was available, it went to sea. The names and locations of the North Sea shoals, Bligh, Terschelling, Schaar, Schouwen, Spon, Thornton and Rabe Banks, with additional light vessels at Maas and North Hinder, and the many friendly buoys, all became daily companions.

Gerth made fifteen voyages down the Bruges Canal to Zeebrugge with *UB 12*. He was in command for 3,107 hours and, of that, spent 1,384 hours at sea, 45 per cent of his available time. Perhaps, most importantly, an almost equivalent time, 41 per cent was spent in maintenance or repairs; several times the boat was forced to return early. Gerth had regular problems with injection valves, and, also on the engine, the fuel pump and valve, the oil pump, noisy cylinders and the manometer, which measured gas pressure. A new radio aerial had to be fitted, the hydroplane became restricted, and the main hatch would not open necessitating a crewman squeezing out through the torpedo loading hatch. The few free hours were spent waiting in Bruges for loadings or sitting out bad weather.

UB 12 saw limited fighting, but lived with daily Allied anti-submarine patrol vessels and destroyers in a seemingly crowded sea. Gerth was in his first action on his second day when he was fired at by destroyers. Once, Gerth took on a British destroyer with a torpedo shot which missed; an eventuality which he blamed on his torpedo crewman. On another occasion, four destroyers with a small cruiser at their centre headed zig-zagging 'at great speed' towards the partly-submerged u-boat. The cruiser passed fifty metres away without seeing the periscope. In all, Gerth was forced to dive twenty-six times and was under attack twice by depth charge, once from aircraft machine guns, and once from the hidden cannon of a Q-ship, which had been disguised as a fishing vessel, and left him with five big holes in his decking. *UB 12* was taken to the sea bed nine times to sit out persistent searches which included being swept by wire and hydrophones.

All ears are laid against the boat's sides to pick up any sound. Everything remains quiet. We repeat the procedure at fifty feet and still hear nothing.[22]

---

22   Niemöller, *From U-boat*, p. 126.

Gerth took two small food steamers after threatening them with his machine gun. One was sunk and the other seized as a prize; one fishing smack was also sunk by explosives.

Rilda was a British steamer, built by R Smith of Preston in 1883, and operated by E Ellingsen of Christiana. She carried 'general cargo', but Gerth claimed it was food. His men rowed to the boat, set explosive charges and handed her crew over to a passing Dutch steamer. There were no casualties. A prize court confirmed the sinking of the ship and the greater part of the cargo as lawful. However, part of the cargo was returned.[23]

Niobe was travelling from Amsterdam when Gerth captured her, took her captain aboard as a hostage, and ushered the ship to Zeebrugge where she was retained with part of her cargo. This was the second time *Niobe* had been taken as a prize. The first was by *U 36*, Kapitänleutnant Ernst Graeff, on 10 May 1915. The owners, NV Koninkl of Amsterdam, appealed to a German Prize Court sitting in Hamburg on 10 July that year which ruled there was no case because the vessel was 'merely brought into Cuxhaven for examination and was then released forthwith'. Vice-Admiral Spindler described the seizure as a 'remarkable achievement' as Gerth had to rely on machine guns and carbines to stop the ship.[24]

Gerth's last success was *Margorie*, a 55-ton British fishing vessel owned by C H Crews of Lowestoft, which was stopped and sunk with explosives. The wreck has never been found; it is estimated to be one mile east of Smiths Knoll.[25] Nobody was hurt aboard *UB 12* during Gerth's tenure, nor were there any casualties from his actions.

Apart from a lack of any great success against enemy ships, Gerth was closely involved in two of the main naval events of 1916, and one minor action. The two major events were of different characters and neither brought any credit to Germany's naval forces.

In the first, *UB 12*, with fellow ub-boats from Flanders, spent an abortive couple of days in August as a part of a second elaborate attempt by Admiral Reinhard Scheer to entice the British Grand Fleet into a u-boat trap.[26] A first

---

23 uboat.net. wrecksite.eu. skipet.no. Spindler, *Krieg sur Zee*, Band 3, p. 231.
24 *TNA*, CO 323/801/4. uboat.net. Spindler, *Krieg sur Zee*, Band 3, p. 232.
25 Lettens, www.wrecksite.eu, accessed 12/3/2017.
26 Scheer, *High Seas Fleet*, pp. 224-31. Tarrant, *U-Boat Offensive*, pp. 32-33. Gayer, *Submarine Warfare*, pp. 19-23.

attempt earlier in the year ended in a 'complete and disappointing failure'. However, it did lead inadvertently, but directly, to the Battle of Jutland.

A few months after that battle, Scheer laid his second trap. He took elements of the High Seas fleet across the North Sea during the night of 18 August 1916 to bombard supposedly military targets around the town of Sunderland the next morning. Scheer anticipated that the British Grand Fleet would then sail to seek combat, but would be forced to approach the town through a broad channel between the coast and the inner edge of three minefields. These large well-charted minefields had been laid by the Germans earlier in the war off the Tyne, Humber and western part of the Dogger Bank. Five 'u-lines', u-boats holding linear formations, with a total of twenty-four u-boats were to be ready and waiting for the Grand Fleet. Two of these lines comprised nine Flanders ub-boats. Separate from the anticipated main action, their task was to guard the southern flank of the High Seas Fleet's advance and to attack light British naval forces from Harwich if they became involved. Gerth and *UB 12* were at the end of U-line II, twelve miles off Texel, the largest and most populous island in the Dutch Friesians.

The operation was mostly a tactical failure. The British intercepted signals announcing the High Seas Fleet's departure and put to sea at 1600 on the eighteenth, before the Germans had actually sailed. Scheer was 'dissuaded from bombarding Sunderland by a false report made by a scouting Zeppelin which mistook the light craft of the Harwich force for a detached squadron of enemy battleships'. He turned away from Sunderland to chase the 'phantom' battleships. That afternoon, with the Grand Fleet closing from the north and the south barred by the Humber minefield, Scheer headed home.

The German navy's reliance upon dirigibles left the fleet constantly at the mercy of fog, wind, sleet and snow, with regard to reconnaissance. Shore command never appreciated that the British not only routinely intercepted their signals to the fleet, but that they expeditiously deciphered them in Room 40 at the Admiralty, with the result that the Grand Fleet was often out to sea before the High Sea Fleet had hoisted anchors.[27]

---

27 Herwig, *Dynamics*, p. 98.

German successes came early the next day, the nineteenth, when u-boats in the first line of attack were on their way to their ambush positions. Two light cruisers in the screen covering the British battleships as they moved south were sunk. At 0445, *U 66*, commander Kapitänleutnant Thorwald von Bothmer, hit the 5,250-ton *Falmouth* with two torpedoes.

'Despite being repeatedly attacked by escorting destroyers and an armed trawler' and suffering depth charge attacks and partial flooding, Bothmer dogged *Falmouth*, firing further torpedoes which missed. At noon, when *Falmouth* which was crawling along under tow, *U 66*, Kapitänleutnant Otto Schulze, fired two torpedoes which finished the ship, killing eleven crew. Schulze survived the war and was appointed Konteradmiral in 1931.

Just before six that same morning, *U 52*, Oberleutnant Hans Walther, fired two successful torpedoes at the modern 5,400-ton *Nottingham* and, half an hour later, a third, which sank her. Thirty-eight men died. Walther died the following year with all hands when *UB 75* was mined off Scarborough.

UB 12 took no direct part in the action, saw nothing of consequence, and, after suffering engine problems, went home to Bruges.

However, strategically, the Scarborough operation was much more successful than Scheer realised at the time. Admiral Jellicoe understood that the whole point of the German operation was a submarine trap. For fear of the u-boats and with two cruisers lost, he saw 'great peril' that could not be risked again.

> *Mines had already made it too dangerous for the Grand Fleet to enter the area south of Horns Reef and east of 5°E. Admiral Jellicoe now reckoned that he ought not to go south of 55° 30'N or east of 4°E at any time and 'only west of the same longitude if a really good chance of action with the High Seas Fleet presented itself'. Furthermore, he did not believe that he should go south of the Dogger Bank at all unless all classes of ship, including light cruisers, had destroyer screens. As he knew he had not enough destroyers for the purpose, it was tantamount to saying that the Grand Fleet would in future have to stay north of the Dogger Bank.*[28]

In the minor naval action, Gerth formed another u-line with three Flanders ub-boats around 18 October and was told that German and enemy naval forces were to be anticipated. German Navy Zeppelins participated in a High

---

28 Hezlet, *Submarine and Sea Power*, pp. 72-73.

Seas Fleet sortie, escorted by torpedo boats, but German and British ships failed to make contact. Admiral Scheer barely mentions this expedition other than stating that he left the most vulnerable part of his fleet in reserve and that he remembered that his torpedo boats could not go as far as planned due to adverse weather conditions.[29] Five Zeppelins suffered serious mechanical breakdowns during the operation.

Mention of Zeppelin raids provides an opportunity to recognise the variety of naval occupations taken by Gerth's colleagues among the sea cadets in his training 'Crew of 1907'.

Among his forty-eight fellow cadets aboard *SMS Freya* in the arduous first ten months of training was Kapitänleutnant Kurt Frankenberg, later commander of the Zeppelin *L 21*. Frankenberg had already flown his airship three times to England in 1916. In November, ten Zeppelins took off on a bombing mission from Nordholz, the Imperial Navy's principal airship base near Cuxhaven.[30] Little damage was done at various haphazard targets as the Zeppelins turned for home or were shot down. Only *L 21* remained. She was rebuffed by guns or baffled by blackouts at Barmston, Leeds, Barnsley and Macclesfield, but dropped bombs on Sharton and Dodworth and a series of impromptu targets in the Potteries. *L 21* was tracked to Yarmouth and had lucky escapes from pursuing British aircraft and anti-aircraft guns.

Then, Frankenburg was found by three Royal Navy Air Service pilots flying *BE 2C* aircraft. The first was Flight-Lieutenant Egbert Cadbury, heir to the chocolate empire, who emptied four Lewis drum canisters into the gasbag with no immediate effect. The second plane's gun jammed in the cold air. The third pilot, Flight Sub-Lieutenant Edward Pulling fired only two shots before his gun also jammed. As he pulled away, *L 21* burst into flames and, said Pulling, 'within a few seconds became a fiery furnace'. The crew of the airship kept firing until *L 21* fell into the sea about eight miles east of Lowestoft. There were no survivors. Pulling received the Distinguished Service Order; Cadbury and his colleague, Flight Sub-Lieutenant Gerard Fane, the Distinguished Service Cross.

---

29 Scheer, *High Sea Fleet*, p. 232.
30 *London Gazette*, 5/12/1916.

4
THE EXECUTION OF CHARLES FRYATT

The second main naval event of 1916 involving Georg Gerth was the infamous 'Captain Fryatt' affair which, in the eyes of the British, summed up everything that was rotten about Prussian Germany and the u-boats in particular. The saga had its roots in the genuine German horror and disgust, borne of the Franco-Prussian war in 1870-71, of the *franc tireur*, the 'free shooter' or civilian gunman. This aversion was extended somewhat tenuously by the Germans to the negation of the rights of merchant and passengers ships to resist u-boat sinkings. The treachery of the *franc-tireurs* became a German 'obsession'.[1]

In 1913, Winston Churchill, then First Lord of the Admiralty, stirred the pot when he proposed that in wartime British merchant ships should be armed in self-defence. He saw no paradox in claiming that if the guns and gunners were provided by the Royal Navy, then the ships could retain their civilian status.[2] The Germans strongly disagreed, but were isolated and reluctantly gave way on the principle of self-defence at a conference held that year in Oxford by the Institute of International Law.[3]

Early in the war, Churchill's rhetoric raised the temperature again. Many remarks have been attributed to him, several unsatisfactorily sourced, and, if

---

1 Blond, *Marne*, p. 39.
2 *Hansard*, House of Commons, Vol. L, 1913, c1776-7.
3 Hall, *Law of Naval Warfare*, 1921, p. 55.

true, probably off-the-cuff.⁴ They included orders to 'immediately engage the enemy, either with armament if they possess it, or by ramming if they do not', that British vessels should treat the crews of captured u-boats as 'felons' and not to accord them the status of prisoners of war.⁵ 'Survivors should be taken prisoner or shot whichever was the 'most convenient'. White flags were to be fired on 'with promptitude'. Any master who surrendered his ship 'will be prosecuted'. The Germans reportedly became aware of Churchill's orders when *U 21*, Oberleutnant Otto Hersing, stopped and sank the British freighter *Ben Cruachan* early in 1915 and found a copy aboard.⁶

More diplomatically, the Admiralty certainly issued a secret order on 10 February 1915, repeated in June 1916, which said that no British merchant vessel 'should ever tamely surrender to a submarine, but should do her utmost to escape', including steering away at full speed if a u-boat was seen on the surface.⁷ If the u-boat appeared suddenly close ahead, the merchant ship was to 'steer straight for her at your utmost speed' and the submarine 'will probably then dive'.

*This order soon became known as the 'ramming order', but the Admiralty had been careful to avoid the use of the word 'ram' in the order because of its connotations of attack rather than defence.*⁸

One of the merchant ship masters who received the Admiralty order was Captain Charles Fryatt of the Great Central Railway Company. In March, as captain of the unarmed steamer *Wrexham*, on the Tilbury to Hook of Holland route, Fryatt turned away from a surfaced u-boat, *U 12*, ordered full speed and, over forty miles, outpaced it. The deckhands assisted the stokers to make

---

4   Among the claimed sources: Churchill, *World Crisis*, pp. 283, 724-5; Coles, *Slaughter at Sea*, p. 114; Griffiths, *World without Cancer*, p. 249; *Richmond Diaries*, 27/2/1915; Simpson, *Lusitania*, p. 36.
5   Simpson, *Lusitania*, p. 36. Richmond Diaries, 27/2/1915.
6   Hersing was known amongst his colleagues as the 'Zerstörer der Schlachtschiffe' - destroyer of battleships: *HMS Pathfinder*, light cruiser, torpedoed off the east coast of Scotland, 1914; *HMS Triumph* and *HMS Majestic*, both battleships, Gallipoli, 1915; *Carthage*, French auxiliary cruiser, Turkey, 1915; *Amiral Charner*, French cruiser, Syria.
7   Hurd, *Merchant Navy*, Appendix A, pp. 436-40. *TNA*, 'War Instructions for British Merchant Ships', *Admiralty War Staff*, 1/6/1916, ADM 137/2832. *TNA*, FO 383/494, p. 613.
8   Jamieson, 'Martyr or Pirate?', *The Mariner's Mirror*, p. 198.

sixteen knots; *Wrexham* arrived at Rotterdam with scorched funnels. Fryatt's employers gave him a gold watch in gratitude.

Later that month, off the Maas Lightship, bound for Rotterdam, Fryatt in the *Brussels* of the Great Eastern Railway Company, attempted to ram *U 33*, after its commander Kapitänleutnant Konrad Gansser had ordered him to stop. The u-boat crashed dived and only narrowly avoided being hit. By the time Gansser surfaced, *Brussels* was gone.⁹ This time, Fryatt's gold watch came from the British Admiralty.

In June, *Brussels* twice escaped u-boat attacks and, in July, was missed by a torpedo. *Brussels* was not allowed to mount a gun because she would be forbidden the use of Dutch ports had she done so.¹⁰

Here the accounts differ. One report notes that Fryatt's 'charmed life and its publicity in Holland angered the Germans and a naval operation was mounted to catch him'.¹¹ On 22 June, five days before Gerth's first patrol in *UB 12*, Fryatt left Rotterdam for Tilbury, calling at the Hook of Holland. There were sinister tales of lights showing from the coast, a flare, a passenger on deck signalling to shore.¹² The next day, *Brussels* was captured by five German torpedo boats from the Flanders Flotilla and taken into Zeebrugge, later to Bruges, and Fryatt and his crew were sent to a civilian internment camp at Ruhleben near Berlin.¹³

British Foreign Office papers state that Fryatt was only forty-eight hours in Ruhleben after which he was taken back alone to Bruges.¹⁴ During his time at Ruhleben, Fryatt was quartered in Barrack No. 1 which was under a man called Turnbull, 'a notoriously pro-German civilian', who claimed Fryatt had boasted to him of his u-boat exploits. Turnbull was given a six-week holiday by his German captors and was then freed.

U-boat historian Termote has a different story. *Brussels* was boarded at sea by crewmen from Torpedoboat *G-102*. An unknown British Admiralty report of 1920 stated that Fryatt had been invited to dine with u-boat officers in the

---

9   *TNA*, FO 383/195, Captain Fryatt's report, 28/3/1915. Hurd, *Merchant Navy*, pp. 308-10.
10 Hurd, *Merchant Navy*, pp. 334-35.
11 Haws, *Merchant Fleets*, pp. 29, 49-50.
12 *New York Times*, 29/7/1916, pp. 1-2.
13 Winton, *Convoy*, p. 38. Coles, *Slaughter at Sea*, p. 149. Cawley and Woodward, 'Charles Fryatt', BBC, 16/7/2016.
14 *TNA*, FO 383/521, pp. 78-80.

cellar restaurant of their casino in a large manor house in Fort Lapin in the Saint-Peters area of Bruges.

> *Bruges, naturally, was not only the rendezvous, but it was also the playground for the Flanders' u-boat men when off duty between raids. The under-sea flotilla chiefs had their headquarters in one of the oldest buildings in the ancient Belgian city [built by the Jesuits] … When meal-time came they adjourned to another place, a sumptuous private mansion, a place of spacious rooms, lofty ceilings, carved woodwork, and crystal chandeliers … an old rathskellar, a cellar which you entered by arched doorways two feet thick … the nightly congregating place … walls decorated with frescoes by a submarine commander. For living quarters they scattered about in private houses deserted by their owners.*[15]
>
> *[The commanders] told [Fryatt] that he was a gentleman and they were on friendly terms up to the moment he saw fit to show off his watch [with his citation for attempting to ram U 33 the previous year]. The atmosphere took a 180 degree turn and he was immediately apprehended and imprisoned.*[16]

Importantly, it was not until 16 July that the Dutch reported that Fryatt had been charged with sinking a German submarine. Termote's version, and the chain of events, does suggest that the plot to capture Fryatt, rather than just the *Brussels*, is an invention. If the Germans knew who they had captured, they presumably would not have sent him to Berlin at all. *U 33*, of course, had not been sunk and, equally, the Germans knew this.

The four-hour trial was held eleven days later, 27 July, at Bruges Town Hall. Before a court convened by Admiral Ludwig von Schröder, the head of the Flanders *MarineKorps*, Fryatt was found guilty of being a *franc tireur* and sentenced to death, which was immediately confirmed. One basis for the charge was his watch inscription. Fryatt claimed throughout that he was attempting to evade an anticipated torpedo and had not tried to ram *U 33*. Gansser was in the Mediterranean and did not appear, but sent his second-in-command. Fryatt was not properly represented and was not informed of his rights of appeal. He was executed by firing squad that evening at 1900. He had a wife and seven children.

---

15 Thomas, *Raiders*, pp. 226-27.
16 Termote, *Krieg unter Wasser*, pp. 173-74.

An execution notice was published in Dutch, French and German, signed by Schröder:

> *The English captain of a merchant ship, Charles Fryatt, of Southampton, though he did not belong to the armed forces of the enemy, attempted on 28 March 1915 to destroy a German submarine by running it down. For this he has been condemned to death by judgement this day of the Field Court Martial of the Navy Corps, and has been executed. A ruthless deed has thus been avenged, belatedly but just.*

The British response was, seemingly, one of surprise and genuine horror. British Prime Minister Herbert Asquith spoke of 'utmost indignation', 'atrocious crime', and being 'impossible to conjecture to what atrocities [the Germans] may proceed'.[17] Lord Claud Hamilton, MP, chairman of the Great Eastern Railway, and aide-de-camp to Queen Victoria for ten years, called the execution 'sheer, brutal murder'. Propagandists 'presented Fryatt as a civilian martyr to be ranked with Edith Cavell', the nurse executed for helping over 250 Allied soldiers in occupied Belgium to get back to England through neutral Netherlands.[18] A war crime was declared and retaliation threatened. The Germans investigated and decided correct procedure had been followed.[19]

After the war, public funerals were held for both returned bodies of Cavell and Fryatt in St Paul's Cathedral, London. A memorial still stands in London's Liverpool Street Station. In the Canadian Rockies, there are two mountains named for Fryatt and Cavell.

Fryatt's story is worth telling both for its own sake and to demonstrate the different values and strength of feeling on both sides of the submarine war, not least among the u-boat captains.

What of Gerth's involvement? The connections are circumstantial, but repay consideration.

---

17 *Hansard*, House of Commons, Vol. LXXXIV (1916), Col. 2080-1.
18 Jamieson, 'Martyr or Pirate?', *The Mariner's Mirror*, p. 200.
19 TNA, FO 383/497, pp. 554-615. A German commission, the Schüking Commission, confirmed Fryatt's sentence on 2/4/1919 as not in violation of International law, but apologised 'most vividly for the hurry in which the judgement was enforced'. Two panel members dissented as they say Fryatt's sentence as a 'severe infringement' ('Regulation of the Council of People's Deputies on the composition and proceedings of the Commission investigating the charges of violation of international law in the treatment of prisoners of war in Germany', 30/11/1918, *Reichsgesetzblatt*), p. 1388. *Deutsche Allgemeine Zeitung*, 3/5/1919.

First, Gerth arrived in Bruges on or about 22 June, the day of Fryatt's capture. He was a new commander who had not yet taken a u-boat to sea in anger when *Brussels* was taken by her prize crew to Zeebrugge and up the canal to Bruges.[20] As a loyal and committed 28-year-old naval officer in a new post, Gerth would have offered his full support to his commanders and been anxious to soak up the style and opinions of his free-booting comrades. If Fryatt was immediately entertained to dinner in Bruges by the u-boat commanders, then it is likely that Gerth was in attendance. He would have heard Fryatt's stories, seen his watch, and felt the icy change in atmosphere in the cellar.

If this part of the story is apocryphal, and Fryatt's connection with *U 33* was not realised until later, then, by July, the whole Flanders Flotilla would have been ablaze with the story of Fryatt's impending court martial. Schröder was Bartenbach's immediate superior and both would have been closely involved in all decisions and, in all probability, instigated them. The military court was held at Bruges Town Hall with five adjudicating officers, one of whom was a serving u-boat commander. The ranks of these men are given, but their names have been omitted from the German report.[21] Might Gerth have attended the court in solidarity that morning along with the few 'unoccupied' commanders in Bruges? He took *UB 12* to sea at 1750 that evening, just two hours before Fryatt was shot.

Did the episode make any impression upon Gerth's Prussian fervour? His involvement in the story is not yet over.

On 4 November, Gerth left Bruges and *UB 12* for a short leave and afterwards went up to the Baltic where his new charge, *UC 61*, was being finished at Bremen. Gerth moved the boat to Kiel and brought it to combat readiness with its first crew.

In November 1916, I was entrusted with the command of UC 70 ... The policy of unrestricted submarine warfare ... led to the design and construction of a new type of u-boat which, [with its] much improved minelaying capacity, did at least boast an

---

20   *Brussels* was used as a depot ship at Zeebrugge by the torpedo arm of the Flanders Marine. On 23/4/1918, she was damaged in the Zeebrugge raid and on 5/10/1918 sunk by the Germans as a blockship at the head of the mole. In 1919, she was raised and taken back to the River Tyne in England. She ended her days running a twice-weekly service for 600 live cattle between Preston and Dublin (Haws, *Merchant Fleets*), p. 50.

21   *TNA*, FO 383/497, p. 592.

> engine plant which brought the whole British coastline within its range. *[The boat]* displaced 450 tons instead of 160 tons, carried eighteen mines instead of twelve, was fitted with one underwater and two surface torpedo tubes, and an 88mm deck gun. The powerful diesels provided a top speed of twelve knots. The boat was capable of remaining below much longer ... and was considerably more habitable.[22]
>
> *[This was]* the busy time of the first diving and steaming trials. No u-boat was allowed to leave for active service till she was in every respect in perfect trim. Finally came the firing exercises at the Submarine School in Eckernförde. To save time, we were towed to the firing position by torpedo-boats. These exercises were chiefly intended to test the ability of the commanding officer. Here he must show whether, under warlike conditions, he not only had his boat absolutely in hand, but also how to attack and how to hit.[23]

Gerth travelled through the Kiel Canal and stopped near the entrance at Brunsbüttel. On one trip, *U 62*, commanded by Ernst Hashagen, was forced to stop over there because of fog. The officers were asked to join the port pilots for a drink, 'mostly old sailing ship skippers, many with white beards and all deep-sea men'.[24] The u-boat men listened to the tall stories of long ago and then responded with their own modern tales:

> When we are on the bottom we can see everything that goes on around us under the sea. A big, curved steel plate is slid noiselessly to one side. A curtain is raised by means of two levers, revealing a dark glass window. Then we press a button, and at a bound the deep-sea night is turned into day in the rays of a powerful searchlight. The thick glass is quite clear and transparent, so that we can distinguish every detail. We see the great curious fishes shooting up, and the crabs, lobsters, and starfish moving among the corals and submarine flowers.

One of the engineers explained that when it got tedious on the bottom, the men often climbed out through the diving lock. It was quite simple, he said, to allow the water in and to bite on the rubber mouthpiece on the diving helmet. It was difficult climbing down the boat's side which was as 'slippery as an eel'.

---

22 Fürbringer, *Legendary*, pp. 69-70.
23 Hashagen, *Commander*, p. 86.
24 Hashagen, *Commander*, pp. 125-27.

'Then we go for our stroll. We all carry lamps and sharp axes in case of danger. A stroll on the sea bottom is a fine affair.'

UC 61 moved down the coast, passed the Netherlands, to be met by an escort:

> German u-boat *UB 4* hove in sight directly ahead, sent by the Chief of the Flanders Flotilla, Korvettenkapitän Bartenbach, to escort us through the German minefields on the Belgian coast. We made Zeebrugge that afternoon, berthing an hour later at Bruges, to be received by the Flotilla chief and the representative of the Naval Corps. That evening Bartenbach made a speech of welcome in the officers' club.[25]

Back in Bruges, on 1 March, Gerth made the customary first short operational cruise for a new uc-boat and crew, five days without mines in the Hoofden off the Dutch coast.[26] *UC 61* was a much more offensive boat than *UB 12*: five torpedoes and a serious deck gun. Bartenbach ordered the boat to a designated patrol square to look out for convoys and to disturb the traffic between England and Holland.[27]

Gerth sailed in the evening, took up his position and, for the next three days in a reasonable sea with good visibility, saw nothing. He was reduced to making practice runs under water. On his last full day, at 0938, ten miles off the North Hinder light vessel, in a quickly freshening sea and rising wind, with visibility cut by snow drifts, he saw a steamer with escorts. Gerth takes up the story in the laconic style of his *Kriegstagebuch*:

> Sighted steamer with two destroyers, dived, ran attack, both engines full speed straight ahead. Realised afterwards it was the English steamer Copenhagen on route to Holland.
>
> Bow shot at steamer, distance about 1,500 metres, steamer speed 16 knots. Hit in the engine room. Steamer stops, lies abeam of the sea, both destroyers circle it. Crew leaves the steamer in ship's boats, destroyers cannot go alongside in the heavy sea. Steamer lies without list; stern significantly lower. Released second torpedo 400 metres from stationary steamer. Failed shot, can only be explained by faulty course of torpedo, probably as a result of the heavy sea. Although going almost constantly full

---

25   Fürbringer, *Legendary*, p. 14.
26   *TNA*, ADM 137/3898, p. 93; ADM 137/3884, p. 55.
27   Gayer, *Submarine Warfare*, p. 5.

> *speed, UC 61 cannot be held at depth, several times whole conning tower comes above water and is apparently being seen.*
>
> *Destroyer approaches UC 61 at great speed. Went to depth, departed. Afterwards headed again towards site of the attack. Sighted nothing else in the very limited field of vision due to high sea [now reported as a gale]. Surfaced very near destroyer, dived. Surfaced. Hatches and thick spars/booms are floating around. Sighted nothing of the steamer. Immediately afterwards sighted two destroyers quite close. Dived. Surfaced. Steamer is briefly visible through fog. Tried to run it down, however steamer is not sighted again.*

What made the *Copenhagen* special for Gerth, Bartenbach and the Flanders Flotilla was that she was a sister ship of Charles Fryatt's *Brussels* in the Great Eastern Railway passenger fleet. That probably was cause enough to enjoy sinking the *Copenhagen*, but there was another reason to dislike and distrust vessels in this fleet: a further sister ship, the Great Eastern's *SS Antwerp*, originally called *Vienna*, was the second Q-ship commissioned in 1915 by the Royal Navy and she was a well-known nuisance to the Flanders u-boats.[28]

> *When there were two of us in the conning tower, there was no room to move, yet when making a torpedo attack the presence of the coxswain was required there. It wasn't easy. I had to work at the periscope, climb up and down, circle round and round and always squashed up against the other person.*[29]

Copenhagen left Harwich for the Hook of Holland at 0400, escorted by the destroyers *Sylph* and *Minos* and was near the end of her passage when hit.[30] The Admiralty received a report of the torpedoing at 0959 from the destroyer *Nimrod*.[31] The crew, passengers and despatches were taken off by *Sylph*, which brought them to Harwich with the destroyers *Matchless* and *Lookout*, arriving at 1400. *Nimrod* was ordered not to sink *Copenhagen*, but to let her drift.[32] Arrangements the next day to send out a search and towing

---

28   Chatterton, *Q-ships*, p. 8.
29   Fürbringer, *Legendary*, p. 18.
30   *Shipping*, No. 144, 2/2002, p. 17. The Great Easter Railway ran train services to from London to Harwich from 1854 and obtained powers in 1862 to connect to their own steamships to Rotterdam and Antwerp.
31   *TNA*, ADM 137/247.
32   Manning, *British Destroyer*, pp. 66, 69, 70, 74, 127-28.

party were abandoned because of continuing thick fog and a rough sea. *Copenhagen* did drift about two miles before she sank. The wreck is lying upright in a trough between two sand waves in about twenty-six metres and with little superstructure remaining.[33]

> *For a moment ... I reflected on the morality of the impending situation. On the one hand, the honourable seamen on that ship, true to the highest traditions of their calling, had willingly placed their lives in the greatest danger to save [others]. And all the thanks they were going to get for it was a German torpedo.*[34]

The 2,570-ton *Copenhagen*, built by John Brown at Clydebank, was by far and away the biggest haul to date of Gerth's short career.[35] The German command placed the boat at about 5,000 tons; figures at this time were being routinely inflated as reports passed up the chain of command. Passenger accommodation was spread over three decks amidships, with room for 320 in first class. There was a full-width sixty-two seat dining room on the lower deck.

The Germans noted that the success on Monday, 5 March, was not observed by Gerth because of the counterattack by the two British destroyers; but the loss was confirmed by newspaper reports.[36]

The sinking was notified by telegram to the Kaiser by the Chief of the Admiralty Staff who explained that 'it was well known that the vessel was permanently cruising in convoy between Holland and England, so it is even more pleasing that the ship was successfully sunk while escorted by destroyers'. Six British crewmen were reported dead, four were married, and all were working in the engine room where Gerth's torpedo hit. Whether they died

---

33   Listed as 'probable': *Diver*, 8/2010. wrecksite.eu/wreck.aspx?75582.
34   Fürbringer, *Legendary*, pp. 94-95.
35   Spindler, *Der Krieg zur See*, Band 4, p. 142. Bendler, *Der UC-Boote*, p. 159. *TNA*, BT 110/279, Ship's Register.
36   *BA-MA*, RM 2/1994, p. 252: Telegram from Admiralty Staff to the Kaiser, 7/3/1917. The Kaiser did read the reports for that of the following month had 'Bravo' noted in the royal hand in the margin.

in the explosion or from subsequent drowning is moot. These were the first people killed by Gerth.[37]

What a difference in attitude nine months made in the submarine war. In July 1916, Fryatt was executed because he tried to save his ship and possibly tried to ram *U 33*. Nobody died. The following February, the Germans declared unrestricted submarine warfare. The next month, *UC 61* sank the *Brussels*' sister ship *Copenhagen* by torpedo without warning in the same area of sea as the attempted ramming, six died, and hardly a murmur was heard.

Actually, there was a little murmur based on some confused information. *Copenhagen* had been a hospital ship and, in some reports, had only reverted to passenger traffic on the day of her sinking, and others suggested she was still carrying wounded. But, this would not be true from neutral Holland, and the story quickly disappeared.

Flushed with the success from the sinking of *Copenhagen*, *UC 61* spent a customary couple of days in maintenance and then moved through the canal to the dry dock in Ostend for repairs to her oil tanks.

---

37 Five names are recorded on the Merchant Navy memorial at Tower Hill in London: Arthur J Atkins, fireman, drowned; Harry Barney, engine donkeyman, drowned; Charles Brundle, fireman, drowned; William Chaplin, fireman, drowned; and Arthur Hammond, fireman, killed. Leonard Rand, fireman, is commemorated at Harwich Cemetery, likely being the only body recovered by one of the destroyers and taken back to their home base (benjidog.co.uk, ancestry.co.uk, accessed 11/2016).

5
NIGHTMARE PATROL

Back in Bruges, Gerth took his eighteen mines aboard for the first time. He was ordered by Bartenbach to lay them in sets off Beachy Head and Newhaven. Afterwards, he was to cruise the Scillies looking for merchant targets.

The u-boat sailed down the canal for Zeebrugge on 17 March in the company of *UC 17* and *UC 65*. *UC 61*'s second patrol was the nightmare voyage, perhaps saved from farce only by an heroic and lucky cruise home to Bruges where all of the torpedoes, and possible the mines, were unloaded and handed back.

There is a small mystery as Gerth does not mention laying mines during his voyage, something he normally noted meticulously both in his war diary and in a separate mine chart. *UC 61* did make the Lizard in its approach to the Scillies so was well past the area where the mines were to be laid.

> *Because a mine cannot distinguish the nationality of a ship that runs into it, The Hague Convention of 1907 had agreed to keep the open seas free of these lethal weapons floating beneath the ocean's surface. Belligerents were permitted to lay offensive minefields only in hostile territorial waters; that is, within three miles of an enemy's coast. Nevertheless, because the North Sea is generally shallow and therefore particularly suitable for moored contact mines, the German navy, preparing for war, began accumulating a large stock with the intention of using them aggressively … from the first day of war German ships and submarines placed over 25,000 mines in*

> the North Sea, most of them in defiance of The Hague Convention ... Britain was wholly unprepared for large-scale mining.[1]

Half way down the English Channel, overcast with a choppy sea, *UC 61* was briefly caught in cross-fire between opposing destroyers with shells landing dangerously close. Gerth went to the sea bed at twenty-six metres, surfaced an hour later, and was quickly caught in a destroyer's searchlight.

> *The one great risk a submarine runs when lying on the bottom is that her tanks may not be absolutely tight. If they are not, a leakage of air or oil may occur through vent valves or seams, and the bubbles rising to the surface may betray her.*[2]

More shells landed nearby and Gerth went to the bottom again. The next morning, he dived twice before destroyers and in the early afternoon spotted a sailing ship and opened fire which immediately brought the attention of five armed trawlers, two of which guarded the ship while the others conducted a search. Trawler *Sapper* flashed an alert to the Admiralty.[3] Two more patrol vessels passed close by while *UC 61* moved under water.

Early that evening, Gerth passed *UC 21*, returning to Zeebrugge, whose jubilant commander, Oberleutnant Reinhold Saltzwedel, would surely have passed on the news of fifteen ships sunk during his patrol, including that morning the 5,225-ton American tanker *Illinois*, scuttled off Alderney. Neither Saltzwedel nor *UC 21* would survive the year.

Next day, Gerth reached the Lizard after brief brushes with a u-boat hunter and several destroyers.

The morning of 20 March was overcast and blowing a gale. Before first light, Gerth's gyro compass failed and he was obliged to take magnetic bearings to the Wolf Rock lighthouse, a lonely rock some eight miles from the Scillies towards Lizard Point. Wolf Rock gets its name from the howling sound made when strong winds blow through its fissures.

UC 61 spotted some steamers, but failed in the swell to get into position for torpedo firing. Funnel smoke signalled the arrival of two armed trawlers which saw Gerth's periscope; the swell had adversely affected his depth control.

---

1 Massie, *Castles*, p. 140. Vincent, *Politics of Hunger*, pp. 39-40.
2 Koerver, *German Submarine Warfare*, p. 134.
3 *TNA*, ADM 137/390, sighting 1400, repeat alert to Admiralty 1922.

The u-boat dived to forty metres to escape the depth charges which followed. The sea was now so bad that any torpedo attack was impossible. The trawlers followed, one either side, tracking *UC 61* with sound detectors.

> *One u-boat, located by hydrophones and then heavily depth-charged, fell silent beneath the waves. Then a propeller was heard faintly turning or attempting to turn ... a slight grating or squeaking such as might have been made by damaged machinery. This noise lasted a few seconds and stopped. Presently it started up again and then once more it stopped. The submarine made a little progress, but fitfully; she would go a few yards then pause. The surface vessels dropped more depth charges and listened again. Then there was a lumbering noise such as might be made by a heavy object trying to drag its hulk along the muddy bottom; this was followed by silence, showing that the wounded vessels could move only a few yards. By now, the surface vessels had used all of their depth charges and could only wait. All night long, the listeners reported scraping and straining noises from below but these grew fainter and fainter. They listened for hours and then, the following afternoon, heard a sharp piercing noise ... Only one thing in the world could make a sound like that ... the crack of a revolver. More of these pistol cracks followed, counted by the listeners above. In all, twenty-five shots came from the bottom of the sea. Then silence.*[4]

Gerth tried a course change and dropped to fifty metres. Then, catastrophe as both electric motors which gave him underwater power began to malfunction. Gerth recorded what happened next in unusual length in his Kriegstagebuch.[5] This story is combined here with a repeat report in July: the trawlers grew into destroyers and, one suspects, other details changed depending upon the audience.

> *The stuffing boxes of the two crank-shafts of the submarine were not tight and were leaking considerably. The torpedo and engine bilge pumps filled with water owing to the negligence of the sailor in charge of the engines who did not report the initial problem. To avoid being rammed, and still more to avoid the depth charges, the submarine dived to a great depth, about sixty metres.*

---

4 Sims, *Victory at Sea*, pp. 153-54. Massie, *Castles*, p. 737.
5 *TNA*, ADM 137/3898, p. 93. *Gosport*, Admiralty report, 'U-Boats: Activities and Losses', Vol. 1, p. 247.

Sixty metres was the tested maximum depth for a uc-boat, 'but they will dive to greater depths in case of serious emergency'.[6] The emergency kit was minimal. 'Every submarine must carry in the second forward and second aft compartment a bag containing appliances for stopping leaks, including at least the following articles: about twenty wooden plugs, ten mallets of various sizes, one hammer, two chisels, two punches of different sizes, one pair of pliers, one box of matches, two candles and tow.'[7]

> The deep dive made matters worse; a serious amount of water was flooding into the boat. Gerth tried desperately to reach the surface. Because of all of the water collecting in the stern, the boat broke through at a sharp angle with, perhaps, a third of the boat pointing out of the water. A sloop opened fire which obliged Gerth to dive again with all speed. The boat's bow now being down, the water which had accumulated aft rushed forward. The boat sank at a twenty-five degree angle to forty metres. The electric motors were completely fused. Gerth stabilised the boat and came to the surface using compressed air. He found himself in a very rough sea with snow and hail gusts and very limited visibility. The trawlers were nowhere to be seen. The oil engines were switched on and UC 61 headed out to sea. The gyro compass, which had stabilised, failed again. Chief Engineer Johannes Giese worked a small miracle to get some electric power through and began to charge the batteries. Some patrol vessels were evaded and UC 61 was forced to dive again at about midnight. The starboard engine began to malfunction and both electric motors were unstable with no chance of repair.

At three o'clock the next morning, Gerth abandoned his mission. He could not make a controlled dive and would be stationary and vulnerable under water so he began a remarkable voyage from Lands End back to Zeebrugge. After a slow day and night's travel, he decided as he approached the pinch at Dover to spend the following daylight hours on the sea bed and he settled to forty-two metres off Beachy Head. However, the boat shifted so badly in the swell that, after an hour, he decided to continue taking the middle channel between Beachy Head and Le Tréport. In one piece of good news, the gyro compass righted itself.

---

6   Friedman, *German Warships*, p. 79.
7   *TNA* ADM 137/3886, 'Appliances for stopping leaks'.

No-one noticed *UC 61* as it crawled up the French coast. Thankfully, one of the net buoys was unlit, but all other shore lights and other buoys were burning as usual. Just after midday on 23 March, *UC 61* moored at Bruges. Gerth had been at sea for a lifetime of just over eighty hours.

6
THE LOSS OF *LITTLE MYSTERY*

UC 61 spent a month in dry dock at Ostend and by 28 April was provisioned and ready for sea.[1] Much of Gerth's spare time was spent in the officers' mess at Bruges and it was here that he was remembered by fellow commander Werner Fürbringer:

> *Among his fellow sailors in the mess, always the burning cigar between his fingers and the red wine in the background, he spread a special atmosphere of comfort, combined with utmost openness for any humour. Reliability of character, high intellectual abilities, unshakable calm and not least his personal courage distinguished him as a first-class human being and an outstanding officer. He enjoyed a maximum of respect and popularity among his peers.*[2]

Gerth left Bruges for the Isle of Wight in the early hours on Saturday accompanied by *UC 65*, which was ordered to the inner Firth of Clyde, and *UC 69*, bound for the steamer passage at Belle Île and Quiberon Bay off the south coast of Brittany.[3] The British intercepted Gerth's radio messages from

---

1 Bendert, *Die UC-Boote*, p. 159. Spindler, *Der Krieg zur See*, p. 142.
2 Cuxhaven, *Georg Gerth*, Obituary, MOV 11/1970.
3 All three of these u-boats were wrecked before the year end. *UC 65* was torpedoed by British submarine *C 15* fifteen miles south of Beachy Head on 3/11/1917. The first torpedo hit amidships, but did not explode; the second blew off the stern, sinking her instantly; twenty-two

the Straits of Dover for both his inward and outward voyages.[4] Because his call sign was recorded, they knew immediately that *UC 61* was on patrol.

Gerth's orders were to lay his mines in the English Channel at a depth and spacing of his choice, 'if possible at the turn of the tide'.[5] He was then to conduct a 'trade war according to special instructions' and to return at the latest after eighteen days 'depending on capability and ammunition consumption'.

Gerth took his boat to the bottom in order to wait for the right tide to drop his mines. Shortly after midnight, he laid two mines at four metres below mean sea level (as with all of his mines) at the Needles; after twenty minutes, four more were laid one and a half miles away; just over an hour later there were three more at Anvil Point; and then three more at St Alban's Head. It was customary for each of these uc-boats to be assigned a particular minelaying area, which formed the primary objective in subsequent cruises.

The losses among the uc-boats of the Flanders Flotilla were disproportionately high. 'This has been said to be due to indifferent diving qualities and to the absence of a watertight hatch between conning tower and hull'.[6] However, the core work performed in the vicinity of the coast and of harbour entrances was inherently dangerous. Mines slid weighted out of the tubes to the sea floor as the u-boat passed overhead; if the mines stuck in the shaft or rose prematurely the u-boat was at fatal risk. At least nine of the seventy-nine uc-boats launched before 1918 were thought to have been casualties of their own mines. Altogether, by information gathered by 2013, some 40 per cent of all u-boats destroyed in WW1 were the known victims of friendly or enemy mines and a further 14 per cent had an unknown fate.[7]

The customary six obliquely mounted bow shafts or tubes discharged a normal load of eighteen mines through the boat's bottom. The German mines operated as follows.

---

    dead, four survivors; career sinkings: 105 ships. *UC 69* was rammed accidently by *U 96* off Cape Barfleur, sinking immediately by the stern; 'its net cutter fouled *U 96*'s bow, for a short time the two boats were locked together. That turned out to be a blessing because most of *UC 69*'s crew made their way aboard *U 96* by going over the bows. Finally, the bows separated. When *UC 69*'s stern hit the seabed, the after torpedo exploded, killing ten men who were in the water' (Messimer, *Verschollen*), pp. 304, 307.

4   *TNA* ADM 137/3886, 'Report from *UC 61*', 15/5/1917, E.I. No. 146.
5   Typed orders signed by Korvettenkapitän Karl Bartenbach, head of the Flanders U-boat Flotilla 23/4/1917.
6   Koerver, *German Submarine Warfare*, p. 116.
7   McCartney, *Maritime Archaeology*, p. 308.

Both mine and sinker went to the bottom, where the dissolution of a soluble plug allowed the partially air-filled mine to float up toward the surface until a hydrostatic device was activated at the desired depth. The line connecting the mine to the sinker was then snubbed. The sinker had arms that swung out when it reached the bottom in order to stabilise it. The drawback of this system was that the two ropes connecting mine to sinker allowed substantial swaying and variance at depth, while the soluble release mechanism at times dissolved as soon as the mine was released, with the result that it came up and struck the submarine. The so-called German 'egg' mine was fitted with the Hertz horn, a lead tube containing sulphuric acid in a glass container. Impact with a ship broke the glass, allowed the acid to flow onto carbon / zinc elements and thus produced an electric current that fired the detonator attached to the explosives.[8]

At 0325, Gerth surfaced in a near-calm sea and started his diesel engines in order to recharge his electric batteries. These batteries powered the boat underwater and also topped up his compressed air containers which provided air for the crew and to clear ballast tanks when surfacing. *Little Mystery* was sighted at 0630.

Half an hour later, its captain, John Greet, spotted the u-boat on the surface two miles away to the north east and closing quickly.[9] Greet immediately threw all his confidential papers overboard in a weighted sack. There was no escort or Allied patrol boat in sight and no radio to call for help. Greet kept to his course for thirty minutes.[10]

---

8   Herwig, *Luxury Fleet*, p. 219.
9   Greenwich Mean Time (GMT) is used where possible. Correlating times from British ships' logs, foreign ships in British waters, u-boat logs, and times ashore is problematic during WW1. These times frequently do not match from one ship to another during known incidents. For instance, the British first introduced British Summer Time (BST) from 21/5-1/10/1916 to save fuel because of u-boat pressure. Three British naval ships meeting a u-boat mid-Channel, and researched for contact with *UC-61*, recorded times in GMT, BST and German summer time, but they were not consistent. See discussion 'U-boat time in 1917', *WW1 Forum*, u-boat.net.
10 The story of the sinking is taken from *TNA*, ADM 137/1295, /2961 & /4120 and *Kriegsarchiv der Marine, Admiralstab der Marine*, '*UC-61 Kriegtagebuch*' *(RM 97*; ex-Naval Intelligence Division PG/61982/NID) and www.uboot-recherche.de. The *Kriegtagebuch* (KTB) was a submarine's war diary, hand-written by the commanders of the Flanders Flotilla in the old German script, translated in the case of *UC-61* for the author by Dr Cathrin Brockhaus-Dark with assistance from her father, Walter Brockhaus, in deciphering the now little recognised cursive handwriting. This contemporary information was checked against uboat.net and pastscape.org.uk (both accessed 17/5/2016); and Larn, *Shipwreck Index*, Vol. 1, Section 6.

UC-61's diesels were stopped. She approached her prey under water, keeping watch through her periscope.[11]

What makes for a favoured victim among the over 7,000 vessels hit by u-boats in WW1? A personal reaction to a curt mention in a list of misery? Something of beauty destroyed for small gain? A famous resistance? A name that promised allure? An unknown grave?

Little Mystery, a wooden two-masted schooner, was built in 1887 by shipwright William Date at his yard on the Dart River near Kingsbridge, Devon.[12] She was bought that July by John Stephens, a Cornish small ship owner and entrepreneur, trading from his home port of Fowey and its sub-ports of Charlestown, Mevagissey and Par.[13] While Stephens and his son Edward with his wife Mary Ann shared ownership of half the boat, the rest was split among another twenty people – 'the butcher, the baker, the master, the manager and by widows and orphans and by local land-owning families'.[14]

One of Stephens' first small schooners, *Little Beauty*, made a profit of £450 in her first year's trading and the money was distributed to the shareholders by one of the owner's sons 'walking through the Fowey streets and the lanes of the surrounding countryside carrying a jingling wash-leather bag of golden sovereigns'.[15]

'By national standards [Stephens] was not an enterprise of importance or particular significance, merely one of the many that were planted, grew and blossomed ... in Victorian England only to fade ... after the Great War.'[16]

However, the Stephens' fleet did last for more than seventy years, managing over fifty vessels during that time. At its largest in 1902, the fleet comprised seventeen ships, averaging just 130 tons gross apiece.[17] Early on, the fleet

---

11   *Naval Staff Monographs*, Historical Staff, Training and Staff Duties Division, Vol. XVIII, 'Home Waters - Part VIII', December 1916 to April 1917 (C.B. 917Q; O.U. 5528[G]), 5/1933, Section 357, p. 448.

12   'William Date, Shipwrights Yard and the Fruit Schooners', *Knightsbridge Estuary U3A Local History Group*, 16/10/2103, u3asited.org.uk/files/k/kingsbridgeestuary/docs.pdf (accessed 18/5/2016).

13   Ward-Jackson *Stephens of Fowey*, p. 5.

14   TNA, BT 110/349/50, *Little Mystery*, Ship's Register (official number 85828). Many shares were mortgaged from time to time; detailing of the consequent transfers of shares would require a chapter in their own right. Also, Greenhill, *Merchant Schooners*, Vol. 2, p. 109, and see pp. 111-15, 120-29.

15   Greenhill, 'The Rise and Fall of the British Coastal Steamer', *The Mariner's Mirror, Vol. 27, Issue 3, 1941*, p. 250.

16   Ward-Jackson, *Stephens of Fowey*, p. 5.

17   Ward-Jackson, *Stephens of Fowey*, p. 5, offers the comparison of the *Cutty Sark* (1869) at 863 gross

became known as the *Company of Little Ships* because some of them had names beginning with *Little* – 'a fleet within a fleet'. 'The distinction had a certain ambiguity since all of the vessels were little, but only ten – but never more than five at once - were *Little*.' All were sailing ships with light crews which included some of the fastest passage-makers of their kind, trading as far as the Indian Ocean and the South Atlantic, though concentrating on the western ocean and, in poor economic times, the coasting business.

The first *Little* in the Stephens' fleet was *Little Beauty*, built at Polruan, Cornwall, in 1875, 'so called because her timber was too small to be used in another ship, the *Ocean Swell*, being built at the same time'.[18] *Little Mystery* was the sister ship of the *Little Wonder*, launched a year before her in 1886 from the same yard.[19] In 1893, *Little Gem* was added to the fleet, another sister ship of *Little Mystery* 'from whose model she was built, the measurements of the two vessels hardly differing'.[20] They were singled-decked, carvel-built boats, eighty-four feet long, 114 gross tonnage when built, and noted for their clean lines, square stern and full female figureheads.[21] In 1894, *Little Mystery* was reduced to 95 tons following the addition of a lower forecastle, sail room, bosun's store, master's room and a chart room.[22]

Little Mystery and her sisters epitomised their half-namesakes, the 'small fry of the ocean', and mostly traded to Newfoundland with salt, returning with dried fish cod.[23] 'Until the beginning of the first world war there were nearly always

---

tons – over six times the size of a *Little*; the full-rigged *Preussen* (1902) at 5,548 tons; and the largest sailing vessel, *France II* (1911), at 5,806 tons (a multiple of almost forty-five).

18 These and following details are taken liberally from Ward-Jackson, *Stephens of Fowey*, particularly pp. 21, 34, 37-38, 76, 84.

19 *Little Wonder* was lost in mid-Atlantic on 24/9/1891. She was on her way from Newfoundland with codfish when in a gale the cargo shifted. The masts had to be cut away and the mate was drowned, though the rest of the crew, lashed to the stumps of the masts, were saved by a passing steamer. Twenty-six people from around Fowey had shares in her (Ward-Jackson, *Stephens of Fowey*), p. 37.

20 84.5 feet x 21.1 x 10.8 (*TNA*, BT 110/349/50).

21 Carvel-built: Wooden planks which do not overlap, as opposed to clinker-built. Gross tonnage at that time was a measure of a ship's cargo capacity.

22 *TNA*, BT 110/349/50.

23 The phase about 'small fry' is from Lubbock, Basil, *Last of the Windjammers*, Vol. 1 (Brown, Son & Ferguson, Glasgow 1927), pp. 455, 460. In John Stephens' day 100,000 fishermen were employed in the Newfoundland trade. 'Making fish, involved hand-cleaning, extracting the liver to rot down into cod liver oil, washing, salting and placing in kegs to pickle in a shore-side shed, then spreading out on racks to dry in the sun, and finally weighing in quintals or 112 pound lots (Ward-Jackson, *Stephens of Fowey*), p. 36.

six or seven of these vessels on the Atlantic.' The Boon brothers of Bideford recalled that maintenance was done at a yard local to them.[24] John Stephens would come from Fowey, sitting in his own small folding chair, watching work in progress on a *Little* or other fleet ship:

> *Of all the schooners we saw, those ships were the most perfect. They were all coloured green under the waterline and painted black above, their decks were scrubbed, their masts scraped and varnished – for they could afford to do those things in those days. The apprentices used to work overtime scraping off the surplus pitch after the caulking and thereby seeking to supplement their five shillings per week. Even then, Mr Stephens would be sitting there ... to make sure that we did a perfectly good job.*[25]

Captain R A Fletcher wrote a love-book to the world of tall ships, but amongst its pages he made space to laud the small schooners which he saw, year in year out, 'thrash their way back and forth' across the Atlantic, chiefly carrying fish from Newfoundland, St Pierre and Miquelon to Gibraltar or to Spanish or French ports.[26] The Stephens' ships performed winter and summer with a 'regularity which spoke volumes for the seamanship of those who commanded them and was a glowing testimony to the strength of their construction, their suitability for their work, and the excellence of their equipment'. Fletcher named particularly *Little Secret* and *Little Mystery* as well known – 'the romance of the sea can never die out while such vessels and such crews as manned them are afloat'.

> *Once I saw one of these ocean-going schooners showing what she could do in a howling North Atlantic gale, with the sea running mountains high ... The sailing ship I was in was under reduced canvas. As the schooner crossed our bows less than half a mile distant we could see her leaning over until her lee gunwale was under water. Her three little scraps of sail, looking not much bigger than handkerchiefs, tore her along at a great pace amid a smother of foam, and clouds of heavy spray and sometimes green water swept her from end to end. We could see two oilskin-clad figures at the wheel; they must have been firmly lashed or they would have been washed away. She seemed*

---

24 The two maintenance yards were Benjamin Tregaskis at Par and at Cleave Houses, on the north bank of the Torridge between Bideford and Appledore.
25 Greenhill, *Merchant Schooners*, pp. 110-11.
26 Fletcher, R A, *In the Days of the Tall Ships* (Brentano's, London 1928), pp. 32-33.

a living, a mad thing as she rushed down the slope of one wave and up the next, bounding ahead in a fashion that even the famous Dreadnought, the 'wild boat of the Atlantic' ... could not have surpassed.

Basil Greenhill, life-long champion of ships like *Little Mystery*, continued the paean: 'These schooners did not often heave-to, indeed they ran often until it was too late to heave-to. Their particular danger, of course, was that of being pooped and swept clean by a fast following sea.'[27] The common method of combating this danger was to tow a hawser behind the vessel in order to slow her down and smooth her wake. 'With a heavy sea, a small mistake would mean lost spars, perhaps a smashed wheel, cleared decks and a broach-to.'

Little Mystery usually carried four or five men drawn from the country around Fowey; West Country men known to the owner. 'Local boys sometimes learned the tricks of this exacting trade in a few years of apprenticeship, and it is said that one small schooner once made an Atlantic passage under the command of a young man only eighteen years old.'

Little Mystery's best known master was John Henry Greet of Plymouth. Born in 1867 in St Blazey, Cornwall, he passed his master's certificate at Fowey in 1894, aged twenty-nine.[28] Greet's own father was blind and lived by teaching the blind. In 1917, Greet's second wife, Rhoda, waited at home in Plymouth with their twelve-year-old daughter, also Rhoda.[29]

On Monday 30 April, Greet, now fifty-two-years-old, and greatly experienced with his ship, was on a south by east course, twenty-five miles south-south-east from Portland Bill on the Dorset coast. *Little Mystery* was alone in a smooth sea and, through the slight haze, she was visible from six miles away. Despite all sails set, she was making only a vulnerable three knots in the light breeze from the north. Her cargo was 168 tons of coal, shipped by Hansa Brothers, loaded at Cardiff and bound for Cherbourg where it was consigned to Messrs Cavroy of Paris.[30]

---

27   Greenhill, *Merchant Schooners*, pp. 113-14.
28   Certificates of Competency, 023292, Fowey: Mate, 18/12/1890, Master 12/4/1894 (*National Maritime Museum*, Master's Certificates). Ancestry.co.uk.
29   Greet's first wife, Elizabeth Hannah Ackland, died after two years of marriage in 1899, aged thirty-four. Greet lodged with the extended Ackland family and, in 1902, married Elizabeth's sister, Rhoda Louisa Ackland, aged thirty-five.
30   *TNA*, ADM 137/1295, English Channel: German submarines, 4/1917.

The area around Portland harbour was busy in 1917 patching up merchant ships, unloading trains with munitions and loading them into transports for the Western front.[31] The Portland naval authorities were also responsible for the controlled sailings in the French coal trade, a lifeline to the French economy since the Germans had captured their north-eastern industrial heartlands in 1914, including seventy-four percent of its coal production.[32]

Two months before, matters became so serious that the French prime minister sent a three-man delegation at a day's notice from Paris to London asking for them 'to be received without delay by Mr Lloyd George and the competent British authorities on questions relating to coal'.[33]

> *The French Government are faced by an extremely grave crisis caused by the coal shortage in France. This shortage has already necessitated the closing down of a number of factories engaged in work of national defence. M. Briand fears that if the present state of affairs is prolonged there will be an interruption in the production of the most important requirements.*[34] *The French Government consider that it is essential to address to the British Government an urgent appeal begging them to make a serious effort capable of remedying this state of affairs.*

Little Mystery's 168 tons of coal may have been a pinprick but, for all her small size, her voyage was a part of the British response to the French plea. The coal was undisputed war contraband at any stage of the conflict notwithstanding the German re-declaration of unrestricted submarine warfare just three months before.[35] It was enough to guarantee her sinking if caught by a u-boat and, if

---

31   Carter, *Royal Navy at Portland*, p. 39.
32   Strachan, *First World War*, p. 59.
33   Translated letter from the French Embassy, London, 20/2/1917 (*TNA*, ADM 137/1392, French Coal Trade, Jan-Apr 1972), p. 249. The importance of the French coal trade to the Allied war effort is shown by two volumes of letters and orders, each containing some 600 pages. David Lloyd George was the Liberal prime minister of the British wartime coalition government.
34   Aristide Briand, French prime minister over eleven terms. He resigned within a month following a letter over disagreements on the conduct of the war. He received the Nobel Peace Prize in 1926 for his work on territorial peace treaties between the Allies and Germany. The delegation was led by René Viviani, French prime minister for the first year of the war.
35   The German Government declared on 31/1/17 that they would resume unrestricted submarine warfare on the following day. Admiral von Holtzendorff and his naval staff calculated that 'if their submarines could sink upwards of 350,000 tons a month when working under restrictions it was reasonable to suppose that when freed from them they could bring the rate up to 600,000 a

British propaganda about u-boat callousness and frequent atrocities was to be believed, or the crew was just unlucky, the intervention could be fatal.

Colliers bound for Cherbourg and ports west, and colliers with speeds under eight knots bound for Brest and the Bay of Biscay ports, assembled at Portland under a French-run scheme.[36] This arrangement precluded small schooners like *Little Mystery*, which was at the mercy of the wind and, on this day, moving at walking pace.

UC 61 surfaced about two hundred yards away on the port side close to the schooner's stern. This manoeuvre was designed to lessen the risk if the u-boat found its prey was actually a trap - a Q ship.

Little Mystery's capture was slightly farcical – no torpedo was loosed as these were too expensive to expend on a small schooner and, besides, there were still six mines aboard; there was no warning shell either from the 88mm cannon. Twenty-nine-year-old Georg Gerth stood in his conning tower when close alongside and fired six or seven shots from his pistol and that was enough.

At the first shot, *Little Mystery* hove to, its crew decided not to return fire with their own hand weapons. A Russian able seaman, Carl Eglit, was hit in the fleshy part of the muscle in his left arm. Greet, Eglit and the three other crew, two British and a Portuguese, immediately got into their 'almost new' boat and rowed across to *UC 61* taking with them as directed their ship's papers.

What the men saw at close quarters was a u-boat with a black hull and large grey conning tower, all in old paint, a canvas bridge screen, one gun and a periscope. An arrangement was noticed in the bows, circular with teeth, like a saw.[37] Three officers and six men were on deck. Two of the officers were in 'duffle clothing', one in a blue uniform. The men were in 'civilian clothes and appeared dirty and unkempt'. One of them had a cap ribbon of the Flanders Flotilla, another wore a ribbon of SMS *Derfflinger*, a battlecruiser of the *Kaiserliche Marine*.[38]

Greet was told by a junior officer who spoke good English that he should have got his boat in the water more quickly. The master was kept on *UC 61*

---

month' (Patterson, *Jellicoe*), pp. 160-76. See also, amongst many, Compton-Hall, *Submarines at War*, pp. 260-68; and Gibson and Prendergast, *German Submarine War*, Chapter VIII.
36 Carter, *Portland*, p. 39.
37 A device for cutting net wires.
38 At Jutland on 28/5/1917, *Derfflinger* was partially responsible for the sinking of two British battlecruisers: with *Seydlitz* she destroyed *Queen Mary* and, with the *Lützow*, sank *Invincible* (Massie, *Castles of Steel*), pp. 588-92.

while a boarding party laid a single explosive device on *Little Mystery*'s waterline. The party also scoured the schooner for food, described in one official report as 'looting'.[39]

> *On the deck a medley of boxes and chests of cocoa, coffee and expensive tea, sacks of wonderful American meal, fresh butter and globes of margarine, cordage, unused nets, oilskins, rubber boots that did not fit the crew, fine white English bread, English marmalade, ham and bully-beef, bacon and beans, two bars of good soap, tobacco and various oddments. All these things, which were now completely strange to us, we had removed from a few paltry enemy fishing-boats, while in Germany the women and children were starving and dying of inanition, or supporting life on vile, injurious, almost uneatable food-substitutes. The poor in Germany thought of old days as they sat over their watery turnips; while in the cabins of these trawlers, which we happened to have sunk just at dinner time, were plates filled with, what seemed to us, lavish helpings of good fresh roast meat and potatoes, such as we only saw in dreams.*[40]

Greet didn't mention any looting except that he claimed that the German commander 'seized my ensign'. He also volunteered that he was allowed to return to his ship to get his compass and was told that he could take some of his photographs as well. 'We saved a few things.'

There was no sign of *Little Mystery* breaking up on the surface; Greet reported her 'sinking stern first'. The charted position is 50° 10'N; 2° 13' 9"W, but as wreck detective Jan Lettens says this could be one kilometre in any direction.[41] It is possible that some of the coal cargo which was all carried in the hold spilled out of the bomb hole in her side on the way down.

The bottom here is about sixty metres with varieties of sand, shell, gravel, pebble and mud. The good timber from Date's Dart River yard is likely wearing well, but the decks will be swept clean, the hull will have settled and, at a hold depth of less than eleven feet, her seafloor silhouette will be slight, swept by currents, but possibly covered in snagged nets, sea urchins, peacock worms, anemones, pouting and pollock.[42]

---

39 *TNA*, ADM 137/1295, p. 114.
40 War artist Bergen, 'My U-Boat Voyage', Neureuther, *U-Boat Stories*, p. 51.
41 wrecksite.eu.
42 'The destruction of wooden wreck sites is especially worrying because after the effects of currents and trawling they typically display little relief above the sea bottom' (Bennett, wrecksite.eu forum,

Little Mystery has no value, is unlikely to show on a sonar, and will probably only be found, if even noticed, by accident.

In the thirteen months fourteen days beginning with Boxing Day 1916, Stephens, *Little Mystery*'s owners, lost ten vessels, of which nine were by enemy action, mostly by u-boats. What seems certain is that these sinkings 'represented a heavy loss for which they received no compensation'.[43]

Greet and his crew pulled towards Portland and, at about 0945, sighted *Royalo*, an armed trawler, which 'from a very far distance' [four miles] opened fire with eight rounds.[44] *UC 61* moved out of sight of *Royalo* above water and after a time submerged showing her periscope. *Royalo* picked up Greet and his crew and took them to Weymouth. It was not yet midday.

John Greet was awarded two war honours in 1919 – the First World War *Mercantile Marine War Medal* and the *British War Medal*.[45] After the war he moved from Plymouth to Middlesex, England, where he lived with his daughter Rhoda and her two children. He died in 1934, aged sixty-eight.

It may come as a surprise that *Little Mystery* lives on. Apart from articles and book references, there is a full hull model on a frame on display at the *National Maritime Museum* at Greenwich, London.[46] The model is decked, with a number

---

15/06/2016). See also Kingsley, 'Deep-Sea Fishing Impacts on the Shipwrecks of the English Channel & Western Approaches'.
43 Ward-Jackson, *Stephens of Fowey*, p. 53
44 *TNA*, ADM 137/675, Weekly Report of Portland Auxiliary Vessels. *Monographs*, Vol. XVIII, fn. p. 448. *Royalo* was mined and sunk off Penzance 1/9/1940 (u.boat.net).
45 *TNA*, BT 351/1/54397, both issued 29/4/1921.The *Mercantile Marine War Medal* was instituted by the Board of Trade to reward the war service of the officers and men of the Mercantile Marine who, while only trained as peacetime mariners, continued to serve while running the risk of being attacked at sea during the war. The *British War Medal* was a campaign medal of the United Kingdom which was awarded to officers and men of British and Imperial forces for service in the First World War (en.wikipedia.org), accessed 27/5/2016.
46 *National Maritime Museum*, SLR1179 (accessed 27/5/2016). The model, dimensions: 860 x 1,174 x 432 mm, was presented to the museum by the builder Max T Davey of Hove, Sussex, in 1969. Other Davey models and prints at *NMM*: two different versions of the mackerel driver *Ebenezer*, 1867, and the sailing brig *Marie Sophie*, 1879 (prints.rmg.co.uk/artist/28383/Max-T-Davey), accessed 27/5/2016; and in the *National Trust Collection*, on loan from *Cotehele Museum*, Cornwall, the *Rhoda Mary* (NT 812819). Davey was a prolific craftsman producing work to a high standard and was known for his style of finishing a model in a realistic fashion compared to the more clinical exhibition style for museum displays. Davey 'also produced accurate and detailed models that could be sailed using radio controlled equipment which was quite rare' (Stephens, Curator of the Ship Model and Boat Collections, NMM, email, 17/6/2016).

of crew in sight, fully equipped and rigged with sails set. So popular is *Little Mystery* that a print and a drinking mug with her image are also available.

The loss of *Little Mystery* may be seen as a part of the hastening of the demise of the cargo sailing ship. Losses to WW1 u-boats identified to the year 2016 total 7,241 in sunken and damaged ships. While it is impossible to clearly categorise all of these, or even to be certain about their propulsion in each case, what is sure to just a few percentage error points is that for every ten ships sunk, three were sailing ships, perhaps some 2,171.[47] However, for Basil Greenhill and the Stephens' fleet, it was not so simple:

> *During the war, there were a sufficient number for convoys to be made up of schooners alone, and such convoys were escorted by armed vessels of their own class. Many were sunk, others fought successful operations with submarines, and some were borrowed for conversion into Q ships. The wartime losses among the sailing coasters were actually considerable ... but nevertheless many survived and these, together with the vessels taken over from the enemy, schooners bought from Holland during the shipping boom, and a few newly constructed ships, must have made quite a considerable fleet ready to resume normal work after the cessation of hostilities.*[48]

More proudly, *Little Mystery* provided her own epitaph as the spur that saved many other schooners on the coal run to France, including some from her home port in Fowey. Less than a month after her sinking, the shipping intelligence officer at Portland wrote to the Admiral's office in Devonport telling him that he had started 'collecting small ketches and schooners and sending them to France as convoys' protected by armed vessels:

> *One lot of eleven left here about three weeks ago and arrived safely, and five left Fowey on 17 May. These latter were French and had one thousand tons of coal between them. They were attacked by a submarine en route, but the attack was beaten off by the escort. It is extremely difficult to obtain escorts, but it would appear worthy of consideration ...*[49]

---

47 Database: Lowrey, *WW1 forum*, uboat.net, 18/5/2016; calculations, the author, 20/5/2016.
48 Greenhill, 'Rise and Fall', p. 256.
49 *TNA*, ADM 137/1393, French Coal Trade, p. 27, letter dated 21/5/1917. An annotation says the admiral agreed on 29/5/1917.

Eight days later, the admiral concurred. Soon, schooners like *Little Mystery* were made up into regular convoys in their own right and were escorted by armed sailing ships.[50]

---

[50] Greenhill, 'Rise and Fall', p. 256.

Georg, right, with his mother, Herwig, and brother, Erich, taken in Berlin, about 1893. *Family archive*

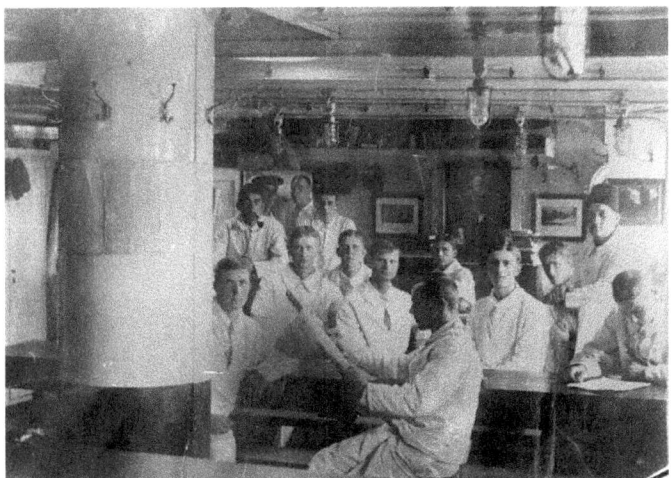

The only picture of Georg in cadet training: centre, staring at camera, about 1907. *Family archive*

Georg's school ship, SMS *Freya*, a converted cruiser.

Naval officer cadet Georg, about 1910, with his mother, Hedwig. *Family archive*

Pre-dreadnought battleship, SMS *Preussen*, Georg's first sea-going appointment before 1911.

Georg's posting in 1912 on the West African station, the gunboat SMS *Panther*.

The opening ceremony for the 'Rider Statue', a *Schutztruppe*, in Windhoek, South West Africa, on 27 January 1912, the Kaiser's birthday. Is Georg in the crowd?

The brutal commander of the German forces in South West Africa, Lothar von Trotha, who led the genocide of the Herero people.

Leopold II of Belgium, responsible for the exploitation of his personal fiefdom, the Congo Free State.

Edmund Morel, uncovered the horror of the Congo and devoted much of his life to ending it.

The light cruiser SMS *Amazone*, Georg's first major posting in the Baltic in 1914.

Roger Casement, honoured in 1905 for his report on Leopold's atrocities in the Congo.

UB 10 and *UB 13*, sister boats of Georg's *UB 12*, lie side by side in the part shelter of Zeebrugge mole. They are painted in camouflage and have 'eyes', typical of the Flanders u-boats. *Tomas Termote*

7

A HECTIC DAY

For the Admiralty and *UC 61* faced a hectic day. Before 1000, Gerth surfaced and successfully topped up his boat's batteries and compressed air. He then moved on to lay his remaining six mines.

UC 61's morning mines had already been spotted even before *Little Mystery* was sunk. The Admiralty moved quickly to clear the mines at St Alban's Head; that speed brought Gerth's second success of the day, although unknown to him until later.

HMT *Arfon*, a coal-burning, ketch-rigged Milford trawler, was requisitioned for war service as part of the general naval mobilisation a few days before war was declared and was converted for minesweeping duties.[1] At 0945, *Arfon*, with the armed trawler *Vera Grace*, swept for the unknown number of mines laid a few hours earlier. One mine was spotted and exploded by rifle fire, a second hit the fore part of *Arfon* and she sank within two minutes; of the crew of thirteen, the ten who worked under cover died.[2]

There was clearly at least one other u-boat operating in the same general area as several reports came in of minor u-boat skirmishes and these are not reflected in *UC 61*'s war diary. All within a few miles of Portland that Saturday: at 1100, SS *Vestalia*, 5,528 tons, exchanged fire with a u-boat until it was driven down by patrols; motor launches 307 and 311 dropped depth charges off Portland Bill at 1130 having seen a wake and claimed a 'kill' which

---

1   *Milford Trawlers*, 'Arfon M223', llangibby.eclipse.co.uk, accessed 18/5/2016.
2   *TNA*, ADM 137/3255, 'Court of Enquiry'.

the Admiralty decided was 'improbable'; SS *Oilfield*, 4,005 tons, managed to outrun a u-boat at 1715; just before midnight a conning tower was sighted near Lulworth; the collier *Querida* sighted a submarine on her starboard beam in the early hours and opened fire as the u-boat disappeared into the darkness.[3]

On his way that afternoon to the Shambles Bank at Portland, Gerth stayed above water while evading a destroyer. At about 1700, he spotted a steamer and headed for it, then dived to let it pass, approached under water and surfaced to fire about ten shots from his canon. This was the Uruguayan SS *Gorizia* of Montevideo, 1,246 tons, from New York via Falmouth for Le Havre carrying 'general cargo', including brass and oranges.[4] The main steam pipe in the boiler room was the only hit causing an immediate loss of power.

Gorizia hove to and the mixed-nationality crew of twenty-two took to their lifeboats and pulled clear. *Gorizia* was boarded and, in the same manner as *Little Mystery*, its American master George Rex was kept on *UC 61* while two bombs were attached. Rex noted the u-boat crew's 'greenish-colour duffle suits'. *Gorizia* sank by the stern within five minutes.

> *The [steamer] sank bow foremost in the usual way; her consort vanished silently by the stern ... The pressure of air and water flung a little cloud of soot from the funnels of both, the so-called 'black soul', the final farewell of a steamer on its way to the bottom of the sea.*[5]

Finding an American master on *Gorizia* was bad luck for Gerth as the Germans remained desperate to keep the United States neutral and out of the war. Gerth, speaking excellent English, listened while Rex protested his American

---

3   Monographs, p. 448; *TNA* ADM 137/1295; ADM 137/442; ADM 137/1296.
4   'Le Havre' was consistently called 'Havre' in Admiralty documents (*TNA*, ADM 137/1295). *Gorizia* was built in 1907 by A Macmillan & Son of Dumbarton, Scotland, as *Glenmount* for the Montreal Transportation Company, Canada, perhaps later SS *Great Lakes*, passing to her last name at the Oriental Navigation Corporation, New York, and, later, Montevideo, shortly before sinking. Sonar contact was established in 1945. In 1988, divers reported the bows blown off (Davies, 24/8/1988, 19/7/1989). Examined by Differential Global Positioning System (DPGS) on 8/5/2003, upright, but partly buried at a depth of forty-two metres at 50° 36'N, 2° 55'W, seventeen miles from Portland Bill (Lettens 27/8/2008; Allen 7/9/2011, wrecksite.eu, accessed 27/5/2016.
5   Bergen, 'U-Boat Voyage', Neureuther, *U-Boat Stories*, p. 50.

nationality and replied with an unemotional, 'I am very sorry, but war is war'.[6] He then told Rex to get back to his ship's boat as an armed yacht had been spotted. The *Lorna* having heard the gunfire approached the confrontation and let off five shells which fell short of *UC 61* by fifty yards. The u-boat dived and all that remained was for *Lorna* to pick up *Gorizia*'s crew and take them to Weymouth.

Gerth finished his twenty-four hours by recharging his batteries before continuing to the Shambles to drop his last mines. On the way, shortly before midnight, he saw a large, unidentified, steamer running with dimmed lights. Gerth was about to shoot when his u-boat was spotted in the moonlight and the steamer turned and made off. A little later, Gerth was forced to dive before a destroyer. At the Shambles, the moonlight was still strong so Gerth dived *UC 61* to avoid being silhouetted in the bright night at the time of his greatest vulnerability; he laid his six mines at irregular distances.

---

6 The Uruguayan *Chargé d'Affaires* quickly took up the sinking of one of its registered ships, looking 'urgently' for further information, but they met the Admiralty 'playing a straight bat' (*TNA*, ADM 137/1295).

8
BALANCE SHEET

What had *UC 61* achieved during 30 April?

Eighteen mines had been dropped in prime Allied shipping lanes. As some of the mines were quickly spotted, dozens of naval craft were diverted to search for them and others.[1] Naval reports suggest that eleven mines had been found by the end of the day and the cost had been high with the loss of *Arfon* and ten men dead.

The confusion did not end there as the next day, Tuesday, 1 May, at 0730, the Commodore-in-Charge, Portland, was forced to close Portland and Weymouth Bay to all traffic 'on account of mines'; at that time only four had been neutralised.[2] The warning was reiterated at 1330, 'no entry, closed until further notice'. The all clear came the next day at 2150, but immediately St Alban's Bay was closed. The disruption to traffic and convoy management was considerable.

Gerth had also sunk the ten-year-old steamer *Gorizia* with its cargo of brass and other metals, probably ordered by the French Government and, equally probably, euphemistically placed on the manifest as 'general cargo' alongside oranges.[3]

---

1 The Commodore-in-Charge at Portland had forty larger vessels at his disposal for convoy escort, minesweeping and anti-submarine activity, as well as over a dozen motor launches (*TNA*, ADM 137/675).
2 *TNA*, ADM 137/442.
3 One unconfirmed diver report says that *Gorizia* was on charter to the French Government, making her a legitimate target. In 1989, divers reported that most of her cargo of brass had been recovered (wrecksite.eu).

And then there was the loss of *Little Mystery*, with her wounded man, and her coal.

And the cost to the Flanders Flotilla of the *Kaiserlichen Marine*? The balance sheet shows a day's u-boat running costs, eighteen mines, no torpedoes, ten 88mm shells, three bombs, and a magazine of pistol ammunition.

One source carefully calculated that Britain's fight against the u-boats absorbed the efforts of 770,000 men (including naval and merchant crews, shipbuilders, dockyard workers, and naval ordnance manufacturers) and diverted from other use some 13,000 naval guns, 3,700 searchlights, nearly 46,000 tons of munitions, and 16,327 kilometre's worth of wire for submarine nets.[4]

---

4   Mulligan, *Neither Sharks*, p. 40.

9
A VISIT TO FRANCE

For Gerth, the following day in contrast was busy, but fruitless. He failed to engage two steamers and three sailing ships. He was fired at by armed trawlers and destroyers escorting a steamer convoy, and, at different hours, evaded four patrol boats, two trawlers, four destroyers, an airship and a plane.

Gerth prudently headed towards Ouessant [Ushant] off the coast of Brittany.

Within hours of arriving at the French coast the next morning, 3 May, Gerth tersely states that he used his cannon to sink two small French fishing boats, an hour apart. French reports initially stated that both boats had been sunk, but this was later corrected to just one.[1]

This was an inglorious episode and left British naval officers wondering whether two submarines were involved because in the first attack 'the Germans showed an appalling ferocity, killing three men and seriously wounding two others'. One wonders whether Gerth was below and had delegated the sinking of this unimportant boat to a junior officer?

> *The necessity for a short, concise, strictly matter-of-fact statement of events dictated our style. Nothing of our sentiments, our inwards selves, found expression.*[2]

---

1 *TNA*, ADM 137/4120.
2 Hashagen, *Commander*, p. 242.

Victorine Helène from Audierne was near the *Ar Men* lighthouse with an excellent catch of skate when *UC 61* was spotted while it was a mile and a half away.[3] The submarine passed 200 metres astern and opened fire without warning, perhaps a dozen shots, and destroyed the vessel's interior. The dead were Jean Guillou, the owner with three children; Jean Guilcher, nine children; and Jean Noel Milliner.[4]

The two injured survivors and an uninjured man stayed hidden in the bottom of the boat for a quarter of an hour while the u-boat left. They tacked east with an oar and used a largely undamaged sail to join a nearby group of fishermen who took them to the Île de Sein where their wounds were dressed. Apart from the unnecessary violence, there is one discrepancy: the fishermen claimed the u-boat used two guns while *UC 61* had only one. This claim is not unusual from inexperienced witnesses under fire for the first time. Also unexplained, is why the boat was not sunk.

Fils du Progrès was another tiny craft, this time from Camaret with a crew of seven.[5] The boat was also fishing for skate using a dinghy to place the nets. *UC 61* was spotted a mile away, the nets cut, and the dinghy recalled. Another boat nearby did the same and fled. At 100 metres, Gerth shouted something to the fishermen which they did not understand. He then made signs for them to gather in the stern; three shots then landed in the bow. *Fils du Progress* sank within five minutes and the men were left in their dinghy.

That evening, Gerth attacked an armed 3,030-ton Italian steamer *Giovannina* carrying oranges from Catania to Liverpool.[6] After several shots hit the boat, its crew took to their boats without casualties. Gerth dived to close with the vessel, surfaced and sent a party aboard to attach two bombs. The Giovannina did not sink immediately so, now in darkness, Gerth put *UC 61* alongside and attached two more. While the boat sank, *UC 61*'s stern came hard against the ship's side. The muzzle door of the underwater aft torpedo tube was buckled and jammed. Gerth spent the next day cruising off the Loire while the muzzle door was freed so that it could be kept shut by water pressure while diving.

---

3   *TNA*, ADM 137/3988.
4   The two wounded men were Maurice Thymrut and Jean Pierre Salaun. A second Jean Guilcher, possibly a son, was unhurt.
5   *TNA*, ADM 137/3988.
6   uboat.net.

Back on patrol shortly after midnight on 5 May, Gerth sighted a steamer in the Loire estuary and gave chase for over five hours. At dawn, now within gun range, he opened fire, hitting twice before his cannon's height adjuster failed, making further shots difficult in a rolling sea.

The steamer was the 1,658-ton *Le Gard* which replied immediately and accurately. Gerth now took his only casualty of the war when one of his seamen was slightly wounded in the foot by shrapnel. Gerth dived *UC 61* for ten minutes and when he resurfaced found the horizon obscured by smoke shells. The height adjuster was fixed and, as the smoke cleared, the steamer was sighted again. Shooting from the height of *Le Gard*'s deck was accurate and landed too close to *UC 61*. Gerth took the pragmatic option and aborted the combat.

The report from the French master of *Le Gard*, Etienne Robert, survives and is a slightly more excited telling.[7] Particularly, Robert claimed that there were two submarines and that he sank one, a claim dismissed by the Admiralty as 'improbable'.[8] Here are some extracts:

> As soon as the first submarine was sighted I ordered the crew to battle stations and three minutes after came the first shell from the submarine's cannon. I ordered 'Open fire'. At the same time, I noticed a second submarine of a lighter colour coming towards us roughly on the first quarter on the port side of the first one and further behind. I then launched seven Berger smoke screens to try and keep the second submarine surrounded by smoke ... At the second shell from the first submarine the main mast was cut and the radio sliced into five pieces; with the seventh shell numerous pieces of shrapnel holed our lifeboats and killed Stoker Pierre Malcoste, grievously wounded the first Stoker Emmanuel Herledan, and lightly wounded Henri Le Guay, Chief Engineer, and Jean Izagard, Second Engineer .... An uninterrupted burst of firing, about thirty rounds, and another shell cut the cables on the aft starboard side peppering the deck and main mast with shrapnel ... I manoeuvred the ship to keep the second submarine within the smoke and to keep the first one astern ... Several shots punctured the gangway and wounded Helmsman Honore Grenier but he did not move from his post ... At the fourteenth firing of Le Gard's cannon we hit the submarine full on at 4,200 metres. Immediately we clearly noticed a vertical flame rising to about twenty

---

7 *TNA*, ADM 137/3988.

8 *TNA* ADM 239/26.

metres, and black smoke, quite different from that of the smokescreen, rising in a plume. The submarine went down quickly by the stern, its nose in the air ... The second submarine came out of the smoke and chased us at top speed whilst firing to which we replied straight away ... I gave the orders to the engines to do the impossible ... The battle started again. We replied shot for shot with eight well aimed rounds which forced the submarine to cease firing and to abandon the fight ... During the fight, all the men acted with admirable composure and discipline ... I would like to bring your particular attention to the good conduct of several members of the crew who did their duty courageously without flinching [twenty-one names attached with details of their deeds].

Gerth then took *UC 61* into Audierne Bay for two days to make repairs. The muzzle door caused ongoing problems and the final solution was to completely shut it and to accept that it would take twenty seconds on the surface for it to be opened and to fire a torpedo. A pressure pump which supplied air to the port engine had been running hot and needed a one-and-a-half-day overhaul, but to no avail. When re-assembled, it ran hot again. Without the necessary tools it was impossible to fix so the starboard engine was adjusted to double up for air supply. Work was regularly interrupted by the need to dive before French patrols.

In the morning of the second day, the French steamer *Nelly*, 1,868 tons, was seen close by and a gun attack made which was 'tenaciously reciprocated'. Here was another case where two, perhaps three, submarines were seen.

Nelly's master, Francois Seres, estimated that about a hundred shells were fired at his boat over half an hour which, if true, would be an extraordinary rate of fire by *UC 61*. *UC 61* scored a lucky hit on an ammunition pile at the rear of the vessel which went up 'in great flames and continuing detonations'. One crew member, gunner Tesseraud, was killed, five seriously wounded and seven slightly.

The master was found slumped in the watch room, weakened by loss of blood, and was helped off the vessel by his mate. The white flag was raised and the crew hastily disembarked in two lifeboats. The master and six men were held hostage aboard the u-boat while Carstensen, an officer and two other sailors searched the ship and then placed six mines.

'The German officer brutally refused permission to go on board to find medication and bandages for the wounded.'

The boarding party was away for three-quarters of an hour and brought back sextants, alidades, a compass, a chronometer, arms and three bundles of foodstuffs. The German sailors also asked by sign language for a small barrel for some wine.

Nelly, from Oran with wine for Rouen, was sunk with blasting cartridges. After two-and-a-half hours, the crew was picked up by the Norwegian steamship *Gustav Vigeland* which showed 'generous sympathy'.

For the first time, detailed personal descriptions of Gerth and his men were provided by the crew of the *Nelly*.

Everyone was dirty. The commander was tall, thin, clean shaven, blond hair, between thirty-five and forty years, and wore a grey-brown suit without insignia and a 'traditional soft hat as German tourists wear, without the feather'. The mate was smaller, agile despite being rather fat, with a moustache and chestnut hair. He was dressed in a dark blue jacket with gold buttons and wore a badged naval cap. The sailors wore dirty blue canvas clothes and fatigues. One sailor was wearing a well-worn leather jacket. Another had a jacket in brown material and wore long rubber gloves. They had sailors' hats with ribbons with writing on them. On one you could read *SMS Flotille Standerberg* and on another *SMS Hannover*. The sailors were armed with long revolvers whose holster was fixed to a board, itself fastened to a hook attached to their clothing.

U-boat men often searched victims for food or showed ingenuity to relieve their diet. Kapitänleutnant Johannes Spieß tells the story of landing on the remote uninhabited Scottish island of North Rona and using its high ground to look for signs of enemy shipping:

> *I looked for a suitable landing place amidst the sheer cliffs and ordered the little rowing boat to be put into the sea and sent the officer of the watch with three crewmen (one of whom was the cook) ashore, armed with guns and orders to do their best. The crew rowed with enthusiasm. They were spotted a little later climbing to the summit. They then looked for birds' eggs, without success, so went off to shoot sheep. Four were shot and hauled down to the launch; only two would fit in so they floated the other two behind. A number of seals and walruses appeared, attracted by the possibility of seizing some of the booty and they weren't frightened off by pistol shots.*[9]

---

9   Spieß, *Six Ans de Croisières*, pp. 220-3, *U 19*, 13/4/1918. Wikipedia repeats the story, but for Kapitänleutnant Walter Remy, *U 90*, who claimed to stop at the island during each of his patrols.

Could North Rona be the only part of the British Isles held by Germany, albeit only for an hour or so, during the Great War?

Gerth returned to the English coast and immediately made contacts.

Just after midnight on 9 May off Start Point, he saw two dimly-lit steamers and gave chase for three hours only to be seen and evaded. At six o'clock he fired a torpedo at another steamer, *Broomhill*, and missed. Gerth blamed the failure on the torpedo 'lying too long in an armed condition'. However, he let the ship pass by until he was able to fire twelve shots without warning, about half hitting home, and one carrying away the wheel and compass.[10] Two men died and one crewman was wounded about the left arm and head.

During the shooting another steamer, the French *Daphne* or the British *Treverbyn*, fired shots at *UC 61* 'from a great distance without a chance', but the shots may have been intended for *UC 17* which was nearby. The survivors of the eighteen-man crew of the Admiralty charter, *Broomhill*, a 1,700-ton collier bound from Penarth to Sheerness, took to their lifeboat which was then used by the Germans, as usual, to place bombs aboard fore and aft.

UC 61 submerged at the approach of the trawler *Caliph* which recovered one body and took the men to Weymouth.

The two men who died on the Broomhill were brothers: Robert, aged thirty-seven, and James Jones, forty-four. Both were 'sett makers', following their father in Caernarvonshire as cutters of small stones for road making, acknowledged as one of the hardest and poorest jobs in the country. Both were married with children. James was injured and drowned getting to the lifeboat; Robert died of his wounds and was buried at Melcombe Regis near Weymouth; his widow and parents were unable to attend the funeral. Both men are commemorated at the Merchant Marine Tower Hill Memorial in London. The 'third' wounded Jones may be duplication and the result of confused reporting.[11]

Today, *Broomhill* is lying on a firm sea bed of sand and chalk. The wreck is intact, lying on the starboard side, mostly collapsed, with the stern pointing south. It is a regular dive haunt. There is a large hole in the hull consistent with being mined: no decking, hull apparently empty, propeller blades missing.[12] Wreck identifier, diver Nick Chipchase, reported being 'absolutely horrified' by

---

10   *TNA*: ADM 137/1296; ADM 137/2692; ADM 137/4114.
11   *CWGC*, Tower Hill Merchant Navy cemetery. *North Wales Chronicle*, 1/6/1917, courtesy of Wendy Williams.
12   wrecksite.eu.

an enormous conger eel that 'reared up above them - like a huge sea serpent - with half its body still hidden within the dark confines of the wreck'.

Just before nine o'clock, *UC 61* surfaced about one and a half miles astern of *Minerva*, a 518-ton Norwegian collier in ballast, and opened fire without warning with some twelve shots one to two minutes apart.[13] In the distance, *UC 17* was shooting at another steamer.

Minerva continued at nine knots towards two loaded, oncoming steamers thinking they might provide cover or diversion. Four shots hit *Minerva*; one struck her boiler with shrapnel causing steam to escape and the ship to stop. Thormod Forland, the master, was wounded in the left eye with splinters; the whole crew abandoned ship in three lifeboats.

One officer and two sailors from *UC 61* boarded to suspend three blasting cartridges from the starboard deck to the water's edge; three or four crew were held on the u-boat while this occurred. Five minutes after the Germans regained the u-boat, an explosion occurred. The ship stood up, stern down, and sank after two minutes in the sight of another Norwegian steamship, the *Freikoll*, 1,169 tons, which escaped. *Minerva*'s account book was seized, but all other papers went down with the ship.

The crew rowed for four hours to Burton Bradstock. *UC 61* went alongside *UC 17* to 'borrow' thirty grenades and then left above water going south, not following the other steamers.

After another frustrating day, *UC 61* was off St Catherine's Point on the early morning of 12 May charging batteries when Gerth sighted several steamers. He dived and moved to attack a trawler. It was the *Maristo*, a Q-ship trap, commander Lieutenant Peter Nicholson.[14]

Gerth could not identify the ship, but he quickly recognised the tell-tale radio masts and then saw a cover near the funnel fall away revealing two guns and, at the stern, a slipway for depth charges. Nicholson had seen the conning tower and watched the submarine dive. When Gerth surfaced, his boat was just twenty-five yards from *Maristo* which attempted to ram. Three depth charges followed; Gerth was forced to break water by the first; the second brought a 'considerable amount of oil' to the surface; the third was set to twenty-five metres to finish the job.

---

13   *TNA*: ADM 137/1296; ADM 137/4114.
14   *TNA*: ADM 53/48473; ADM 239/26; ADM 137/1296.

At thirty metres, *UC 61*'s fuses were partly blown, the bilge pumps were failing and the boat sank to the sea bed at thirty-five metres. Fuses were reinserted and *UC 61* crept away.

Gerth surfaced almost an hour later in hazy weather. He found that the ventilation valve for the stern oil bunker had opened despite a lock and oil was gushing out. Problem fixed, he moved on to Portland before having to dive before some destroyers.

Nicholson, a 'cool and reliable officer not given to exaggeration', claimed a sinking; the Admiralty thought he was probably right, but only allowed a damaged u-boat.[15] However, Nicholson was awarded the Distinguished Service Cross and was asked to recommend two of his crew for Distinguished Service Medals: Second Hand Alexander Robertson and Leading Seaman George Bremner. The Commodore at Portland also awarded a £200 bounty to be distributed among the eighteen-man crew. Nicholson got £40:12:6, well over £3,000 a century later, and the two lowliest telegraphists Atholie Atkinson and Eric Hartman £4:18:9 (almost £400 today, nearly a month's wages) each.[16]

> *A u-boat captain drew upon his individual character, skills, training, and experience to master the challenges of seamanship, battle tactics, and above all leadership of his men. Every combat patrol tested a commander's abilities daily, whether in the intricacies of manoeuvring to obtain the best firing position, the split-second decisions in eluding a depth-charge attack, or the constant effort to maintain his crew's morale and efficiency. His severest test required him to set the proper example while under attack, cracking a joke or ostentatiously reading a novel as depth charges detonated around them. As one commander recalled, 'If you had the confidence of your crew, you were almost a god.'*[17]

The following day was dense fog until the evening when it suddenly cleared. Gerth tried, but failed, in a torpedo attack on a convoy and received a depth charge for his effort. There were patrols, destroyers and planes all around.

---

15   *TNA*, ADM 137/1296.
16   McCartney, 'Paying the Prize', *Mariner's Mirror*, 2/2018, pp. 42-43, explains that to keep details of the anti-u-boat war secret the Admiralty suspended all prize payments until after the war.
17   Mulligan, *Sharks Not Wolves*, p. 2.

> *The lighthouses at Cap Gris Nez and Dungeness, greatly dimmed, shine across at us … Off Cape d'Alprecht we are forced to dive, confronted by a host of vessels … at periscope depth we worm our way through various small steamships, tugs, and patrol-vessels. Soon after midnight we can see the surface again: all hands remain at diving stations. At high speed we approach the barrage … When ten minutes have passed I observe … a submarine chaser. In less than half a minute, the sea has closed smoothly above us: and yet, too late … the thunder is tearing the silence to pieces. All around us roar the bombs. In spite of the still considerable range, we experience a most violent concussion in the boat … We must take our last remaining chance: remain submerged and dive under the whole area of nets and barrage … which was still ten miles off … The giant hull of the boat is humming along close above the bottom. Every now and then it hits the bottom with a jerk that throws us from our feet … Surely it must get deeper soon … We steer down again, always with the feeling that we must 'duck our heads' as low as possible to get under the nets. This time our impact with the bottom is unpleasantly severe … At that moment, the starboard side scrapes heavily against some object on the bottom. There is a thunderous hammering as if great blocks of rock were rolling over us. The boat lists over heavily, rights herself, strikes bottom heavily again … Either we find deep water within a few minutes, or else we run into the deadly arms of the nets and mines … Again, the boat strikes bottom: 95 feet. The boat is taken back to her old course. At the last minute, it seems, we have found the gap. Now we are under the barrage. A loud explosion behind us: the stern gives a heave, and the starboard propeller starts to turn irregularly. But otherwise all is still. We stop engines and drift on. We are alone, and through.*[18]

Two days later, 15 May, after brushes with more aircraft in the channel, Gerth moored *UC 61* at Bruges. The boat then spent over a month in dry dock at Ostend.[19] The repairs included the water pump which had run hot at sea as the cooling chambers had been half filled with fine sand. Pistons pins on each engine were examined; the metal shells had broken and when all mountings were checked all displayed the same condition.

---

18   Hashagen, *Commander*, pp. 193-95. Hashagen's account is much abbreviated and occurred after *UC 61*'s stranding. The barrage Hashagen ran from Cap Griz Nez across to Folkestone was not installed until late in 1917. However, the strain and the terror brings to life the few casual lines in Gerth's log.
19   *BA-MA*, RM 3/11186, pp. 21-23.

10
LUCKY MINE AND A MISHIT

Gerth's penultimate patrol, indeed his whole war effort, was disdainfully dismissed by a Royal Naval officer.

> *The results of [UC 61's] war on commerce, though not absolutely verified by us, seem to have been but mediocre; they were approximately as follows: a couple of sailing vessels, one British two-masted barque and one or two steamers sunk by gunfire. Two torpedoes were fired, but missed. There was again damage to the machinery which, though not serious, involved a day and night of repairs. One of the compressors, by the negligence of the engine-room crew, heated for want of water-cooling. The packing rings and segments of the piston had to be changed immediately, and the compressor was entirely overhauled on the return to Bruges.*[1]

Of course, that was all true as far as it went, but Gerth was less forthcoming about a French armoured cruiser and a British destroyer.

His next voyage did not start well. Gerth was scheduled to sail from Bruges on 3 June with *UC 47* and *UC 48*. The plan was for *UC 61* to lay mines off Brest and then to attack shipping in the western exit of the English Channel.[2] Gerth left Ostend a week late on 11 June and set off from Bruges the next day. Late evening, he tested the u-boat's trimming and the hydroplanes jammed so it was

---

1   *TNA*, ADM 137/3898, p. 94.
2   Spindler, *Krieg zur See*, Band 4, p. 320. Bendert, *Die UC-Boote*, p. 159.

back to Bruges then down the canal to Ostend for repairs. That took another week.

On 21 June, he was back in Bruges to load his torpedoes and mines. The next day, he found the gauge cock of the front starboard bunker had become detached due to a poor fastening.

Gerth finally sailed on 23 June, twenty days behind schedule and after a total of thirty-eight days' inactivity. After he had checked his trimming, passed the Channel net barrier and reached the Colbart light vessel, he was undertaking regular evasion tactics with three separate destroyers and an airship.

> *We naturally have to frequent places where patrols are particularly active in guarding steamer routes, and these prowling trawlers, yachts and destroyers make it difficult to get within torpedo range of any steamers. We abandon many a promising target because the patrols make it impossible for us to break surface and our under-water speed is too low to enable us to take position to attack ... They hunt us with hydrophones, which pick up the beat of our engines, and when they think themselves close enough, they drop their depth charges, which have to be taken far more seriously than the 'crackers' we knew in the summer of 1916. We lose an enormous amount of time in consequence before we can think of another attack. The zig-zagging of ships has also become compulsory, while the intelligence service and convoy discipline have been perfected to an astounding extent.*[3]

The next day, 25 June, was overcast with intermittent rain as Gerth made his way towards Brest. At half past one the next morning, Gerth laid his first set of six mines at Chenal du Four off Ouessant and about the same time the following morning two more sets of six off the Pierres Noires Lighthouse on the approaches to Brest.

Within an hour, Gerth picked up an uncoded radio message: the French armoured cruiser *Kléber* had run into his mines.[4]

Kléber, after service in the Dardanelles, had made an uneventful voyage from Dakar to Brest where she was to be placed in a reserve squadron. One of Gerth's mines was seen drifting on the port side. Captain Lagorio ordered

---

3   Niemöller, *From U-boat*, pp. 66-67.
4   *Le Petit Journal*, 30/6/1918. uboat.net. forum-auto.com. '*Un Livre d'or de la Marine Française*', *Guerre 1914 1918*; 14-18-marine-livredor.wifeo.com/kleber-croiseur-cuirasse.ph, accessed 1/2/2017.

battle stations and reduced speed, but at once struck a second mine below the waterline on the starboard side by the rear boiler room.

Sub-lieutenant Thoreux, aboard since the start of the war, described events: 'The resulting fire spread to the coal bunker and soon the cruiser was shrouded in smoke whilst water rushed into sections causing her to take on a list.'

The vessel plunged at the bow immediately; the forward boiler room flooded together with the coal bunker which separated it from the ammunition bunkers; water rose quickly onto the deck and filled the second boiler room; electric light, pumps, speaking tubes, electrical control of the helm and telephone network were all lost.

As soon as the mine explosion took place, the captain gave the order to stop and put out a distress call on the radio. The engines were put into reverse to move the vessel, but there was limited room for manoeuvre because of the first mine. As *Kléber* gradually settled, arriving ships were unable to attach two lines because of the raised stern. The situation rapidly worsened; the vessel suddenly shuddered when all the forward bulkheads gave way.

Despite good order, abandoning ship proved difficult as lifeboats were damaged. Life rafts were launched and men slipped into the water; ten men were killed when the wireless antenna fell onto them. Fifteen men died in the boiler room and several others in the explosion. In total, forty-two men lost their lives.

> *No State, not even America, thought it against the dictates of humanity to build submarines for war purposes, whose task it should be unexpectedly to attack warships and sink them with all on board. Does it really make any difference, purely from the humane point of view, whether those thousands of men who drown wear naval uniforms or belong to a merchant ship bringing food and munitions to the enemy, thus prolonging the war and augmenting the number of women and children who suffer during the war?*[5]

UC 61 had slipped away into the dawn where Gerth met an unnamed u-boat at a pre-arranged meeting point, dodged some destroyers and, because the weather was worsening in the Bay of Biscay, made for the English coast.

---

5   Scheer, *High Sea Fleet*, p. 268.

> ... lockers broke away from the bulkheads and lay all over the cramped compartments; the galley gave up all cooking and if anybody was hungry or even had any appetite – most people refrained from eating, as being devoid of purpose – he just ate odd bits of bread, spread with anything that came to hand.[6]

At Start Point, Gerth lined up the Norwegian schooner-rigged steamer *Edith Fische*, but cancelled the torpedo because at 1,132 tons the ship was too small for the expense. Instead he opened fire with six rounds. One shell hit the bow and another the after deckhouse.[7]

> We held up the vessel from a distance by means of a warning shot, gave the crew time to leave their ship, and then destroyed her by means of explosive charges, by shell-fire on the water-line; or if we were in a hurry, with a torpedo. But every torpedo fired cost a thousand pounds. And, above all, we only had a limited number of torpedoes on board. So we used them sparingly.[8]

Two men were slightly wounded. Eighteen crew rushed to the boats and two jumped over board. Gerth failed to see approaching trawlers, which he blamed on a misty periscope. He came under fire and was forced to dive. Two distant depth charges followed. The men in the water were picked up by the trawler HMT *Lois* and returned to their ship. *Edith Fische*, in ballast, made it safely to Newport after salvage by the tugs HS *31* and *Herculaneum*.

The weather worsened again with thick fog and Gerth sat it out on the sea bed at thirty-eight metres. The next day he saw a big, empty tanker with some trawlers and, from his stern tube, fired a torpedo which malfunctioned.

A destroyer and some patrol vessels were evaded and Gerth went to the sea bed again at Beachy Head to see out the fog, surfacing every two hours to check conditions. In the evening of 30 June, he met *UB 40*.

The next three days were full of destroyers, patrol vessels and armed trawlers and two further failed torpedo shots and an interrupted gun attack against steamers.

On 4 July, Gerth stopped an unescorted Norwegian steamer which he named as *Ran*. It was the *Ole Lea*, 534 tons, christened *Peritia* in 1880, *Ran* in 1907, *Tosca*

---

6   Niemöller, *From U-boat*, p. 25.
7   *TNA*, ADM 137/1341. uboat.net.
8   *Hashagen, Commander*, p. 65.

in 1914, and *Ole Lea* in 1915, having six owners during her life. Her last owners bought the ship about two months before the sinking, intending to rename her *Ull*, but had not yet done so.[9] The master at sea was clear that he was sailing the *Ole Lea*.[10]

In any event, *UC 61* approached on the starboard side from the west, steering in the same direction, but faster, while *Ole Lea* continued on course. Gerth fired three rounds at 3,000 yards, hitting twice. *Ole Lea* stopped engines and the crew left the ship in two lifeboats and rowed towards land. Some sources say *Ole Lea* was sunk by torpedo, but only Gerth was present and he is specific that he scuttled the vessel with 'blasting cartridges'.

The crew were picked up at five in the morning by a British patrol boat that had heard the firing and were taken to Weymouth.

The well-broken-down wreck of *Ole Lea* is lying in a sandy gravel bed; there is no apparent cargo, but an amount of debris particularly on the port side; a four-bladed propeller. The midships engine and boiler, with remains of a funnel on top, plus forward and stern winches, are easily seen.[11] In 1995, a steam whistle was recovered from the wreck so it became known as the 'whistle wreck' among the South Coast diving fraternity.[12]

Later that day, Gerth missed with another torpedo shot against a steamer, the third failed attempt of this patrol.

> *How incredibly difficult it was, after calculations and manoeuvres that might last hours, to carry out a successful attack and get in a position to fire a torpedo at a ship protected by fast, well-handled, heavily armed escorts. And even at that point came the art of accurately firing the costly instrument after only a second's aim, with one eye, through a periscope constantly dipping up and down with the movement of the water and thus cutting off the field of vision. If the periscope, that was used so cautiously and rarely appeared above the surface, or its inevitable trail of foam, or the course of a moving torpedo, were discovered too soon by the enemy, the chance of success was gone. The enemy, too, was experienced in the arts of defence, in attack, in deceptive manoeuvres, and in steering zig-zag courses that were hard to calculate. On all the enemy's surface vessels there were many practised eyes on the lookout for u-boats; they*

---

9 skipet.no/skip/skipsforlis; miramarshipindex.org.nz.
10 *TNA*, ADM 137/1341. uboat.net.
11 wrecksite.eu.
12 Hinchcliffe, *Dive Dorset*, p. 54.

were set upon our destruction, and there were tempting honours and rewards for every success. What with their u-boat chasers, destroyers, aeroplanes, nets, depth-charges, u-boat traps of all kinds, u-boats, and many other devices, they pressed us very hard. There were mishaps on both sides that for many meant the end.[13]

The next day was spent charging batteries, waiting for targets and diving frequently before patrols. On 6 July, there was at last, for Gerth at least, a change for the better. In the midst of frequent traffic, one of his torpedoes finally hit and sank a steamer. It was the unescorted 2,900-ton armed collier, *Indutiomare*, flying Belgian colours. *UC 61* was not seen and fired from her second bow tube while under water. The torpedo's wake was spotted by *Indutiomare*'s master and second mate coming from the south on the starboard side about 200 yards off. The ship's helm was put hard-a-starboard. The torpedo hit, three men were killed, and the remaining twenty-two crew took to two lifeboats.

Indutiomare sank within two minutes. *Indutiomare*'s gunners did not have time to fire, nor did they have a target. The survivors were picked up by the French steamer *Thisbe* and were landed at Portsmouth that afternoon by HMS *Seahorse*. *UC 61* stayed submerged for the next five hours and did not find another target that day.

The final victim of *UC 61*'s career came in the morning of 7 July with another torpedo hit, but it was not as Gerth described the action:

Beachy Head: Dived before destroyer. Stayed under water in order to wait for steamer. Sighted convoy consisting of a middle-sized passenger steamer and a deeply loaded steamer with four masts, numerous cargo booms/derricks, size at least 6,000 tons, shepherded by four destroyers, two u-boat hunters and some trawlers. Shot out of first tube at steamer. Hit. Boat is rammed by escort. Went to periscope depth. The attacked steamer has sunk. Slightly astern lies a destroyer bow heavy up to the front funnel under water. Mast and bridge are missing. The whole escort goes at high speed around the damaged destroyer. A hit against the destroyer instead of the attacked steamer is out of the question. It had probably been damaged by ramming.

Gerth got it wrong. Four destroyers, *Landrail, Beaver, Forester* and *Ettrick*, and four patrol boats, *22, 25, 32, 54*, were escorting a convoy (HH4) of five steamers from

---

13   Bergen, 'U-Boat Voyage', Neureuther, *U-Boat Stories*, pp. 18-19.

Hampton Roads in Virginia, USA, at nine knots.[14] The convoy commander on *Landrail* ordered *Ettrick*, which was astern the convoy, to swop places for *Landrail* to chase up a convoy straggler. *Ettrick* increased speed to seventeen knots to effect this. *Landrail* turned to meet her and spotted a torpedo track crossing half a mile in front, breaking surface three seconds later.

Just before eight o'clock, the torpedo struck *Ettrick* by the galley behind the fore bridge, cutting the vessel in two. The fore part turned turtle, remained afloat about five minutes, and then sank after an explosion in the magazine killing all forty-nine men who were at breakfast in that part of the ship. HMT *Sheldon* took off the survivors.

P 25 took *Ettrick* in tow by the stern as the six men who remained on board fought to keep the ship afloat. The three ratings who remained on Ettrick until she docked were commended for their conduct: Henry Bell, Bertie Sadler and William Beard. HMS S*eahorse* took over the tow while tugs *Sturdy* and *Alert* used salvage pumps. The remains of *Ettrick* were brought safely to the North Railway Harbour at Newhaven at half past seven.

The convoy commander thought *UC 61* fired at the British oiler *Madrono*. *Ettrick*'s lieutenant thought *Ettrick* was 'evidently' the target. The court of enquiry found that Lieutenant Athol Gudgeon, captain of *Ettrick*, who gave evidence at the naval hospital at Gosport because of his injuries, was 'partially to blame' having only two lookouts instead of the required four, but that 'in view of the state of the surface of the sea ... it was unlikely that the torpedo would have been seen in time to avoid it'. No disciplinary action was taken. Gudgeon died of his wounds one month later, aged thirty-two.

Ettrick was not repaired and was hulked until the end of the war when she was sold for scrap.[15]

When is a wreck a wreck? *Ettrick* does not appear on any wreck list as the bulk of the ship was towed to dry dock. However, her bows can be dived on - if they are ever found.

The Chief of the German Admiralty Staff sent a report of Gerth's sinkings to his Commander-in-Chief. In the margin of the telegram, the Kaiser wrote 'God'.[16] Gerth moored at Bruges just before midday on 8 July.

---

14   *TNA*: ADM 137/3283; ADM 340/60.
15   27/5/1919 to James Dredging Company.
16   *BA-MA*, RM 2/1996, p. 27. 'As late as 1918, Wilhelm still read the war diaries of his submarine commanders and marked each one with his famous marginal notes' (Herwig, *Naval Officer Corps)*, p. 28.

11
GERTH'S SEA WAR

After 148 days in command, Gerth had spent 48 days, some 32 per cent, operational, the great majority of the remaining two-thirds under repair and much of that in dry dock. Adding the 108 days for training and delivery from Kiel to Bruges since putting formally into service, *UC 61* was operational for 19 per cent of its life.

At a build price of around two million Reichsmark, the boat cost the German people nearly 42,000 Reichsmark a 'patrol day' to which must be added the expense of a twenty-six-man crew for training, wages and food (with one man injured); u-boat running and repair costs; and munitions and management overheads.

It was an expensive war.

The return from Gerth from both *UB 12* and *UC 61* was 26,764 tons of shipping with total crews of 862 men, twelve ships sunk including an ageing armoured cruiser, four ships damaged including a ruined destroyer. Amongst the total were three sailing ships, including *Little Mystery*.

Disruption was caused by mine alerts and sweeping on, perhaps, twelve days, with some ports closed in the south of England for six of these.

There was also the considerable overall cost to the British of combating the u-boats, including mines and net barriers, a dedicated and extensive anti-submarine fleet, as well as aircraft and airships, the raids on the Flanders ports, and the human and munitions burden of the third battle of Ypres.

Gerth and his two u-boats killed 118 men and wounded twenty-one others.

Interestingly, in Gerth's u-boat career, he may never have seen a dead body.

12
ON THE BEACH

The sand around the wreck of UC 61 is studded with pieces of black peat from a submerged forest which crumble in the hand. The forest is fifty to sixty feet below the sea bed and, at this point, does not expose fossilised tree stumps. It extends across the Channel to England and therefore dates from when England was joined to the Continent as one land mass. This was about 8,000 years ago, between 6225–6170 BC. It is thought that three underwater landslides off Norway, the Storegga Slides, triggered one of Earth's biggest tsunamis. A landlocked sea in the Norwegian trench had burst its banks. The water struck the north-east of Britain with such force that it travelled twenty-five miles inland, turning low-lying plains into what is now the North Sea and, also, marshlands to the south into the Channel.[1]

The canal from Bruges, Belgium's inland port, to the sea at Zeebrugge is seven miles long. It is over 200 feet wide, relatively straight and comfortable enough for two large motor craft to pass at ease.[2]

In 1917, as today, it was lined with many regularly-spaced trees and ran through flat, uninspiring Flemish farmland. Most of the trees were and are Canadian black poplars planted by a proud country for the official opening in 1907.[3] Because of its scenic route, the area bordering the canal was generally

---

1 Bondevik, et al, 'Storegga Slide Tsunami'.
2 11.5km x 70m (110m maximum) x 7m. Currently named *Canal Baudouin*, it is classified 'Class VI' and open to ships of more than 2,000 tons with a draft of 5.5m or less.
3 Populus x Canadensis is a hybrid *Black Poplar* frequently seen along riversides, roadsides and in parks and grown for ornamental planting and timber production. It originated in France in the eighteenth century.

quiet. Housing was sparse. There was no large village or heavy industry and the main road and railway to the sea was a mile or so to the west. Local people about their errands occasionally paced the footpath. The adjoining fields were intensively worked, but manually or with horse-powered machinery and transport. There was little activity on a hot afternoon in late July.

However, twenty-five miles away to the west, one of the major bombardments of the war had been underway for four days.[4] General Douglas Haig's British 2nd Army was preparing the German trenches in front of Ypres for a major attack to begin on the last day of the month. The first objective was to push a salient as far as the village of Passchendaele; the second the main railway line to Ostend when, if the army could advance to Roulers, it would command the key German railway junction in the northern half of the Western front; the third was the two canals from Bruges to Ostend and to Zeebrugge, including those three towns, and an end to u-boat activity in Flanders.

Four months later, the British offensive petered out around Passchendaele in shell-cratered ground churned into mud by heavy rain and became for the British the 'embodiment of the First World War's waste and futility'.[5] There were over half a million British and German casualties and it was here that the Germans used mustard gas for the first time. As a result of the stalemate, six long-planned, daring, amphibious landings of over 13,000 British troops and nine tanks on the Belgian coast and aimed at the u-boat bases were cancelled.[6]

Shortly after lunch, the local quiet around the canal was shattered. There were few things noisier than the twin diesel engines of a u-boat. On a quiet night at sea, the clatter could be heard several miles off as if in invitation to patrolling Allied anti-submarine craft.

The racket was appalling. The noise was so loud in the dangerous quiet that the longer it went on the less comfortable I felt about it.[7]

---

4   The front-line trenches began on the coast near Nieuwpoort and snaked inland to Ypres. Ostend, also connected by canal to Bruges, is about eleven miles north-east of Nieuwpoort and Zeebrugge about seventeen miles further.
5   Strachan, *First World War*, p. 245.
6   Bacon, *Dover Patrol*, pp. 184-205.
7   Fürbringer, *Legendary*, p. 35.

The passing of today's submarines could be anticipated: for over two years u-boats usually went out to sea on war patrols on a Wednesday or Thursday, but seldom setting out on a Friday or the 13th of the month which were both well-known to bring bad luck.[8] This Wednesday, 25 July, there were two modern minelaying uc-boats, *UCs 47* and *61*, travelling on the same afternoon from Bruges North Port.

After its fourth successful if particularly hard-fought voyage, *UC 61* spent eleven days in repair docks at Bruges and Ostend while Gerth took leave to celebrate his promotion to Kapitänleutnant. This was Gerth's twentieth trip down the canal in two days short of a year of u-boat captaincy.

Gerth's previous visit to Ostend the month before had been eventful. In 1917, there were regular if often ineffective attacks on all the u-boat dock areas by Allied aircraft and by naval bombardment. During February, in three separate air raids on Bruges, thirteen houses were destroyed, fourteen civilians killed and many more injured; more than 1,200 bombs were dropped on the city that year.[9]

On 5 June, *UC 61* was one of four u-boats in Ostend for repairs.[10] At 0320, the British opened a forty-minute bombardment from two monitors, *Erebus* and *Terror*, causing considerable damage to the dockyards, but no casualties.[11] *UC 61* was in a u-boat shelter for work to her engines, rear torpedo tube and front hydroplane and escaped damage; however, *UC 16* was hit and *UC 70* sunk because it was moored alongside a lighter carrying petrol which was struck by a heavy shell.[12]

> *A whistle blew from the deck of UC 70. It had been good to feel the solid earth beneath our feet again, but now the time was up; and not a man of our crew was missing. The seamen were on deck, and the mechanics at their engines and dynamos. All the*

---

8   Koerver, *German Submarine Warfare*, p. 196.
9   Termote, *Krieg Unter Wasser*, pp. 172, 187.
10 *TNA*, London, ADM 137/3818, p. 20. The other boats were *UC 16*, *UC 65* and *UC 70*.
11 MA-BA, Freiburg, RM 88/1 FdU Flandern KTB, p. 23. See also Newbolt, *Naval Operations*, Vol. V, Chapter 9; Bacon, *Dover Patrol*, pp. 108-11. A monitor was a relatively small warship, which was neither fast nor strongly armoured, but carried a disproportionately large gun.
12 *UC 61* Kriegstagebuch (KTB), Cuxhaven; interrogation of Lead Stoker Friedrich Becker (SHD, Cherbourg, SSTe35). Many of the pen pictures of the crew which appear in this book are compiled from the same source – the original handwritten notes in French and German made at the crew's formal interrogation.

lights on deck were extinguished; only an occasional flash of a torch betrayed where the cables were being cast off. The boat slid down the Bruges Canal to Zeebrugge.[13]

Among the pigeons which rose and settled on the canal at the din from the two u-boats, one bird might set off at a steadier pace and fly determinedly to the north-west.[14] Many homing pigeons were parachuted into the occupied territories in baskets strapped to Allied agents. Their target was one of a line of Admiralty stationary pigeon lofts spread on the east coast of England from Newcastle-on-Tyne to Hastings. Up to sixty miles, pigeons were practically infallible; more than 95 per cent of the messages sent by pigeon post during the war were safely delivered.

As a result, Admiralty Intelligence knew the timing and number of u-boats making for the sea before the day was out and, often, because of identifying marks and other long-gathered data, and radio intercepts, which boats they were and who were their captains. The unknown source of this information was a continuing worry to the u-boat high command.

A great disadvantage of [the German] situation is how easily enemy agents can observe us. There are probably agents and spies everywhere, but never is gathering information about an adversary as easy as when, for all intents and purposes, he possesses only one harbour and at all times must return to this one port ... While all the intelligence reports that we receive out of England are unreliable – though when reliable, always days late – English intelligence in all cases reaches England within a few hours.[15]

---

13   Neureuther, *U-Boat Stories*, p. 134.
14   Osman, *Pigeons in the Great War*, pp. 7-8, 17-27, 45, 50. 'At the outbreak of the war the Belgians had no doubt the finest pigeon service in the world, with headquarters in Antwerp, but before the city's capture on 8 October 1914, Commandant Denuit, chief of the Belgian service, had the lofts and birds all destroyed, thus preventing the Germans using a service that had taken years to become efficient.'
15   Wegener, *Naval Strategy of the World War*, pp. 172-73. See also Führer der Unterseeboote Hermann Bauer, briefing, 1/2/1917 (*TNA*, ADM 137/3886): 'Intelligence received from England proves that the British are kept continuously and most accurately informed regarding our submarines and their movements. The greatest reticence is therefore demanded, particularly in public places, in trains, etc ... Crews are to be instructed repeatedly and explicitly on this matter.'

There was a small irony here as all u-boats carried a few pigeons.[16] These flew in the opposite direction and alerted the u-boat command of Flanders Flotilla in Bruges of significant success or failure. The Flanders u-boats also carried radio, but it was used sparsely and the greatest restrictions on giving movements and positions while at sea were enforced for fear of the British direction-finding radio masts; security on the Flanders boats was by far the strictest of the u-boat flotillas.[17]

'The effect of this secrecy is to reduce the amount of first-hand evidence as regards details of cruises.'

The Germans were greatly shocked when they discovered after the war that the British not only had direction finding equipment, but also the codes used for u-boat transmissions; every message that was sent was read by their enemies. *UC 61*'s telegraphist, Otto Bock was aged twenty-two from Hoisbüttel. He completed seven months' radio training at Wilhelmshaven, joined *UB 12* as his first sea posting and with Seaman Willy Neumann were the only two men who transferred with Gerth to *UC 61*.

Orders to the two uc-boat commanders were handwritten, dated on Tuesday, the day before, and delivered in person by their leader, Korvettenkapitän Karl Bartenbach.[18] The orders were brief and left matters greatly to individual discretion; Bartenbach was well-known for allowing unusual flexibility to his men both on and off duty.[19]

First, the commanders were given their day of departure and warned that British submarines were currently operating off the coast of Flanders. Second, they were each told to lay their eighteen mines at a spacing and depth setting as they wished, if possible at the turn of the tide, in designated general areas. Third, they were then to conduct 'trade war', sinking any vessel within another broadly named area. Finally, the boat was to return 'according to capability', but at the latest after twelve days. In adopting this managerial approach, Bartenbach followed the tactical doctrine of *Auftragstaktik*: at every level of military command, operational orders took the general form of defining

---

16 In his later years, Georg Gerth kept a caged canary (interviews with Georg Gerth's daughter, Christa Gerth, 15-16/11/2016).
17 Koerver, *German Submarine Warfare*, p. 190.
18 *MA-BA*, RM 120-95, Flotilla Order No. 264, 24/7/1917.
19 Koerver, *German Submarine Warfare*, p. 197.

the objectives and leaving the details to be worked out by the subordinate commanders.[20]

'Control was decentralised – essential for opportunistic u-boat warfare – and both the local knowledge and the initiative of subordinate commanders was given full play.'

Bartenbach's orders instructed a third uc-boat, *UC 21*, to join *UC 61* and *UC 47* on the trip to Zeebrugge and from there to lay mines at Exmouth, Berry Head and Dartmouth, but by the time *UC 21* arrived from Ostend at Bruges to take on armaments, it needed repairs to its cooling water pump and was delayed for four days. *UC 47*'s mines were destined for the Channel Islands, and those of *UC 61* for the shipping lanes near the *Royal Sovereign* lightship off Eastbourne and for Newhaven and Brighton.[21]

The course Gerth always laid to pass through the Channel, and shown by his contemporary hand-drawn maps, hugged the French coast whereas many of his fellow captains chose to sail close to the English side where the water was deeper.[22] There is a continuing misconception that travelling by the French coast meant a French Atlantic destination.

> *Reports had been received that the enemy had sealed the Straits of Dover by means of anti-submarine nets which stretched from Dover to Calais. The investigation of the matter had fallen to Oberleutnant Haecker [UB 6], and on completion of this dangerous mission he had been able to report that, whereas the Straits were almost totally netted off, there was a definite gap close under the French coast between Calais and Cap Gris-Nez.*[23]

There has been much confusion about *UC 61*'s destination and it is often claimed that it was heading for the sea lanes around Boulogne or Le Havre.[24] This misinformation was largely caused by Gerth who lied several times in interrogation about his route, where he intended to drop his mines and his operational area. These lies were intended as diversions and were disproved

---

20 Offer, 'Bounded Rationality', p. 196.
21 *UCs 21, 47* and *61* Kriegstagebuch (KTBs), Cuxhaven.
22 Termote, *Krieg Unter Wasser*, p. 112.
23 Fürbringer, *Legendary*, p. 15.
24 Grant, *U-Boat Intelligence*, pp. 113-14.

quickly by the British and French interrogators, but have proved long-lasting in subsequent histories.

In fact, after mine laying on the English south coast, Gerth was ordered to the area between the Isle of Wight and Portland Bill, his regular sinking ground. These destinations are supported by Gerth's written orders which are held in Germany and by papers and maps later found aboard his boat.

It was *UC 47* that was headed for Le Havre after mine laying at the Channel Islands; *UC 21*'s later target area was between Land's End and in front of the Bristol Channel. Neither vessel nor their crews would survive the year.[25]

In its career, *UC 47* sank fifty-seven ships and damaged eight others. In turn, the submarine was rammed just forward of its conning tower by patrol boat *P57* off Flamborough Head on 18 November; it was then depth-charged twice. British divers recovered its log and charts.

UC 21 was one of the most successful u-boats of the Great War, ninth on the list of ships sunk with ninety-nine vessels; fourteenth on the list of tonnage sunk at 134,063 tons. Less than two months later on 13 September, *UC 21* again left Zeebrugge, this time for the Bay of Biscay and was lost by unknown cause a few days later.

There is one lock on the Bruges Zeebrugge canal, a sea lock, which the u-boat crews had to operate and which often gave departing u-boats a reason to travel together.

In early afternoon, *UC 61* arrived in Zeebrugge harbour where up to two dozen ships could shelter in stormy weather. The boat was already fully fuelled, armed and provisioned, but there was a power supply to allow the u-boat's electric motors to be recharged.

UC 61's crew of twenty-six probably remained on board as the 'seaside village did not offer many facilities'.[26] Included was one supernumerary, Max Pucknus, aged twenty-eight from Tilsit, who served as a boatswain with the rank of petty officer first class. Pucknus was on a month's loan from the battleship SMS *Schleswig Holstein* in the second squadron of Germany's High Seas Fleet. It was his first cruise in a submarine.

These visits by officers of the Fleet were latterly introduced by the German Admiralty to 'vary the monotony of the existence of personnel in large ships

---

25   uboat.net, accessed 14/12/2016. Messimer, *Verschollen*, p. 286.
26   Termote, *Krieg Unter Wasser, pp. 156-63.*

and to interest the whole of the navy in the life of submarine crews'.[27] With increasing and high casualty numbers, volunteers for u-boat service had begun to dry up. Eleven obsolete pre-dreadnought battleships were demobilised in the summer of 1916 to release seamen for submarine duty.[28]

By the end of 1916, the voluntary system of recruiting for the submarine service was 'entirely abandoned owing not so much to the danger as to the hardship and discomfort of the life, for which the high pay and good food failed to compensate'.[29] From this time onwards the authorities seem to have had considerable difficulty in selecting suitable officers to man the increased number of u-boats. In addition, it became regular practice to 'transfer up to 15 per cent of each crew after every two patrols to assure a continuous flow of experienced men for future u-boats'.[30]

In March 1917, an urgent demand for submarine officers was circulated among the ships in the Baltic and, subsequently, the records show many ships being sent insistent calls for the transfer of young officers.

> *The instance of this man [Pucknus] ... is typical and shows the immobility of the personnel on board the [large ships]. This man shipped on board the iron-clad as [a seaman] in 1908, and gained his stripes one by one. He has not been moved since that date, and made no complaint of having been kept nine years on the same iron-clad, every nail of which he knew. The case of this PO does not seem to be exceptional.*[31]

Despite all of the upheaval, Gerth had a relatively stable and experienced, if young, crew. The average age of twenty-three was kept up by Gerth and his helmsman, Andreas Nagel, both twenty-nine, and the oldest man aboard, navigator Hubert Lengs at thirty. Most of the crew had joined up in the first few months of the war. Eighteen of the men had been with Gerth since around the time of the commissioning of *UC 61*; on average each had fourteen months' u-boat experience and half had also served in another boat.[32]

---

27 *TNA*, ADM 137/3818, p. 109.
28 Koerver, *German Submarine Warfare*, p. xliv.
29 Koerver, *German Submarine Warfare*, p. 213.
30 Mulligan, *Sharks Nor Wolves*, p. 39.
31 Koerver, *German Submarine Warfare*, p. 23.
32 These figures are compiled from information given by the crew during the initial interrogations after capture at Wissant (SHD, Cherbourg, SSTe35).

Gerth paused at Zeebrugge to complete formalities and then made his way at 1525 towards the end of the curving thirty-five-metre-high mole, a solid stone breakwater more than a mile long which contained a railway terminus, a seaplane station, and large sheds for personnel and material.[33] One of the mole's cannons was mounted on a platform which could be rocked to imitate waves. Flanders Flotilla gunners used it to practise firing at towed targets at sea.[34]

> At the seaward extremity of the mole was installed a coastal battery equipped with 88mm rapid fire cannons under the command of Oberleutnant Schutte. His post was in fact the outermost artillery emplacement of the entire Western Front and by reason of his isolated existence at the end of the two-thousand-metre-long breakwater he was known universally as 'The Pope of the Mole'. He was also the most decent fellow in the world. Crewmen aboard u-boats putting to sea or returning were able to obtain from him all their requirements, including drink. Virtually every u-boat passing the mole would pull alongside the molehead to greet the Pope.[35]

This mole, and the sea lock Gerth had just passed through, were the targets in the famed Zeebrugge raid of 1918. This access of the u-boats of Flanders Flotilla to the North Sea remained a preoccupation of the Allies throughout the war.

After the failure to break through to the Belgian canals during the last battle around Ypres, the British sought to land a specially-raised force of Royal Marines on the mole from an ageing HMS *Vindictive* on 23 April 1918. In a vicious fire fight, a third of the men were lost.[36]

The marines were to provide support and cover while three blockships entered the canal. The crews succeeded in sinking the ships at angles to the canal by blowing out their bottoms, releasing tons of cement to the canal floor. The operation was instantly declared a great success; senior Admiralty officers

---

33 Newbolt, *Naval History*, p. 127.
34 Termote, *Krieg Unter Wasser*, p. 91.
35 Fürbringer, *U-Boat Commander*, p. 50.
36 British casualties were 214 killed, 383 wounded, nineteen taken prisoner. German losses were ten killed, sixteen wounded (Bacon, *Dover Patrol*), p. 223. Eleven Victoria Crosses were awarded, some later by ballot of the participants. One survivor was the author's great uncle, Tom Heal.

waited for the returning men on the quayside at Dover in order to hand out gallantry medals.

In fact, the raid was largely a failure as a smaller u-boat, *UB 16*, was able to pass through the canal two days later at high tide.[37] Larger u-boats temporarily diverted to the sea through Ostend but, by month's end, the average sailings were back to normal.[38] The Germans removed two wooden piers on the western bank of the entrance to the canal near to the sunken ships.[39] Using dredgers, they scooped a fifteen metre-wide passage and the obstructions, bought with so much blood, were nullified.

Vice Admiral Sir Reginald Bacon, fired the previous December as head of the Dover Patrol, described the blocking as 'gallantly carried out, but useless'. The Government was forced to admit after the war that the attack had failed and that the 'incorrect information issued to the Nation by the Admiralty was responsible for the elation of the population and the halo which has surrounded this unfortunate operation'.[40]

In the later afternoon, when Gerth left the relative safety of Zeebrugge harbour, he first faced the danger of what the German's called the 'exclusion area', a double row of 1,500 mines, reinforced by nets full of explosives, which had been laid in April 1916.

The British laid a line of defence directly in front of the Flanders base. It was a line of mine-studded nets and patrol boats placed eighteen miles out from Zeebrugge and extending for thirty-five miles along the coast from the shallow water outside Dunkerque to the shallows of the Scheldt. There was not enough water at the ends for the U-boat to dodge around the barrier. Nor was it possible to dive under the nets. The water along the line was not deep enough. So it had to be a case of slipping through on the surface at night and trying to give the patrol boats the slip.[41]

---

37 Jellicoe, *Submarine Peril*, pp. 92-93.
38 Jellicoe, 'Foreword' to Bacon, *Dover Patrol*, p. 11. Tarrant, *U-Boat Offensive*, p. 62.
39 Termote, *Krieg Unter Wasser*, p. 161.
40 Newbolt, *Official History of the War, Naval Operations*, Vol. V, pp. 274-77; and, Newbolt, again, *Naval History*, pp. 127-31.
41 Thomas, *Raiders*, p. 230. Also, 'two lines of moored deep contact mines forty miles long and fifteen miles of mined nets had been positioned thirteen miles off the Belgian coast' (Grant, *U-Boat Intelligence*), pp. 61-62.

Gerth always ran the same course from Zeebrugge, travelling at night, and following where he could the route prescribed for merchantmen. He aimed first for British Buoy 4 on the Outer Ruytingen Sandbank (almost halfway from Dunkerque to Nieuwpoort) then picked up the last buoy of the barrage and the Snouw shoal (26 D), guided by the Dyck Lightship off Gravelines. 'This allowed *UC 61* to round the barrage without passing below or above it.'[42]

Gerth passed south of the Dyck lightship, and intended to go north of Buoy 5, between Calais and Cap Gris Nez, well to sea, but near to Wissant. All these buoys, especially another buoy numbered 2501 twelve miles off Calais, were familiar to the u-boats.[43]

'In the course of time these beacons became the most trusted friends of the submarine flotilla; they were all numbered, and were the greatest navigation aid in the passage of the Straights of Dover.'[44]

Gerth then planned to hug the French coast, go through the Dover Straits and then to turn south at Cap Gris Nez, passing the Le Colbart Light Vessel. However, there was another major task; he had also to slip round the end of another net barrier filled with mines, laid between September and November 1916, and which stretched from the Goodwins, passed the Outer Ruytingen Bank to Snouw.[45] The nets were reinforced by 2,010 deep mines laid in three rows to the south. Despite having heavy moorings, the tide sometimes dragged the mines into the nets. Also, as the net sagged in many places, it allowed u-boats to pass over. Submarines could easily distinguish the floats of indicator nets and could avoid them in daylight.[46]

On the surface at a maximum speed of almost ten knots, *UC 61* had a range of 3,000 nautical miles, or when cruising at six knots, 5,290 miles. Under water, *UC 61* relied on the 1,124 cells of its battery-powered electric motors which were limited to a range of thirty to forty nautical miles at six knots. There had to be a reason to submerge: stealth, safety from attack, positioning

---

42   Washington, DC, *National Archives (NARA)*, U Boat Campaign (Enemy): U-Boats, 'Interrogatoire de L'Équipage de *UC 61*' [Interrogation of the Crew of *UC 61*] (45/520/JU/Box 572).

43   Buoys 4 & 5: UK Hydrographic Office, Chart 1872, archive series B24, 'Calais to the River Schelde' at 51° 5' 37"N, 2° 28' 15"E. For Buoy 4, see also Fleet Notices 93, 19/2/1917; 141, 19/9/1917; and 698, withdrawn, 1/12/1917. With thanks for the search by UKHO staff.

44   Gayer, *Submarine Warfare*, p. 13, 'the 'German post-war authority on the submarines'. Also quoted in Bacon, *Memoirs*, p. 155.

45   Gibson & Prendergast, *German Submarine War*, p. 117.

46   *TNA*, ADM 137/3876.

for a torpedo strike, and for rest for the crew, probably stationary and settled on the bottom. Even then, the electric motors were needed to replenish the oxygen supply.

> *To break through the barrage on a dark night, on the surface, gives the best prospects. The positions of the net and mines are not exactly known and are constantly altered. Should one be forced to pass through under water, the net must be dived under, in the deep-water channel ... For the Flanders boats it was their daily bread, so to speak. On every cruise from Zeebrugge to the western approaches of the Channel they had to pass through, outward and inward bound. Consequently, they knew the position of the barrage, the individual buoys, the tactics of the patrols, and the alterations in the whole barrage-system. They had experience. They were smaller and handier; and from their base close to the Straits they constantly got up-to-date information, and slipped through on the surface, at a favourable moment in darkness and fog. In spite of all this, the Straits of Dover remained, even for them, a permanent source of the greatest danger.*[47]

In between the mines and the nets, the u-boat lanes were constantly patrolled by a steady stream of deadly searchers: fast destroyers able to ram, armed trawlers with depth charges, spotter airships, aircraft with bombs, submarines with torpedoes, and many smaller craft with effective guns:

> *The motor boats in pairs with a steel net between them searched through the channel where they suspected that u-boats were lurking. Every time we stuck up our periscope cautiously in order to look around a bit, it never failed that we had one of those searching parties right in front of us, so that we must submerge in a hurry to a greater depth in order not to be caught by the dangerous nets.*[48]

Gerth described the weather as 'initially hazy'. But, even before he reached the buoys of the barrier net, dense fog set in. Fog was prevalent at this time of year, especially in the early hours of the morning. That same day, the British consular general in neutral Rotterdam asked the Admiralty whether to delay the sailing of British ships.[49]

---

47 Hashagen, *Commander*, pp. 179-82.
48 Spiegal, *Adventures of the U 202*, p. 48.
49 ADM 137/485.

I learnt the value of the comparative invisibility of the submarine. The silhouettes of the Englishmen slid by like wraiths, only a few hundred yards away; often indeed so close that we were afraid they would hear the dull hum of the Diesel engines, or have their suspicions aroused by the spray as it flung itself from our bows, dashed over the conning-tower and faded into the darkness astern.[50]

By the time Gerth was within the mine area, he decided that continuing 'did not carry a greater risk than lying on the bottom or returning'. Before crossing the barrage on the surface, commanders watched for the surveillance measures and the lights marking the line of buoys and then moved at a favourable moment.[51] *UC 61* carried at the bow great wire scissors for cutting the nets if the boat became trapped.

Gerth's story was supported by Engineer Sub-Lieutenant Johannes Giese. Giese, aged twenty-six, and like his commander from Berlin, was an experienced u-boat man. He had some twenty-one months aboard *U 6*, which he left, ironically, just before it stranded on the Maas River and the crew were interned, and on *U 74*, before joining *UC 61* from its commissioning.

Gerth wrote that he was 'at complete invisibility' and had to assess his positioning by dead reckoning shaping a course along the coast between Gravelines and Blanc Nez.[52]

By one of those strange coincidences, Gerth's men were heard at this task, but not seen. The story was told by twenty-three-year-old Ensign Louis Guichard, who wrote several books after the war romanticising his experiences.[53] Guichard was leading a patrol of four small wooden motor boats each with six men. He was trying to catch some sleep below on a small seat when he was called to the deck by a Breton called Bourhis who had heard something strange. They were about two miles from Buoy 4 at two o'clock in the morning.

---

50   Hashagen, *Commander*, p. 44.
51   *SHD*, Vincennes, *Nautical Bulletins*, 'Observations by submarine commanders on crossing the submarine nets of the Pas-de-Calais' (MV SSZ 18, Sous-marins ennemis), pp. 4-25.
52   There is a point at each end of Wissant Bay before leaving the Channel: Cap Blanc Nez (White Nose) and the larger Gris Nez (Grey Nose) towards the open sea.
53   Guichard, *Au Large*, pp. 135-38. Guichard was born in Saint Nazaire; he moved to a destroyer after a mandatory eighteen months on patrol boats; by the end of the war he was ashore as a marine fusilier. He left the navy as a frigate captain (*SHD*, Vincennes, MV CC7 4e moderne 3257-9).

Very gently, we move forward in the dense fog; the night is perfectly calm; the slightest sound of a voice must carry more than a mile. Leaning over the gunwale we strain our ears; the characteristic hum of a combustion engine crosses the night, then stops, very close. We listen intently with beating hearts. A hoarse voice cries out a command in which I distinguish clearly the words 'rechts [right]' and 'auf [left]'. The Germans are very near ... The voice dies away. The submarine is probably trying to grope its way. The hum of the engine resumes, decreases, distancing itself, and we vainly try to follow. After a quarter of an hour the trail is lost.

Gerth was below and had delegated the navigation of *UC 61* to Warrant Officer Hubert Lengs, from Dortmund, 'feeling quite confident of his course'. It was Lengs' watch and he was 'on duty near the conning tower'. Although Lengs had been through comprehensive training since the winter off 1915, it was his first voyage on a submarine on active service. Perhaps it is a little strange to understand, but it was normal practice for u-boat commanders to leave all navigation matters to those like Lengs with the skills – even in thick fog.

The navigation of submarines is entrusted to a warrant officer, who is a specialist in the subject, and is known as a Steuermann. These navigating warrant officers are well up to their work and reliable in taking star and sun sights. In addition, many boats carry a second Steuermann, or a war pilot, whose special qualification is knowledge of the locality in which the submarine is to operate. These war pilots are usually ex-mercantile officers, who obtained an intimate knowledge of Allied ports by years of trading to them in time of peace. The commanding officer does not as a rule interfere in the navigation or concern himself greatly with it. He gives the navigating warrant officer direction to follow a certain route or to work out the course and speed to reach a certain point at a given time. These warrant officers are the right hands of the submarine commanders.[54]

Close at hand was Gerth's number two, Leutnant Karl Dancker, an experienced ship's officer who, when the war started, was in New York serving on the *Hamburg Amerika Linie*. After a period as adjutant on the obsolete pre-dreadnought battleship SMS *Kaiser Friedrick*, Dancker volunteered for submarine duty in

---

54   *TNA*, ADM 186/407. Also, Koerver, *German Submarine Warfare*, p. 134.

February 1916, served on *UC 24* from October for two months, and then joined Gerth on *UC 61* at its commissioning.[55]

The practice of taking along officers of merchant vessels as military pilots proved successful over time, especially with their knowledge of neutral and enemy shipping. 'After these pilots had gained war experience with tried submarine commanders, they were admirably suited to act as advisers to commanders newly assigned to duty at the front.'[56]

> *With an agility to which I am now accustomed, I swing myself on to the floor. There are only sea-boots to put on, for the rest of one's clothing is worn, day and night, during a voyage that may last weeks. Thus, one's toilet is extremely simple, if not particularly thorough. Indeed, washing and shaving are seldom practised of a morning. It becomes easy to study the luxuriance or otherwise of our respective hair and beards ... Water and soap are very precious on board a u-boat. Morning cocoa and bread and marmalade taste delicious under such conditions.*[57]

Lengs was contouring, carrying out soundings with a weight on a line, knowing that if he kept the boat's depth constant he knew his distance from the shore on the portside and would avoid grounding. The shape of the sand banks off Dunkerque on the way to Cap Gris Nez support this as *UC 61* would have to follow a narrow channel with shallow water either side. This was a similar practice to that used by u-boat commanders 'lost' in the Channel who would ground their boat on the bottom to measure their depth and then assess their position against their detailed charts.

Gerth thought he had by dead reckoning travelled one hour passed Cap Griz Nez and changed course a little further southwards – 'I do not recall the exact course' – in the middle between Colbart light vessel and the French coast. Immediately afterwards, he said, he stranded at five in the morning (French reports say at 0420, with which Gerth later agreed) near the village of Wissant

---

55   It is likely that Dancker left the *Kaiser Freidrick* when she was withdrawn from service in February 1915. She was eventually decommissioned in November, thereafter being employed as a prison ship and later as a floating barracks. She was scrapped in 1920. *UC 24* was based in Bruges and moved in February 1917 to the Mediterranean Sea. In May, it was torpedoed by the French submarine *Circé* off the entrance to Cattaro harbour with twenty-four dead and two survivors.
56   Gayer, *Submarine Warfare*, p. 5.
57   Bergen, 'My U-Boat Voyage', Neureuther, *U-Boat Stories*, p. 17.

at high tide. High tide that morning was scheduled at 0457; by low water at 1209 the sea had fallen five and a quarter metres.

Gerth's excuse to his superiors was that 'the fault in my ship's position by dead-reckoning can be attributed in my view to the fact that during the previous days there had been an easterly wind which on the evening of my sailing out had turned into a strong westerly wind. The back-flow of the impounded water must have caused an unusual counter current flow.'

Gerth attempted to release the boat by using his engines at full power. When this failed he reduced weight by blowing the buoyancy tanks; firing three torpedoes, one from each tube; throwing artillery ammunition over board; and pumping out some bunker fuel. He was hampered by the boat's construction from doing more: compressed air could not be blown into the oil bunkers.

There are significant, but not vital, differences between the information that Gerth gave his interrogators in Calais on the day of grounding, and that given to his superiors three years later. These differences may not be surprising, but everything that Gerth said has to be weighed. He clearly lied several times.

First, he ordered his crew to say that *UC 61* had left Zeebrugge on 15 July and 'passed round Scotland to Wissant without laying any mines or committing any hostile act'. All of the prisoners, bar one, obeyed this order, but, afterwards 'acknowledged their obvious lie'. Even Gerth was 'easily convinced' that his story was 'too implausible to pass muster'. He had invented it to hide his passage through the Channel barrage.

He then claimed that his destination for mine laying was Boulogne and Le Havre, another lie which was taken at face value by his interviewers, newspaper reporters and, later, historians.

Gerth said that around 0420, *UC 61* 'jerked several times and stranded in the open sea', but was actually high on a long beach.

The surface motors failed to move the boat, first full speed ahead, then astern. Then, the electric motors were coupled to the diesels without effect. The two loaded torpedoes were fired from the bow tubes, not three as Gerth later claimed. A firing from the third submerged aft tube risked an early explosion on the sand. Two self-propelled torpedoes were found drifting before midday in the sea off Wissant and Admiral Bacon, Vice Admiral of the Dover Patrol, was alerted by telegram.[58]

---

58   *TNA*, ADM 137/2096, 26/7/1917; *SHD*, Cherbourg, SSTe35.

The two spare torpedoes could be loaded from inside of the boat into the after tube but, as that had not been emptied, time and special equipment would be necessary to raise them through the conning tower for external entry into the empty bow tubes. This became important many years later.

While the crew worked, the water was falling. The bay at Wissant Bay is an eight kilometres long picturesque sweep of slowly sloping sand popular as a bathing resort since the nineteenth century.[59] Its tidal speed is considerable; several hundred metres of flat beach are uncovered in a few minutes. It is also the most rapidly eroding shoreline on the French mainland with up to half a kilometre lost since 1917.

For Gerth it was a hopeless task not helped by him still not knowing where he was as the fog was hours from clearing. At first, he thought he had stranded on the Bassure de Baas, a lengthy shoal around the corner of Cap Gris Nez almost seven and a half nautical miles away.[60]

There are many contemporary photographs of *UC 61* aground. She lay almost parallel with the dunes which line the shore in front of an uninhabited area about 800 metres east of the village, near to the tiny hamlet of Strouanne, with her bow pointing to Gris Nez. She was travelling from the east, from the direction of Calais, and from Zeebrugge beyond.

Wissant's small fishing fleet was tucked up close to the high tide mark near the village. The u-boat's arrival had not been heard. Today's maritime chart suggests that *UC 61* had bad luck for there is a depression in the sand leading from the north-east up the beach, only just worth the recording, but large enough to accommodate a u-boat heading in *UC 61*'s precise direction.[61] This took *UC 61* much further towards the shore than would otherwise have been possible. As the sea receded, she was left isolated in a little pond. No amount of weight loss would have got her off.

---

59 Sedrati, 'Emblematic case of Wissant Bay', pp. 483-494.
60 The northern end of Bassure de Baas is three miles south from Cap Gris Nez, less than one mile from the French coast, nearly opposite Ambleteuse. It is 'shallowest at its northern end, perhaps three to four fathoms; its east and west sides of the bank are steep, rising from about twelve fathoms'. It is here that there is a knoll of twelve feet of water, half a mile in extent in the vicinity of Cap d'Alprech lighthouse 'upon which the sea breaks with violence' (Ogden, *Sailing Directions of the North Coast of France*, 1908), p. 3.
61 SHOM chart 7323.

13
COASTGUARD SERIN AND THE BELGIAN CAVALRY

Gerth instructed telegraphist Otto Boch to send a wireless message to Bruges: 'Have run aground apparently Boulogne. Hopeless. *UC 61*.'

German monitoring at 'E-Stelle West' of French radio traffic showed that the boat had stranded at Wissant at high tide and 'there was little chance that it would come free again, especially as it has already been noticed by the enemy'. About three hours later, the Calais radio station reported that the boat had come free, 's'est fait courir'. Shortly afterwards, the Eifel Tower station set the record straight reporting that the crew were captured and the interior of the boat aflame.[1]

Gerth had given orders to blow up *UC 61*. He prepared for the explosion with two torpedoes and thirty blasting cartridges (which were intended for use on captured Allied merchantmen). Some of the bombs, 'in particular, were placed near the reserve torpedo under the locker in the engine-room between the motor bearings and close to the shell room'.

At around 0600, Gerth noticed four supposed English destroyers, which anchored as close as possible; Belgian cavalry; and 'one or two companies' of Belgian infantry. Much of this information was exaggerated, but, together, did

---

[1] RM 88/1, pp. 39-41. There were several other intercepted and conflicting telegrams over the next few days. The Kaiser was not told about the loss until 5/8/1917 when a personal telegram was sent to him in Berlin by the chief of the admiralty staff of the navy (RM 2/1996).

support his 'hopeless' radio signal. The report of the destroyers' arrival was repeated in the classic u-boat history by Harald Bendert.[2]

> *About 0700, the cartridges were attached [effected under the direction of Karl Dancker] ... Secret books and notes were destroyed ... I instructed my men on what they should say [under questioning] and, with the water level still around 1.20 metres and the Belgians about to come aboard, then went with my crew ashore. The detonations ripped the boat completely apart. Accumulator and oil bunker fires completed the destruction.*

On a, perhaps, slightly lighter note, it may be that *UC 61*'s pigeons were set free in good time. One of the crew was charged with their welfare and would hopefully have been aware of a recent German admiralty staff instruction that carrier pigeons were not to be shot 'unless there is absolute proof that they are not ours'. This, of course, was not the case. The problem was that the German Naval Air Service had 'not enough good carrier pigeons at present returning to its pigeon houses'. Captured or dead pigeons were to be 'searched for news and handed in to the 2nd Naval Air Division'.[3]

The crew jumped overboard and 'swam ashore easily' [some reports say 'waded'] and gave themselves up. The first bombs were fired just as the Belgians arrived. Later reports suggest that the cavalry captain wanted to go aboard, but Gerth cautioned him. 'I beg you do nothing. We are all here and my boat will blow up in a moment or two.'[4]

Eight to ten minutes later the bombs exploded and, claimed an interrogator, entirely destroyed the central part of the vessel and starting a fire which burnt out the 'whole interior of the hull'. This was not correct: the complete front of the u-boat which contained her mines was untouched and there was only limited damage to the central control section under the conning tower. The fire was extinguished by the sea at 1400 at the next high water.

The response to Ensign Guichard's radio alert to the French Admiralty on his encounter with a German submarine arrived at daybreak: 'Go to Wissant where an enemy submarine has run aground.'

---

2 Bendert, *Die UC-Boote*, p. 159. See also ADM 239/26; ADM 3918; *Naval Staff Monographs*, Volume XIX, (C.B. 917R; O.U. 5528[H]), August 1939, p. 207.
3 *TNA*, ADM 137/3886.
4 Chatelle, *Calais Pendant La Guerre*, p. 164.

The telegram wires from Dunkerque to Admiral Bacon in Dover were humming.[5] The first alert was despatched at 0650: 'Hostile submarine ashore at Wissant at 0600.'[6] French light craft are being sent at once. At 0745, news that the crew of three officers and twenty-three men were prisoners, 'but ship damaged by explosions'.

After half an hour at full speed, Guichard's flotilla arrived in front of the dunes which were shrouded in mist, and they 'contemplated the hull of an abandoned submarine which smoked sadly under a lowering sky'.

Sadly, for Gerth, these four small boats were his exaggerated four English destroyers, a type Gerth knew well from numerous encounters over the last six months. No English vessels were recorded at the scene. The 'one or two companies' of Belgian infantry never did arrive; some of the Belgian cavalry arrived on bicycles. Guichard registered his disappointment:

> *We had hoped that we would need to attack the submarine in order to capture it, but we cannot, alas, do anything: the whale lies dry, surrounded by land on all sides. To its right, the small beach town appears vague between two banks of mist: between them and the submarine … And in front of this surreal landscape we float on the swell, while from invisible Gris Nez the semaphore station siren solemnly bellows its two blasts each minute.*

Guichard's enthusiasm for a fight was misplaced. His 'flock' of four new motor boats, recently arrived from America, were viewed by all as like new toys with doll's house living quarters. They would have stood little chance against *UC 61*'s highly-trained crew with their 88mm canon had Gerth decided to stand his ground.

> *You remember our old toy motor boats which cost 29 sous? In the bow a little lead cannon, then a mast with its tin flag, and then in the stern, above the two portholes which had been painted in, the hole for the key to start the engine? At this moment I commanded boats which seemed just like them.*[7]

---

5   *TNA*, ADM 137/2096.
6   There was an hour difference between French and English times.
7   Guichard, *Au Large*, pp. 82-83.

The motor launches were part of an order for 580 vessels to *Elco* (Electric Launch Company Inc.) of Bayonne, New Jersey, and, because America was still neutral, were ordered by the Royal Navy through the Canadian Vickers company and assembled by them in Montreal and shipped across the Atlantic as freight.[8] Forty of the boats were passed to France and Guichard was the proud 'owner' of the first four, ML 114-117, renamed with élan by the French as V1-V4.

Guichard signalled to the beach that his flotilla was returning to their sector. As they did a u-turn, an explosion occurred on the coast 'throwing a puff of yellow smoke out of the submarine'.[9]

Throughout, the lookouts at the lighthouse and radio station at Cap Gris Nez sent regular telegrams to Dunkerque.[10] At 0720, they heard a 'really big explosion without being able to distinguish in which direction'; at 0830, another explosion to the east in the direction of Wissant. First sight of the u-boat from which thick smoke was pouring came when the weather started to clear at 1200. Two torpedoes floating at sea were reported at 1215. And, at 1610, lookouts noted that the u-boat's bow was resting 'very high in the water which was up to the rear of the conning tower'. The stern was 'completely submerged' and the fire 'seemed extinguished'.

After the pragmatic, if inconsistent, German view of *UC 61*'s stranding, the French story of the happenings on the beach was both more romantic and more dramatic. For the Belgians, a little later, perhaps, it was an attempt to move centre stage. This was a surreal event because it was hampered at least until late morning by the mists slowly burning off in the July sun.

Serious work was needed to glean secrets from the wreck and its crew, and both needed guarding. Considerable armaments, jettisoned and lying all about, had to be made safe.

The inhabitants of Wissant decamped to the sands and milled around excitedly requiring protection for both themselves and for the remains of *UC*

---

8   Over twenty of these motor launches received battle honours, the majority of them in the blockading of Zeebrugge in 1918. ML 135 played a part in the sinking of *UC 49*, sister ship to *UC 61* on 8/8/1918. The launches cost £8,600 each without armament and 200 were sold after the war for about £275 a boat; those used in the Mediterranean went for £50. Reportedly, many were used for smuggling (Colledge and Dittmar, *Index to British Warships*, naval-history.net, accessed 23/12/2016).

9   Guichard, *Au Large*, pp. 82-83.

10   *SHD*, Cherbourg, Bundle 4, folder of telegrams.

61. Regardless, fisherman dragged boats to the sea for a morning's work. Local dignitaries arrived and made the town hall available for official matters. There was talk of a musical band. Customs officers and coastguards, and Belgian and French military, all armed, strutted to and fro. The squad of forty Belgian cavalry brought their horses and their bicycles. Alerted in Calais by telephone, the most senior officers of the coastal forces were on their way in motor vehicles to take charge and with them brought their official news teams and photographers – and a film cameraman. British allies, who led the local fight at sea against the u-boats, had to be informed and allowed their proper role.

Luncheon would be a serious logistical matter for the few local inns; opportunities for a quick profit abounded among those with provisions to sell. Over the next days, journalists arrived in numbers, many instructed to attend from head offices in Paris, and all requiring accommodation, insight and exclusivity. Above it all, heroes were to be found and recognised in this sorely needed national triumph.

It is not surprising that, amongst the hyperbole and daily clamour for new information, and the writing and rewriting, especially many years later in semi-official histories, and on the internet, the truth became somewhat opaque.

Picture this: It is shortly before five in the morning. Apart from the steady ripple of the waves on the flat beach; it is fog quiet. This is the time to take the shrimps that have come up with the tide and are trapped in sand pools as the sea falls back. A young shrimp girl, 'une pêcheuse de crevettes', bare-footed, skirt tucked in her bloomers away from the cold water, the pole of a wide-headed net held in both hands, gently scoops her prizes and tips them into the fish bag across her shoulders, her thoughts, as every other morning, elsewhere. Several hundred metres along the coast, as she crosses the bottom of a little bay formed by the lowering tide, a fifty-metre submarine slowly appears.[11]

Thinking she had found a French ship, the unnamed and unsung heroine ran straight to the nearest semaphore and customs post, where M. Charlemagne Honvault was on duty – the same M. Honvault who was eleven years later to play the leading part in the fate of *UC 61*'s carcass.

On her way to the semaphore, the shrimp girl met a coastguard who she told of her find. This was Coastguard 2nd class Stanislas Pierre Louis Serin, shortly to become a national hero. The coastguard was tasked with cracking

---

11 Taken, a little freely, from 'L'échouement du sous-marin boche', *Le Petit Calaisien*, 28/7/1917.

down on contraband and collecting everything the tide brought ashore on the sand or on the rocks.[12] By good fortune, Serin's hand-written statement on an official form and made two days after the stranding survives in the French military archives at Vincennes Castle, east of Paris.[13] In it, Serin describes being alerted by Honvault at 0445. There is no mention of the shrimp girl.

> *I went to the beach straight away and was joined by the brigadier of customs [Lambert], head of the post, he was accompanied by [two] customs officers [Under Brigadier Delcroix and Officer Tedellec] armed with their guns and I had my revolver. We were taken along the beach up to the submarine (port side) by M. Jean Ternisien, owner of the lugger No. 461.[14] There was a thick fog and we could only vaguely distinguish what had happened ... The crew were busy throwing ammunition into the sea, but were doing this on the starboard side – the side facing the open sea – we were unable to see properly what they were doing ... The commander was at his post on the bridge, a large number of the men had their life belts on – one held in his hand a life buoy with the writing 'Unterseeboot'. The engines were still running.[15]*
>
> *At the first inquiry by the brigadier of customs, 'Do you speak French?', the commander said, 'Yes'. [It was noted in many reports that Gerth spoke excellent French.]*
>
> *Second question: 'What nationality are you?' No reply. 'English?' Same. Me: 'German?'*
>
> *As I know from long experience the manoeuvres necessary to refloat a steam ship, [everything] confirmed to me we had an enemy in front of us and with the agreement of the brigadier I made ... the owner of the boat put us ashore at the closest point to go and telegraph Calais. It was then about ... hours when an order came by telephone from the Place de Calais [ZAN: Northern Army Zone headquarters] to get the crew to disembark immediately. I gave the order to the boat owner Ternisien to put to sea again. When we arrived, the crew were getting into the water and after around fifteen minutes the vessel exploded. It was 0730.*

Over the next few days, various official letters from higher and higher up the chain of command, even to Vice Admiral Pierre-Alexis Ronarc'h, supreme

---

12 *Le Petit Journal*, 29/7/1917, p. 1.
13 *SHD*, Vincennes, Box MV SS Gr 43, 28/7/1917.
14 Elsewhere in the telegrams: No. 841 HS, a small, masted fishing boat.
15 Underlined in original text.

commander of the ZAN at Dunkerque, and to the Ministry of the Marine in Paris, particularly praised the actions of Serin and Ternisien. It was pointed out that neither of the men hesitated to approach the enemy submarine 'even though its situation was still unclear, and a refloating could have been envisaged'. The two men had 'bravely done their duty without any fear for what could happen to them and it was not certain in the first instance whether they would be exposed to gunfire'. Things turned out peacefully, but 'this was not certain until after the event'. The Commander of the Marine at Calais, de Bon, put forward both men for 'official recognition of satisfaction'.

At the extreme, it was the Belgian cavalry which claimed the day. The lancers of the 5th Regiment spent the summer 'resting' on the coast near Wissant and, after Serin had effected his capture, were called on to guard the prisoners who were taken to Wissant Town Hall.[16]

The exaggerations reached their peak in a newspaper article which turned Coastguard Serin into a Belgian lancer who challenged the submarine.

'The response was hubbub. A shot was fired.'

The article continued, 'Cavalrymen first of all, charge at the attack. In a wave, the squadron resolutely entered the water. They had not gone more than twenty metres when the crew, as one man, threw themselves in, too, but with their hands up. We approached them furiously, cries, scuffles, jostling, splashing around, the victorious and the prisoners reached the sand and stopped there dripping wet.'[17]

The Lancer regiment was quickly given the life-time soubriquet, 'Submarines'. It wasn't long before this reporting transmogrified and, later, typically, appeared on the internet in an otherwise largely correct web report as 'Quand la Cavalerie belge captura un sous-marin allemande'.[18]

The coastal commander from Calais, Captain J Rigal, was contacted at 0620 by Calais town hall, which also alerted the Intelligence Service.[19] The commander made arrangements for every eventuality: mobile artillery to

---

16   *Royal Museum of the Armed Forces and of Military History*, Brussels, AU 9089/2, p. 108. See also 4th Regiment HQ correspondence (Box 308, 26/7/1917).
17   Museum Cabour WOII & 2/4 Lancers, Adinkerke, Belgium, framed cutting, 'Le Sous Marin', *Le courier de l'Armée*, 30/11/1919.
18   *www.1914-1918.be/insolite_sous_marin.php*, accessed 8/12/2016. 'When the Belgian cavalry captured a German submarine.'
19   Rigal became the French naval attaché in Washington in 1912 and where he wrecked his car in a road accident. He and his car are recorded at the *Library of Congress*, LC-USZ62-108182.

destroy the submarine from the land; two loads of gun cotton explosives; men armed with guns; trucks and cars to take them quickly to Wissant.

He travelled by car with the marine commander of Calais. On arrival at 0740, Rigal instructed the locking up of the three officers and twenty-three men of the crew with a twenty-man armed guard. He assessed the fuel fire as 'unwise' to approach and unstoppable as it moved forward up the boat and reached the conning tower at 0745; there were explosions every fifteen minutes.

'When the tide put out the fire … I reckoned that the submarine had been completely disembowelled by the numerous explosions inside it and ravaged by the fire with the exception of the compartments with the mines.'

The commander eventually saw to the taking off of the machine gun and small arms and their ammunition, and the collection of the many shells and bombs which lay about after being thrown overboard.

Rigal made some other decisions, one with surprising consequences many years later. While he set the marine commander to carry out a preliminary interrogation of the three officers, he organised the customs officers to search all of the crew. The officers gathered eleven wallets, some money, photographs and several cards and personal papers.[20] The prisoners were allowed to keep their clothes, their food (bread and sausage) and tobacco and cigarettes.

Almost one hundred years later at Chateau de Vincennes in Paris, as part of the searches for this story, a brown envelope was opened and out tumbled many of these confiscations. The money was in two parts. First, three notes from the Chamber of Commerce in Oran were found in the wallet of Stoker Christian Carstensen, age twenty-three from Flensburg. Carstensen had been aboard *UC 61* when a boarding party scuttled the French steamer *Nelly* which was carrying wine from Oran to Rouen the previous May. Second, one franc banknotes issued by the Chamber of Commerce at Boulogne were found in the wallet of navigator Hubert Lengs, who, it was noted, spoke French well. Also inside the envelope at Vincennes, taken from Gerth's wallet, was a poem about the u-boat war, *U-Boote heraus!*

---

20   *SHD*, Vincennes, MV SS GR 43, p. 6.

U-boats are out![21]

You stormy weather sound,
Now you flow through the lands
It is as if your brazen urge
Now breaks all chaining bonds:
U-boats are out!

As if through snow and winter rage
A spring storm burst –
Now will the rolling, icy flood
A wildest dance spray through:
U-boats are out!

Now will after strangling fear and pain
After heavy, wavering thoughts
To spread the iron seed
The sowing day begin:
U-boats are out!

Now will the wall wrought from ore
Bind even more unbreakable
When the glorious password flies above
As with mighty rattling winds:
U-boats are out!

Now forwards you heroes too big for words
Drive out and bring it to an end
Now we lay Germany's future fate
Into your hero hands:
U-boats are out!

---

21 Gustav Schüler, *U-Boote heraus!*, translation Cathrin Brockhaus-Clark. In 1914, Schüler (1868-1938) published a patriotic volume of poems and songs 'Wider die Welt ins Feld'; some of these were set to music and became popular with German soldiers during WW1. Early In 1917, a German propaganda film 'U-Boote heraus!' was released.

There is no reason to believe that French instructions for interrogating naval prisoners were much different from those issued by the Germans to its own officers.[22] In any event, as a potential taker of prisoners, Gerth would have known these orders and therefore what might happen. He expected his officers and men to be separated immediately and for this reason had given unrecorded instructions to his assembled men before they left the u-boat. This immediate separation by the French was so that the crew had 'no opportunity of talking over their evidence or of influencing each other's statements' because 'the mere presence of officers is liable to make the men more silent and reticent'.

Letters, notebooks, and any other documents were to be taken from the prisoners at the earliest opportunity and nothing must be thrown overboard or destroyed. There should be a search for secret books. The first interrogation was to take place immediately after capture as 'experience has shown that gratitude for rescue makes [the prisoners] more communicative and trustful than at any other time'. The second interrogation would depend primarily on the capability with which it is conducted and it was therefore 'important to select suitable men for the purpose'. For officers, this also meant equivalence of rank, language skills and familiarity with the enemy's naval organisation.

Général Ditte, military governor general of Calais, hero commander of the Moroccan division at the Battle of the Marne, arrived at 0815; Vice Admiral Ronarc'h at 0900 to take control of the wreck site. There were now three putative authors present. Guichard was shortly to depart in his patrol vessel. Ronarc'h wrote several books, but, sadly, only the first part of his memoirs which concluded at the end of 1916. He had a stellar naval career and had commanded the legendary soldier fusiliers - 'the girls with red pompoms' - which fought at Dixmude and the Yser in the first months of the war, before taking command of the Navy in the North, the ZAN.[23] Général Ditte's history of Calais during the war dealt sparsely with *UC 61* confirming the general events and adding that only Gerth was given a summary interview at Wissant.[24]

After looking to the safety of the many onlookers, Ronarc'h first task was to make *UC 61* safe; wreck it may have been, but the u-boat still carried much of its considerable arsenal.

---

22 *TNA* ADM 137/3886.
23 Boniface, *SHD Library*, Vincennes, GR 16N 2466. Chapter 2.
24 Ronarc'h, *Souvenirs De La Guerre;* Ditte, *Calais*, pp. 111-12 (a rare copy is held at the *Archives départementales du Pas-de-Calais* in Dainville, Arras).

The uc-series boats had five ways to sink enemy ships and these set Admiral Ronarc'h's priorities.[25]

UC 61 was firstly a mine-layer. The whole area forward of the conning tower was taken up by six slanted 100cm mine shafts, open to the sea, that each carried three mines, one on top of the other, and all eighteen were in place.[26]

Two forward torpedo tubes high on the deck each carried a 50cm torpedo ready loaded, but these should not be fired until all of the mines were laid for fear of premature explosion; and yet, they had been fired on stranding and found floating at sea. Were the mines unstable as a result? There was also a rear tube below the waterline, also possibly with a ready-loaded torpedo. Room within the boat was at a premium and it was assumed in intelligence reports that no spare torpedoes were carried; and yet two were carried ready to be loaded in the after tube: one was lashed to the roof of the petty officers' quarters; the other was stowed under the locker in the engine room between the bearings of the two diesel motors.[27] All torpedoes had to be lowered into the boat using special cranes; it was no easy matter to take them out again back at Bruges if unused, and especially not on a beach and potentially under fire.

On the deck, forward of the conning tower, was an 88mm cannon which could be used for fighting armed steamers, stopping unarmed ships or sinking smaller ones. Standard issue was about 120 rounds 'but this was often considerably exceeded'.[28]

If the cannon was deemed 'overkill', *UC 61* had a detachable 13mm machine gun and numerous small arms. Gerth had, earlier in the year, captured the schooner *Little Mystery* with only shots from his pistol.

Once aboard a stopped vessel, and with the enemy crew moved to lifeboats, *UC 61* carried a large number of explosive devices with timers, hand bombs, which could be attached to a vessel at the water line and set to explode when the boarding party had safely left.

Ronarc'h firstly ordered the giant net scissors to be detached from the bow and thrown onto the sand so that a wooden crane and pulley system could be installed to remove the cannon and send it with its ammunition to Sevran-

---

25   *MA-BA*, RM 3872, technical data, 25/5/1916.
26   Gröner, *German Warships, Vol. 2: U-Boats and Mine Warfare Vessels*, pp. 51-52.
27   *TNA*, ADM 137/3818, p. 7.
28   *TNA*, ADM 186/383, 'German Navy, Part 3, Submarines', 3/1917.

Livry, north of Paris, for testing.²⁹ At the same time, he asked for the mines to be taken off.

On 2 August, the u-boat was 'shaken up by bad weather' and had, supposedly, said the lighthouse watchers, turned right around and was facing south. Only one mine had been removed by 13 August, but it had to be sunk at sea, where it possibly remains, because it was impossible to remove the detonator. The work also had to be halted because of the placing of the crane to remove the cannon. The tilt of the wreck made matters worse and the men were nervous of pulling the mines out half-sideways because little was known of the model and its sensitivity. By 1 September, *UC 61* was sinking further into the sand halting the extraction of the mines and their removal to Calais; ten remained on board.

An enemy submarine on the beach of a tourist village, even in wartime, cannot be hidden. It is not going anywhere and can be seen from any number of vantage points. Quickly, local people, Belgian cavalry officers, and tourists from Calais and beyond were out with their cameras.³⁰ In a few days, postcards were on sale. The French authorities were obliged to issue press statements within twenty-four hours and then keep making almost daily statements for the next two weeks.³¹ *UC 61* was to remain a tourist attraction for many years to come.

Following the initial story of the wreck and the capture of the crew, the main excitement was the march of the German sailors to Calais Citadel for interrogation and incarceration. For this event, a local man, Marius Alix, scooped his competitors and sold his stories as a 'Special Envoy' to the Paris edition of *Le Petit Journal*, one of the four major French daily newspapers.³² Alix had his

---

29   *SHD*, Vincennes, MV SS Gr 43, letter 1/8/1917 confirming telephone agreement 30/7/1917.
30   The photographs, taken by an unnamed Belgian cavalryman, were included in a personal photograph album which covered family and military service before 1917 and, later, in the Congo (*Royal Museum of the Armed Forces and of Military History*, Brussels, Est I/2322), p. 5.
31   The bulk of the remaining press coverage can be found at *The Departmental Archives of Pas-de-Calais* in Arras: *L'Avenir de Marquise*, 2/8/1917 (PG 190/6); *Le Boulonnaise*, 28/7/1917 (PG 49/27); *Croix de Pas-de-Calais* (PG 76/12); *Journal de Berck* (PG 197/9); *La France du Nord*, 30-31/7/1917 (PG 16/96); *L'Independent du Pas-de-Calais*, 29, 31/7, 4/8/1917 (PG 229/34); *Notre Belgique* (PG 106/1); *Patriote de l'Artois* (PG 65/5); *Le Petit Calaisien* (PG 60/16); *Phare de Calais* (PG 8/38); *Reveille de Boulogne* (PG 188/2); and *Le Telegramme*, 27, 29/7/1917 (PG 9/28).
32   The others were *Le Matin*, *Le Petit Parisien* and *Le Journal* and all carried good coverage. From being France's largest selling newspaper in the 1860s, *Le Petit Journal* was in relative decline by WW1. However, it still produced almost one million copies helped by a large colour rotary press that could print 200,000 sheets an hour and subsequently had a cover price of five centimes, a third the cost of its competitors (wikipedia, accessed 27/12/2016).

first stubs printed the day after the wreck, Friday. On Saturday, he provided additional information, mostly of good accuracy. He knew, for instance, that the wreck was caused by navigational error, how it was fired, that the crew had reached shore without difficulty and that no mines had been sewn.

His main coup reached the paper's Sunday edition and described his visit to the submarine at the same time as Ronarc'h and Ditte, the arrival of the crew in Calais, and a personal interview with Gerth, perhaps just a passing shouted exchange in the street.[33] A number of his descriptive passages are worth recalling:

> *The normally calm streets of Calais filled about two o'clock in the afternoon with swarms of people. This is the hour when the throng of these little lace making fairies return to their workshops.*
>
> *Framed by Belgian lancers, twenty-two German sailors and two officers paraded past them. Monocle riveted in place, with a surly air, one of the officers seemed satisfied with the curiosity they were creating.*[34] *[The monocle represented, beyond all other badges of rank, the affectation and assumed superiority of the Prussian officer class.]*[35]
>
> *I wanted to see where this enemy boat was stuck, or what remained of it. Leaving Calais, we took the road, which follows the twisting coastline, past Sangatte, Escalles, and there we were at Wissant, a small town of 900 inhabitants. Everyone, naturally, was on the beach and I could see very clearly, about 600 metres away, the huge wreckage. From afar it looks like some marine monster vomited up by the sea which lay, disembowelled, on its side.*
>
> *A cordon of troops keeps the curious at a distance because there is continuing concern about a possible explosion from a forgotten explosive device inside it.*
>
> *The brave customs officer, a little nervous – who wouldn't be when twenty-four Germans come out of the water towards you and there is only you to receive them – aimed his weapon and warned the officer that if he or his men tried to escape, he would shoot without hesitation.*

---

33 La Bibliothèque nationale de France, gallica.bnf.fr/ark:/12148/cb32895690j/date. The coverage in *Le Matin* and *Le Petit Parisien* is from the same source.
34 Three officers and twenty-three men were captured.
35 'New Society' cartoon in Feldman, *Army, Industry and Labour*, p. 479.

[Gerth] *responded to the ultimatum from the customs official with the word immortalised by Cambronne [merde].*[36] *The customs official had the good taste not to respond and the German, happy with that and after having confirmed that he was giving himself up, turned back to his crew. The men bustled about the boat a bit then with the water up to their middles reached dry land.*

This prize, although pretty much unusable, was pleasing for ... it rid us of a dangerous pirate; a crew trained in submarine warfare since they say – are they bragging - we have sunk **seventeen** *ships.*[37]

The German commander, who speaks our language very well, explained that when he had stopped on the bottom of the seabed to allow his crew to rest they were far from the coast but he had not taken account of the low tide which he believed was not that strong at this location and, furthermore, the falling tide had moved a sandbar against which his boat had rested. Moreover, that morning, thick fog had prevented an accurate assessment of distances.

It is with visible frustration the German officer recounted to those who questioned him the superhuman efforts he made not to fall into our hands. He was no doubt dreaming, seeing himself captured, of the many attacks which were now impossible to commit.

But did his frustration not, above all, give such pleasure to the little lacemakers of Calais who saw him and his crew as evildoers paraded between the Belgian police?

The crew passed through the hamlets of Hervelinghem and Saint-Inglevert. They made a sensational entry into Calais, dressed in black oilcloth suits and the men wearing berets of the same fabric. They took the boulevards Gambetta and Jacquard which led to the Citadel, a multi-walled fortress begun in the late sixteenth century, and moved through the main gate with its portcullis housing and arrow slots.[38] There remains sufficient barred windows and steep steps on

---

36   Pierre Cambronne was one of Napoleon's most experienced generals and accompanied him to exile on the island of Elba and then played a leading role in the 'Hundred Days' – the return of Napoleon. He was immortalised in French language for his supposed response, 'Merde', to a demand to surrender the remnants of the Old Guard at the Battle of Waterloo. The response, which Cambronne always denied using, was among the many myths celebrated by Victor Hugo. Gerth's reply was described by Serin (although nowhere is this recorded officially) as 'in the language of Cambronne'.

37   Original emphasis. Twelve ships recorded sunk and four damaged in *UC 61*'s KTB.

38   The Citadel still stands with a narrow walk on top of its inner walls. It is now a large sports complex, *'La Stade du Souvenir'*, and picnic area with a picturesque second sea gate, 'La Porte de Neptune'. The main gate holds two plaques which commemorate the over 500 French and British soldiers who died in the defence of Calais in 1940.

the inside of the internal wall to give a good impression of the cells awaiting the men. The major interrogations, each lasting about one hour, took place here. In a few days, the crew was moved to a number of prison holding camps for dispersal.

No self-respecting senior military officer travelled to an opportunity like Wissant beach without their personal official photographers nearby. One photographer made it to the beach on the day of the stranding. A picture, not dramatic, but first, was taken at about midday at some distance along the beach, and shows smoke still rising from the wreck.

The four official military reporters arrived at the wreck early in August and produced glass plate pictures in black and white which are now held by the French military's audio-visual archive.[39] The first three, Jacques Agié, Edmond Famechon and Charles Winckelsen, were present on the 4th and the fourth, Albert Moreau, on the 6th.

While the captions on the photographs are modern, the original 'Légende' still exists detailing the reporters own notes and dates of travel. They show, for instance, that Agié was already in Flanders. Famechon and Moreau came from Picardy. Winckelsen arrived from the Aube and went on to the Oise.

Agié's pictures are dramatic and cover the whole wreck under guard at low tide. Famechon concentrated on the fire power of *UC 61*: the mine shafts and the removal apparatus for the canon, and also the damage caused by the explosions. Moreau called in at Calais Citadel first to take a picture of one of the removed mines and then captured an inspection by French and British senior officers who clambered, some with difficulty, up to the deck using flexible rope and metal ladders. Winckelsen covered the same visit, but with close-ups of the officers, who moved among casual French sailors on the deck.

Despite the excellence of these pictures, many of which have been copied and appropriated without reference on the internet, pride of place goes to a film of the wreck taken by Cameraman Daret, also on the 6th.[40] The film lasts one minute thirty-two seconds and shows, in remarkably good quality, *UC 61* under guard at low tide.

---

39   *ecpad*: *The Etablissement de Communication et de Production Audiovisuelle de la Défense*, Ivry-sur-Seine: Agié SPA 52 X 1995-2000; Famechon SPA 97 R 3524-3534; Moreau SPA 212 M 4196, 4202-4205; Winckelsen SPA 6 OS 81-87.
40   *ecpad*, 14.18 A 708.

How much should all of this considerable information about the sixteen hours or so of *UC 61*'s last voyage be believed? Was it possible for a u-boat to be so hopelessly wrong in its position after so short a journey? The answer, according to Captain Chris Phillips, formerly of HM Submarines, using contemporary charts and tidal information, is 'Yes'.[41]

'I have not made a definitive reconstruction of the boat's movements, but taken a good, educated guess based on my understanding of the conditions, likely performance of the submarine, contemporary charts and tables, and my knowledge of the area. In answer to your question: I am pretty sure this would have been an accidental grounding. This is not just because the conditions all point in that direction, but also because I can't see what he would have gained from grounding deliberately.'

Should Gerth have been on the bridge at the time of grounding? The answer, given the then practice in the Imperial Navy, and given where he thought he was and his reasonable confidence in his navigating warrant officer, is 'No'.

Even in good visibility, as Gerth is going out on patrol, he would need to conserve his fuel for the patrol as well as keeping some reserve of speed for any emergencies. I reckon on five to six knots passage speed in the better visibility at the start of the voyage, dropping to three to four knots when he entered the fog. Even if he had revolutions set for more speed than this, it is quite possible in the strong westerlies which he mentions that his speed would have been reduced further by the effect of the wind on the submarine and the short, choppy waves which would have been thrown up by the wind. At the time of grounding, it was high water, but by no means slack. In fact, in the vicinity of Griz Nez at this state of tide, the tidal stream is at its maximum strength, and Gerth would have been pushing into it since around midnight. So, for most of the period during which he had been in restricted visibility, he would have navigated by dead reckoning. I expect in the circumstances it would be quite easy for him to overestimate his ground speed. I doubt that he would have been going backwards at any stage, but was just being slowed and set more than expected. I deduce that he reached the offing of Dunkerque, and the east end of the mined netting barrage, in better visibility between 2200 and 2359, and then reduced speed marginally due to the restricted visibility at that point.

---

41   Phillips, Lieutenant RN retired, master of the sail training ships *Lord Nelson* and *Tenacious*. Assessment delivered by email, 6/8/2016, with addenda 8/8, 12/8, 4/9, 4/12/2016.

> *Making about four knots through the water, the combined effect of the two and a half knots tide and the strong westerly wind have reduced the speed over the ground by more than what he allowed. His dead reckoning position is out.*
>
> *Where he thinks he is altering course out in open water (as he says, an hour beyond Gris-Nez and halfway between Colbart light and the French coast) to continue his transit of the strait, he is actually still well to the east of Gris Nez, halfway between today's Abbeville and CA3 buoys. Had he been where he thought he was the tidal stream, albeit adverse, would have been in a reciprocal direction and would not have affected his course over the ground significantly. However, as he was further east, there was more of an east-going element to the tidal stream, which would have pushed him to the east and hence he grounded off Wissant.*

Captain Phillips added a proper and important caveat. He was confident in his deduction 'unless there is another context of which I am not aware'.

Gerth said in his interrogation that on stranding he thought he was on Bassure de Baas over seven miles away. If true, Captain Phillips' work shows that Gerth's mistake was entirely possible. Remember, also, that on stranding Gerth signalled to his headquarters in Bruges that he thought he was near Boulogne which is consistent with stranding on the Bassure de Baas. This information, for background, explains why so many histories, written after war, show the wreck of *UC 61* near Boulogne, well around the corner of Cap Gris Nez.[42] This error is repeated to current times.

If a lie, and Gerth lied often and usually understandably, mostly to deceive his enemies, then Gerth thought he was somewhere else. A reasonable assumption in this case is that Gerth knew exactly where he was and he was there for either an undisclosed or a hidden purpose. Gerth later claimed to Marius Alix that he had 'stopped on the bottom of the seabed to allow his crew to rest'. He had then stranded because of a series of errors and because the retreating tide had 'moved a sandbar against which his boat had rested'. The idea of a tired crew after leaving port just twelve hours before is not credible. Even if true, and *UC 61* was on the bottom near its final resting place, the sea was so shallow that it could never have submerged more than a few feet and this would have been immediately evident inside the boat.

---

42 For instance, Gibson & Prendergast, *German Submarine War* (1931); p. 222, facing; Banks, *Military Atlas* (1975), p. 263; Humphreys, *Dover Patrol* (1998), p. 109.

There are a number of other possibilities which can be reasonably rejected. A first thought is that Gerth was, in fact, surrendering, having had enough of the danger of the submarine war. The rate of u-boat losses was increasing after the easier days of 1916. The German navy lost fifteen u-boats between May and July 1917, but the ratio remained favourable: fifty-three merchant ships were sunk for each u-boat sunk. Moreover, twenty-four u-boats replaced the fifteen lost.'[43]

Even the brashest of commanders based in Bruges knew that they were unlikely to survive the war and that their death, while glorious, would probably be slow and unpleasant. This inevitability was regularly discussed under drink in the officers' mess. And, yet, despite the probability of death, morale amongst the officers of the Flanders Flotilla remained remarkably high to the end of the war; it remained in many ways the most popular posting. Few officers survived to tell of their experiences.[44]

From the force of 1,400 that began the war, approximately 18,000 men passed through the submarine combat and support services by war's end, of whom perhaps 11,400 actually served in u-boats. During the war, 5,132 u-boat officers and men were killed or died of wounds, and an additional 729 captured – a loss rate of over 51 per cent ... Of 457 u-boat commanders, 152 were killed and thirty-three captured, for a total loss of over 40 per cent.[45]

Across the submarine service, numbers of officers suffered from nervous breakdown or were incapacitated by heart trouble or eye-strain, and the case of *UC 39*, which surrendered on her first cruise after the explosion of a depth charge near her which caused only slight damage, is 'eloquent of both lack of training and shaken nerves'.[46]

Certainly, the French interrogators recognised that almost to a man the crew of *UC 61* 'felt little grief for her loss. On the contrary, [the crew] were plainly well pleased to see the end of a life which had assuredly proved rough, uncomfortable and full of danger'. The interrogators agreed that, with the

---

43   Massie, *Castles*, p. 738.
44   Fürbringer, *Legendary*, p. ix.
45   Mulligan, *Sharks Nor Wolves*, pp. 39-40. The numbers vary with sources, but they are sufficiently accurate to make the general point.
46   Koerver, *German Submarine Warfare*, p. 197.

exception of a few hardened 'East Prussians', 'no side or bravado was shown'. There was a 'want of enthusiasm and ardour' which was a great contrast to the 'fine military spirit' shown by the crew of *UB 26* the previous year.[47]

If Gerth was planning to give himself up, it was unlikely to be something that he would have shared with his crew for fear of disclosure, disgrace and arrest. If true, Gerth would have ensured he was conning the vessel and not settled below at the crucial moment unless, of course, he already knew before he went below that *UC 61* was committed in Wissant Bay and would never round Cap Gris Nez. It would, at the end, have been spontaneous for he could not plan for the dense fog and, if the fog had not been there, his deck crew would have seen the shore lights. There is nothing in the general papers, interrogations, Gerth's subsequent behaviour or actions or at the court of enquiry in 1920 that adds any support to this theory.

Finally, anyone reading about Gerth's war career or his later attempts to escape imprisonment must be impressed by his courage and tenacity. This was not a man tempted to give his boat and crew to the enemy.

For an opposite point of view, there is one press article written two weeks after the wrecking, when fresh news was fast becoming difficulty to find. Eugene Tardieu said in the *Echo de Paris* that he was told that the Gerth 'wanted to blow up the boat with himself and the crew rather than be taken prisoner'. Tardieu also claimed that the crew included deserters who had been recaptured and put forcibly aboard and that they had threatened to kill Gerth.[48] This suggestion is unsupported by any British, French or Germany testimony. The crew records show that most of them were volunteers and none of them were deserters. The whole article smacks of over-excited reporting.

For Albert Chatelle, writing in 1949 in his long, lucrative series about seaside towns in war, the finding of one franc banknotes on Navigator Lengs was potentially crucial.

'We don't really know whether the grounding was purely accidental or if the submarine had to come dangerously close to shore to land an officer who

---

47 *UB 26* achieved no sinkings. The boat was on only its second patrol when on 5/4/1916 it became entangled in nets from the French destroyer *Trombe* in Le Havre roads. *UB 26*, commander Oberleutnant Wilhelm Smiths, surfaced and scuttled with twenty-one survivors who were imprisoned in France. The wreck was raised, repaired and commissioned by the French on 3/8/1916 as the *Roland Morillot* (uboat.net, accessed 29/12/2016).
48 *SHD*, Cherbourg, 'Echo de Paris', 8/1917 (SSTe35).

was in excess of the normal complement and on whom was found currency notes issued during the war by the Chambers of Commerce of Boulogne and Calais.'[49]

Was this just a journalistic fishing trip? There are three immediate errors in Chatelle's interpretation: the money was found on the u-boat's navigator, Lengs, not on supernumerary Pucknus; there was only one note; and the note was issued solely on Boulogne, not jointly with Calais. If Lengs had truly been, even momentarily, considered a spy, his interrogation would have gone differently from that of the rest of the crew and there is no indication of this in any record.

The only evidence of different treatment for Lengs is that he was the one crew member moved to the prison camp at Serres-Carpentras where he remained until 1920.

At this time, the records are full of summary executions by the French of individuals accused on flimsy evidence of spying. Feelings at large were running high. The case against Lengs is dismissed for want of further evidence.

But where did he get his solitary note?

This was his first trip aboard *UC 61*; his time beforehand was concentrated in North Germany. If Lengs was not a spy, the case for Gerth moving too close to a beach to either pick up or drop off a spy also falls. There is no mention in Bartenbach's orders of a 'black op', but then there never were hints of this sort of work while there were surely many clandestine operations for the Flanders Flotilla.

In fairness to Gerth, he was not the only commander to hazard his boat in the North Sea in 1917 in difficult weather. In May, *U 59*, Kapitänleutnant Freiherr Wilhelm von Fircks, searching for navigational signals in the fog, ran onto a German mine net south of Horns Reef off the Danish coast and lost thirty-three men.[50] In November, *U 48*, Kapitänleutnant Karl Edeling, drifting while waiting for a full moon, and *U 94*, in heavy seas, both ran aground on the Goodwin Sands.[51] *U 48* was discovered at dawn the next morning by British patrol craft. After a brief exchange of gunfire, scuttling charges were set and the crew abandoned the boat leaving nineteen dead. *U 94*, Kapitänleutnant

---

49 Chatelle, *La Base Navale du Havre*, pp. 235-36.
50 Gayer, *Submarine Warfare*, p. 27.
51 Gayer, *Submarine Warfare*, p. 28. uboat.net.

Alfred Saalwächter, managed to free himself by following Gerth's example and considerably lightening the vessel.[52]

For *UC 61*, there remains one possibility, publicly evident at the time and yet barely mentioned officially by the Allies. It is so relevant, that its omission and lack of subsequent investigation or comment is challenging. *UC 61* had been hit in the conning tower by a shell which did not explode, but could have caused real damage. And, supposedly, Gerth was never asked about it by his interrogators or never mentioned it even to his own superiors.

Could this be possible?

On the evidence, the first person to mention the shell hole was Royal Navy Commander Henry Spencer of HMS *Arrogant*, accompanied by Engineer Lieutenant Commander Edwards, quickly sent from Dover for an inspection of the wreck. Spencer's observations were typed up on 29 July, possibly on return to Dover, for Sir Reginald Bacon, who received the document the next day.[53] Overall, the report comes a little short and is not hopeful of much that might be of use to the Allies. To be fair, this was an early inspection and Spencer found the interior of the submarine 'a complete wreck'. It might be possible to get more details of remaining intact gear 'when the debris is cleared away'. There is one almost throwaway paragraph deep within the report:

> *The conning tower appears to have been struck by a projectile, as there is a small hole such as a projectile would make on the starboard side of it. Although there is no trace of any further damage inside. This may have been the reason for the grounding of the submarine.*[54]

The next mention was by military reporter Edmund Famechon during his visit on 4 August. In the general caption to his eleven photographs, he typed for his legend, '*UC 61* wrecked at Wissant after having been hit by an English shell and scuttled by her crew.' He added in his own handwriting, 'From information that I could gather, it is assumed that the submarine was hit by a shell to the

---

52 Several u-boats were stranded during the war, including one commanded by future u-boat Führer Karl Dönitz who ran *U 25* aground and stuck fast on rocks on the Dalmatian Islands. An Austrian destroyer was summoned and pulled the boat off the next day (Padfield, *Dönitz*), p. 82.
53 *TNA*, ADM 137/3898, pp. 132-37. HMS *Arrogant* was used from 1915 as the base flagship for the Dover Patrol at Dover. She also served as a submarine depot ship.
54 ADM 137/3898, p. 133.

conning tower (as shown in photo number nine) and came inshore to perform the necessary repairs.'[55]

Photo number nine is a posed close-up of a Frenchman in uniform (hopefully, it is the famed Serin; the gentleman appears in many of the pictures by several photographers) leaning forward and staring intently at a clear round breach of the conning tower, the metal bent inward through impact. The impact is forward and on the right-hand side. There is no evidence of an explosion.

The press got to the story when one of the writers for the Paris edition of *Le Journal* visited the wreck on 13 August: 'It was as a result of a fight that the submarine grounded. It carried, on the left side of the conning tower, a shell hole through which in high seas, waves entered the submarine. To make a repair at night, the pirate came to hide from the waves behind the headland [Cap Gris Nez]. Here it touched a sandbank and grounded.'[56]

There are a number of errors: the hole is on the starboard side; the sea was calm and not choppy enough to throw 'waves into the submarine' through a three-to-four inch hole four feet above the deck; it was no sandbank, but the beach. But, however, the general point is made.

Finally, *Le Miroir* on 19 August carried a full-page picture and caption, headlined 'The *UC 61* Had Been Hit by a Shell'.[57] This picture, not one recorded by the official photographers, was clearly taken in the first few days as the u-boat's canon was not yet removed. The caption was headed: 'A cross on the conning tower indicates the hole made by a projectile.'

In our last edition, we published two photographs of the German submarine, which had just been grounded in the Pas-de-Calais and whose crew were captured. Interest in this catch has doubled by the fact that the U-61 [sic] did not ground following a steering error but because it had been seriously damaged by allied patrols. You can see here a hole in the conning tower of the vessel made by an English or French shell.

A later report by the Royal Navy added that the conning tower was built of steel plating about half an inch thick and its fairing had been penetrated by a small projectile making a jagged hole about three inches in diameter. This UC

---

55 *ecpad*, 97/3532.
56 *SHD*, Cherbourg, *Le Journal*, Paris edition, 0500, 16/8/1917, article datelined 13/8/1917 (SSTe35).
57 *Le Miroir*, 19/8/1917, p. 14.

II class of submarine was developed in 1915 when construction speed was of the essence. They suffered a 'decisive construction error: there was no hatch between the conning tower and pressure hull so that the exposed conning tower became the weakest part of the hull'.[58] As there was no lower conning tower hatch, the pressure hull plating had been covered with a layer of cement up to within one and a half inches of the top of the conning.[59] In other words, if the conning tower pressure hull was penetrated, *UC 61* would not be able to dive without substantial repair.

David Townsend qualified as a Royal Navy Shipwright Artificer involved with ship construction and design and then served on both conventional and nuclear submarines as a Seaman Officer.[60] His practical experience is fundamental to his informed view as to the likely source and effect of the shell hole.

It is likely that UC 61 sustained a hit from a coastal vessel's 3.5 - 4 inch gun through the starboard for'd fairing of the fin that streamlines the conning tower.[61] The shell was probably an impact fused version that failed to explode because of the very thin mild steel superstructure. However, there are a number of essential service pipes and the hatch of the conning tower that could have been damaged by the shell. If the inner hull was breached, the importance of the damage would have forced the commanding officer to seek shelter to attempt repairs. Because of fog, dead reckoning navigation and a high tide, the vessel grounded at the top of the tide and was left stranded.

The casing superstructure is made from light metal (possibly five to ten pound) and the pressure hull is twenty-pound plating. A Royal Navy engineer officer would have worked on the basis that a one-inch thick plate is forty pounds, and therefore

---

58 Koerver, *German Submarine Warfare*, p. xxxviii.
59 *TNA*, ADM 137/3898, p. 122.
60 Townsend passed a full four-year shipwright artificer apprenticeship in HMS *Fisgard* and HMS *Caledonia*, before serving as one of the two shipwrights onboard HMS *Plymouth* for two years on an extended global deployment. Following promotion, David trained at the *BRNC Dartmouth* and HMS *Dolphin* before taking up various appointments in HMS *Otter*, HMS *Resolution*, HMS *Repulse* and HMS *Revenge* as the torpedo / anti-submarine officer and then as the temporary executive officer of HMS *Revenge* in refit, the temporary first lieutenant in HMS *Walrus*, and finally as the analysis officer (RN) at the Joint Acoustic Analysis Centre. Following retirement from the Royal Navy, David spent some time as the volunteer project leader at the Chatham Historic Dockyard restoring the submarine HMS *Ocelot* using past contacts and foraging in shipyards to obtain missing equipment needed to complete the restoration.
61 The fairing is called a 'fin' in the Royal Navy and the 'sail' in the US Navy and is 'faired' for hydrodynamic effect.

the pressure hull would be half an inch thick and the superstructure casing could be as little as one-eighth of an inch thick. The discrepancy in the thickness of the plate is because the casing is 'free-flood' and so not under pressure when dived and merely provides streamlining and protection to external fittings and the conning tower. However, as noted by the RN inspectors, efforts were being made to save metal at this stage of the war.

A failed explosion from a shell fired by any warship would have caused no surprise at the time. The rapid increase among the Allies in their requirement for artillery shells had 'overtaken the procedures for quality control'.[62]

In January 1915, one German observer reckoned that half the shells fired by the French were duds, some because of incompetence and haste, but others because of profiteering and fraud. At the Battle of the Somme in July 1916, 30 per cent of shells failed to explode.

Townsend feels that regardless of the lack of explosion, the submarine could have been prevented from diving for three reasons.

First, the shell severed a compressed air pipe that passed through the fin on the starboard side between the external compressed air tanks. These pipes were used for surfacing by blowing water from the ballast tanks II and III and used to dive and surface the boat.[63] Second, the shell severed the venting lead air cocks situated in the fin which led from the forward oil fuel tanks to the external oil fuel tanks. This could potentially lead to contaminated diesel oil wrecking one of the two diesel engines, or allow diesel to leak to the surface giving the position of the submarine away.[64] Third, the shell may have disrupted the watertight integrity of the upper hatch of the conning tower leading into the submarine. As no lower hatch was fitted for safety as in modern submarines, the boat would have filled quickly with water had the submarine dived with the leak undiscovered. 'Should the submarine be in a collision with a ship passing over the top and damaging the conning tower as it is proud of the pressure hull, there would be no way to isolate the rest of the boat.'

---

62   Strachan, *First World War*, p. 167.
63   Friedman, edited, *German Warships of World War 1*, description of the compressed air services, p. 315, technical drawings, pp. 356-57.
64   Friedman, *German warships*, technical drawings, pp. 358-59.

The restriction to one hatch in the UC-series boats was at best a major design compromise, at worst a serious safety fault.[65] If Gerth had come ashore to effect a vital repair to a compromised conning tower, he would have found on inspection, says Townsend, that it was impossible. The fairing gave only an inch or two of space to allow access to the rounded surface behind it and, in this space, would need to be fitted a patch capable of withstanding rapid emergency diving to a depth of, perhaps, four of more atmospheres.

Townsend contends that *UC 61* was hit from a vessel while at sea. The shell would have arrived from the seaward side of the u-boat as it travelled southwest. This makes immediate sense. The possibility that the shot was fired after *UC 61* was beached needs brief consideration, but this option can be swiftly discounted. Nobody knew that the submarine was on the beach until it was spotted by the prawn fisher girl. The fog remained dense during the contacts between Gerth and his crew, and a shrimp girl, the coastguard, customs officials and, eventually, the Belgian lancers. Before the fog lifted, the beach was crowded with military and townspeople and remained so. The only Allied vessels ordered to the scene were Ensign Guichard's patrol boats and they did not fire.[66] If a shot was fired from the distance necessary, and to hit *UC 61* at the angle at which it did while lying stationary on the beach, the gun would need to have been in the vicinity of Cap Gris Nez, facing inland and not out to sea, and be fired blind into a crowd of people. Remember, the Gris Nez lookouts could not see *UC 61* until midday.

There was one other mention of the shell hole over ten years later. In 1928, as a side remark to another story, the newspaper *Le Miroir*, described how *UC 61* arrived in Wissant Bay to 'undertake a small repair to its conning tower'.[67]

Townsend only speculates when he suggests possible serious damage. There remains the question of who fired the shot? The vessel could have been French or British. However, most patrols, especially away from the immediate coast, were carried out by the Royal Navy. Contacts with enemy submarines were carefully recorded by the navy for tracking and intelligence purposes. No

---

65 The reason for the lack of a bottom hatch was a combination of the method used for lowering torpedoes into the boat and of the hoist used for raising and lowering the periscopes which themselves had to pass through the conning tower pressure hull (*TNA*, ADM 137/3898), p. 120.
66 *TNA*, ADM 137/2096.
67 *Le Miroir*, 'On découvre une torpille dans l'épave du sous-marin allemand échoué à Wissant', 'A torpedo discovered in the wreck of the German submarine beached at Wissant', 30/6/1928 (*SHD*, Cherbourg, Box MV SS Gr 43).

contact, not even a nearby contact, has been recorded for the necessary hours. Why would any warship keep quiet about a contact or be told to keep quiet about a contact? Why was Gerth not questioned on the matter by the French, or later by the British? Why is there nothing of consequence in the records to reflect the declarations in the Press?

The best answer is that the Allies did not know what happened, but they had been responsible. Something unusual was afoot the night that *UC 61* struggled through the fog and the activity was planned to have a major impact on the u-boat war. Admiral Bacon decided to reinstate the coastal net-barrage fronting Zeebrugge, which had been allowed to lapse during the winter months of 1916-17.[68] Bacon was accompanied by Admiral Ronarc'h aboard HMS *Broke*, a Faulknor class destroyer leader, to witness the laying. Admiral Ronarc'h was therefore unwittingly present off Zeebrugge at the beginning of *UC 61*'s last patrol and then witnessed its aftermath at Wissant. Bacon wrote proudly that twelve miles of nets were laid in one and a half hours.[69]

> *It was painfully apparent that the Goodwin-Snouw nets were failing to debar the use of the Straits to u-boats. Admiral Bacon believed that the only way of so doing was to lay a mine barrage across the Channel; but no mines were available. He therefore laid a barrage similar to the coastal mine barrage of 1916. Early on the morning of 25 July [1917], a minelayer laid 120 deep mines along a line about eighteen miles off the coast, and then the drifters laid fifteen miles of mine-nets in position. On 27 July, the line of nets was prolonged still further. This barrage had to be patrolled day and night. Although it acted as a deterrent, the barrage did not prevent submarines from emerging from their base. Actually, on the very day it was laid, UC-61 (Gerth) left Zeebrugge and passed both this obstruction and the Goodwins-Snouw barrier at night.*[70]

The nets were laid by Admiralty drifters which were fired on by German destroyers, but HMS *Broke* and two others, HMS *Terror*, an Erebus class monitor, and another destroyer leader, HMS *Nimrod*, drove them off.[71] The remainder of the nets were laid on 27 July and a daily patrol started. The Admiralty did

---

68 Jellicoe, *Submarine Peril*, p. 13.
69 Bacon, *Memoirs*, p. 143.
70 Gibson and Prendergast, *German Submarine War*, pp. 193-94.
71 Bacon, *Memoirs*, pp. 143-44.

not try to keep the new minefield secret. On 28 July, *UB 20* hit a mine and sank with the loss of all hands while on a diving trial off Zeebrugge.[72] On 29 July, *Le Petit Calaisien* reported from The Hague that the Dutch marine ministry had been told by the British Government that minefield limits had recently been extended and, as a result, the 'safe channel is so narrow that passage cannot be entirely guaranteed'. 'All possible measures' would be taken to ensure safe passage for vessels returning to the Netherlands.[73]

There are two other pieces of evidence. Gerth was inside Zeebrugge mole on the same day as *UC 47*, commanded by Paul Hundius, just appointed Kapitänleutnant. Hundius left Zeebrugge in the haze at 1650 perhaps an hour later than Gerth and was soon signalled by a German destroyer.[74] Two sea areas were being blocked by newly-laid barrier nets; 'ahead there are destroyers in combat with English armed forces'. Hundius therefore turned north of Thornton Bank away from the danger in company with *UC 65*. At 1930, Hundius dived *UC 47* to check trim, but it wasn't until 0100 the next morning that he turned south by the Goodwin Sands. When he passed the channel net in deep water by Buoy 2 (2501), the fog was so bad that he decided to stay in the deep channel, taking regular soundings. The fog began to clear around 0700 and, an hour later, Hundius was forced to dive before two monitors and, at 0900, an aircraft.

UC 65 also managed to get through the fog. It was commanded by one of the u-boat aces, Otto Steinbrinck who, by war end, had sunk just over 200 ships, a surprising number of them small fishing boats. Steinbrinck had returned early to Zeebrugge as he had run out of torpedoes after a successful trip to the English south coast. Pausing only for light repairs and to restock, he was told in Bruges of a 'coastal alarm' with British monitors and destroyers standing south-west of Thornton Bank (and that, on his return, he would be switching command to *UB 57*). After passing the Zeebrugge mole, meeting *UC 47* and being warned by the same German destroyer, Steinbrinck also travelled to the north. By 0100 on 26 July, the sea became calm and smooth and, in a dense fog, *UC 65* 'lightly rammed a fastening buoy of the net barrier'. Undamaged, Steinbrinck turned south where 'other sea signs are neither heard nor seen'. Towards morning, a breeze developed and it became clearer.

---

72 Terraine, *Business in Great Waters*, p. 76. uboat.net.
73 *Le Petit Calaisien*, 30/7/1917.
74 *UCs 21, 47* and *65* Kriegstagebuch (Cuxhaven).

As Gerth was surrendering at Wissant, *UC 65* torpedoed HMS *Ariadne*, a cruiser minelayer, off Beachy Head, killing thirty-eight crew.[75] Including *Ariadne*, the Allies had thirteen ships hit on 26 July; the Germans lost two u-boats, *UC 61* and *UB 23*.[76]

So, this would seem to be the simple answer to the hole in *UC 61*'s conning tower? While the u-boat was creeping out of Zeebrugge harbour to start its patrol, it missed the warning from a destroyer and turned left as planned, rather than right as did *UCs 47* and *65*, and sailed through the edge of a major British minelaying operation. From behind, German destroyers rushed out from Zeebrugge and engaged British warships protecting the mine-laying drifters.

UC 61 received a probable stray hit, possibly friendly fire.[77] If the perpetrator was a British destroyer this is also a ready explanation as to why this engagement with a submarine was not reported. The scrap between destroyers is recorded, but no u-boat is mentioned. It was because no ship saw or aimed at *UC 61*.

Why was the successful hit on *UC 61* not investigated or publicised by the Allies when they later found a hole on the beached wreck? What damage did the shell do?

When the first British officer, Henry Spencer, briefly examined *UC 61* and its projectile hole on 29 July, he reported there was 'no trace of further damage

---

75   HMS *Ariadne*, 11,000 tons, one of seventy-four ships over 10,000 tons sunk by u-boats during the Great War (uboat.net). 'The wreck is blown over a huge area of seabed, nothing sticks up more than one or two meters at the most. We occasionally do it as a second dive with a bit of tide running to cover more of the area' (www.wrecksite.eu/wreck.aspx?10756, accessed 11/1/2017). The next day, Steinbrinck torpedoed the 6,482 British passenger steamer *Candia*, one dead, and the 3,919-ton British steamer *Bellagio*, one dead. In January 1918, Steinbrinck broke down through exhaustion and, on recovery, became first staff officer to Karl Bartenbach.

76   Schooner *Bertha*, Portugal, cargo ship *Locksley*, Norway, barquentine *Venturoso*, Portugal, all scuttled off Villa do Conde, near Oporto (all *UC 69*); schooner *Blanchette*, Italy, and sailing vessel *Gesu E Maria*, Italy, both scuttled off Cape Corse, Corsica (both *U 33*); passenger cargo ship *Carmarthen*, British, near The Lizard, Cornwall, torpedoed, but sank under tow, and Portuguese naval trawler *Roberto Ivens*, mined off Cape Espichel, fourteen dead (both *UC 54*, mining presumed); steamer *Ethelwynne*, British, mined, but towed to port, and French steamer *Flore*, probably mined, both off the Shetlands (both *U 71*); cargo ship *Ludgate*, British, mined off County Cork, twenty-four dead (*UC 51*); passenger steamer *Mooltan*, British, torpedoed off Tunisia with two dead (*UC 27*); refrigerated cargo liner *Somerset*, British, torpedoed off Finistère, France (*U 54*). *UB 23* (fifty-three ships) was depth charged off the Lizard by HMS *PC 60* and put in at Coruña, Spain, three days later where it was interned (uboat.net).

77   On 17 March 1917, Gerth was caught in a similar situation and, with shells landing too close to *UC 61* for comfort, had to dive to escape fire from two opposing destroyers in the North Sea.

inside'. *L'Illustration* may have been first with the story on 18 August when a journalist wrote that there were several holes in the 'light sheet metal of the conning tower', none of which apart from the main projectile hole are visible in over thirty photographs. This may be true for small holes to the rear of the structure where the bombs were set, but not for the projectile hole facing forwards.

'If the submarine had really been hit by shells from one of our patrols,' said the journalist, 'the Ministry would have not missed an opportunity of announcing that our sailors had contributed to the loss of the enemy.'[78] *Le Miroir* published the story with a definitive picture the next day. In other words, the projectile hole had been missed by most among the wider post-explosion damage.

Why did Gerth never mention it? The hole appears nowhere in his interrogation. In 1920, when the loss of *UC 61* was investigated perfunctorily by the German Admiralty staff, Gerth does not recall it. Gerth does give a detail conjecture or how he was misled by tides and shifting sands. He was looking naturally for excuses so that the matter of the stranding would be dropped. As a part of his explanation, he turned Guichard's four 'toy' boats into English destroyers. He would surely have grasped the opportunity of a damaged boat that could not dive, especially one that could no longer be inspected.

There is one answer that deals satisfactorily with all the seemingly conflicting information, improbable as it at first seems. Gerth didn't know his u-boat had been hit. On his way south, for whatever reason, probably the sound of the destroyer fight, he may even have sighted a British destroyer, Gerth dived *UC 61*. This would have been an almost unremarkable event. On previous voyages through the channel he had dived *UC 61* over a dozen times to avoid enemy encounters. It would not be something he would remember three years later. There was no log as it burned in the ship. As the ship dived, hatch closed, everyone below deck, the stray shell hit. It pierced the outer fairing on the conning tower, hit the inner structure, failed to explode and rolled harmlessly through the open gap at the bottom and into the sea.

At the time of diving, the noise in the u-boat was extreme, air tanks, water tanks, diesel engines, electric motors, loud commands, men rushing to stations. Someone may have heard a dull thump, but there was no damage to the

---

78   Dufossé, *Wissant, 1914-1918*, unpaged, f. 9, quoting *L'Illustration*, 18/8/1917.

u-boat's water integrity. Everyone got on with their job. When *UC 61* later surfaced, there was no evidence of damage inside the conning tower, and the ship was in fog. The hole was out-of-sight on the outside of the conning tower. The imperative was navigation by dead reckoning and checking the boat's depth. The lack of knowledge of the hit also explains why Gerth did not turn back. From his and the crew's perspective, nothing had happened and there was no reason to cancel the mission. When he arrived at Wissant, still in dense fog, the hole was still not seen in the excitement of the moment.

The cannon hole in *UC 61*'s conning tower becomes a tantalising, but real, red herring. The shell was fired unknowingly by a warship, either British or German. It was a dud that caused no damage that impaired the boat or could readily be seen by those aboard. Nobody knew that it had happened. *UC 61* pushed on down the channel and, once free of the Goodwin Snouw barrage, and, as was thought, safely past Cap Griz Nez, was turned south for the open sea. Because of faulty navigation in thick fog and slow speed against a racing high tide, Steuermann Lengs blindly ran the boat ashore. Gerth thought he was stuck on the Bassure de Bass near Boulogne.

Instead, he was trapped on the beach at Wissant.

14
INTELLIGENCE GIFT

The [British] cloak of tight secrecy remained until the early 1990s when the Admiralty finally returned captured documents to Germany. By that time, American authorities had made a good number of German [u-boat] logbooks available on 35mm microfilm. The absurdity of the Admiralty's dogged tightness can be further illustrated with the fact that copies of a number of the logs in their possession could be viewed in the United States and in German libraries while those in London were still closed to the public.[1]

Newly-promoted Kapitänleutnant Georg Gerth, commander of *UC 61*, had a cursory chat with his captors at Wissant Town Hall. Serious interviews did not take place until later that day when all the crew were safely marched to Calais Citadel and placed in cells. At least two bilingual French officers, likely more, interrogated the men for about an hour each.[2] It is probable they had experience of interviewing German submariners for their final report reflected first-hand on the lesser enthusiasm for the war of the crew of *UC 61* compared to that of the twenty-one crew of *UB 26*, entangled in nets and scuttled off Le Havre in March of the previous year.

Handwritten notes were taken in French and German, depending on the interrogator and the language skills of the crew member. These notes were correlated into a formal report, typed up on 8 August, translated into English,

---

1   Showell, 'Preface', p. x, in Doenitz, *Memoirs*.
2   Interview with Matrose Paul Schindler, Seamen's Hospital, Brest, 13/3/1918 (SHD, Cherbourg, SSTe35).

and sent on 11 August to the British liaison officer in Paris. The liaison officer then distributed copies widely to the senior echelons of the Royal Navy.

Reginald Hall, the Director of the Navy Intelligence Department (NID), received his copy on the day it was sent and asked that the thanks of the British Admiralty be conveyed to the French for the 'very valuable information obtained from these prisoners'.

The original handwritten interview notes survive, given no security classification, as well as early copies of the initial 'Confidential' French 'interrogatoire', and of the English translation, immediately classified 'Secret' by the British.[3] These documents, and further copies, are widely dispersed today in Cherbourg, London, Paris and Washington, DC, the latter sent via the American embassy in Paris to the Force Commander, US Naval Forces, European Waters.

By 11 August, eighteen days after the stranding, the report was mostly too late. Urgent intelligence action had already long been taken: traps set, mines laid, ships sunk, convoys re-routed, codes changed, secret files and assessments of u-boats and officers updated, the wreck three times assessed, armaments, equipment and, even, oil distributed for inspection, and the crew dispersed to prison camps across France.[4]

On the day of the stranding, Admiral Bacon in Dover sent a telegram with no time stamp through the commodore in Dunkirk to his opposite number, Admiral Ronarc'h.[5] Bacon said that the Admiralty 'think the French interrogation so good that they could not improve on it'. Ronarc'h was asked to send a copy of the results 'in due course'. Even then, there were fifteen mistakes, several important, in translation from French into English in the formal report sent on 11 August; it is likely from the style that there was more than one translator at work at the same time.

Contrary to a seemingly overall leisurely process, this was an impressively quick set of interrogations and, from what followed within a few days, the telegram sounds more diplomatic, even deliberately misleading, than a true statement. It also shows that there were many early reports long before the more measured document was sent almost three weeks later.

---

3   Original notes, *SHD*, Cherbourg, SSTe35; French 'interrogatoire', *National Archives*, Washington, 45/520/JU/Box 572; English translation, *TNA*, London, ADM 137/3818.
4   *ICRC*, P 24350, officers; P 24301-3, other ranks.
5   *TNA*, ADM 137/2096.

So far, so simple: a u-boat crew captured on a French beach and taken to a French fortress for close examination by French officers who freely share their information with their allies in Britain and America; the French are cordially thanked for the efficiency.

The crew was sent on its way, the three officers to a depot at Montoire-sur-le-Loir where they arrived on 5 August and the twenty-three 'other ranks' to holding camp *Gefengenen-Kompagnie 84* in the French military zone, probably in the Department of Oise about fifty kilometres from the front line.[6]

However, there is another aspect which only gradually becomes visible and, even when recognised, remains partly opaque. This aspect is the hand of the British NID. Three deficiencies are immediately apparent: the lack of details of the interview with Georg Gerth, compared with his two junior officers, especially as he was reported to have been the 'most talkative'; the absence from the reports of any mention of actions stemming from the most important findings; and the lack of any indication of a serious attempt to collate and to monitor the intelligence gain from aspects of the boat and its fittings.

In today's Admiralty files that are released for public inspection, there are a large number of crew interrogations and also inspection reports of other u-boats, mostly either captured by the British or dived on within a short period of sinking. After reading them all, it is possible to make comparisons about the way u-boat intelligence material was gathered and reported.

UC 61 was treated in a strikingly different way. Importantly, its material was gathered mostly in its own files separately from all the other boats. It is as if the information was held back and intended for release at a much later date. Over eighty pages are missing. Obvious subjects are not covered or are covered casually. As an example, the Admiralty collected in typed books carefully annotated lists of the information discovered from survivors of each class of u-boat. The book for the uc-class has almost one hundred headings listed, from aircraft attacks through to zigzagging, for fifteen uc-boats from March 1916 to June 1918.[7] It is an impressive piece of work. *UC 61* is not mentioned.

The large amount of important information that was collected is scattered around dozens of files in a way that is not common to other reports and

---

6   *ICRC*, P 24350 and P 24301-3. At Montoire-sur-le-Loir on 24/10/1940 the famous handshake between Adolf Hitler and Maréchal Pétain took place signifying the start of organised French collaboration with the Nazi regime. The meeting took place in a railway carriage (wikipedia).
7   *TNA*, ADM 137/3876.

Charles Fryatt and his ship, *Brussels*, captured by five German torpedo boats in 1916.

Ludwig von Schröder, Georg Gerth's commander as head of the Flanders MarineKorps, signed Charles Fryatt's death warrant; 'iron man' told to suppress the Kiel naval rebellion.

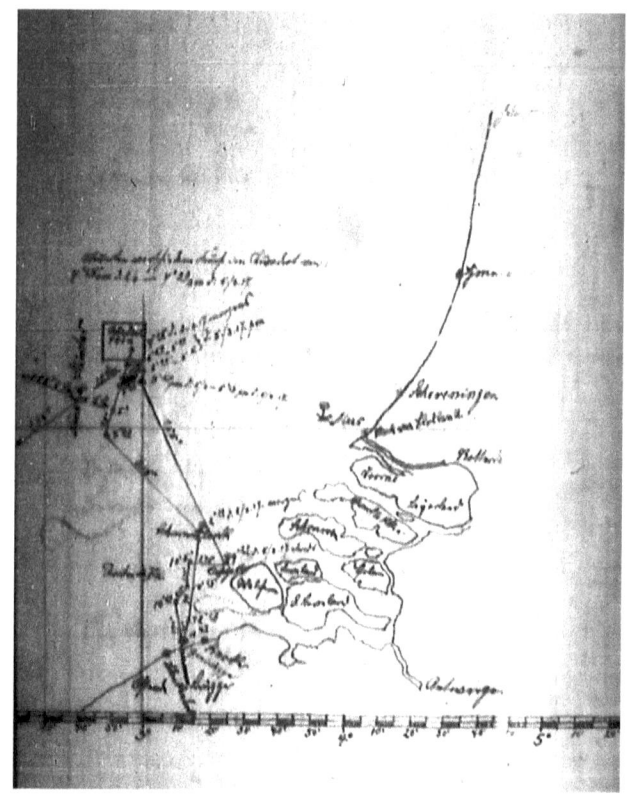

Georg's hand-drawn chart of his first voyage as commander of *UC 61* in 1917 showing the sinking of the *Copenhagen*.

Ludwig von Schröder, left centre, and Karl Bartenbach, surrounded by their officers on the steps of the casino at Bruges, 1917. Perhaps Georg is pictured? *Tomas Termote*

UC 58, a sister ship of Georg's *UC 61*. *SHD, Vincennes (MV SS Z 18)*

A UCII boat in the Bruges Zeebrugge canal showing its forward wire cutters and the covers of three of its six mine shafts. *Tomas Termote*

The mole and harbour of Zeebrugge, approached from land through a sea lock. *Tomas Termote*

HMS *Ettrick* in dry dock after her front was blown off by accident by Georg's torpedo.

18 MARINE DE GUERRE. — Le " Kléber " (Croiseur cuirassé). — LL.

The French armoured cruiser, *Kléber*, which hit one of Georg's u-boat mines in 1917; forty-two men died.

UC 61 on Wissant beach, photographed on 4 August 1917 by Edmond Famechon, about a week after stranding. The bows, blown off by the crew's sabotage, have drifted some distance away following high tides and stormy weather. The derrick was built to detach the boat's cannon which was then taken for examination. The unexploded shell hole can be seen in the centre of the picture. ©*Edmond FAMECHON/ECPAD/Defense*

Coastguard 2nd class Stanislas Pierre Louis Serin (probably), hero of the stranding of *UC 61*, inspecting the shell hole in the fairing that streamlines the u-boat's conning tower. ©*Edmond FAMECHON/ECPAD/Defense*

Reginald Bacon, the 'cleverest man' in the Royal Navy, charged with blocking the Dover Straits to u-boats; maximised the intelligence gain from Georg's *UC 61*.

One of *UC 61*'s mines taken from the wreck in 1917 to Calais Citadel.

Georg's copy of the Signalverkehr, dated 1911, with the complete hand flag signalling system between the military and merchant ships of the German Navy. The charred book was found in the bottom of *UC 61* in 1917 and re-found in the French military archive in 2017. *SHD, Vincennes (MV SS Gr 43)*

Documents confiscated from the crew of *UC 61* at Wissant Mairie in 1917, also re-found in 2017. *SHD, Vincennes (MV SS Gr 43)*

Georg and his crew escorted by Belgian lancers from Wissant beach to Calais Citadel in 1917. Georg is centre, mid-stride. *Royal Museum of the Armed Forces and of Military History, Brussels (Est I/2322)*

interrogations. One possibility is that the lack of administrative rigour may just be a result of much of the work not originating in Britain and, therefore, entering the filing systems in an inconvenient way. This doesn't sit well with the efficient organisation within the NID. The British quickly took control of the many intelligence activities emanating from *UC 61* after stranding. Another possibility is that there is a further file not found, perhaps destroyed or not yet released. The period following 2017, one hundred years after the event, may see some movement in the naval archives at Kew near London and a document will appear quietly in the listing.

Immediately on stranding, Commander Herbert Spencer accompanied by a senior technical expert was despatched from Dover for an inspection additional to the work by the French. Within a few days, almost certainly while *UC 61*'s crew was still at Calais, Bernard Trench interviewed Otto Bock, the u-boat's telegraphist. Working under Reginald Hall, Captain Trench, with Commander Brandon, headed the German section of naval intelligence in Room 40 at the old Admiralty Building in London.[8] After leading a team to interrogate survivors and to recover codebooks from shot-down Zeppelins, Trench was primarily concerned with the u-boat war and put together a team of divers to examine wrecks.[9] He was also the top interrogator of u-boat prisoners.[10]

Under interrogation by this most senior of Britain's naval intelligence experts swiftly despatched to Calais, Bock revealed his 'procedures and details of the German Admiralty's system for communication with the u-boats'.[11]

Commanders were instructed to listen to the 'Great Bruges Station', one of the captured Belgian broadcasting facilities, at set times each day when they were on the surface and were able; each u-boat sent at least three messages: on arrival, on leaving its operational area and when approaching home so that the torpedo boats and coastal gun crews could be alerted to their return. In addition, of course, u-boats could transmit in dire emergency as Gerth had done from Wissant beach.[12] Bock was ordered to listen to the Bruges station

---

8   Preface, 'Behind the mask'. Patrick Beesly, *Room 40*, pp. 32-33. Because of the war-time increase in Trench's work, Hall announced to everyone's consternation, that he would enrol women. 'Women in a department dealing with secret matters was something quite new.'
9   Admiral Sir William James, *Code Breakers of Room Forty*, p. 121. David Ramsay, *Blinker Hall*, p. 232.
10   James, *Code Breakers*, pp. 8-10. Beesly, *Room 40*, p. 266.
11   Ramsay, *Blinker Hall*, p. 233.
12   'In practice [u-boats] sent very many more [messages]. It was often necessary to signal that they had laid a minefield, were short of fuel, had an engine breakdown or had run out of torpedoes or

at 0100, 0500, 1000, 1500 and 1800 GMT. He also had to listen for special communiqués to submarines which were sent at 1100 through the German Admiralty Station at Nauen in Brandenburg, and for the instructions for all submarines at sea which were sent at 1700 each day from the cruiser *Arcona*, a u-boat support vessel moored in the Ems estuary.[13] The *Arcona* was a sister-ship of the *Amazone*, Georg Gerth's brief posting in the Baltic in 1914.

There was a greater reason why German military radio traffic received close attention. In 1912, the British Committee for Imperial Defence (CID) decided that all German-owned transatlantic cables were to be cut immediately following a declaration of war.[14] Early on the morning of 5 August 1914, the cable ship *Telconia* raised and cut each of the five German cable systems connecting the port of Emden with Spain, Africa, and North and South America and, shortly afterwards, a Royal Navy cruiser dragged up two German-owned cables near the Azores. In addition, nine German wireless stations around the world were destroyed by September leaving only two, isolated In Windhoek in German West Africa and Tsingtao in China, with no-one to talk to. Only one German cable system, a joint venture with an American company operating between Monrovia in Liberia and Pernambuco in Brazil survived the determined and successful assault, but this was cut early in 1915.

The CID's decision paid Britain a dividend far greater than could have been envisioned and its results were to shape the course and the eventual outcome of the conflict. With the loss of its cable systems at the very outset of the war, Germany was forced to communicate by wireless with its embassies and overseas stations, particularly those in Spain and the Americas.

The 1914 British Naval Annual asserted that there was no threat of interception of radio traffic. However, at that time wireless telegraphy was 'new' technology and its vulnerability to interception seriously underrated. The listening times

---

ammunition. Operational information which could be of value to other u-boats was also signalled …' (Hezlet, *Electronics and Sea Power*), pp. 141-42.

13   *TNA*, ADM 137/3818, p. 99. The Nauen station in the Brandenburg region of Germany was opened in 1906 by Telefunken and was the oldest radio transmitting installation in the world, initially powered by a 35HP steam tractor. See also, *SHD*, Vincennes, Box MV SS Gr 43.

14   Hezlet, *Electronics and Sea Power*, pp. 83-84. Kennedy, 'Imperial Cable Communications', *War Plans of Great Powers*, pp. 75-98. Ramsay, *Blinker Hall*, pp. 27-28. Devlin, *Too Proud*, p. 183.

supplied by Bock of *UC 61* were quickly married to three German naval codes which were assembled by luck by the British in the first few months of the war.

The capture of the codes was the stuff of legend, so much so that the navy code breakers in Room 40 dubbed the findings as 'the miraculous draught of fishes' and others, later, wondered whether the stories describing the captures had been made up to cover 'skulduggery'.[15]

The first code, the *Handelsverkehrsbuch* (HVB), was used between the German Admiralty and their merchant ships, and was discovered by a Royal Australian Navy captain who tricked the German skipper of the steamer *Hobart*, off Melbourne, who did not yet know that war had begun, into revealing the document's location behind a secret panel by his bed.

The second, the *Signalbuch der Kaiserlichen Marine* (SKM), was, supposedly, taken from the clutching arms of a dead German sailor after the light cruiser *Magdeburg* was sunk by two Russian cruisers off the coast of what is now Estonia. The SKM codes were used for major naval operations and by German flag officers to communicate with the army and other units.[16]

The third, and most unlikely event, involved the sinking of four old German destroyers during which the books for the VB code, *Verkehrbuch*, were thrown over the side in a weighted trunk, only to be dredged up by accident six weeks later by a British fishing trawler. Through 'monumental good fortune', all main German code books were collected 'without the Kriegsmarine realising what had happened ... the German admiralty complacently concluded that no serious consequences are feared here from the possible loss of [one of the] codebooks'.[17]

It was, principally, the HVB code that was used by the u-boats.

As soon as a u-boat began to operate in our waters, her presence and her position was known, as a rule, first vaguely by wireless or other information, and then in some detail a day of two later when attacks were reported or when survivors from sunk ships had been landed and questioned.[18]

---

15   Boyle, *Before Enigma*, pp. 26-27.
16   Wegener, *Strategy*, p. 73, fn. 3. Boyle, *Before Enigma*, pp. 22-7. Beesly, *Room 40*, pp. 3-7. Ramsay, *Blinker Hall*, Ch. II, pp. 23-38. Koerver, *War of Numbers*, p. 42.
17   Ramsay, *Blinker Hall*, pp. 30-33.
18   *TNA*, ADM 116/3421, p. 298.

UC 61 was lost at the end of July 1917 and, although the tide of u-boat dominance was just turning, few realised it. Many politicians and admirals were close to despair. Having, for the first time through Bock's information, the precise listening times for u-boats at sea, and their transmission stations, proved a time-saving and mind-concentrating assistance to the British u-boat hunters. Early in 1915, Room 40's efficiency had been further improved by the development of a network of direction finding stations.[19] Positioning was imprecise, accurate only within a five to fifty mile radius, but that was enough to give the Navy a tactical advantage.

> *Direction finding had originally been developed by Marconi from 1911 onwards ... During January 1915, the first weekly maps based on DF information were produced for Military Intelligence, originally detailing German wireless positions and later indicating movements not only of troops but of Zeppelins and aircraft ... Hall reasoned that giving the existing wireless stations DF capability would enable them to track the course of German warships.*

Marconi set up a direction finding station on the coast at Lowestoft, the first of a chain of six stations covering the entire North Sea. By May 1915, Room 40 had successfully followed the track of a u-boat across the North Sea from the time it had sailed from its base at Emden. Vice-Admiral Sir Arthur Hezlet later claimed that radio intelligence was assessed as the 'most important single factor in the defeat of the u-boats', giving the Admiralty a fairly complete picture of where the u-boats were, what they were doing, and where they were going 'and the routing of traffic clear of them'.[20]

The arrival of Trench in Calais for the interview with Bock deserves further attention. All of the *UC 61* crew had already been interviewed by the French, reportedly satisfactorily. Why would it be worthwhile for Trench to hop over to Calais only for one interview with Bock? Tench must have reasoned there was more important information to be gained.

One of Trench's many strengths was his ability to draw information from the u-boat officers that fell into the Allies' hands. Trench's red-covered files on u-boats and commanders, assembled with detailed care, were one of

---

19 Ramsay, *Blinker Hall*, pp. 36-37.
20 Hezlet, *Electronics and Sea Power*, p. 143.

the treasures of the NID.[21] Many a u-boat commander was 'amazed at the amount of information about their Service and its personalities possessed by their interrogators'.

I was warned to say nothing whatever [in interrogation] whether secret or not ... As officers, we had not allowed our thoughts to contemplate the possibility of capture and our crewmen had not been instructed on the pitfalls to avoid while under interrogation ... When I heard this [British] officer speak freely ... it dawned on me suddenly that the British espionage system in Bruges must be far more efficient than any of us had suspected. The man spoke as though he had been among us in the mess, listening to our chatter. If only I could get a message to Bruges from here![22]

Trench must have taken the opportunity to interview Gerth while he was in Calais and, perhaps, *UC 61*'s other two officers, Karl Dancker and Johannes Giese. This would explain the lack of a serious interview report on Gerth in the main French files. This conjectured dossier was perhaps lost or kept elsewhere because of its important content.

The French interrogation team found the prisoners from *UC 61* 'quite willing to answer questions' and compiled a full list of their names, ranks ages and job descriptions.[23] Only one, Stoker Franz Goosman, the youngest crew member at nineteen years, and a volunteer, refused to give further information.

Not surprisingly, there were several spelling errors, particularly with the surnames, and one crewman, Stoker Michael Weidner, was left out of the crew list although this was corrected later. This omission explains the inconsistency in the total crew numbers: there were three officers, Gerth, Dancker and Giese; eight petty officers, juniors and non-commissioned officers, Barthold, Bodrich, Gerigk, Kleinsorg, Lengs, Nagel, Naumann and Zäbisch; one supernumerary, Pucknus, who ranked as a sergeant in the French prison system; and fourteen crew members.[24]

Most of them spoke easily about their previous ships and their submarine training, but were 'entirely silent' on confidential military matters. Commander Gerth was one of the most talkative of the prisoners and 'answered the most

---

21   James, *Code Breakers*, p. 121. Beesly, *Room 40*, p. 266.
22   Fürbringer, *Legendary*, p. 127.
23   *TNA*, ADM 137/3818.
24   Appendix 1, 'Crew of *UC 61*'.

indiscrete questions quite willingly' almost apologising for not knowing more about subjects like new u-boat construction. The crew were not well acquainted with the state of affairs in Germany or even the general results of their submarine campaign.

'The Flanders submarine crews lead an isolated existence and their only means of knowing what is going on at home is through carefully censored correspondence and newspapers.'

However, the crew was quite open with information about the commissioning of *UC 61*, the training of officers and men, how crews were made up and replaced, and about some of the boat's war voyages. The overall impression from the report is that the French interrogators were somewhat easy-going and sometimes misled. They failed to uncover *UC 61*'s most successful cruise and were left with the impression that this cruise 'though not absolutely verified by us, seems to have been but mediocre'.

Gerth gave freely of his consistent route through the Goodwin Snouw mine and net barrage on each of his five cruises through the Dover Straits. This information had serious consequences for the Flanders Flotilla, as will be discussed shortly. He also described the effectiveness of the Allied bombardments of Ostend and Zeebrugge the previous June, and particularly mentioned the number of dud shells; explained the orders and procedures for laying mines; and gave his opinion on the Allied actions against u-boats which had become far more difficult to deal with since the end of 1916. Boats were now obliged to 'stay constantly on the alert' with the destroyer as the most dangerous enemy. The seaplane and dirigible were the least feared and were 'like tiresome mosquitoes which force the vessel to dive, but whose stings are only superficial'.

> *Our u-boats were safe from sky attack. Small craft, it was possible to build shelters for them. We had regular u-boat stables, quite roomy structures where as many as twenty-five craft could be run in side by side. The shelters were covered with a roof of cement, iron, and gravel more than six feet thick. Bombs which, exploding in soil, would dig a crater nine feet deep would scarcely make a dent in these well-constructed roofs.*[25]

---

25   Thomas, *Raiders*, pp. 233-34.

Bacon jumped on Gerth's comments.[26] In a secret letter to the Secretary of the Admiralty, dated 16 August, he said that he was delighted that Gerth's interview showed that not only was his assessment of the damage caused by the Ostend and Zeebrugge bombardments correct, but that also a submarine and a trawler were sunk. However:

> *The remark re high explosive shell having many blinds is very painful. After enormous labour to bring off a bombardment on one of the very few days it is possible – faulty fuses appear to have largely reduced the damage done. There should have been no excuse at Zeebrugge as the majority of the ground is firm. I suggest that perhaps our direct action fuses are a mistake in that it is conceivable that the fuse may be deformed on impact before the striker has time to act.*

The response and style of the Admiralty can be seen in the initial response to this Bacon broadside. On 5 September, twenty days after Bacon wrote, a gentleman called Henley, for 'DINO', asked 'CINO' to remark on the paragraph. Duncan, 'CINO', replied two days later suggesting a reply asking Bacon to supply the calibre of shell and number of fuze [sic] and whether they were fitted with false caps 'before any useful remarks can be given'. The next day Henley wrote back concurring that Bacon be asked for details.[27]

Bacon then moved to the attack on Gerth's preferred method of passing the channel barrage as 'of great interest'. He saw the fact that Gerth had passed to the east of Buoy 26D as 'rather a criticism of the French patrols', including, one assumes, Ensign Guichard and his toy boats. He criticised the French interrogators for their lack of confidence, 'Nous gardons l'impression …'

> *The captain of UC 61 having free choice chose the Snouw end five times in succession. I believe the Goodwin end used to be used, but was stopped by the thousand-yard length of net thrown up to the north … I have laid a similar length on the Snouw bank with white bottles and painted buffs so as to be nearly invisible. Of course, it is next to impossible to <u>stop</u> the end of a barrage short of running the ends ashore and having gates.[28] Gates in tideways are objectionable and lead to accidents. Flanking nets are the only alternative.*

---

26   *TNA*, ADM 137/1383, p. 114.
27   *TNA*, ADM 137/1383, p. 116.
28   Bacon's underlining.

Here Bacon was at loggerheads with Winston Churchill, First Lord of the Admiralty, who issued the minutes, and gave detailed guidance to his admirals, from a conference held in 1915.

> *The first step should be the closing of the Straits of Dover by lines of nets drifting to and fro with the tide, and each section watched by its respective trawlers and with a proper proportion of armed trawlers and destroyers to attack any submarine entangled. In this moving barrier there should be a gate through which traffic can be passed and it appears necessary that this gate should be so arranged as to force a submarine to come to the surface to pass through it. Destroyers and other armed craft should continually watch the approaches and passages through this gate, and be ready to attack any submarine showing on the surface.*[29]

Possibly pausing for breath, Bacon then agreed entirely with Gerth about the relative effectiveness of destroyers and aircraft. 'Destroyers are all important, and aircraft only of use to make the submarine dive, but not to destroy it.' This time, Churchill claimed the strategic credit, 'The first British countermove made on my responsibility was to deter the Germans from surface attack. The submerged u-boat had to rely increasingly on underwater attack and thus ran the greater risk of mistaking neutral for British ships and of drowning neutral crews and thus embroiling Germany with other Great Powers.'[30]

Using the collection of personal notes, official forms and photographs, and the rest, confiscated from the crew at Wissant, *UC 61*'s interrogators then produced a comprehensive and valuable breakdown of the current twenty-five boats of the Flanders Flotilla and their operational status; their commanders, including their experience and assessments on their competence; and a list of the presumed dates and method of loss of twenty-seven u-boats.

Time and again in later Admiralty records dealing with individual submarines and their commanders, there is an asterisk followed by a legend similar to, 'Confirmed by prisoners of *UC 61*'.[31]

To this breakdown was added detailed discussion by the prisoners of a further six u-boats which the French considered unlikely to still exist, although

---

29 'Decision of 11/2/1915 Protection of the Channel Communications', Churchill, *World Crisis*, pp. 285-86.
30 Churchill, *World Crisis*, pp. 724-25.
31 For example, in *TNA*, ADM 137/4154, see *UC 16*, *UC 18*, *UC 64*, *UC 65*, *UC 70*.

some did. These lists were assembled from the comments of the whole crew. All of these deductions were backed by information from a well-placed German spy, the 'disgruntled and avaricious' Dr Karl Krüger.[32] From the earliest days of the war, Krüger delivered a monthly trove, over fifty reports of accurate intelligence information detailing the prevailing situation in all German shipbuilding yards.[33] 'In March 1917, he delivered his masterpiece: the exact numbers of the submarine construction programme.'

Most of the crew's photographs and receipts are annotated on the reverse by the interrogators in French and German with family names, home and military locations, ranks, dates, training and previous war boats. These documents were clearly used to prompt the crew to discuss their personal histories and, in turn, to plot the movement of German vessels and their commanders, and also the experience of their crew members.

Taken together, it is, even today, remarkable how many of *UC 61*'s crew's careers can be understood. It is a master class in patient reconstruction. It is also a salutary lesson of what not to take on a military mission where capture is a possibility. None of the items, most illegally withheld, were returned to the crew.

The reduced crew examination report covers thirty-two pages; there are copious details on a wide variety of military subjects including the cross-Atlantic submarine merchant cruiser *Deutschland*, German naval forces in Flanders, battle cruisers, light cruisers, minelayer cruisers, armaments, specialist training for torpedo and wireless personnel, and general pay and living conditions.

When the mess on the floor beneath the conning tower of *UC 61* was cleared, it was soon evident that the interior of the u-boat forward of the engine room, the whole living space, was not the burned out wreck that was at first supposed or, perhaps, pretended.[34] Several documents, charred around the edges, but still completely readable, came to light including the latest Channel charts and up-to-date codebooks.[35]

Gerth's radio assertion to Bruges that secret papers and notebooks were destroyed was incorrect. One document was Gerth's own copy of the *Signalverkehr*, dated 1911, with the complete hand flag signalling system

---

32 Koerver, *German Submarine Warfare*, p. xix.
33 *TNA*, ADM 223/637. For submarine numbers see, also, *TNA* CAB 24/8, pp. 328-29, 24/3/1917.
34 *TNA*, ADM 137/3898, p. 96.
35 Ramsay, *Blinker Hall*, p. 233.

between the military and merchant ships of the German navy. This was not vital information, but still a most useful acquisition.

As with the personal belongings of the crew found in Vincennes, the signal book slid from another brown envelope in 2016, this time with separated pieces of burnt edging falling to the desk.[36] All of the documents found were handed at Wissant on 28 July to a representative of French naval intelligence sent especially for their collection.[37]

However, the most useful item was a small black bound notebook, full of handwritten notes in pencil, mostly messy and, today, partly illegible. This was Gerth's own notebook. Its contents read like a check list for readying a u-boat for war: postage tariffs, a 1917 calendar, crew details, engine ignition rings, uniform checks, sea boots not handed in, meeting the dockyard accountant, acquisition of carbon dioxide and carbonic acid bottles, dockyard entrance arrangements, visiting the instrument department, washing basins, oil and torpedo receipts, and many more. Interspersed are notes on other u-boats of the Flanders Flotilla: *UC 16*, lost on mines off Zeebrugge; *UC 17*, then commanded by Werner Fürbringer, friend and u-boat ace who wrote Gerth's obituary; and *UC 26*, sunk by the British destroyer HMS *Milne*.[38]

A copy of the original German with a French translation was sent on 4 August by d'Andrey, the chief of Military Intelligence, ZAN, with a covering letter, and from there, with two hastily scratched and frequently altered pencil translations into English, to the British authorities at Dunkirk, and thence immediately to Dover.[39]

The notebook clearly held vital information.

Gerth stated that steamers left Newhaven between 2000 and 2100; this statement was then crossed out. 'Course for entering Newhaven 225°.' Gerth then described, amongst other notes, for instance, Admiralty instructions for vessels 'passing through the channel [they] should shape course from a point eight miles southward of Newhaven and the parallel of 50° 39' N until the *Royal Sovereign* light bears true north'. Four areas where German mines had been reported by the British were listed: a circular area east of Beachy Head on 23 July, northwest of Cherbourg on 21 July, south of Brighton on 16 July, and

---

36   *SHD*, Vincennes, MV SS GR 43.
37   *SHD*, Vincennes, MV SS GR 43, p. 6.
38   Gibson & Prendergast, *German Submarine War*, p. 180.
39   *TNA*, ADM 137/2096, Dover Patrol Operations Packs, Vol. III; ADM 137/3898.

northwest of Fécamp on 10 July.[40] Evidently, the Germans had read encoded Admiralty warnings of u-boat mined areas. There was also a sketch that showed the mines laid by *UC 62* near the *Royal Sovereign Light Vessel* on 23 June; this last was one of the areas that Gerth was ordered to mine on his current, but last, patrol.

Three days later, Vice-Admiral Bacon sent an encrypted telegram to the Admiralty about the implications:

From papers found in UC 61 it is evident that she had information of the danger areas declared on the 23 July when she left on the 24 July [25 July]. This shows that the auxiliary code or vocabulary signal book is useless as a code. She also had good information regarding the routes of vessels in the vicinity of Newhaven.[41]

That same afternoon, Bacon following his telegrams with an explanatory letter in which he said that the route information could have been obtained from a neutral or by intercepted Allied wireless transmission; the danger area information probably by intercepts. He advised that warships passing through the Dover area should in future not use wireless, but should get the latest information by visual signalling with different arrangements for east and for west bound traffic. He added:

It is necessary to continue to signal the area as soon as they are known to be dangerous, but I have given orders that the fact of any danger area being declared clear *is not to be passed by wireless transmission. It will be sufficient if vessels are informed in ordinary cases when they return to harbour.*[42]

So, within a week, the German's important advantage from code breaking was nullified and an alternative signalling system put in place.

Reginald Hall evidently relied on Bacon's discovery when he telegraphed Paris that evening:

Vice-Admiral Dover reports that documents from UC 61 show that Germans have information about our minefields, etc, which they probably got from one of our codes

---

40   Also quoted in Grant, *U-Boat Hunters*, p. 53.
41   *TNA*, ADM 137/2096, 7/8/1917.
42   *TNA*, ADM 137/2096. Bacon's underlining.

being compromised. Please procure me either original or true copies - not translations – of documents – matter is urgent.[43]

A Hall memorandum of 9 August was also based on Bacon's work. 'It would appear that the Germans have decoded our signals ... The codes concerned can be ascertained from Vice Admiral Dover. Five days later, the Signal Section reported having taken 'necessary steps', a possible euphemism because of what followed.[44]

Robert Grant, doyen of u-boat historians, noted that the Admiralty 'had moved faster than that, for by 10 August, the German Admiralty Staff concluded that the British knew that their cipher for the Auxiliary C-14 Code was compromised, since the British had undertaken a wholesale change of ciphers. The German Admiralty Staff asked Bartenbach at Bruges if *UC 61* was carrying decryption materials which might have fallen into British hands. The reply was that the Commander Gerth was a former radio officer and officer on the Admiralty staff and must surely have destroyed secret documents of this sort.[45]

In fact, in 1931, u-boat historians Gibson and Prendergast suggested that the British moved even faster again, and more clandestinely. It was evident that as soon as a minefield was cleared by the British minesweepers and the clearance was announced by code to shipping controllers, the Germans often moved back to the cleared area and re-laid the field hoping to catch now freely-moving shipping unawares.

Gibson and Prendergast's version was that a field laid off Waterford in Ireland was carefully chosen and left intact, but it was announced through the broken code that it had been swept. Kurt Tebbenjohanns, commander of *UC 44*, received his written orders to lay mines at Waterford on 30 July, just four days after *UC 61* stranded. In that time, the team at Room 40, had to have found Gerth's notebook, got it to London, realised its significance, devised a plan, put in place safeguards to shipping close to Waterford, and then announced that the harbour entrance area was cleared.

---

43 *TNA*, ADM 137/645.
44 *TNA*, ADM 137/2096, 3898.
45 *TNA*, PG 62061.

Clearly, if this was the case, the notebook was found quickly and all inside *UC 61* was not the hopeless mess that it was supposed to be. If true, it was fast work.

The most likely explanation is that plans for the Waterford subterfuge had been in place for some time before *UC 61*'s stranding, but that the discovery of Gerth's notebook added piquancy and certainty. Further poignancy was provided by a strong link between Tebbenjohanns and the Gerth family. Erich Gerth, Georg's brother, another uboat captain, was a member of the same sea cadet intake as Tebbenjohanns – the 'Crew of 1905'.[46] Both were assigned as part of a group of fifty-two trainees to the fully-rigged, coal powered training corvette *Stein* in May 1905 and spent the next ten months living cheek by jowl in port and in arduous cruises in the Baltic, the Mediterranean and into the Atlantic.

The idea of a subterfuge sinking gained traction. Secrets often eventually will out and closing a harbour is not a private matter. Grant added in 1969 that the previous minefield had been laid on 14 June by *UC 42*.[47]

David Ramsay, official biographer of Sir Reginald 'Blinker' Hall, wrote in 2008 that 'Hall dearly loved a ruse and never more so when he could wreak havoc on the detested huns'; and confirmed the devious story as an example.[48]

William James, who had privileged access to Hall's partly-finished autobiography, said that Hall arranged with Sir Lewis Bayly, the commander-in-chief at Queenstown, Ireland, to 'close the port secretly for a fortnight after the last mines had been laid'. If Grant's mine-laying date of 14 June was right then, that not only rules out *UC 61*, but also suggests the fortnight closure was well over by 4 August.

Patrick Beesly suggested the subterfuge did happen, but was connected with interpretations of intercepted broadcasts rather than *UC 61*'s disclosure.

Richard Compton-Hall described the affair as 'something like a practical joke'.

Gibson and Prendergast were not to be out-done:

---

46 *BA-MA*, MSG 2/18641.
47 Grant, *Intelligence*, p. 115.
48 Ramsay, *Blinker Hall*, p. 231. See also Beesly, *Room 40*, p. 265; Compton-Hall, *Submarines*, p. 305; Dorling, *Swept Channels*, p. 128; James, *Code Breakers*, p. 116; Kemp, *U-Boats Destroyed*, p. 31; Messimer, *Verschollen*, pp. 282-84.

> *Patrols rushed to the scene, and picked out of the water the commander ... and a very angry man was he ... his boat blew upon other German mines, laid previously to his arrival. Bitterly did he complain about British carelessness in not clearing the area properly and rendering it safe for his operation. The mine-sweepers had actually made a 'dummy counter-mining sweep': they had not cleared away the last-laid patch of German mines.*[49]

From Tebbenjohanns' quieter personal account, this narrative may be somewhat excited. Historian Grant changed his mind about *UC 61*'s inadvertent involvement. He decided on fresh research that *UC 44* had blown itself up on its ninth mine which had exploded under the stern; the other eight mines were all collected by British minesweepers.[50]

> *Her stern is blown up. Bulkhead at after end engine room crumpled and practically the whole of stern abaft the bulkhead wrecked. Damage to bottom extends well forward under engine room.*[51]

Unfortunately, Grant told no-one publicly of his change of heart. It was not until 2003 that his new research came to light when his publisher finally persuaded him to allow a third book he had written in 1971 to go to print.[52]

However, Professor A Low, writing in 1940, was able to explain Grant's new concern and confirm Gibson and Prendergast's interpretation. Low said that Tebbenjohanns was puzzled as to the reason for the explosion which had blown off the stern of his ship. His first thought was of a premature mine, but enquiry showed he had 'fallen into the trap set for him, for the ninth mine had struck a mine laid on a previous occasion'.[53] Low was clear that Tebbenjohanns was watching outside Waterford, as usual with the Flanders flotilla, as the minesweepers cleared the port, trailing their sweeps and dropping their buoys. The British knew this because of occasional skirmishes between u-boats and minesweepers and also because of the alacrity with which new mines were

---

49 Gibson & Prendergast, *German Submarine War*, p. 196.
50 Grant, *U-Boat Hunters*, p. 55.
51 *TNA*, ADM 116/1632.
52 Grant, *U-Boat Hunters*, pp. 54-55.
53 Low, *Mine and Countermine*, pp. 149-51.

laid. This time, however, the mine sweeps were dummies and 'the last thing the flotilla wanted to do that day was to bring up a live mine'.

Dusk came and *UC 44* crept forward, nosing her way down the 'swept' channel. *UC 44* hit a mine laid previously by *UC 42* just as she laid her ninth 'new' mine, the two mines exploding together.

The story will not quite go away. Despite all the due respect owed to Grant for his copious original research, in this case the weight of evidence, and Low's explanation, suggests he came to the wrong conclusion.

UC 44 was searched by divers with the 'principal object of recovering all books and documents' and copies and originals of those found are in the archives.[54] After weather delays, *UC 44* was eventually salvaged in September as damage was now viewed differently and considered 'slight'. The British Admiralty deemed that it was 'also most important that no information should get out as to how or where she was destroyed'. Why would that be secret if she had blown up on her own mine?

The importance of *UC 61* to NID was again sidestepped.

UC 61 stranded on 26 July and was immediately available for inspection. The explosions and fire, despite statements to the contrary, were largely confined to the engine room. *UC 44* was sunk five days later and not raised until September. Yet:

> *It was the recovery whole of UC 44 (using two divers who worked on UC 5) which proved for the Salvage Section [of the NID] to be the intelligence coup of 1917. Undoubtedly this was a key milestone in the understanding of what intelligence treasure troves sunken u-boats could yield.*[55]

Far more likely, it was the appreciation of the full treasures of *UC 61*, which drove the Admiralty to return with some urgency to the *UC 44* wreck and to raise it before winter set in.

Among the many recovered papers on *UC 44*, there was a record of the conference in January 1917 when u-boat commanders were told of the re-imposition of unrestricted submarine warfare, and also the u-boat's *machinery history* book, published quickly in January 1918.[56] Among the attendant orders

---

54   *TNA*, ADM 137/645.
55   McCartney, Tin Openers.
56   *TNA*, ADM 137/3875.

found were the instructions that all u-boats were to pass through the English Channel, navigating by Buoy 2501 and the other light buoys, 'without being observed and without stopping' and that u-boats going around Scotland were to 'let themselves be seen as freely as possible in order to mislead the British'.[57]

It seems, therefore, that Gerth's implausible claim that he had travelled around Scotland to reach Wissant was a matter of ordered disinformation and, while easily disproved, was not as naive as his interrogators thought.

As a result of Gerth's hapless information, on 21 August, Captain W Fisher, Director of the Anti-Submarine Division, reported to the Chief of Naval Staff that the stranding of *UC 61* and its previous five passages showed it was a 'delusion that submarines operating in the Channel proceed thither north about'.[58] Fisher's evidence included a table showing that from January to August, twenty-seven u-boats were certain to have passed through the Straits, thirty-nine were probable, and thirteen possible.

Grant reported that despite the evidence of *UC 61* and *UC 44*, Bacon paid no attention and insisted that the old barrage east of Dover had been a success.[59] Bacon was fired as head of the Dover Patrol at year end, in part because submarines were getting through the channel, and was replaced by Acting Vice-Admiral Roger Keyes.[60]

In an extraordinary passage in his *Memoirs*, Keyes recounts that on taking up his new appointment, he was greeted initially with hostility by Bacon's staff as they denied to a man that 'enemy submarines were passing through the Straights in any numbers ... and to support this view they pointed out that there had been no sinking nor minelaying by submarines in the Dover Patrol area for some time'.[61]

Keyes had opened Bacon's safe and passed over to his new staff the information from Fisher's division, and that taken from *UC 44*.

'It is no exaggeration to say that they were astounded when confronted with this very definite evidence.'

---

57   *TNA*, ADM 137/3866.
58   *TNA*, ADM 137/1382. Grant, *U-Boat Hunters*, pp. 63-64.
59   Grant, *U-Boat Hunters*, p. 64.
60   For more impartial and detailed views, see Marder, *Dreadnought to Scapa Flow*, Vol. IV, pp. 323-349; Patterson, *Jellicoe*, pp. 177-209.
61   Keyes, *Naval Memoirs*, Vol. 2, pp. 156-57.

If Keyes is to be taken at face value, it was over five months since *UC 61* proved the point that the 'terrible losses on shipping south of the Channel and in the western approaches were caused by submarines streaming passed Dover' and it was five months lost. The failure to sink a u-boat on the old Dover barrage seemingly proved to Bacon and his team that there were no submarines there in the first place.

However, this is far from the whole story and Keyes' account must be questioned. The antipathy between Bacon and Keyes became legendary. As Bacon's friend, Admiral of the Fleet Earl Jellicoe wrote the foreword to Bacon's *Memoirs*. Jellicoe was quite precise:

> *It was recognised by Admiral Bacon in 1917 that the net barrage was not effective in denying the passage to submarines, although it had its uses and caused the enemy considerable loss. Therefore in February 1917 he placed before me plans of a ladder mine-field barrage to be laid between Folkestone and Gris Nez ... A statement to the contrary in Volume V of 'Naval Operations' is incorrect ... It was, of course, the existence of Admiral Bacon's ladder mine-field with its patrol which led to the destruction of twelve German submarines during December 1917 and the year 1918, and to the partial closing of the Straits of Dover to vessels of this type. As so often happens, the credit for this success was given to the Admiral's successor [Keyes] instead of to him.*[62]

In contrast, Jellicoe wrote in one of his own memoirs that it was not until early 1917 that it was realised that 'practically all outward-bound submarines' were adopting the English Channel route.[63] 'Until a short time before this, it was quite the exception for this route to be taken, but it now appeared to be the rule.'

Hew Strachan described Jellicoe as 'a worrier, a centraliser and a hypochondriac'. For him, the German u-boat was always a 'potent threat'; he would never have kept Bacon in post if u-boats rampaged past Dover ignored and unchallenged.[64] By contrast, American Rear-Admiral William Sims, who had been a friend since service together in China in 1901, described Jellicoe

---

62 Bacon, *Memoirs*, Jellicoe, 'Foreword', pp. 10-11.
63 Jellicoe, *Submarine Peril*, p. 50.
64 Strachan, *First World War*, pp. 202-3.

as an indefatigable worker, unostentatiously dignified ... all courtesy, all brain, none more approachable, more frank, or open-minded'.[65]

This was a palace coup; Jellicoe, well-liked, but deemed 'old school', was fired by letter on Christmas Eve, 1917. For his part, Bacon fought back:

> *The fact that submarines were passing through the channel was the lever used by certain influences at the Admiralty to oust me ... My differences of opinion with the Barrage Committee, due to my accumulated experience, were used to further the idea that I was obstructive and impossible to work with; yet, in every case, results proved that my contentions were correct and the Committee wrong, which was not to be wondered at as I had had nearly three years' local experience and they had none.*[66]

The Barrage Committee was a device set up by railways chief Sir Eric Geddes, recently appointed First Lord of the Admiralty, supposedly to light a fire under Bacon. Geddes was one of Prime Minister Lloyd George's 'men of push and go', revolutionising in turn small arms production, shell production, and the military ports and railways, before being sent to the Admiralty which he found in disarray.

Gerth's description of his five voyages through the barrage had further consequences. From 30 July to the end of the year, four days after *UC 61*'s stranding, Grant suggests that minelayers began working close to Zeebrugge, 'precisely on the u-boat route' described by Gerth. During August, three fields of forty mines were laid, roughly eleven miles to the north and north-west of Zeebrugge, and on 22-24 September, the effort was intensified with a further eighty-five mines.[67] The admiralty's private compilation of mining activity notes that there were twelve days of new mining in the appropriate area in July, eight in August and ten in September.[68]

Collectively, these new mines may have accounted for three u-boats: *UC 21*, due back in early October, never returned from a relatively unsuccessful voyage, its only reported sinking was the scuttling of a sailing vessel off Ushant on 16 September; *UC 14* did hit the mines just north of Zeebrugge with the

---

65 Sims, *Victory at Sea*, pp. 7-8.
66 Bacon, *Memoirs*, p. 167.
67 Grant, *Intelligence*, p. 65.
68 *Royal Navy Library*, Portsmouth, Leith, *History of British Minefields*, appendix. Only three copies of this work of over 500 pages were produced.

detonation logged at 2215 on 3 October, all seventeen crew were lost; the day before, *UC 16* sailed for Boulogne and is presumed lost on the Zeebrugge mines on 4 October after the body of its watch officer was washed ashore in Holland.[69]

Together, during their careers, these three u-boats are credited with sinking 156 ships and damaging twelve others. Whichever side one takes in the debate about *UC 44* off Waterford, and whether Gerth's declared u-boat route from Zeebrugge would have been mined sooner or later, and to greater or lesser intensity, the whole suggests that the cost to the Germans of *UC 61*'s intelligence was beginning to mount.

Before the end of WWI, 375 u-boats of thirty-three separate classes belonging to seven general types had been commissioned. The Admiralty, from spies, from captures, wreck inspections and interrogations of survivors, had gathered a considerable amount of information. Manuals circulated with details of each type and of its armament. The basic information was all in place. However, this was a time of dramatic innovation. Each side jostled for any advantage in offensive and in anti-submarine measures. No less than winning the war was at stake. All of the sunken or captured boats that could be reached carried potentially important information and equipment and this importance increased with the arrival of any new class of u-boat and with the passage of time. The need to review any u-boat which became available was urgent.

Amidst all the classes and sub-classes of WWI u-boats, the important difference came down to three types: the u-boat, which became a long-range raider; the ub-boat, a coastal torpedo attack boat; and the uc-boat, a coastal mine-layer which, after dropping its mines, became a coastal raider.

There were three series of uc-boat; fifteen boats in the early Series 1 (*UC 1 - UC 15*), all built by 1915; sixty-four boats in the mainstream Series II (*UC 16 - UC 79*); and sixteen boats in the more advanced Series III (*UC 90 - UC 105*), which only came into service from July 1918.[70] While Series II was a

---

69   *UC 21*: ninety-nine ships sunk and six damaged, the fourteenth most successful u-boat of WW1; *UC 14*: fourteen ships sunk including the Italian battleship *Regina Margherita* with 675 dead; *UC 16*: forty-three ships sunk and six damaged (uboat.net). *UC 16* and *UC 21* were two of the four boats in Ostend with *UC 61* during the bombardment of 5/6/1917; *UC 21* was the 'third' boat, delayed by repairs, which failed to travel down the Bruges canal on 25/7/1917 with *UC 61* on the latter's last voyage.

70   *UC 80 - UC 89* played no part in the war. Only three were launched with the others were not

continuous series, the thirty-one boats after *UC 49* might be considered the more advanced. Their production was spread across five constructions yards and it was the day-to-day lack of cohesion between these yards that led the leader of *UC 61*'s fitting out party, Petty Officer Peter Kleinsorg, to complain about the many and confusing design differences.[71]

UC 61 was one of four boats built for a cost of around two million marks each at the Weser Yard in Bremen. For the Allies, the first capture of a Series II uc-boat would be a major coup; so much detail was unknown or guessed.

Three Series 1 uc-boats provided information before *UC 61*'s stranding. *UC 2*, off Yarmouth, and *UC 12*, off Taranto Harbour, Italy, were destroyed by their own mines with all hands lost in June 1915 and March 1916. *UC 2*, which was also later rammed, was examined by Royal Navy divers and parts of the boat were raised; *UC 12*, was raised, re-commissioned by the Italians and named *X-1*.[72] The third Series I boat, *UC 5*, was by far the most famous of its day. *UC 5* was the first u-boat to penetrate the English Channel, laying mines off Boulogne. After a twenty-nine-patrol career in which thirty ships were sunk and seven more damaged, *UC 5* grounded on the Shipwash Shoal, near Felixstowe, in April 1916. The boat was scuttled, but the explosive charges caused limited damage.[73] Little intelligence was discovered as much material had been destroyed by the crew.[74] After securing two mines which were bumping about inside in two-feet of water, the holed boat was patched up and towed to dock. *UC 5* was later taken to Temple Pier on Victoria Embankment in London and opened to the Press, including the naval correspondent of *The Times*.

---

completed and broken up on the slipways at war end. U-boats *UC 106-192* also played no part in the war being either commissioned in 1919 and surrendered without engines or torpedoes, uncompleted, broken up, or had their contracts cancelled (Gröner, *German Warships*), pp. 34-35.

71 Germaniawerft, Kiel; Kaiserliche Werft, Danzig; AG Weser, Bremen; Blohm & Voss, Hamburg; and Vulcan in Hamburg (Gröner).

72 uboat.net. *UC 12*: The Italians discovered that this u-boat had been constructed in sections at the Weser Yard in Bremen (*UC 61*'s yard) and then shipped by rail and assembled at Pola, and that her crew was German (Compton-Hall, *Submarines*), p. 219. 'The knowledge that Germany, technically their ally, was assiduously mining their naval bases was a contributing factor in Italy's decision in August 1916 to declare war on Germany' (Kemp, *U-Boats Destroyed*), p. 17.

73 uboat.net. *West Sussex Record Office*, Druitt MSS/429. *The Times*, 22/7/1916, p. 3.

74 McCartney, *Tin Openers*, p. 21.

> *Several requests for permission to photograph the UC 5 having been received, the Admiralty announce that there is no objection to such photographs being taken, both while she is on her way up [The Thames] and while she is moored.*

Many postcards followed; *UC 5* was taken on a publicity tour which ended in Central Park, New York, and the hull, later used to stimulate war-bond sales and recruiting, was sold for scrap in Montreal in 1923.

On 22 May, nearly a month after stranding, the Admiralty instructed that all books and papers recovered from *UC 5* should be send to NID.[75]

> *Unlike UC 2 and UC 12, this small minelayer was virtually intact, and her construction could be studied intensively. Such study was important because some features of the smallest minelayers would be preserved in the designs of her newer and larger sisters [the Series II uc-boats].*

Grant listed five uc-boats from which during the war 'divers took special materials' which were therefore 'highly significant'; he added to the list *UC 12* in Italy and *UC 61*, which needed no divers.[76] There were four Series II boats from which information was gathered before *UC 61*'s stranding, all in 1917, and a brief examination of the circumstances of their demise allows the importance of *UC 61*'s inspection to be placed in context.

UC 39 was forced to the surface by depth charge and hit by gunfire by destroyer HMS *Thrasher* off Flamborough Head on 8 February with seven dead and seventeen survivors.[77] The first u-boat men on deck, including the commander Oberleutnant Otto Ehrentraut, were killed by a shell. HMS *Thrasher* kept firing because the u-boat kept her engines running even though the men on deck had their hands up in surrender. When the skipper of a Swedish steamer, held captive from that morning, waved a white flag and the engines were switched off by a petty officer, the firing stopped. *UC 39* didn't sink for a further two hours and thirty-five minutes after capture. The affair was a great embarrassment to the Royal Navy who had the boat in tow - and the event was kept secret.

---

75 Grant, *U-Boat Hunters*, pp. 49-50.
76 Grant, *U-Boat Hunters*, p. 32.
77 uboat.net. *TNA*, ADM 156/28. *TNA*, ADM 137/3876.

Following a court of enquiry on 13 February 1917 into the sinking of the interestingly-named HMS *UC 39*, Lieutenant L Ommanney, the commanding officer of the destroyer HMS *Itchen* which had the tow, was sent to court martial. Ommanney 'received distinct orders by signal to make sure that *UC 39* would float or to beach her'. He did neither. The boat was boarded and documents taken off including the engineering officer's notebook, but it was admitted that no effort was made to search for or to patch up the damage.[78] After over an hour of towing when shallow water could easily have been made, and during a towing manoeuvre, *UC 39* suddenly and quickly sank in deep water.

The commanding officer got off on a legal technicality because of the framing of the charges; the Admiralty was not happy about the acquittal which the fourth sea lord saw as 'very fortunate' for the *Itchen*'s captain. 'This officer probably did his best, but his best was not good enough; and he didn't rise to the occasion.' This was the Admiralty's first chance to get hold of a complete Series II uc-boat and they lost it.

A few days later, Hall received a letter with a crumpled piece of paper picked up in the street.[79] It was orders from the submarine school at Kiel from January, 'without doubt dropped by a *UC 39* crew member when they were being conveyed across London', thought Hall. Sixteen months later, a diver visited *UC 39*, but 'it was thought too old to be worth investigating'.

A few weeks later on 23 February 1917, *UC 32* blew up on its own mines near Roker Pier lighthouse off Sunderland; there were twenty-three dead and three survivors including her captain, Herbert Breyer. That month, the newly-formed NID team, led by Trench, inspected their first uc-boat wreck, lying in thirteen metres of water in three broken sections.[80] 'Items' were recovered, including a torpedo.[81] The machinery history book was recovered and published in May.[82]

The survivor's interrogations have not been found, but the interview with one of *UC 32*'s crew, acting warrant officer Bernhard Haack, is on record.[83] On 25 January, Haack was in a boat travelling to a stopped British trawler, the

---

78   *TNA*, ADM 137/3875.
79   Grant, *U-Boat Hunters*, pp. 51-52.
80   Grant, *U-Boat Hunters*, pp. 52-53.
81   McCartney, *Tin Openers*, p. 22.
82   *TNA*, ADM 137/3875.
83   *TNA*, ADM 137/3060.

Mayfly, with the intention of sinking her with bombs when *UC 32* was attacked by *Speedwell II* and quickly submerged leaving Haack behind. Haack gave his interrogators reasonable detail concerning *UC 32* and other u-boats that he knew.

On 8 May 1917, *UC 26* was rammed and depth charged by British destroyer *HMS Milne* while in the act of submerging.[84] The u-boat's commanding officer was 'dilatory' and could have got away, but was slow down the hatch and his boat was hit in the conning tower. *UC 26* hit the bottom at forty-six metres with a 'considerable bump'. The second in command, sub-lieutenant Heinrich Petersen, and others managed an escape when compressed air allowed the hatches to be open; he rose slowly owing to his heavy clothing and suffered just a mild attack of the 'bends'.

The incident has relevance for two reasons: first, Petersen, one of the two survivors, kept a diary which survived with him, and he also gave on interrogation useful information of uc-boats; second, the Dutch press carried reports received from Germany that eight crewmen had reached the surface of whom the English deliberately only saved two.[85]

A translation of Petersen's diary was distributed amongst the Dover Patrol on NID's suggestion 'as it is thought that this diary would make encouraging reading for our patrols'.[86] Hall of the NID instructed that all letters home from the two survivors were to receive 'special examination' and 'any doubtful letters' were to be forwarded to him personally.[87] Commander V Campbell of HMS *Milne* received the DSO; Lieutenant L Pearson, the DSC; and four crew, the DSM.[88]

The last opportunity was an encounter with *UC 29* whose sinking was another exploit in one of the most lauded careers of the Allied naval war.[89] On 7 June, *UC 29* attacked HMS *Pargust*, a Q-ship commanded by Commander Gordon Campbell, who had already been awarded the DSO for sinking *U 68* and the Victoria Cross for sinking *U 83*.[90]

---

84 *TNA*, ADM 137/1287.
85 *TNA*, ADM 137/3897.
86 Letter NID, 14/5/1917 (*TNA*, ADM 137/3897).
87 Letter NID 15/5/1917 (*TNA*, ADM 137/3897).
88 *TNA*, ADM 137/1287.
89 ADM 137/3897.
90 Chatterton, *Q-ships, pp. 21, 39-46, 109, 161, 192-208, 246.*

Pargust was hit by a torpedo. Lured in close, *UC 29* submerged when hit by *Pargust*'s suddenly-disclosed deck guns, and then reappeared and was hit by some forty shells; Germans came to the deck and waved and Campbell ordered 'Cease Fire'. 'In a typically unsportsmanlike trick', *UC 29* then made off 'at a fair speed' so Campbell reopened fire and sank the u-boat.

Pargust did not sink due to her deliberate cargo of heavy timber. Campbell received a bar to his DSO; two other men received VCs by ballot.[91] Two men who came to the deck early on to man the u-boat's gun had been washed overboard in the heavy seas. They were the only survivors and gave limited information, but one, Leutnant Hans Bruhn, disclosed that Series II engine cylinders were being carefully checked since May because 'a submarine failed to return when all of her twelve cylinders had failed'.[92]

UC 26 left Ostend at the end of April 1917 to lay mines and 'this boat suffered from continuous defects'.[93] *UC 31* had also turned back in November with engine problems and again in December when two cylinders failed. Robert Grant noted that these engine problems, as well as the mining difficulties of five more minelayers, all occurred in submarines built by Vulcan at Hamburg, and all belonged to the First Flotilla, stationed at Heligoland.

Could sabotage have played a part?

Admiral Reinhard Scheer admitted that, in any event, after each cruise every u-boat needed docking because of the large amount of technical apparatus which needed careful overhauling and the damage due to the voyage or to enemy attacks had to be repaired. 'Generally speaking, after four weeks at sea a boat would need to be in the dockyard for the same length of time for repairs'.[94] Constant breakdowns also caused a great diminution of the total efficiency.

By the time of *UC 61*'s stranding in July 1917, a fully-equipped Series 1 boat had been captured, another dived, and a third raised by the Italians. Since then, the navy had 'lost' a captured Series II boat at sea, and interviewed twenty-four survivors from four other boats, a few of whom gave useful information. *UC 61*

---

91 Campbell received a second bar to his DSO for a famous later exploit in HMS *Dunraven*, yet another Q-ship, after an eight-hour duel against *UC 71*, which escaped undamaged. *Dunraven* was sunk (Gibson & Prendergast, *German Submarine War*), p. 197.
92 Grant, *U-Boat Hunters*, pp. 128-29. 'Believed to be *UC 30*' (ADM 137/3897), p. 60 (4).
93 Gibson & Prendergast, *German Submarine War*, p. 180.
94 Scheer, *High Sea Fleet*, pp. 316-17.

was therefore the great coup, the first Series II uc-boat to be captured and to be inspected fully by NID teams.[95]

Despite the damage to *UC 61*, and it may have been in everyone's interest to play it up, the boat was going to be inspected with a fine-tooth comb.

> *The divers who visited the then recently sunken u-boats did so for the sole purpose of intelligence gathering. Intelligence came mainly in the form of charts, codebooks, call signs, technical and personnel data. The intelligence war against u-boats was secret. Little except hearsay emerged until 1969-70 with the release of much of what is now known as ADM 116 and ADM 137 to the National Archives [in the UK]; within which is a rich source of data. The information vacuum which lasted for over half a century after WW1 was fertile ground for rumour and hearsay; some of the legacies of which have endured to the present.*[96]

In his preliminary inspection of the wreck of *UC 61* on 31 July, Commander Spencer felt that much of the information already held by the Admiralty on *UC 61* was 'largely correct'.[97] He cited the boat's armaments (although quoting four torpedoes rather than the correct five). There existed good outline drawings, two pamphlets with the main details and two books of plans were issued, and a third book with detailed descriptions was 'in the press'. He also notes that *UC 61* was built at the Weser Yard in Bremen which was a different yard from the boats from which previous information was gleaned and there might be points of minor difference.

In fact, the engineering officer, Johannes Giese, made a point of complaining during his interrogation that these uc-boats were built at several yards. As a part of his training for commissioning, he visited *UC 74* at Blohm & Voss's yard at Hamburg for a month from 26 November 1916 and then *UC 71* in the Vulcan Yard at Hamburg from Boxing Day for two weeks. Giese said that he had to make a fresh study of the details of the mechanism in each boat 'on account of the radical difference in their arrangement'. Spencer concluded his letter that accompanied his report to Bacon:

---

95   Ramsay, *Blinker Hall*, p. 233.
96   McCartney, *Tin Openers*, p. 19.
97   *TNA*, ADM 137/3898, pp. 128-37.

> *These minelaying boats are of course greatly inferior to the regular ocean-going type in both offensive and defensive qualities, but details of their fittings, etc, may prove worthy of study, as they are of such recent construction and there is no doubt that in general the fittings adopted will closely resemble those in the larger boats.*

One wonders how Spencer's dismissive views on the uc-boat's offensive capabilities were received. The uc-boats were primarily coastal minelayers only able to engage with their five torpedoes after all mines were laid. However, apart from all the damage, disruption and chewed up resources in management time, money and constant use of resources by all these mines – and this was considerable, and the benefit of computer hindsight some one hundred years later, sixty-four uc-boats conservatively sank 1,867 vessels and damaged a further 218, putting out of action some 3.4 million tons of shipping.[98] Twenty-six vessels were taken as prizes. Series II boats made 559 patrols and in them 981 men lost their lives, an average of over fifteen men per boat.

As a result of Spencer's report, a more thorough inspection for the NID was made by three officers led by Commander A Sommerville on 3 August.[99] By this time, the wreck had sunk bodily into the sand so that the lower portion was inaccessible 'even at dead low water'. The wreck listed heavily to starboard and the after end, mostly blown off in Gerth's explosion, was now severed by recent rough weather and was lying some distance from the main part and was almost full of water. All small fittings and electrical gear were burnt out. However, Sommerville noted the good standard of workmanship, the use of metal where steel could have been used, 'there appeared to be no effort to save metal', the number of safety appliances in the fittings, and the salvage equipment.

David Townsend, who examined the evidence of the shell hole in *UC 61*'s conning tower, was also asked to assess the main findings made by Sommerville and his team. Because of the difficulty in obtaining iron ore and the capacity of smelters during war time, steel would have been used for the pressure hulls. However, felt Townsend, savings could be made by using mild steel on unpressurised structures such as the casing. Mild steel is not as strong or as hard as steel.

He found the mention of safety appliances in the report interesting.

---

98   Figures derived from a spreadsheet constructed from information on u.boat.net, accessed 8/1/2017.
99   *TNA*, ADM 137/3898, pp. 117-27.

These could range from isolating valves, to lifejackets, or hatch securing latches. There may have been some type of escape breathing hoods, but this is unlikely as there were no escape hatches. The main safety appliance would have been a wired buoy that could be made to float by compressed air and released to indicate the submarine's position on the seabed. Later ones may have been fitted with a telephone so that surface ships could communicate with a stricken submarine.

Bacon asked immediately for one of the boat's two periscopes for inspection and Ronarc'h, back in his office in Dunkirk after taking control of the beach at Wissant, replied immediately offering to 'lend' one 'as soon as they have been dismounted'. In fact, he sent the periscope on the day of stranding.

Bacon also asked on 30 July for details of a mine, which was thought to be of a new type; for one of the torpedoes found floating in the sea; and for details of watertight ammunition holders.[100] In order to have ammunition readily available upon surfacing, a ready use locker of ammunition was fitted outside of the pressure hull, close to the 88mm cannon.

'It would be interesting to the Allies,' said Townsend, 'to know how many shells could be fired before more ammunition had to be brought up, or the boat had to dive out of a gun action.'

If the ammunition holders were kept dry, literally by bungs, what effect would dived pressure have on those bungs? Would they be hard to remove if the submarine had been deep, thereby preventing immediate firing of the gun? De Bon, marine commander at Calais, needed first to check with Ronarc'h whether he approved sharing information with the British Admiralty about the munitions box. Ronarc'h replied to the effect that de Bon should get on with it.[101] The gun mountings were taken off and sent to Paris, while the gun and its ammunition was sent to French national ammunition factory at Sevran-Livrey, for testing.[102]

On 15 August, the British commodore at Dunkirk reported to Bacon that Ronarc'h had sent him a bottle of engine oil taken from *UC 61* at the request of the Admiralty.[103] The French had been asked for five bottles, but 'only one

---

100 Periscope reference: TNA, ADM 137/2096. Mine reference: *DRASSM* report, No 2014-105, relating to submarine archaeology operation OA2533, 24/7/2014, courtesy of Alain Richard.
101 *SHD*, Vincennes, Box MV SS Gr 43, p. 29.
102 *SHD*, Vincennes, Box MV SS Gr 43, p. 2.
103 *TNA*, ADM 137/2096, 16/8/1917.

could be obtained as the oil tanks were practically burnt out'. The bottle was despatched on that day's duty destroyer. Oil for analysis was important as, by determining the type and level of impurities in fuel, assessments could be made of the origin and quality of available fuel. Also, the amount and size of tiny shards in the oil sump would indicate the quality of metal being used in engine production and might help in assessments of the effectiveness of the British blockade on iron ore, especially that imported from Sweden by the Germans. The intelligence describing engine failures on uc-boats added weight to this type of investigation.

It should be noted that Bacon, in Dover, through whom many of NID's requests in addition to Bacon's own were sent, and Ronarc'h were firm friends.

I look back on my cordial relations with Admiral Ronarc'h as one of the brightest spots in a somewhat uphill and arduous command. He possessed great experience and shrewdness, yet he was always ready to enter into the spirit of a new adventure ... He was ever ready to smooth a local irritation and help our vessels as fully as his own.[104]

Altogether twenty-nine aspects of *UC 61*'s construction and operations were investigated. Of these, in an impressive report, Sommerville noted sixteen features that were different to the general practice in use by the British, or were completely new. These would be of interest to NID to improve Allied combat effectiveness or to help improve British designs. He also made a good number of measurements, discussed details of construction work and listed another twelve lesser, but useful, features.

Here, half of Sommerville's main observations are provided for interest and, in some cases, combined with information from Spencer's report, with Townsend offering his comments.

The jumping wires were primarily used to lift nets or booms out of the way as the submarine found a way through harbour defences and net barrages, although in this case they doubled up as a wireless aerial. *UC 61* had double jumping wires which 'may relate to parallel wires for additional backup or that they were rigged fore and aft. As submarines developed, became quieter, and sonar became more sensitive, jumping wires were found to vibrate giving out detectable noise.' The jumping wires worked in tandem with a wire net

---

104   Bacon, *Dover Patrol*, p. 233.

cutter (the 'scissors'), shown in a pen picture, and taken off *UC 61* at Ronarc'h's orders These consisted of 'two flat bars about ten feet long and secured at an angle of thirty degrees to the superstructure with ten short knife edges clamped between them'.[105]

Gyro and magnetic compasses were fitted. The straightforward magnetic compass 'gives the last resort for navigation but needs variation, deviation and magnetic influences to be taken into account'. A gyro compass involves spinning discs that use the gyroscopic effect to keep it balanced and level to point to true north as opposed to magnetic north. As it is electrically driven, it is possible to have gyro repeaters in different positions for steering, navigation and attack solutions, something that cannot be done with a magnetic compass binnacle.

UC 61 had twin propellers driven on the surface by twin diesel engines. The steerage way is caused by the propeller flow over the rudder so, 'by placing a rudder behind each propeller maximum steerage can be obtained, and with smaller blades'. It would have also been possible to steer the boat by adjusting the speed of each propeller and even turning the submarine around by going ahead on one and astern on the other.

The inspecting officers and the Press were much interested in *UC 61*'s two hydrophones which were housed in a small recess in the starboard side of a well in the superstructure between the conning tower and the mine shafts. This equipment enabled those in the boat to detect sounds from attacking surface and underwater craft. Spencer drew a pen sketch of the apparatus. The hydrophones were about twelve inches apart, one facing to starboard, one to port, and were mounted on rubber, which was an advance to stop internal machinery noise interfering with the hydrophone results. Wires from each led to a common junction box and thence in an iron tube through the hull.

The much-copied journalist Marius Alix who first told the story of the stranding of *UC 61* was allowed an early tour of the u-boat:

> *And finally, in the forward part of the vessel and left untouched by the fire, a curious acoustic system was found that allows a crew, even during travelling underwater, to*

---

105   *TNA*, ADM 137/3898, p. 135.

hear all outside noise in a given perimeter. This is an invention from which, hopefully, we can profit.[106]

The inspectors also found another well with a lid near the bow and drew a pen picture of it. The well was home for a folding boat, useful as quickly ready for inter-ship transfers, taking moorings to buoys, getting ashore, or even a means of escape for some of the crew in an emergency.

'One of the top makers was the *Klepper* company that also produced canvas and wood kayaks that were still being used by the British Special Boat Service in the 1970s and 1980s.'[107]

The main ballast tanks were flooded by opening a vent at the top of the external tank, allowing seawater to flood in. When the boat needed to surface, the vents were closed and, in the case of *UC 61*, high pressure air at 2,350 pounds per square inch (psi) was passed through a reducer to a lower pressure air of 176 psi and then blown into the ballast tank, displacing the seawater.

When tied up alongside, a submarine needs mooring bollards (Samson posts) situated proud of the casing. But, when dived, 'these posts would make noise and disrupt the hydrodynamic efficiency'. By twisting the bollard, it can be dropped down into a housing so that it is flush with the casing deck.

Under tow, *UC 61* needed to be able to slip the rope quickly in an emergency. This would normally be done in other boats from the foredeck. However, 'small submarines have notoriously dangerous casings that are often awash when underway, and so being able to slip the tow rope from the safety of the fin is quite important'.

Word of the treasure trove available aboard *UC 61* spread slowly through the British Admiralty; u-boat historian Paul Kemp described the intelligence haul as 'immense', without offering more proof than the periscopes and the minefield charts.[108] Veteran u-boat archaeologist Innes McCartney claimed 'much of the wreck was undamaged in the scuttling and was taken away for examination'; although no detail or evidence is given.[109]

On 16 August, the Board of Invention and Research (BIR) said that 'it would be of material assistance in connection with the work now in hand' if copies

---

106   La Bibliothèque nationale de France, *Le Petit Journal*, 28/7/1917, p. 3.
107   klepper.com/en/company.html, accessed 4/1/2017.
108   Kemp, *U-Boats Destroyed*, p. 30.
109   McCartney, *Maritime Archaeology*, p. 322.

of both the crew interrogation and the report by 'English' officers could be made available.[110] The BIR committee was responsible from 1915 for soliciting expert scientific assistance to solve tactical and technical problems.[111] Chaired by Sir Jackie Fisher, former First Sea Lord, the BIR recruited scientists working in six science and technology divisions, which assessed and evaluated invention proposals from the public, with a view to applying them to naval technology and tactics.

Even after *UC 61* had been long filleted by the French navy and by the British Intelligence service, there was still more information that the wreck could provide.

A major and obvious problem had dogged the Allies since the beginning of the war: how to sink a u-boat; in particular, what weight of explosive was needed to penetrate a u-boat's skin and how close did it have to be when it exploded? The problem came to a head in January 1916 when the British began work on two new 'Type D' depth charges for use from fast and slow ships.[112] As well as being constrained by pre-set depth mechanisms, 'the effectiveness of these prototypes was also limited by the fact that they did very little material damage to submerged u-boats unless they exploded within a short distance of the target'. The depth charges were usually simply dropped from the stern of the attacking ship so the 'degree of accuracy needed was difficult to achieve'. After some successful work by June, the problem again became urgent when the weapon was extended to use by smaller craft.

Perhaps, *UC-61*'s hull could provide additional answers?

During August and September, only a few weeks after the stranding, a series of firing tests was organised to establish how much explosive was needed to penetrate *UC 61* when it was submerged at high tide.[113] It was a meticulous operation with details recorded of the size of the boat, its position and the depth of the pit into which it had sunk in the sand.

Preliminary tests in late August and early September used 75mm shells to fire from 1,000 to 4,000 metres. Two stationary bombs were tried close to the hull. Later, a new Belgian 70mm mortar, the Van Deuren, designed by General

---

110 *TNA*, ADM 137/1383, p. 156a.
111 Schneider, *Operations Research Applications*, p. 13. During its operation from 1915 to 1918, the board evaluated over 41,000 submissions.
112 Tarrant, *U-boat Offensive*, p. 27.
113 *SHD*, Vincennes, Box MV SS Gr 43, pp. 1-37.

Pierre van Deuren, was given a trial.[114] Photographs were taken after each firing and copies of these and of the tests have been found at the French naval archive at Chateau de Vincennes.

Everyone was well aware that ten mines remained trapped on board in twisted shafts, but it was hoped that they were not 'ultra sensitive to shocks' as they were deep in the water.

On 4 September, twenty mortar bombs were fired from 550 metres directly at the part of the submarine containing the mines. No explosion resulted. At low tide the next day, the hull was examined closely, but no damage could be found. At high water, nineteen bombs with seventeen kilos of high explosive were fired. The fifth bomb did not explode; the tenth bomb appeared to trigger another explosion which was possibly the fifth bomb. The fifteenth bomb produced a powerful blast.

Observers standing on the dunes thirty metres from sea level saw 'the line of the horizon cut the plume at least half of its height from its base'. Inspection next morning, 6 September, showed a total destruction of all of the forward part of *UC 61* up to the conning tower. All of the mines had exploded.

A commission which observed the tests authored a report in Calais, signed by their President, Biseuil, on their findings. On the final explosion, they wrote:

> *The characteristics were these: a vast and compact plume of water and sand with a zone forty metres diameter at the base, fifty metres high, which was maintained for [ten or more seconds] as though by a constant pressure at the base. That a spectator had the time to take away his photographic equipment is a case in point and he took a photograph at the moment when the plume was still at its maximum height.*

The commission estimated that an exploding shell of 75mm could be used effectively against a submarine on the surface or semi-submerged. The fragility of the projectile had raised concerns that it would break in contact with the thick steel of the hull of the submarine. However, although several traces of incomplete explosion had been noted, [one] firing showed that shells pierced without fracturing the thin steel of the superstructure and its cement ballast and that ... it was susceptible to perforate either with a delayed explosion or with an explosion on contact. In either case, the 'damage produced was major'

---

114 landships.activeboard.com/t38307173/the-van-deuren-mortar, accessed 4/1/2017.

and would cause the loss of the vessel or put it out of action for some time and 'prevent it diving through ingress of water with or without internal disruption'.

The conclusion from the tests was that a charge of six kilograms exploding in contact with the hull in five metres of water 'damages the hull causing a tear which would cause the loss of the vessel'.

The report was sent on 15 September to Ronarc'h who wrote tersely on the bottom: '*UC 61* can no longer serve as a useful experiment.'

15
PRISONERS OF WAR

> *France's actions were completely contrary to those of the other Allied countries. Their evil intentions became clear – they wanted to exploit the prisoners as long as possible. No single measure of the French government would create more hatred than the cruel treatment of German POWs in the reconstruction zones from December 1918 … As a consequence, a new protest movement arose in Germany accusing France of the 'murder of the souls of our prisoners'.*[1]

The immediate interrogators at Wissant thought that the crew of *UC 61* was relieved to have finished with the discomfort, stress and every day danger of life in a u-boat. In truth, the French interrogators found the crew a little disappointing. There was almost none of the 'East Prussian' arrogance that was shown the previous year by the crew of *UB 26 captured at Le Havre*.[2] 'No side or bravado was shown.' Only one junior member of *UC 61* was defiant and refused to answer questions.

Since the declaration of unrestricted submarine warfare in January, the rate of loss among the coastal submarines of the Flanders Flotilla had risen. The simpler and safer days of 1916 would never return and crews knew that their chances of survival were decreasing. With hindsight, these u-boat personnel now had less than a 50 per cent chance of staying alive until the end of hostilities.

---

1   Rose, *Krieg nach dem Kriege*, pp. 170-184.
2   *TNA*, ADM 137/3898.

'The men of the fleet reckoned that a submarine rarely survived its tenth trip.'³

Another piece of hindsight would have given the crew of *UC 61* further pause. Three of their number would be dead before release and the remainder would all be incarcerated for almost a thousand days, half of which time would be after the armistice.

As the twenty-six men waded ashore, there was no evident animosity. Curiosity, certainly, as the village population moved to the beach; perhaps some respect, tinged with a little fear. None of the guards, when they were eventually found, had to hold back an angry crowd of local people. The crew stood idly outside the town hall while they waited for the first decisions as to their future. The slight illegality of losing personal papers perhaps still rankled, but the crew were allowed to keep their tobacco and pieces of bread and sausage. After the early morning excitement, UC 61 was no longer their responsibility.

The announcement that they were to walk more than twenty kilometres to Calais in a rising summer sun may have caused surprise as they watched French military vehicles stream into Wissant. The cars, though, held senior French officers and the lorries contained men and equipment concerned only with making safe the still burning u-boat and the dozens of munitions lying inside and outside the craft. The crew with an average age of twenty-three were all fit submariners less than a day into a patrol.

Their Belgian mounted cavalry escort arrived importantly and prepared to herd the captives to their destination. One can imagine some choice exchanges with the lancers. Many of these men were survivors from the retreat from Belgium into France of 1914 and had seen no action since then.⁴ Some carried thoughts of families left behind in their occupied homeland and of friends dead in scattered horseback skirmishes; all these memories would have been leavened with a strong resentment based on the numerous horrific tales of German atrocities against supposed Belgian *franc tireurs*. However, pictures of the country walk to Calais through the villages of Hervelinghen and Saint-Inglevert suggest more of a stroll than of a tense affair with bayonets at the ready.⁵

---

3   Bouton, *Abdicates*, pp. 89-90.
4   *Royal Museum of the Armed Forces and of Military History*, Brussels, AU 9089/2, p. 108.
5   *Royal Museum of the Armed Forces and of Military History*, Brussels, Est I/2322, p. 5. *SHD*, Cherbourg, Box MV SS Gr 43, picture caption, p. 1.

The crew reached Calais in good order with some evidence of haughtiness, enjoyment even, as they marched along busy boulevards. Gerth's monocle caused comment. The lunchtime crowds, brought quickly by the news of the capture, were interspersed by a large number of gawping young female lacemakers.[6] This spectacle was in sharp contrast to Germany where from 1914 the streets would be cleared before the transport of military prisoners and, later, laws were passed to prevent any fraternisation.[7]

> *Whether in Germany or in France, the passage of prisoners in a town raised curiosity, and often hatred amongst the population, particularly if it was a question of a town near to the front.*[8]

Perhaps the first sight of the impressive walls of the Calais Citadel gave the crew some concern. This was unmistakably a medieval prison fortress: a cobbled entry through tower and portcullis, arrow slots in thick stone double walls, windows with iron grilles, and a teeming interior full of motor transports, weaponry and many hundreds of potentially hostile enemy soldiers. However, imprisonment and twenty-four hours of close examination may not have been so immediately distressing for a group of men used to the conditions inside a cramped submarine.[9]

But what next? How long before they were moved? Where to? Would they go as a group? When would they be separated from their officers? Would they be punished for their avowed wartime trade of starvation? Some foodstuffs were already difficult to find locally. Prices were rising. Everybody seemed to know someone who knew someone who had been killed by a u-boat. Would treatment of imprisoned submariners be different from that meted out to soldiers captured in land battles?

> *Why didn't you stay at home? Why did you go to sea when you know what threatens? Why do you or your governments force us to destroy your ships wherever we can find them? Do you think we are going to wait until our own women and children starve and let you keep your bread baskets full before we defend ourselves? You have started*

---

6   *Le Petit Journal*, 29/7/1917.
7   Becker, *Oubliés de la Grande Guerre*, p. 41.
8   Dufour, 'Prisonniers du guerre', p. 11.
9   Interview, Schindler, Seamen's Hospital, Brest, 13/3/1918 (*SHD*, Cherbourg, SSTe35).

it. *You are responsible for the consequences. If you would discontinue your inhuman way of carrying on the war then we would let your sailing ships and steamers pass unmolested when they do not carry contraband. You have wanted war to the knife. Good, we have accepted your challenge.*[10]

Direct expectations of the sailors came from news of their comrades who had already been captured. Prisoners of war were generally encouraged to send postcards and a fixed number of letters a month. Prisoners were allowed to write to whomever they pleased and that often included letters directly to friends and officers in their home units and also, in the case of commanders, to the families of dead crew. These letters were scrutinised and censored for militarily valuable information about tactics, units, equipment, commanders and morale as well as for news about broader concerns, particularly the three-year Allied blockade and its effects on industry and civilian life.

Captured u-boat men reported prison conditions in England that were more boring than bad. Food was said to be better and more plentiful than at home. However, the unknown for the crew of *UC 61* was the condition of prison camps in France for most u-boat men who survived the loss of their vessel were taken to Britain. This was because much of the responsibility for patrolling the merchant shipping lanes, certainly those leading to the English coasts, and also for dealing with German maritime sorties into the North Sea and the English Channel, was the province of the Royal Navy. When the Royal Navy fished enemy sailors out of the water, they took them home with them.

Many u-boat officers were placed at Donington Hall in Leicestershire, which Kapitänleutnant Freiherr Edgar von Spiegel von und zu Peckelsheim, commander of *U 93*, found was the 'best prison camp in England, and if there were any better they must have been de luxe places indeed. It was one of the most beautiful country seats in England, a great grey castle in a perfect setting on green lawns and oak trees. Sheep were grazing on the meadows and birds singing in the trees.'[11] Peckelsheim was left in the water when his boat went down on being hit by a Q-ship. He was greatly surprised when he heard later that the boat had survived and been brought over 2,000 miles back to

---

10   Spiegel, *202*, p. 64.
11   Peckelsheim, '*U 93*' in Thomas, *Raiders*, pp. 189-92.

Wilhelmshaven by Leutnant Wilhelm Ziegner, 'scarcely more than a boy', on his first cruise.

Engine-room Petty Office Walter Gach of *U 48* wrote home in December 1917:

> *You notice nothing of the war here. We were sent by rail to London and we shall shortly be leaving here for the camp. I have been here for eight days already, and we are very well off and could not wish for anything better. I am in a large room with five of my comrades and we do nothing else but eat and smoke and look out of the window. You see plenty of life here; there are no wooden soles or bicycles with wooden tyres here yet, and the butchers' shops have rows and rows of pigs hanging up. There is no prospect of starving England. I am glad the war is over for me.*[12]

Indirect expectation was a more concerning matter. Prisoners of war were used in various ways from early in the war as retaliatory bargaining chips: withholding access to food parcels or exercise, forcing punitive and dangerous labour or placing prisoners in the front line as human shields. Both sides publicised their retaliations widely in order to shame the enemy or to force a change in policy or behaviour by exciting public opinion.[13] This publicity would certainly have reached u-boat crews as newspapers from both sides were generally available to them.

For example, on 15 March 1915, Winston Churchill when First Lord of the Admiralty, described as 'pirates' thirty-nine men captured that month from two scuttled u-boats. *U 8* was trapped in nets, forced to surface and fired on by HMS *Ghurkha* and HMS *Maori*; *U 12* was rammed and shelled by a British destroyer off Fife Ness leaving twenty dead.[14] While the men awaited a threatened trial at the end of the war for their alleged piracy, Churchill had them segregated in isolation in naval detention barracks at Chatham rather than placed in prisoner-of-war camps.[15] The conditions at Chatham were later acknowledged by the u-boat men as far from Spartan.

---

12 *TNA*, ADM 186/38, p. 19, Gach to Fräulein Walpurin, Breslau, 2/12/1917.
13 Jones, 'Prisoners of War', in Winter, *First World War*, Vol. II, pp. 274-76.
14 uboat.net.
15 Jones, *Violence*, pp. 83-86.

However, compare Werner Fürbringer's view after being depth charged in *UB 110* in 1918 and before being sent north to a camp at Colsterdale near Manchester:

I was held for four weeks in the Detention Barracks, four gruelling weeks in solitary confinement, beset by agonising worries and a sense of grinding outrage.[16]

Churchill's emotional and badly thought through response to unrestricted submarine warfare sought a quick and dramatic headline. The Germans responded in kind with the same number of carefully chosen upper-class British officers, some wounded, placed in much tougher conditions in German camps. They endured weeks of solitary confinement, primitive sanitation, restricted exercise and semi-starvation. The outcry in the British Parliament was quick and intense.[17]

Churchill's decision, with which he was not immediately identified by the Government, was called a 'great mistake' and a 'piece of absolute folly'. Serious charges of 'special treatment', apart from segregation of u-boat men at Chatham, were denied. British parliamentarians were appalled, indignant and powerless at what they 'knew' as retaliations ordered personally by the Kaiser, 'the ever-present nightmare of the Slavonic force which besets the heart of the average German [and accounts] for the present frenzied lunacy of the German people. In these bestialities, they are playing the game of angry children; we will not follow them in that.'

Charges of piracy could not be sustained.

'On a purely practical point, a u-boat with a small crew crowded into a cramped space, could not possibly commit the essence of piracy, which surely was to board a prey, carry off its cargo and capture the vessel. U-boats had no hands to spare for prize crews and not much space for extra cargo or prisoners on board.'[18]

---

16   Fürbringer, *Legendary*, p. 129.
17   *Hansard*, House of Commons debates 1915: 27/4, Vol. 71, c544 cc572-5, cc623-92; 5/5, Vol. 71, c1087, cc1201-30.
18   Winton, *Convoy*, pp. 8-9.

Churchill was forced into a humiliating climb down which gave his many domestic enemies further and sufficient ammunition to remove him from office soon afterwards.[19]

From then on, Britain largely avoided carrying out any reprisal against prisoners of war. The Director of the Department of Prisoners of War at the War Office even viewed reprisals as un-British: 'Our national characteristics are opposed to the ill-treatment of a man who has no power to resist and this especially in the case of one who is not personally responsible for the acts complained of.'[20] U-boat personnel were still given 'differential treatment' in prisoner-of-war camps although nobody quite specified what this meant. King George made his own protest to the Prime Minister about Churchill's instruction. The king, George V, with a German wife and first cousin to the Kaiser, favoured 'generous and magnanimous consideration to our prisoners-of-war'.

Most captives had been taken on fluid battlefields which, on the western front, meant during the German advance and the French response of 1914. Trench warfare provided fewer and fewer opportunities for surrender. To obtain intelligence, patrols were despatched to drag individuals by force through the Allied lines.[21] From the beginning of 1915, French prison camps were, therefore, relatively stable in numbers except during the big offensives.

By chance, official figures for the number of German non-officer naval and military prisoners held in France were released the day before *UC 61*'s crew was captured: there were 44,016 of which 876 were in hospital, almost parity with those held in the United Kingdom.[22] It was not until the German Spring attack and subsequent collapse of 1918 that numbers rose dramatically. 'The British Army made more captures in 1918 than it did in the previous three years of the war combined.'[23]

However, taken over all fronts, 'the scale of captivity was staggering' and was almost the same as the 'risk of death'. In this, the Great War was different from previous conflicts. The huge number of eventual prisoners was a phenomenon

---

19   Willis, *Prologue to Nuremberg*, pp. 17-22. Hull, *Scrap of Paper*, pp. 297-98.
20   *TNA*, FO 369/1450, Major General Sir Herbert Belfield, 'Report on Directorate of Prisoners of War', 9/1920, pp. 57-58.
21   Dufour, 'Prisonniers du guerre', pp. 9-10.
22   *TNA*, FO 383/261, 25/7/1917.
23   Jones, 'Prisoners of War', pp. 267-79.

without precedent in history involving between six and a half and eight million men, about one in every ten soldiers of all the nations involved. Eventually, there were 530,000 German prisoners held on French soil.[24] The sheer numbers forced the introduction of mass, industrialised, militarised captivity. Defensive battlefield technological advances were adapted in the construction of prisoner-of-war camps to ensure prisoners could not escape – barbed or electrified wire, sentry towers with machine guns, floodlights and guard dogs. Sophisticated railways ensured that food supplies regularly reached camps.

'The way prisoners are treated is also a way of waging war.'[25]

French and German experience of managing prisoners came from the Franco-Prussian war of 1870 and initially they used the same camps, but these were soon found to be insufficient. There were too many prisoners to hold without causing epidemics and protests.

In the first period of WW1, there was much improvisation. The French constructed pre-fabricated 'Adrian' barracks from light wood panels with tar paper roofs which were difficult to heat in winter. There were nearly 500 detention sites, either in mainland France or in its colonies. The main urban centres and their suburbs or the ports united several detachments under the one authority. The communes of less importance, or those in rural areas, grouped together prisoners who were then taken daily to factories, work sites or agricultural work. Each work company was to contain 425 prisoners 'not to be employed within range of enemy activity'.[26]

The number of Germans employed in labour companies rapidly increased. By 26 January 1917, 22,915 German prisoners were working directly for the French war effort.[27] Combatants were required to operate their prison camps according to common law and military codes enhanced by external rules such as international conventions or rules adopted by the warring parties after agreements between them. Visitors to the camps, sent by neutral powers and humanitarian or charitable organisations, found that the methods employed did not always meet legislated standards.

The prisoner had become useful as a currency of exchange, as a hostage, and as an object of retaliation. Above all, the prisoner became a worker in

---

24   Dufour, 'Prisonniers du guerre', pp. 8-9. Kramer, 'Prisoners', pp. 76-77.
25   Delpal, 'Prisonniers de guerre', pp. 144-46.
26   Jones, *Violence*, p. 139.
27   *SHD*, Vincennes, 16 N 525, '*État des Prisonniers se trouvant dans la Zone des Armées le 26 Janvier 1917*'.

the service of the economy of the country where he was held prisoner.[28] The requirement for manpower everywhere was too great to let this pool of prisoner labour remain unused. Prisoners could no longer be fed for doing nothing so, as a minimum, they could 'replace farm workers and other workers gone to the front, the wounded, the dead or those themselves prisoner of the adversary'. This supply became indispensable.

> *In rural areas, German prisoners were a blessing for the farmers. Amongst them there were many who had worked the land in their own country and it was with a real sense of pleasure that in captivity they took up their former occupations with agricultural machinery under the watchful eyes of the territorial guards. Throughout the war this foreign work force which carried out agricultural work benefited from excellent living conditions.*[29]

The Red Cross calculated that at least two thirds of prisoners in France and Germany were sent to work detachments, sometimes far from the camp at which they were registered and to where their parcels were sent.[30] Conditions for prisoner-of-war labour companies attached to the French army were frequently poor often due to supply problems which dogged, particularly, the newly established camps.

> *However, cultural attitudes also played an important role; the indifference to these captives' welfare indicates a certain attitude that prisoners were expendable – revealing an ongoing process of brutalisation. Although never justified as an official reprisal, the treatment was also certainly perceived in terms of retaliation by the French personnel involved.*[31]

While conceding this criticism, many French historians insist that the situation of German prisoners could never be compared to that of the French in the German zone.[32] From the end of 1916, the treatment meted out to prisoners in Germany became 'more and more rigorous'. French and English doctors

---

28   Becker, *Oubliés de la Grande Guerre*, p. 111.
29   Dufour, 'Prisonniers du guerre', p. 17.
30   Canini, 'L'utilisation des prisonniers de guerre comme main-d'oeuvre'.
31   Jones, *Violence*, p. 148.
32   Becker, *Oubliés de la Grande Guerre*, pp. 116-122.

not only accused their German colleagues of not being on top of things, but also to have provoked epidemics by willingly mixing Russian prisoners carrying typhus with other soldiers.

'One sees here how war is carried out by all means. Each one being persuaded by the determination of the other to beat them. The *war of the lice* counts as much as that of the cannons.'[33]

Quickly, prisoners became dependent on the laws of the state which captured them. 'All appeal by prisoners for the regulations and laws of their own country would be useless; the prisoners being currently under just the laws of the captive government.'[34]

The Geneva Convention of 1906 allowed prisoners to be put to work, but excluded officers, civilians, churchmen, health workers, invalids, wounded and the incapable. Camp commanders spontaneously gave the prisoners tasks concerned with hygiene, cooking, laundry for the common good and to guard against idleness. Day-to-day life could change at any moment if the men were caught in a tornado of maltreatment inflicted upon them as retaliation.

'To the end of the war this menace hung over all camps and detachments ... The life of a prisoner went very slowly, sadly and exhaustingly.' Sexual frustration also afflicted prisoners 'although this was largely a taboo subject'.[35] There were also cultural fears that prisoners would lose their virility or return after the war with homosexual tendencies. Efforts were made in many camps to provide courses in reading, gardening, letter writing, sport, camp newspapers, theatre, music, choirs, hobby workshops, and learning a foreign language.

Minimum rules of laws of war agreed in various pre-war conventions, ratified by the British, French and German governments, had to be respected. There were regular bilateral agreements as the opposing governments struggled to find formulas to deal with the numbers. One of the new arrangements between the French and German governments, negotiated at Bern, Switzerland, came into force on the day of the capture of the crew of *UC 61*. The main points of The Hague Convention on Land Warfare of 1899, modified in 1907, quickly became outdated.[36]

---

33   Becker, *Oubliés de la Grande Guerre*, pp. 105-22.
34   Becker, *Oubliés de la Grande Guerre*, p. 91.
35   Jones, 'Prisoners of War', p. 286.
36   Kramer, *Prisoners*, pp. 76-77.

> *Prisoners were not to be seen as captives of individuals, but of the captor state; they were not to be treated as individuals, but as legal, disarmed enemies. Prisoners 'must be humanely treated' and allowed to keep all their private property with the exception of arms. They could be employed in work, so long as it was not related to war operations, nor should it be exhausting or humiliating. The captor nation was responsible for feeding and clothing the prisoners on the same peace footing as that of its own soldiers. Prisoners were not to be compelled by force to impart information about the military situation or their nation ... prisoners should be removed immediately after capture to camps at least thirty kilometres from the firing line.*

Some of these agreements were quickly put aside, for instance on the level of feeding. By 1915, the Allied blockade was beginning take insidious effect. To emphasise the immorality of depriving civilians of food, the Germans decided to feed prisoners of war at the same level as German civilians.[37] Generally, German troops almost throughout the war received better rations that the civilian population.

In response, the Allies fully utilised the right of prisoners to receive food parcels to ensure their men held prisoner by Germany were protected to some degree from their blockade's impact. Across western Europe, a complex and effective food parcel scheme developed. German prisoners held in France and Britain also received parcels sent from home.

'However, as the war progressed and the blockade's impact tightened, it became more difficult for families to send individual parcels; increasingly they received care packages bought directly from the International Red Cross.'

Many prisoners, especially officers, could also receive money sent by bank mandate to purchase food locally.

'Overall, prisoners of war were the subject of a mammoth charitable aid effort during the war which encompassed both domestic and international organisations such as the International Committee of the Red Cross at Geneva, the Vatican and the Young Men's Christian Association.' This process drove a 'rapid modernisation of wartime humanitarian aid delivery and charity lobbying techniques'. With feeding of prisoners no longer solely the responsibility of the captor state, prisoners' access to food became a 'lottery,

---

37   Jones, 'Prisoners of War', pp. 273-74.

based on how well served their location was by rail and by how much food either charities or their home state could provide'.

Throughout the war there few naval men amongst prisoners taken by the French: while men from the *Kaiserliche Marine* could be counted in tens, and fliers by the handful, it was the German army that was counted in hundreds of thousands.

This may have been a saving grace for the crew of *UC 61* because initial conditions for soldiers taken at the front by the French were usually not good. The rarity of u-boat men and the importance of their equipment and practices meant in-depth interrogations were far more likely than if they were foot soldiers. It also meant that there was no discernible special treatment or navy camps for sailors. Because their capture happened away from the trenches they were often taken to prisons either in metropolitan France or behind the front in the military zone.

Newly-taken prisoners in the military zone were 'kept in large collection centres where conditions were generally overcrowded with very rudimentary sanitation' before being sorted into different categories for divergent treatment – Alsace-Lorrainers, Poles, officers, and skilled and unskilled workers.[38] There were regular claims of random beatings by guards.

Prisoners were quarantined for fifteen days in these holding camps before moving to permanent wooden barracks with bunks or beds with sacks filled with straw and a blanket and no heating. Daily rations were meagre: ¼-¾ litres of coffee; up to two litres of noodles, rice or soup; 400-500 grams of white bread; sometimes with added beans, potatoes or lentils. This food had to suffice for a ten-hour day spent on heavy manual tasks such as forestry, road or railway building, quarrying or loading stores.

Even though many aspects of French prisoner of war labour companies are well documented, there is no complete cohesive plan of the entire French camp system or of its inhabitants.

Broadly, camps fell into two categories, those run by the Army behind the front line and known to the Germans as *Gefengenen-Kompagnie* (G-K) companies, and those in regions in metropolitan France run by the formal prisoner-of-war system. Some sources suggest that all the G-K companies were in the military zone and used for military labour. The Germans compiled and published an

---

38   Jones, *Violence*, pp. 241-43.

atlas in May 1918 of the eighteen metropolitan French regions and their many constituent camps.[39]

For instance, in Region XVIII there were seven depots. Georg Gerth was imprisoned in one of these, the Île d'Oléron which was centred on Fort La Galissonnière. The depot was responsible for three camps at Jotonnière, Saint-Pierre-d'Oléron and Saint-Georges Chéray, together containing 192 prisoners.

Other regions had dozens of depots, and some depots had dozens of camps. The atlas included the numbers of prisoners in each region and each camp was mapped. In the French military archives at the Chateau de Vincennes, there are boxes of haphazard records. Many days can be spent on off-chance searches. By 1 June 1918, France had captured 243,590 German prisoners.[40] Of these, 46,664 were working in prisoner of war labour camps for the French army.[41] The remainder had been assigned to work in the French interior or consisted of prisoners who were exempt from working because they were officers or wounded.[42]

Today, there is a burgeoning record of millions of individual prisoners being developed by the International Committee of the Red Cross (ICRC) in Geneva.[43] All of the crew of *UC 61* were entered quickly into the system after capture showing a necessarily efficient process.[44]

UC 61's officers were quickly separated from the men.[45] The two sea officers, Gerth and Karl Dancker, the second-in-command, and Johannes Giese, the engineering officer, were received at Montoire-sur-le-Loir by 5 August. The twenty-three crewmen were taken to G-K 84 holding company, probably in the Oise, this move being recorded on an ICRC fiche on 27 August. These fiches identify individual *UC 61* crew members so that there is no doubt about provenance. They also give full name, rank, date and place of birth, and name and address of next of kin which has proved useful in discovering more information about individuals and their families. Individual fiches in the

---

39   Bern, Deutsche Kriegsgefangenen-Fürsorge, *Atlas der Gefengenenlager in Frankreich in neun Karten*, 15/5/1918.
40   *SHD*, Vincennes, 16 N 525, '*État des Prisonniers se trouvant dans la Zone des Armées*', *1/6/1918*.
41   Jones, *Violence*, pp. 238-39.
42   *SHD*, Vincennes, 7 N 1993, '*Ministère de la Guerre, Sous-Secrétaire d'état la Justice Militaire, Note pour les Directions et Services*', 29/5/1918.
43   grandeguerre.icrc.org.
44   *ICRC*, P 24350, officers; P 24301-3, men.
45   Delpal, 'Prisonniers de guerre', pp. 148-152.

ICRC files, when found, often contain 'P' numbers, which provide online links to further documents, which mostly concern camp transfers and details of illnesses.

For German naval personnel, there is a short cut. Each combatant country was required to report to their adversary the whereabouts of captives held and also to report any movements between camps. German naval archives with limited numbers to track still hold some of the alerts received from the French.

The first German prisoner-of-war record found that includes the crew of *UC 61* is dated 15 May 1918 and lists u-boat crews held in France.[46] There is a second list, dated 10 July 1918, which shows that nine crew members had been moved, including Gerth to a more secure officer's camp following an escape attempt, while Max Eggers and Andreas Nagel joined Max Pucknus at port locations, and Paul Schindler was in hospital in Brest. These stories are covered later. The remaining five men, Otto Bock, Georg Gerigk, Adalbert Neumann, Willi Sänger and Michael Weidner, changed their work camps.

By far the most complete list is dated 31 March 1919, over four months after the end of the war.[47] It is typewritten and compiled by German naval staff from information sent to them by the French, and includes the date of entry of each man into the French prison system. This date is the same as the date of capture for those taken on the mainland or near the French coast; for men captured overseas the date indicates the time of landing in mainland France. Handwritten annotations have been made in pencil and pen as new information on individuals was received. The first date of registration on the list is 17 December 1914, the latest date is 27 May 1918. There are 471 captives named, officers and men, who are held in seventy-five named camps and eight separate numbered G-K companies with a small number of men whose work camp location was not known. This level of dispersal, especially for officers, suggests a policy of deliberate separation rather than chance allocation. The list may well be as far as possible complete because every expected vessel that provided prisoners can be found.

The great puzzle of the lists is to find the location of the G-K companies. A G-K company, each with an alphanumeric identifier, is almost always a collection of small camps in a locality. Even if the general location of a G-K

---

46 *MA-BA*, Freiburg, RM 86/18: RMA 10139, p. 128.
47 *MA-BA*, Freiburg, RM 20/504, pp. 73-88.

company is known, placing an individual prisoner in one of its constituent camps is all but impossible.

Many of the prisoners in the German list dated 31 March 1919 were from marine infantry and artillery regiments and were captured in the fluid fighting near the coast in December 1914 after the Battle of the Marne. The three principal ships' contingents were from the armed cruiser SMS *Kaiser Wilhelm der Grosse*, a converted passenger liner; the light cruiser SMS *Königsberg;* and SMS *Möwe*, a survey ship.

Kaiser Wilhelm der Grosse eluded the British blockade and, for a few weeks in August 1914, operated as a commerce raider. On the 26th, just three weeks after breaking out into the Atlantic, she was surprised by the British light cruiser HMS *Highflyer* while lying in Spanish Saharan waters off the Rio de Oro. *Kaiser Wilhelm der Grosse* sank from gunfire in shallow water with the surviving crew putting ashore in the boats.

The *Möwe* was scuttled at Dar-Es-Salaam, the administrative and commercial centre of German East Africa, later British Tanganyika and then independent Tanzania, under threat from British cruisers. The *Möwe* was intended to supply *Königsberg*, which met her fate from British monitors after hiding deep in the Rijufi River, about 200 miles south of Dar-Es-Salaam.

What is remarkable is that the crews of these three ships who were able to reach land were only and gradually captured over the next two years. The crews of the *Möwe* and the *Königsberg*, in particular, took their ships' guns and joined with the *Schutztruppe*, the colonial troops in the African territories of the German colonial empire in east Africa. They fought the Belgians and the British on Lake Tanganyika and also with Lieutenant Colonel Paul Emil von Lettow-Vorbeck, known to the Germans as the 'Lion of Africa', who commanded the one German force to invade British imperial territory.[48] Lettow-Vorbeck surrendered his much reduced and emaciated East African force only at the end of the war.

The three u-boats represented were crews from *UB 26*, entangled in nets and scuttled off Le Havre in the March of the previous year, twenty men; *UC 38*, depth charged by French destroyers in December 1917 in the Ionian Sea, eleven men; and *UC 61*, twenty-six men.

---

48 Hoyt: *Germans who never lost, Möwe*, p. 52, *Königsberg*, pp. 145-9; and *Guerrilla: Colonel von Lettow-Vorbeck*. Zimmer, 'Crew of the *Möwe*'.

Six naval flying officers from the seaplane station at Zeebrugge were held at different camps. One of the fliers, Joseph Kaspar, was held at the Montoire camp on the Loir River near Orléans with three other officers, Karl Dancker, *UC 61*'s second-in-command, Johannes Goldermann from the Flanders Flotilla torpedo boat *A 19*, and Hans Gayer of the Zeppelin *L 49*.[49]

Torpedo boat *A 19* was rammed and cut in two by the British destroyer HMS *Botha* on 21 March 1918.[50] It was part of a German force intercepted while bombarding Dunkerque as part of an investigation of defensive artillery to see whether the port could be captured.[51] One of a few survivors was named as Köller, held in the PoW company *Gefengenen-Kompagnie 84* at an unknown location alongside seven members of the *UC 61* crew, stokers Friedrich Becker, Christian Carstensen and Wilhelm Starke; radio operator Otto Bock; machinist Fritz Bödrich; seamen Willi Sänger and Johannes Giese, the naval engineer.

The presence of Giese, who gave evidence at a court of enquiry in 1920 into the loss of *UC 61*, suggests that there was, at least, an engineering officers' section at this camp. In the German navy at this time there was a 'decided effort to suppress and thwart the drive toward advancement of inferior social groups such as engineering officers and warrant officers'.[52] Naval engineers were looked down upon as technical personnel. In 1911, the inspector of the navy's education department suggested that engineers should be drawn from families of 'lower than middle-class background in the future' so that they would 'give up their social pretensions' and content themselves with the position 'they deserve'. Whether this subjugation by his own people extended to officer Giese's standing in his French prisoner-of-war camp is unclear.

The final large contingent of prisoners on this 1918 list of German marine prisoners in France was the crew of two Zeppelins, seen as naval craft, eleven men from *L 49* and fifteen from *L 50*. *L 49* provided one of the iconic pictures of WWI when it crashed nose down into woods at Bourbonne-les-Bains and became the first German airship to be captured intact. It was photographed the next day surrounded by French peasants by Albert Moreau.[53] Moreau was

---

49   The Loir River is a tributary of the River Sarthe.
50   Newbolt, *Naval Operations*, Vol. V, pp. 224-227.
51   Karau, *Naval Flank*, pp. 180-83.
52   Horn, *Mutiny*, pp. 7-8.
53   Keyzer, *Unseen Glass Plate Photographs*, pp. 176-77. Moreau joined the conflict at the Marne where he recorded the second Battle of Champagne in September 1915. He was noted for photographs of prisoners of war, trenches and corpses after which 'confusion' became his art-historical theme.

one of the French army photographers who attended the stranded *UC 61* on the beach at Wissant.[54] *L 49* and *L 50* were part of a group of eleven Zeppelins that bombed England on the night of 19 October 1917. On their return, they ran into headwinds and fog and eight accidentally crossed into central France. Four were lost, two destroyed by Allied gunfire, and two, *L 49* and *L 50*, were forced down by the French *Crockodile* squadron. 'Engineers took the *L 49* apart and developed a series of blueprints and reports to evaluate design improvements since 1914 ... The plans served as the basis for the development of airships after the war.'[55]

Eight of *UC 61's* crew of twenty-six are accounted for at Montoire and G-K 84. Georg Gerth, the commander, was at Boyardville officers' camp on the island of Oléron on the French Atlantic Coast; Max Pucknus, the petty officer on loan for a single patrol from the battleship SMS *Schleswig Holstein*, was at Rouen-Croisset, possibly after early internment at Dieppe; reserve navigator Hubert Lengs was at the hamlet of Serres-Carpentras near to Avignon in the far south; machinist Paul Barthold at G-K 13, a community of camps including Bellinglise, Coup-Gueule, St Leger-aux-Bois and Choisy Aux Bac in the Oise region; stoker Paul Schindler at G-K 25; and the remainder, bar two, at G-K 90: seamen Max Eggers, Paul Ihn, Kurt Koch and Adalbert Neumann; machinist mates Georg Gerigk, Peter Kleinsorg and Alfred Naumann; stokers Franz Goosman, Karl Raabe and Michael Weidner; and b'swain's mate Andreas Nagel.

The second b'swain's mate, Franz Zäbische, was at G-K SA5 in 1918 which was at Pont-Sainte-Maxence and, again, in the Oise region, seventy kilometres from the front. In 1919, Zäbische was in Paris at the 'Bureau de renseingnements', literally an information office, or more probably the intelligence section of the French Deuxième Bureau counter-espionage section, which makes for an unsolved puzzle. What could a twenty-two-year-old junior petty officer have known that was of particular interest and required special attention in the French capital in 1919?

There is just one oddity in Zäbische's war-time career offered up to his interrogators, his service on SMS *Vineta*. This posting may have confused

---

    Keyzer's book of first world War photographs contains a section on Moreau, pp. 171-192, which begins with a picture of *UC 61* 'washed up' on the beach at Wissant.
54   ECPAD, SPA 230M4573.
55   Syon, *Zeppelin!*, p. 85. *Illustrated London News*, 17/11/1917, Issue 4100, Vol. CLI, pp. 5-10.

or interested the French. In an effort to maintain security, a second SMS *Möwe*, a commerce raider that was causing great concern in the Atlantic, was temporarily renamed *Vineta*, after another auxiliary cruiser which had been withdrawn from front-line service. In this guise, *Möwe* set out on a series of short cruises during the summer of 1916 to attack Allied shipping off the coast of Norway. But then, this posting was equally claimed by one other *UC 61* seaman, Paul Ihn, who had no recorded special attention.

The final crew member was the one man not on the German prisoner list of 1919, seaman Willy Neumann. Neumann was twenty-three-years-old and had been with Gerth on *UB 12*, the only witness to all of Gerth's operational patrols. Neumann died less than three months into captivity on 17 October 1917.[56] The rapidity of the death of a supposedly fit young man so soon after capture offers just a hint of accident or brutality.

The two other crew members to die before release were Karl Raabe on 23 January 1920, of whom nothing further is known except that by the time of his death he had been moved to G-K 80B, and Paul Schindler on 26 July 1918 who has a most interesting story. The imprisonment of Max Pucknus and, later, Andreas Nagel at Rouen is part of an important wider tale of retaliation.

Finally, the attempted escape by Georg Gerth by u-boat from his island prison needs detailed investigation.

Most prisoners survived captivity in western Europe.[57] About 25,000 German prisoners died in France. Death rates for British and French prisoners in Germany were around 7 per cent, Germans held in France had a death rate of 6.4 per cent and Germans held in Britain had a death rate of 3 per cent.

'Most significantly, too, these death rates were almost entirely other rank prisoner deaths.'

In general, the main home front camps saw little disease except for the major typhus epidemic of 1915, which killed millions in Russia and Easter Europe particularly, and the 1918 influenza epidemic which was even-handed.[58] The death rate for the crew of *UC 61* was 11.5 per cent, but this is too small a sample from which to draw any conclusions.

---

56 Spindler, *Der Krieg zur See*, Band 4, p. 547.
57 Jones, 'Prisoners of War', pp. 283-86.
58 Arnold-Forster, *Blockade*, p. 29.

Paul Schindler was born in 1895 in Kleinzschocher near Leipzig in Saxony, an unmarried son of Gustav and Mary.[59] He joined the 1st Werf Division at Freiwilly in October 1915 for ten months training and then attended the School for Stokers in Kiel. After a spell at the u-boat base in Zeebrugge, he was ordered to Bremen to join his first u-boat, *UB 29*, and from there in December 1916 to *UC 61* for her commissioning. Schindler's timing was exemplary as on *UB 29*'s next patrol after he left, it was sunk by two depth charges from the destroyer HMS *Landrail*, south of Goodwin Sands, with all twenty-two hands lost.

Schindler died in Davos-Wiesen, Switzerland, a year to the day from his capture at Wissant. He was first taken on his own from Calais to G-K 25 which was headquartered at Roye, thirty-seven kilometres from the front line. Roye provided workers for two sugar beet refineries at Baurin and Wawignies, close to the Belgian border, at a claimed sixty and seventy kilometres from the front. Under the auspices of the agricultural authorities of the Somme, the company also provided workers for Tilloloy and Crépy-en-Valois where the furnaces were heavily bombed by the Germans early in 1918.[60]

Schindler was moved by 13 March 1918 to the Seamen's Hospital at Brest.[61] He had bronchitis, but there is good reason to suspect that it developed into tuberculosis.

While in Brest, Schindler underwent a searching interview which was a little unusual, first because he was in hospital presumably because of the condition that was to kill him within four months and, second, because this was a long time after his initial interview with the rest of the crew at Calais.[62]

The interview was conducted by Lieutenant de Vaisseau Cariou, commander of the French submarine *Sirène*, who used Engineer First Class Tasizza as his interpreter. Their handwritten report was discovered by chance in archives in Cherbourg. Cariou's command of the *Sirène* suggests this was an opportunistic encounter, more to do with his wish for personal knowledge rather than any official French naval request. *Sirène* was the first of four submersibles in its class, laid down in 1900 in Cherbourg and launched the following year. By 1918, these craft were antediluvian, indeed all were scrapped the following

---

59 Davos Archives, Death Register, 9/232/176.
60 *SHD*, Vincennes, 'Emplacements des Camps de Prisonniers de Guerre', 16N2466, 16/11/1917.
61 *ICRC*, P 34594.
62 Interview with Schindler, written by mistake as 'Schurdler' (*SHD*, Cherbourg, SSTe35).

year. They were torpedo boats with four tubes which could go under water to just thirty metres. However, diving took six to nine minutes and was achieved by flooding the space between the inner and outer hull.

One imagines that any commander of one of these vessels would have been keen to learn what a modern u-boat could achieve. It is interesting, though, that Cariou spent little time discussing *UC 61* with Schindler and moved quickly on to a detailed and lengthy investigation of the capabilities of *UB 29*, Schindler's first posting.

'Given that the prisoner had been on board the grounded submarine at Wissant and thinking that all possible information had thus been gathered on this vessel, we decided to concentrate this interrogation on *UB 29*.'

Schindler's condition worsened quickly. As a result, he was accepted for participation in a great humanitarian experiment which was universally described as 'one of the few good things to have come out of the war'.[63]

Article 2 of the Geneva Convention allowed the warring sides to send home prisoners incapable of taking up arms again because of their wounds. Repatriations could only happen through a neutral territory and needed the involvement of the president of the Swiss Confederation, Giuseppe Motta, and the papal nuncio, Eugenio Pacelli (a close contact after the war of Georg Gerth's brother, Erich).[64]

Only the idea of humanity has given to the vigilant neutrality the character of compassion and human tenderness and without these general human qualities neutrality would have remained unsubstantial and lifeless.[65]

The French-German exchanges, the first to be organized, began through Switzerland in March 1915 and those between Germany and Britain followed in December through the Netherlands. Under the auspices of the Swiss Red Cross, very sick soldiers, amputees, the blind, the deaf, those paralysed or gassed, and those wounded about the face, and with advanced syphilis, were considered as non-combatants and transferred to their home country. As the war continued, the grounds for repatriation were gradually widened from purely physical to recognising the 'good of families' and also that, after eighteen

---

63   Kramer, *Prisoners*, p. 86.
64   Becker, *Oubliés de la Grande Guerre*, pp. 201-8.
65   Motta, 13/9/1915, quoted in Kühnis, 'Deutsche Kriegsinternierte in Davos', p. 3.

months, 'captivity seemed to become almost impossible to put up with', which produced a category which became known as 'barbed wire psychosis'.

In the main camps, the prisoners suffered from a feeling of being crushed, overwhelmed, and at the same time they did not want to make a new life because of the monotony of their life with its limited horizons. Real life was elsewhere. Torn between a refusal to accept the camp, which was their personal defeat, their capture and the desire to live in the best possible way under their unfortunate circumstances, they often fell into what was called depression, which developed in some of them, certainly as the years passed, into a 'barbed wire psychosis', which transformed itself into a nervous illness.[66]

Negotiations concerning men with tuberculosis and other long-term diseases began in February 1915. These were men who could not be healed in less than a year. 'The authorities were under no illusion as to the possible duration of the war and needed to be assured that a tubercular patient, once cured, would not return to arms. 'Thus was born the original idea of internment in a neutral country like Switzerland, for those prisoners not sick enough to be repatriated, but too sick to be left in POW camps.'

Men were chosen from the POW camps by joint nationality medical commissions for internment in the Swiss mountain resorts of Leysin, Montana and Davos and also in Denmark, Netherlands, Sweden and Norway.[67] From 1916, Switzerland received the greatest number of French and German soldiers, about 30,000 a year. Prisoners were interned for the duration of the war, their own countries agreeing to return any who escaped.[68] In parallel, doctors and priests inspected the sanitary and spiritual requirements of the prisoners and sought ways of fighting epidemics, particularly typhus and tuberculosis.[69] In all, 219,000 prisoners were exchanged or interned in a neutral country during the course of the war.

More than 1,200 volunteer workers with the International Committee of the Red Cross dealt with all the requests for information on prisoners of war.[70]

---

66 Becker, *Oubliés de la Grande Guerre*, p. 97.
67 Dufour, 'Prisonniers du guerre', p. 21.
68 Lindsay, edited, '*Swiss Internment of Prisoners of War, Experiment in International Humane Legislation*', p. viii.
69 Delpal, 'Prisonniers de guerre', p. 154.
70 Dufour, 'Prisonniers du guerre', p. 20.

Each day the agency received 8-10,000 letters which they acknowledged and forwarded as quickly as possible. The archive of information grew to 400 metres long. Today, six million files have been restored and computerised.

Schindler followed a well-worn and successful path.[71] Initial tests were carried out at his prison camp where he put himself up for internment. All those selected were brought to Lyons where they were examined by a Commission of Control. Schindler passed and, together with other successful internees, went at 1525 by daily train from Lyons-Bretteaux under the guard of an officer, an NCO and seven soldiers to arrive at Geneva at 1930. Here, carriages were separated and sent to allotted destinations. For Schindler and other Germans this was Davos-Wiesen. The French were taken to Leysin-Montana.

The first group of one hundred German internees taken from French camps, all suffering from tuberculosis, arrived in Davos on 26 January 1916.[72] There was a temporary reduction of internees in April 1917 due to a new agreement that soldiers cured of tuberculosis could go home on condition that they should not be ordered to fight again. By July 1919, 2,500 German prisoners had been interned which translated to a German colony of about 1,400 at any one time.

The men were quartered in hotels, boarding houses and sanatoriums.[73] Special consideration was given to 'hotels in distress because of the war' and it was necessary to choose those that were little frequented by foreigners to avoid 'promiscuous association'. 'These establishments in no way resembled hospitals; sleeping accommodation for large numbers are rare; the rooms are bright and attractive and can, as a rule, receive two, three or at the most four occupants.' Proprietors were paid six francs for the officers and four francs for the soldiers with an increase for tuberculosis patients for whom extra food on a planned menu was necessary.

The Swiss arranged an impressive array of educational courses for the German prisoners. Those who were students before the war or for whom a change of career would be necessary because of disability were encouraged to travel to the university towns and were enrolled for free.[74] It is unlikely that Schindler was well enough for this option, but around 400 men enrolled

---

71 Lindsay, *'Humane Legislation'*, pp. 15-19. Yarnall, *Barbed Wire Disease*, Chapter 11, 'Exchanges, Internment and Agreements'.
72 Kühnis, 'Deutsche Kriegsinternierte in Davos', pp. 6-13.
73 Lindsay, *'Humane Legislation'*, pp. 20-24.
74 Lindsay, *'Humane Legislation'*, pp. 25-28.

for a vocational college, the *Deutsche Internierten-Fachschule*, which was managed by the local German-language school in their own building or in the Davos Dorf Casino or the community centre.[75] There were seven classes, including general education and foreign languages, commercial studies, craftsman apprenticeships, examination studies, academic subjects at higher levels, practical hand skills, and a library with drawing facilities.

Internees like Schindler who died at Davos were initially buried at the Waldfriedhof Davos Platz.[76] Early in 1917, plans were made to establish a separate cemetery near the Wolfgang pass. The German Sanatorium, *Deutsche Heilstätte*, made available a plot of woodland which was inaugurated on 27 October 1918. The remains of forty-six internees, including Paul Schindler, were transferred to the new *Soldatenfriedhof*. Initially the graves had wooden crosses which were later replaced by granite stone with individual names carved.

There is a small hall of honour where a commemorative plaque reads, 'Here rest in peace German warriors. In hospitable foreign parts far from home they also died for their fatherland.'[77]

The likely experiences of the three crewmen of *UC 61* who found themselves based at French port cities was decidedly tougher, especially at Rouen and Le Havre. Their captivity smacked much more of the German retaliation applied to Churchill's thirty-nine 'pirates' held at Chatham. Luckily for the *UC 61* crewmen Eggers, Nagel and Pucknus, their involvement came towards the end of the episode. Again, it was actions by the French and the British which sparked the crisis.

It seems only right that if the utilisation of prisoners can be made to prove beneficial, it should be the whole body of the people, ie, the state alone which should benefit by it. German labour belongs to the whole country; the whole country alone has the right to profit by it. Therefore, when prisoners are placed in ports where the dockers are paid six, eight or ten francs a day, the contractors should not be permitted to benefit by prison labour at one franc fifty a day.[78]

---

75   Kühnis, 'Deutsche Kriegsinternierte in Davos', pp. 15-19.
76   Kühnis, 'Deutsche Kriegsinternierte', p. 22.
77   The cemetery is open to the public and is located behind the *Hochgebirgsklinik Wolfgang*, the former German Sanatorium.
78   *TNA*, MUN 5/139, 'Memorandum on the Employment of German Prisoners in France', 26/9/1916.

In 1915 and 1916, the French decided, first, to put German officers on hospital ships as human shields as a response to u-boat attacks and, second, to send German prisoners-of-war to less sanitary camps in North Africa to ease overcrowding in France.

Then, the French and the British began extensive long-term employment of German prison labour near the front, including the French use of German prison labour to work under shell-fire on the Verdun battlefield. The British changed their practice of always carrying their battlefield prisoners across the channel. They diverted some 1,500 carefully-monitored German prisoners of war from the UK to work in Rouen and Le Havre from April 1916.[79] These German prisoners formed the first permanent British prisoner work units in France and were intended to load and unload French ships and to ease congestion in French ports. In exchange, the French gave the British army direct access to forests and quarries, to be worked with prisoner labour. This helped overcome a tonnage crisis in spring 1916 caused by German submarine warfare and the difficulties of bringing wood and stone from the UK to the British army in France.[80]

There are copious reports of the Rouen work parties in the British Foreign Office files.[81] The prisoners' principal complaints concern being forced to work, day after day, in all weathers. 'Ceaseless rain was falling. We were given no choice, but to work. We were told that if we did not obey the signal within ten minutes and go to work, every tenth man would be court-martialled and shot ... Here you must either work or die.' The order applied equally to men with no experience of manual labour during which they were expected, for example, to carry sacks of flour weighing 200 pounds. Camps were rudimentary. Men lived in sheds without floors, the ground consisting of loose cinders. The roofs were not watertight. The walls had no lining and were 'very draughty'. There were no tables or seats.

'What began in 1916 as a limited German reprisal clearly deteriorated in the winter of 1916-17 into something much more ruthless.' German reactions may have been measured, but they always raised the stakes.[82]

---

79   Jones, *Violence*, pp. 137-38, 140.
80   Ferguson, *Pity of War*, p. 371.
81   *TNA*, FO 383/185, 'Prisoners, Germany Files', 1916.
82   For a review of the legality of reprisals on prisoners of war, see Hull, *Scrap of Paper*, pp. 276-310.

> *Germany employed French prisoners from middle-class intellectual professions in marshland drainage work in a reprisal action in 1915. Yet it was the German army which carried out the most extreme reprisals of the Western Front belligerents. In 1916, it sent thousands of French and British prisoners to work on the eastern front, near the front line, in sub-zero temperatures in reprisal for the British decision to use German prison labourers [at French ports]. This 1916 action was followed by an additional German reprisal in 1917 when the German High Command ordered that all newly captured British and French other ranks, taken prisoner unwounded, were to be held near the front line and between 10,000 and 20,000 French prisoners from camps in Germany were to be sent to join them. They were to have 'no provision of protection from the weather; no hygienic care; only meagre food; long and exhausting work without any restrictions, including transport of munitions and fortification work under enemy fire'.*[83]

Allied soldiers were used as human shields in the front line. The French, particularly, could see their comrades labouring in front of them in the direct line of fire and, after some military indecision, this caused the deliberate loss of their own men. There was a great deal of resentment. As with the 'pirates', the Germans carefully publicised their retaliatory actions. This punishment was to be highly visible, carried out symbolically upon French prisoners whose real suffering would 'chastise the metaphorical body of the French nation for its misdeeds'. Outgoing post from French prisoners was forwarded with speed. 'In a very real way, therefore, the German spring reprisals of 1917 used violence as a spectacle and theatre.'[84] The French received a German ultimatum that, if France did not withdraw all German prisoner of war labourers to at least a distance of thirty kilometres behind the front, Germany would increase its retaliation.[85] The withdrawal of German prison labourers was to be carried out as swiftly as possible and completed by 5 May 1917.

> *The prisoner reprisals came at a very tense phase of the war for both Germany and France. Following the massive losses in the Somme and Verdun battles of 1916, the German military leadership decided to retreat to a stronger defensive position on the*

---

83 Jones, 'Prisoners of War', pp. 274-76. Jones, *Violence*, pp. 151-59.
84 Jones, *Violence*, pp. 151-59.
85 *The Times*, 22/1/1917, p. 9.

western front and to focus upon the outcome of the unrestricted submarine warfare campaign.

The French Commander-in-Chief, George Robert Nivelle, was adamant that the French should establish their own reprisal camps for German prisoners in retaliation. Nivelle also publicised the reprisals to his troops to deter French surrenders. 'The irony was that although ordinary soldiers endured hard labour under shellfire, this was seen as culturally acceptable. When demanded of prisoners, on poor rations, by the enemy, however, it was perceived as violently abhorrent.'

Even without a perceived need for retaliation, all sides introduced prisoner-of-war labour close to and at the front and it 'marked a deterioration in prisoner-of-war treatment'. Prisoners suffered 'physically and psychologically; they were often hit by shells from their own side and forced to work directly on their captor's war effort in breach of international law'. The International Red Cross at Geneva arranged prisoner exchanges, inspected camps and monitored prisoner treatment. However, such inspections were restricted to the home front: no neutral power or humanitarian agency was allowed access to prisoners of war working directly for armies at or near the front line. Eventually, the agreement that prisoners should be held at least thirty kilometres from the front was reinstated. From then, the French carefully recorded the distance of their camps from the trenches in their official documents. However, an order from the French 2nd Army command on disciplining prisoners stated:

> *Treatment ... must be conceived of in reprisal for the sufferings which our own have experienced in camps ... Any act of indulgence, any regard whatsoever for a Boche prisoner is a punishable act of weakness and will be the object of severe sanctions by the higher command. Any misdemeanour by a prisoner must be punished with the greatest severity and the punishment must be immediate and without mercy.*[86]

It is impossible to say how closely the crew of *UC 61* were caught up in the dockyard work. Max Pucknus, the supernumerary, was initially at Dieppe, but was later moved to Rouen-Croisset. Andreas Nagel was from Krautsand, near

---

86 *SHD*, Vincennes, 16 N 2468, D. 4, f. 140, Copie de la Note 2515, SP46, 15/9/1916, 'Ordre donné par Groupement ABC de la IIe Armée à titre de compte-rendu, aux armées le 22/10/1916'. Jones, *Violence*, p. 149.

the entrance of the Kiel Canal onto the River Elbe. His first postings were on the sister pre-dreadnought battleships ships *Kaiser Wilhelm II* and *Kaiser Friedrich III* before he volunteered for the u-boat service. Nagel served in both *U 11* and *UC 17* before *UC 61*. Nagel was originally in camp G-K 90, transferred to G-K 80B and, finally, to Rouen-Lev. Some prisoners were highly critical of conditions in Rouen including being spat on by French civilians in the street.[87] Seaman Max Eggers from Grömitz, near the city of Lübeck on the Baltic coast, went from G-K 90 to Le Havre Abattoirs. His patrol aboard *UC 61* was his first and last voyage.

It was only in the autumn 1917 that those British reprisal prisoners working on the Russian front were finally sent back to camps in Germany when Britain ceased using German prisoner labour units in French ports. However, the British continued to expand its use of German prisoner labour companies across France.[88] This latter was likely the fate of most of the crew of *UC 61*. Twenty of them at some time lived in a numbered, unplaced work company, whose actual location possibly languishes is some administrative record in the Chateau de Vincennes.

---

87   Jones, *Violence*, p. 138.
88   Jones, *Violence*, p. 143.

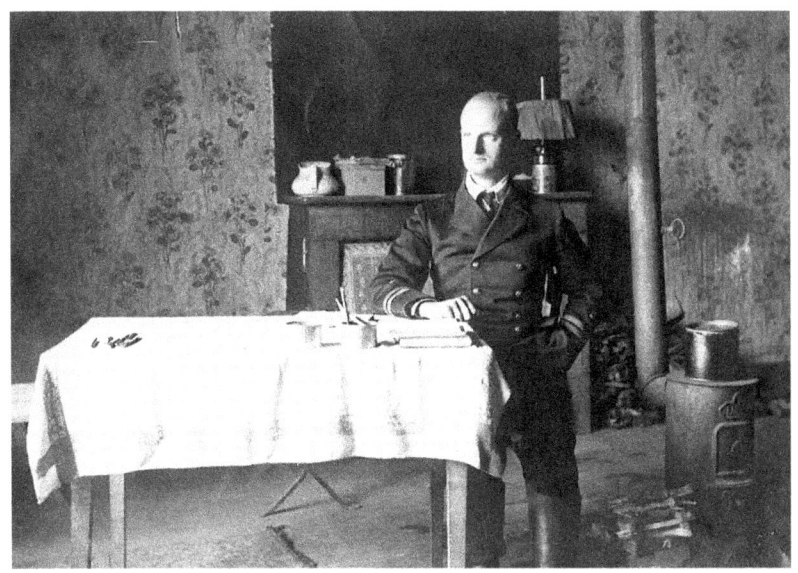

Georg in his officer's cell in the fortress prison at Carcassonne, probably 1918. *Family archive*

Käthe Kollwitz's famous etching of 1924 shows German children with their food begging bowls as a result of the British hunger blockade. The Kaiser refused Kollwitz a artist's gold medal because 'medals were for men'.

The live torpedo found in the blown-up wreck of UC 61 on the beach at Wissant in 1928. *SHD, Cherbourg (MV SS Gr 43)*

Georg's wife Maria and her three daughters; Christa-Maria is the youngest. *Family archive*

The Beobachtungsuhr, an observation watch, Georg's sole remaining possession from his time in the Kaiserliche Marine. *Frédéric Gerth*

During the night of 16 March 1945, RAF Bomber Command dropped 256 heavy bombs and aerial mines on Würzburg followed by 300,000 incendiaries. The fire storm reached 2,000 degrees Centigrade and produced a proportionately higher rate of death and destruction than during the attack on Dresden the month before.

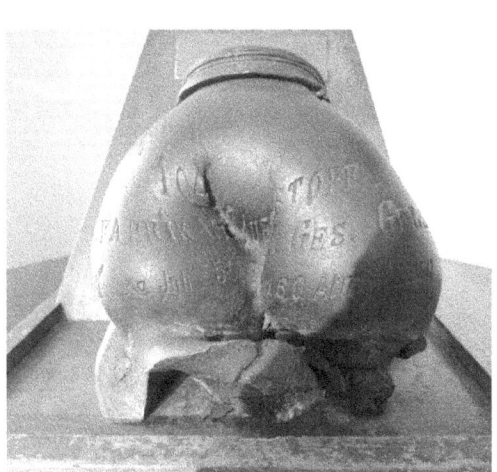

The mysterious 'compressor head', thrown out of UC 61 in an explosion, and presented to the 4th Belgian Lancers in 1958. *Jacqui Squire*

Georg in later years; he died in 1970.
Family archive

The gravestone of Georg and his wider family in Würzburg. Georg and his wife, Maria, are recorded bottom right. *Author*

The remains of UC 61 at low tide on Wissant beach in 2016. *Alain Richard*

After ringing the bell, the author waits for entry to the atmospheric 'UC-61' bar in Rue de l'Arc de Triomphe, Paris. *Jacqui Squire*

16
GERTH'S CALL FOR HELP

The threat to life of the enlisted men, whether through retaliation, brutish behaviour or hunger, was a long way from the world of the captured officer that Georg Gerth lived through.

Central to how captivity was structured in 1914 to 1918 was the dominant belief that captured officers should receive a better standard of treatment than other-rank prisoners. This overwhelmingly led to captured officers being held in separate officer prisoner-of-war camps where they were allocated other-rank prisoners from their own country as orderlies. Conditions were far better than in the men's camps.

Officer prisoners were exempt from working.[1] 'In those days of rigid class hierarchies, enemy officers were generally, if not always, treated with dignity and given pay according to their rank, provided with comfortable, heated lodgings inside separate areas of camps, sometimes even in hotels, and provided with a manservant.'[2]

Nonetheless, it was claimed, officer prisoners suffered particularly from apathy, depression and a sense of shame at spending the war in captivity.[3]

The island of Oléron owed its initial importance to its position relative to the island of Aix which guarded the approach to the great port and arsenal of Rochefort. Cannon on Oléron could reach only half way to Aix. Engineers

---

1 Jones, 'Prisoners of War', pp. 283-86.
2 Kramer, *Prisoners*, pp. 77-78.
3 Jones, 'Prisoners of War', p. 286.

handed Napoleon a report advocating the construction of a 'stone ship' built on a sand and rock reef and capable of mounting guns able to bridge the gap. Construction work began in 1804 and used the small village of Boyardville for storage of men and material and port access to the site. The project was dogged by heavy storms, poorly-positioned rocks and British attacks.

A second attempt in 1809 failed and it took another thirty years, after repeated tensions between the French and British, for work to restart. Fort Boyard finally appeared in the late 1850s by which time artillery range had increased and the fort's forty-seven cannon were redundant. Fort Boyard eventually became a prison and by the turn-of-the-twentieth century fell into disrepair. The French Navy chose the small, but bustling, Boyardville for underwater defence and, later, a torpedo training school, and built a naval academy there in 1876.[4] It is interesting that Gerth should be imprisoned next to a functioning torpedo school, his military speciality.

The various Napoleonic buildings, barracks for the hundreds of Napoleonic construction labourers, large fortifications and Fort Saumonard (formerly Fort Galissonnière and Fort Napoleon), provided ideal prison camps.

At the time of Gerth's arrival at Boyardville, Oléron had a small importance for its tourism, fishing, salt extracted from the marshes, good brandy, and for pine resin taken in the Saumonard Forrest and distilled on the mainland to provide turpentine and rosin.[5] In the way of rubber farmers, the *resiniers* placed a terracotta pot under cuts in pine trees.

In 1990, *Fort Boyard* became famous as the site of an eponymous and popular French TV game show. *Crystal Maze* was created as an alternative format for the UK market.

The 'other ranks' were held in the old barracks at Boyardville alongside the torpedo school. Sixty-one officers were settled in a 'very good' prison camp on a 'charming and healthy site', either in town or in bungalows on the sea front near the port, and were served by thirteen batmen.[6] 'These *Messieurs* install themselves for games, taking in an ideal view and sunbathing whilst studying or reading books which are sent to them from Germany.' Small gardens for

---

4   Admiral Amédée Courbet commanded the *École des Défenses Sous-Marines* (School of Underwater Defences) at Boyardville from 1874 to 1877. Ledieu, *L'Amiral Courbet, 1889*; Michon, *Guide Répertoire des Écoles de France*, 1896; Trève, *Quelques Pages de le Vie d'un Marin*, 1887, pp. 42, 59, 71.
5   Berbudeau, *L'Espion de Boyardville, Une Plage Inconnue*, 1893.
6   Dufour, 'Prisonniers du guerre', p. 15.

flowers and vegetables were maintained 'with care' by the orderlies and by the officers. Recreational activities included reading, walks where the officers wanted within a limit of four square kilometres, music (pianos, violins and guitars) and chess.

Boyardville was inspected during a Red Cross tour in 1915. Lieutenant-Colonel Dr C Marvel noted that relations between the French guards and the interned were 'particularly good on the Isle of Aix and at Boyardville'.[7] The two daily meals were taken in two restaurants; the pension was sixty to seventy-five francs per month. A typical menu included coffee and bread for breakfast, a salad of haricot beans and potatoes at lunch and macaroni for supper. 'Several of them buy what they need and make meals themselves.'

After Georg Gerth's capture at Wissant, interrogation at Calais and move to Montoire, he was sent ten days later, 15 August 1917, to Boyardville.[8] For Gerth, this meant a move well away from the trenches, but ironically one which took him much closer to his own front line, which he had patrolled in *UC 61* a few weeks before.

> *We in the officers' mess raised our glasses and drank toasts to one another and to the beautiful u-boat: 'Rich spoils! A happy journey home! Long live the u-boat!' That is the u-boat toast.*[9]

In 1949, Albert Chatelle, interrupted by the second world war, continued his lucrative employment of writing war histories of the French coastal towns. It was the turn of Le Havre and Chatelle remembered his books on Calais and Boulogne of twenty years before when he wrote of the wreck of *UC 61* at Wissant.[10] He turned the last patrol of Gerth's u-boat into a Le Havre story, 'Un mouillage de mines et une évasion manquée'.[11] The city was a main port of entry for British soldiers into France; an estimated 1.9 million Tommies passed through. The port was heavily protected with warships, but the u-boats waited outside and several ships were torpedoed in the roadstead. The suburb

---

7   Comité International de la Croix-Rouge, Marval and Eugster, 'Rapports sur leurs visites aux camps de prisonniers en France et en Allemagne', 5/1915, p. 19, grandguerre.icrc/fr/Camps/Quiberon/304/fr, accessed 1/2017.
8   ICRC, P 27882.
9   Spiegel, *202, p. 34.*
10 Chatelle, *Base Navale du Havre*, pp. 235-36.
11 Mine laying and a lucky escape.

of Sainte-Adresse on the cliffs with fine views overlooking the port and the Seine estuary was the seat of the Belgian government-in-exile from October 1914 until the end of the war.[12]

> *In the second fortnight of July 1917, Le Havre harbour narrowly escaped a major mine laying. UC 61 sailed from Zeebrugge on 25 July about 1300 in the afternoon, for her fifth cruise. Her orders were to lay mines in front of Boulogne and Le Havre and then to cruise along the Atlantic coast. UC 61 never arrived at Le Havre. In the night following her departure, she ran aground at low tide on the beach of Wissant, not far from Cap Gris Nez.*

Chatelle was mostly right, except that the *UC 61*'s mines on this patrol were destined for near the *Royal Sovereign* lightship off Eastbourne, and at Newhaven and Brighton on the English south coast.[13] There was no 'Le Havre' story. Chatelle was also still trying to turn *UC 61*'s stranding into spy speculation:

> *We don't really know whether the grounding was purely accidental or if the submarine had to come dangerously close to shore to land an officer who was in excess of the normal complement and on whom was found currency notes issued during the war by the Chambers of Commerce of Boulogne and Calais.*

This was even less right as the supernumerary was Max Pucknus and the one-franc banknotes were found on Hubert Lengs, the navigator / steersman, someone whose skills would be lost to the boat if he was put ashore as a spy.

However, Chatelle's story then changed into a discussion of an escape attempt by Gerth from Boyardville. This story appears nowhere else and it was only after much searching that records of the extraordinary event were found in French naval archives on long-term loan from the Chateau de Vincennes to the depository at Cherbourg.[14] The following chronicle is constructed from the Cherbourg documents, which were written by French intelligence officers, and using background material as appropriate.

---

12   Sainte-Adresse is a sought-after location today, especially as a grateful Belgian king granted a large sum to defray the local taxes of residents.
13   *MA-BA*, RM 120-95, Flotilla Order No. 264, 24/7/1917.
14   *SHD*, Cherbourg, SSTe35, pp. 79-100.

The French claimed that Gerth's camp at Boyardville contained many u-boat officers although that seems more than doubtful as they held very few throughout the war; the French captures involved *UB 26*, *UC 38* and *UC 61* and, of the latter, only Gerth was held there.

Almost immediately, Gerth 'hatched a plot' to escape from Boyardville by u-boat. From 1917, following agreement between the French and German governments, a postal service using special postcards was organised with deliveries once every two months.[15] Officer prisoners were allowed to send two letters and four official postcards each month. Gerth wrote on 1 September to Leutnant Suadicani at Flanders Flotilla headquarters at Bruges and included a message written in secret ink. This request was made within two weeks of arrival so one can assume Gerth and other u-boat officers had received escape training.

In the [French] postal report for July 1918, the censor noted that a proportion of prisoners expressed their dissatisfaction with captivity and their despair at being out of the German offensive. Yet, prisoners, the censor noted, were not depressed. Many were still 'filled with an unquenchable faith in the right arm of Hindenburg (Ludendorff) and are still religiously respectful of the Kaiser', awaiting some action by them which would bring about the final victory.[16]

The recipient of the secret message was Leutnant Günther Suadicani, commander of *UB 17* for just nine days in 1916. As this was Suadicani's only command and he sank no ships, one can assume that for some reason his suitability to command was questioned.

Clearly not disgraced, Suadicani joined Korvettenkapitän Karl Bartenbach as his senior staff officer.[17] In this position, he was the appropriate man for Gerth to write to and who would take the escape plan to Bartenbach for a decision.

Also within the two weeks since his arrival, Gerth had signed up a co-plotter, described by the French as German officer, 'le Ct. Schwerdteger'. The surname is probably a misspelling of 'Schwerdtfeger', of which the Red Cross archives

---

15   Becker, *Oubliés de la Grande Guerre*, p. 37.
16   Jones, *Violence*, p. 245.
17   Suadicani stayed in the German Navy: Kapitänleutnant 28/4/1918, Korvettenkapitän 1/4/1927. He died 11/6/1953 (uboat.net).

have more than one hundred. As all the ranks given in the French documents were French, the 'Ct.' could stand for a capitaine in the French Navy (German, kapitän) or a commandant (German, major) in the French army. None of the three Schwerdtfegers in the German naval officer list was taken prisoner.[18] In any event, no more is heard of Schwerdtfeger.

Gerth's letter was read by French intelligence as were all messages from prisoners. The secret ink was discovered, the letter let go, and the following exchange of letters monitored.

Gerth said that he would be able to escape on a u-boat if he stood within several hundred metres of the Chassiron lighthouse. He asked for the u-boat to be there for five consecutive nights as 'only one night seemed to him to be very risky'. If the weather prevented boarding, he would signal by long flashes of a lamp. Gerth had a weak pocket torch. Gerth also asked Suadicani to indicate any better alternative pick-up point precisely.

One Suadicani response was dated 5 January 1918, intercepted by the French on the 10th and delivered to Gerth about the 14th. Time was already slipping away because of the delay caused by the French.

Dear Gerth

During the nights of 12–18 January, a submarine will cruise abeam of the Chassiron lighthouse and will wait for you to come out about 100 metres south of the lighthouse at low tide. You will have to climb as high as you can on the rocks and signal with your pocket torch. Possibly you will give your surname as a sign of recognition. The berthon will be launched and come and fetch you. On 13 January, low tide is around midnight. The mission will only be possible if there is very calm weather; for a rescue to be made it would be at around five miles from the coast. In bad weather, this plan could not be attempted.

In case the plan cannot be executed during this fixed period, a new attempt will take place during the period of the following new moon. A better place for an escape then could perhaps be the west buoy situated to the west of Fort Boyard near the

---

18   Ehrenrangliste, 1914-1918, lists three German naval officers with a last name of Schwertfeger. They are Hans Schwertfeger, born 1880, Crew 1898, korvettenkapitän 1915; Paul Schwertfeger, born 1892, Crew 1900, kapitänleutnant 1910; and a possible twin, Hermann Schwertfeger, born 1892, Crew 1901, kapitänleutnant 1912. None was a prisoner of war. Paul Schwertfeger underwent u-boat training in 1918, including time as the commander of the training boats *U 21* and *U 22*.

Saumonards Point? But for that it would need you to indicate to us as to whether we should count on this place, if it's surveyed and whether, to the right of this place, there are surveillance ships and warships moored. In addition, Rudi is currently on his way to this location to get information for a repeat trip in February. Further news follows.

A Berthon was a small collapsible boat carried on u-boats, designed and built from 1877 by the Reverend Edward Lyon Berthon of Romsey in southern England, as collapsible lifeboats. Berthon was prompted in his work by a fellow cleric who survived the sinking of the passenger ship SS *Orion* in 1850. One assumes that the Germans had developed their own version. The boats had double linings of canvas, sectioned in two watertight envelopes; the deck could also double as a life raft.[19]

The plan was for Captain Prulières of the French Army secret police to carry out 'special surveillance' and either take the place of the escapees or let the men make their signals and seize them and the crew of the Berthon at the last moment. Gerth was apprehended by Prulières after he signalled with his torch from the rocks. The exact night is not given, but it would have been the 14th or one of the following four days. No Berthon or u-boat was seen. Within the month, Gerth was moved from Boyardville to the inland fortress prison at Carcassonne.[20]

The French list in detail their 'reception committee' which included a submarine and numbers of torpedo boats and patrol boats. The sea patrols were to be fitted with Walser apparatus, a type of hydrophone for picking up underwater noises.

'Through the good offices of the Gascony Patrol division, I would kindly ask you to take every measure to watch these places with discretion during the period indicated with the view of surprising if possible the submarine which is going to attempt this operation.'

Did any u-boats attempt to rescue Gerth and, if so, were they sunk on the way there or did they make it to Boyardville, reject the mission, and were they sunk on the way home?

---

19 wikipedia. The Berthon Boat Company still operates in 2017 on the same site in Lymington, where the business moved in 1918, with a skilled workforce of one hundred specialising in the refit and repair of small yachts.
20 *ICRC*, P 33851, 16/2/1918.

No mention has been found of a rescue operation in the *Kriegstagebuch* of possible u-boats, but this is not unusual. Special operations were often not mentioned or mentioned only cryptically. The coded note from Suadicani suggests two visits, one to attempt the pick-up and a second, which is 'in addition', to scout information for a repeat trip the next month if this should be necessary. 'Rudi' was currently on his way for this back-up mission.

For Rudi to be identified with his short-form first name suggests he was known to Gerth. The only possible 'Rudi' was Rudolph Seuffer, commander of *UC 50*, which sailed from Zeebrugge on 7 January 1918 and was ordered to lay mines near the Loire and the Gironde and was in the Bay of Biscay at the right time conducting trade warfare. Seuffer would probably have met Gerth as they both received command of their uc-boats in the Flanders Flotilla in December 1916. Also, Seuffer was in the same sea cadet year, Crew 1905, as Georg Gerth's elder brother Erich and the two were the best of friends as evidence of a photograph and its caption shows.[21]

However, Seuffer's *UC 50* was 'originally assigned to the High Sea Fleet's I Flotilla and wasn't reassigned to Flanders until July 1917, just a couple of weeks before Gerth took *UC 61* out on her final patrol'.[22]

UC 50 did not return to Zeebrugge. U-boat historian Robert Grant declared that it was 'highly probable' that *UC 50* blew up the day after sailing when the drifter *Brothers Jem* on watch in the Straights of Dover felt a heavy explosion and 'soon found a large quantity of oil and dead fish'.[23] The drifter was unable to investigate further because of bad weather. Messimer's *Verschollen* says that *UC 50* was rammed and depth charged off Dungeness on 4 February 1918 by HMS *Zubian* while homeward bound on the surface with the loss of all twenty-nine hands, but this is successful refuted by u-boat experts.[24] Michael Lowrey of uboat.net explains:

---

21   Photograph of Erich Gerth and his 'best friend' Rudi Seuffer, both in uniform in a 'relaxed' pose with alcoholic drink in, possibly, an officers' mess in 1917. Photograph captioned later by Eva, Erich's wife (Family collection, shared 2018).
22   Lowrey, correspondence 11/8/2016 and following (uboat.net, WW1 forum).
23   Grant, *U-Boat Intelligence*, p. 79.
24   HMS *Zubian* was a composite destroyer made of the front end of HMS *Zulu* and the rear and mid sections of HMS *Nubian*. 'For now, the HMS *Zubian* sinking claim for *UC 50* is the standard, post-war British claim. The maximum patrol length for a Flanders UCII patrol through Dover however was only twenty days, which is a major red flag. Luckily, we don't need to rely upon that to reject the *Zubian* sinking claim, as Zubian's attack was clearly against the homebound *UC 79* there is a clear match in *UC 79*'s *KTB*' (Lowrey, uboat.net). Also, Grant, *U-Boat Intelligence*, p. 81.

What actually happened to UC 50 is very unclear. It is one of the two most missing of the Flanders-based submarines that did not return from patrol. By most missing, I mean that at this point, all we can say is that it sailed and did not return. In most other cases of missing Flanders-based U-boats we at least have some contact after they sailed (typically a ship sinking). Unfortunately, we aren't going to be able to use ship sinkings to determine whether UC 50 got to her assigned patrol area in the Bay of Biscay. UC 50's patrol area overlapped with that of the larger U 84 and U 93, neither of which returned from patrol. While some attacks on shipping were clearly conducted by U 84 or U 93 (and in one case clearly by U 93), there aren't any cases that are clearly attributable to UC 50 as there are no survivor statements describing a UCII. However, that may not mean much as several ships were torpedoed without the u-boat being observed.

The likelihood is that Rudi never made it to check out potential pick up points around Boyardville. The loss of *UC 50* cannot be attributed to Gerth's escape attempt as the u-boat would have been sailing anyway, but it was the fifth u-boat to have an association with the demise of *UC 61*, alongside *UC 44* off Waterford and the three uc-boats sunk when new mines were laid on Gerth's u-boat route south of Zeebrugge the previous year.

Was there a second u-boat intended to collect Gerth and Schwerdtfeger from Boyardville? Or was *UC 50* attempting both missions? If there was a second u-boat, it was not from Flanders Flotilla as they are all accounted for, either in port or not in the Bay of Biscay. The previous boat in the area was *UC 17*, which arrived back in Flanders on 15 January. The next boat operating in the Bay of Biscay is probably *UB 59*, which only sailed on 20 January. There are only two candidates, already mentioned as in the vicinity, *U 84* and *U 93*, both of which were lost at around the right time to unknown causes.[25]

The problem with the involvement of either of these is that they were High Seas Fleet boats. Suadicani would have to arrange any escape attempt from Bruges with officers based in Germany. Lowrey feels that 'this seems a bit unlikely'. The fractured nature of the various u-boat commands and the difficulty of co-ordinating missions are accepted. However, Suadicani would not be operating without direction and, presumably, Karl Bartenbach would have the rank and reach to contact another command. There was an overall national

---

25   *MA-BA*, Freiburg, KTBs: *U 84*, RM 90/v/96; *U 93*, RM/97/1021; *UC 50*, RM 97/1034.

imperative to get experienced u-boat commanders back to sea as quickly as possible to meet the monthly sinking targets; and there was the attraction of further rescues if this first was successful. A larger u-class boat that was going to the area anyway would be convenient and be better provisioned to keep station for five consecutive nights while active during the day. A u-boat would have more room for two extra men and, also, might carry a larger collapsible Berthon to handle the five miles from boat to shore estimated by Suadicani.

U 84, commander Kapitänleutnant Walter Roehr, was lost around 15 January and was found near Penmarch, Finistère, in 2014. *U 84* was assigned to operate between Penmarch and Île de Ré. The wreck of what is probably *U 93*, commander Kapitänleutnant Helmut Gerlach, lies in the eastern English Channel which fits its ordered patrol area from the Channel Islands to Penmarch.[26]

---

26 Michael Lowrey, WWI forum, uboat.net, 2/1/2017: *U 84*, *U 93*, and *U 95* all sailed within a few days of each other — 1/1/1918, 29/12/1917, 27/12/1917 respectively — from Germany. We also know that all three of these boats successfully got through the Straits of Dover outbound. First of all, *U 95* is not an option for a Bay of Biscay POW rescue mission. U 95's patrol area was the western English Channel (Spindler, *Krieg zur See*, Vol. V, p. 45). In recent years, the wrecks of three large u-boats have been found. The first located is off Hardelot. I was among the people involved in trying to identify this wreck. The submarine in question is of the *U 93* type. (By design, this could be *U 93*, *U 95*, or *U 109*). It was clearly lost while homebound and has massive damage to the stern (internal torpedo explosion?). The propellers were scrubbed and clearly exclude *U 109*. Based upon dates on the propellers, Axel Niestle concluded that the wreck was most likely that of *U 95* (propeller dates after *U 93* was launched, but before *U 95* was launched). The 16/1/1918 date was the apparent last contact date from Royal Navy files (but further west). This is what uboat.net's listing reflects. Then, a few years later, Innes McCartney dived a U 93 class wreck near the Lizard. Innes was of the opinion that the wreck off the Lizard is likely *U 95* and sunk on 7/1/1918 by ramming. (This was the attribution for *U 95* before the Hardelot wreck was found.) The Hardelot wreck, despite the propeller markings must thus be *U 93*. The Royal Navy 16/1 mention could easily be a misattribution or otherwise made in error. Also, from an operational prospective, the odds are higher that *U 93*, with its patrol area along the French coast, would return via Dover as compared to *U 95*, which was assigned to operate in the western English Channel. Innes' hypothesis is pretty strong. However, the alternative theory would be that the Lizard wreck is that of *U 109*. (It is hard to get *U 93* to off the Lizard.) The wreck Innes found is within a mile of a British minefield. The sinking claim for *U 109* is via mine off Griz Nez while sailing outbound through Dover on 26/1/1918. Upon closer examination, there really isn't all that strong a sinking claim there. *U 109*'s patrol area was the St George Channel, and the Lizard would be along the way for her. Finally, the wreck of *U 84* was found off Penmarch about three years ago. I was involved in identifying that wreck. One area of particular concern was making sure the wreck was not *U 93* — and based upon certain design characteristics, we ultimately determined the wreck had to be *U 84*, not *U 93*.

One other page in the French escape reports may shed light as it contains submarine contact reports thought relevant by them for, probably, 5 January 1918 (so not *UC 50*). Ten miles from the Chassiron lighthouse, on the northern point of the island of Oléron, a French aircraft, one of a pair, threw a bomb by hand at a submarine (no bomb launcher); the submarine replied by firing a machine gun which hit the wing of one of the planes, and then 'dived quickly and disappeared'. The same afternoon, about 1500, three French aircraft found 'the same' u-boat engaged in a fight with a British steamship. One plane attacked and 'fired a bomb straight on the bow of the submarine at ten metres'; the submarine dived and disappeared.

The reason for Gerth's move to Carcassonne was clearly well known among his fellow officers. On the same day, 16 February, that he arrived at his new prison, another coded letter was sent from Boyardville to Suadicani in Bruges and intercepted. It purported to come from a 'Capitaine' von Niessen. There was later correspondence:

> *The escape attempt by Lt Gerth has failed as the escape was discovered. The French know nothing about the way in which the escape should have been carried out. Gerth has been taken to the mainland and asks you to be kind enough to now place on me all the goodwill that you had shown to him up to now as several officers here would like to once again have the chance to fight on the front and in particular Cap. von Dewall, former commander of the fighting squadron (Army High Command). The possibility of an escape is guaranteed.*
>
> *If you agree with us as we hope we would ask you to take into consideration the following: Fixed term for the new undertaking the nights of the new moon 10-15 May, the nights of 10-15 being included. The place for the escape remains that for the January escape. Delay for letters is fixed at five weeks. If the sending of the reply is no longer possible before the 5 April please put back the operation to the nights of the new moon in June, that is to say the nights of 7-12 of June, those of the 7-12 being included.*
>
> *The reply will take place solely by the same method as the current letter if possible simply encoded according to the key: Üb immer Treu und Redlichkeit.*
>
> *In haste*

The prophetic code key *Üb' immer Treu' und Redlichkeit*, 'Always practise loyalty and honesty', deserves more than a footnote. It is the first line of the poem

Der alte Landmann an seinen Sohn, 'The old countryman to his son', by Ludwig Hölty.[27] The lines became popular as the words to the tune sung by Papageno, *Ein Männchen oder Weibchen*, 'A little man or little woman', in Mozart's opera *Die Zauberflöte*, 'The Magic Flute'.

When Friedrich Wilhelm III became king of Prussia in 1797, his wife Queen Luise ordered that the carillon of the Potsdam Garrison Church should play every hour her two favourite tunes, that played on the half hour was *Üb' immer Treu' und Redlichkeit* as an emblem of Prussian soldiers' virtues. The song became the unofficial Prussian national hymn.

On 21 March 1933, the ceremony for the opening of the new Reichstag after the German federal election was called the *Day of Potsdam*. Adolf Hitler took his oath of office in the presence of President Hindenburg in the garrison church. Twelve years later during the *Night of Potsdam*, a British bomb attack caused the church bell tower to collapse and the carillon with its forty bells fell to the ground while constantly playing the tune *Üb' immer Treu' und Redlichkeit*.

Hauptmann Job-Heinrich von Dewall, von Niessen's accomplice, was a pilot and the commanding officer of KagOHL 2 who did not return from a bombing mission over Châlons in Champagne on 23 March 1918.[28]

This second attempt at escape from Boyardville by u-boat in May 1918 also failed and Dewall was quickly moved from the sea coast to Montoire.[29] ICRC records indicate that Dewall was moved from a camp at Auch, the historical capital of Gascony, back to Boyardville on 27 October 1918.[30] Dewall was finally released in March 1920. He went on to work in several senior positions in the German aircraft industry and in the Luftwaffe.[31] In 1942, he was appointed Generalleutnant, air marshal, when he became a freelance member of the war science department in Berlin. Ironically, Dewall died in September 1945 after going missing near Karlsbad, a presumed Czech prisoner of war.

Captain Prulières of the French Army secret police returned to carry out his 'special surveillance' and was landed covertly because it was 'important not to raise awareness in the camp at Boyardville which remains ignorant of this operation'. The French reception committee was even more involved and

---

27   wikipedia.
28   *ICRC*, P 18454. theaerodrome.com/forum.
29   *ICRC*, P 36281, 15/5/1918.
30   *ICRC*, P 30318.
31   Hildebrand, *Die Generale der deutschen Luftwaffe 1935-1945*, pp. 190-91.

explicit than for Gerth's attempt. The French Minister of the Navy and his chief of staff, Vice Admiral Ferdinand-Jean-Jacques le Bon, intervened to organise the subterfuge. The submarine *Brumaire* with its eight torpedoes left its base at La Pallice each day of the escape period to be in position for the evening and returning the next morning at 0200. Would this 1906 boat, finally launched in 1911, have been a match for a modern u-boat in an open fight? Torpedo boats followed *Brumaire* an hour-and-a-half later each day. Two patrol boats, 'if possible armed with Walsar apparatus', to the west of Pertuis Strait, between the island and Rochefort, moved at slow speed in order to use their hydrophones.

> *If the weather allows, [Brumaire] to moor as close as possible to the land in the south west of the lighthouse [Chassiron]. It will be ready to cast off immediately and hold itself only on a kedge anchor and a cable, ready to go, with a buoy. The ship must offer the smallest silhouette possible and ... to be ready for every eventuality it will be semi-submerged. If the Brumaire needs help it will launch rockets of whatever colour.*

This time, the u-boat was seen, not during the failed May operation, but in the June repeat, word of the failed endeavour and capture in May of Niessen and Dewall not having reached Suadicani. This latter operation has the hallmarks of a French trap. Semaphorists at Chassiron lighthouse first saw a fixed white light on 9 June, thirty miles west of the La Coubre lighthouse on the mainland, and then a u-boat was seen keeping watch, but not approaching Boyardville immediately. The white light was seen twice more from Chassiron that night at 2300 and 2345.

There is one other recorded escape attempt by u-boat, not off France, but off north Wales. In 1915, Korvettenkapitän Max Valentiner, commander of *U 38*, from Heligoland, was ordered to pick up three German officers who had broken out of their prison camp. Valentiner waited three days for the signal from shore and at dawn on 16 August he 'abandoned the mission, not knowing that the officers were hidden by a projecting rock on a beach five hundred yards away'.[32]

---

32   Coles, *Slaughter at Sea*, p. 53. Valentiner was later branded a war criminal while operating in the Mediterranean. Wilhelm Canaris took over *U 38* at Pola.

Gerth arrived at the barracks in Carcassonne Castle to join 200 other officers on 16 February 1918 where the incomplete local files have no record of his stay.[33] The previous year, the imposing prison was occupied by internees, but in November 1917, the castle was handed over to the French General Directorate of POWs and the internees left for new accommodation. This was a matter of 'extreme urgency' for lodging officer prisoners.[34] Gerth might have reflected on similarities with his short stay at Calais the previous year where high towers and medieval walls with arrow-slits guard passageways to the barbican and the river. Much time seems to have been taken up, according to prison records, with complaints about the sugar ration from 1917 to 1921. Fifty-two German officers signed an urgent request for sugar ration cards shortly after Gerth's arrival.[35]

Georg Gerth's family have recently recovered a picture sent home to Germany from Carcassonne where Gerth is seated at a table with wine and reading by a petroleum lamp.[36]

Gerth was able to indulge his life-long interest in philosophy, particularly at that time works by Hermann Hesse, Immanuel Kant, Friedrich Nietzsche and Rainer Rilke. Kant, thought to be Gerth's preferred philosopher, particularly condemned British imperialism and methods of trade.[37] During his solitary readings, so typical of his later reclusive character, Gerth may have expanded this condemnation to imperialism in general, and therefore, a gradual longer-term disassociation with the trappings of his own imperial ruler.

> *Enlightenment is man's release from his self-incurred tutelage. Tutelage is a man's ability to make use of his understanding without direction from another. Self-incurred is this tutelage when its cause lies not in lack of reason, but in lack of resolution and courage to use it without direction from another. Sapere aude![38] 'Have courage to use your own reason!'. That is the motto of enlightenment.[39]*

---

33   ICRC, P 33851. Email, M Claude-Marie Robion, Archives d'Aude, 1/3/2107, 25/4-1/8/1918.
34   Ministry of War, telegram, 66693-3/11 of 29/10/17 (SHD, Vincennes, GR 16N 2472).
35   Archives d'Aude, 9R/1, 10R/17 &20, 'Prisonniers de Guerre Enemis', Ref. 354a/AD-2017.
36   Interviews with Georg Gerth's daughter, Christa-Maria Gerth, 15-16/11/2016.
37   Koebner, *Imperialism*, p. 276.
38   'Dare to know!' (Horace, *Ars poetica*). This was the motto adopted in 1736 by the Society of the Friends of Truth, an important circle in the German Enlightenment.
39   Kant, *Foundations of the Metaphysics*, p. 85.

The family believed from what Gerth told them that he was well treated in his French prison. But then, they did not know that he had tried to escape and was sent quickly to a more secure site. Gerth briefly described this time in his curriculum vitae attached to a dissertation he wrote in May 1923 while studying at the University of Würzburg.[40] Note, particularly, his claims to 'two' escape attempts, which is not disputed, but not proven by research, and to 'severe special treatment' that did not happen at Boyardville before the escape attempt, but may have happened later.

After the destruction of my boat in late July 1917, I became a French prisoner of war. Two attempts to escape which I undertook to return to the service of the fatherland failed and this, in addition to my previous occupation as a submarine commander, resulted in severe special treatment. However, during my two-and-a-half years of captivity, I had the opportunity to study philosophy in which I have always had a special interest.

Gerth's escape attempt may have solicited some unpleasant repercussions. The most serious crimes for any prisoner were trying to escape and refusing to work.

[Escape] rarely succeeded; most of the fugitives were re-captured. Throughout 1918, French headquarters produced instructions for stopping escapes, many of which could be explained by the relaxing of surveillance, an 'excessive familiarity with prisoners … and serious breaches of camp rules'.[41]

Prisoners were unable to refuse work allocated to them and, although they were theoretically entitled to a subsistence wage, in accordance with international law, due to be paid to them at the end of the conflict, most never received it because of chaotic conditions at war's end.[42]

Perhaps there was a greater expectation that officers, as a matter of honour, should try to regain their countries. This was certainly more likely since the

---

40   'The brandy industry of the Saar territory since application of the Versailles Peace Treaty', Inaugural dissertation written and submitted to the Faculty of Law and Political Science of the Bavarian Julius-Maximilian-University Würzburg in order to attain the degree of Doctor of Political Science by Georg Gerth, retired Lieutenant Captain, from Berlin, Würzburg 1923.
41   Delpal, 'Prisonniers de guerre', pp. 152-53.
42   Jones, 'Prisoners of War', p. 282.

abandonment of the parole system soon after the start of the war. Lower level escapees were often placed in special camps known as 'security measures'.

At the end of a 'terrible year' in November 1917, French premier Clemenceau was alarmed 'about the growing, unstoppable and truly abnormal number of escapes by German POWs'. He was worried that the 'enemy can obtain precious and true information on our projects and at least on our troop movements; it makes a laughing stock of our surveillance, and such frequent escapes could lead us to believe whether they are led by criminals around the camps'.

Clemenceau was told that successful escapes were much less than he believed, thirty escapees out of 19,000 prisoners in the military zone in December 1917, for example. 'But this idea of a prisoner/spy was widespread at a moment when both at the front and behind the lines morale had dropped.'

> *In December 1917, the Northern Army produced a resumé of all the escapes from 6 October to 6 December comprising three columns, 'Circumstances of escape', 'Responsibilities and sanctions', and 'Measures taken to ensure more efficient surveillance'. Sixty-nine prisoners escaped alone, in twos or threes and up to six at a time in twenty-four escape attempts. Fifty-one were retaken and were interrogated for the reasons and the circumstances of their attempt. In fourteen cases, the motive for escape was given as 'nostalgia', to which was twice added insufficient food. All these prisoners worked on detachments in the department of Oise and the Somme, in quarries, saw mills, sugar beet processing plants. They were not complaining of the hours they worked, nor of having been located so close to the front line. Their placements were quite reasonable at forty to fifty kilometres from the front. But this distance was not so great as to not be able to cross [the front line], with luck in one or two nights, which explains the number who definitely escaped.*[43]

The French became preoccupied by a 'sort of general relaxation' in 1918 in the management of the camps and the work regime, attributing it to a growing tendency amongst the military that guarded the camps as 'not seeing in the prisoners but a loyal and upright soldier to whom the fortune of war was against'.[44]

---

43 Becker, *Oubliés de la Grande Guerre*, pp. 127-30. SHD, Vincennes, 16 N 2477, Arcis-sur-Aube, 12/12/1917.
44 Delpal, 'Prisonniers de guerre', p. 153.

The *Deuxième Bureau* called on everyone connected with the camp system to understand the atrocities committed by the Germans to French prisoners to 'dissuade them from excessive compassion'. 'It is necessary to show them the truth about our adversaries of whom nobody in France, after three years of war, could be ignorant of their treacheries, savageries and crimes.'

Perhaps, towards war end, the 'spontaneous practice towards German PoWs was developing in a humanitarian way' and chimed with the new approaches of the charitable, religious and humanitarian organisations, particularly the International Committee of the Red Cross.

There was one known interruption to Gerth's stay at Carcassonne.[45] Gerth was a victim of a 'phenomenon which touched every region of the world in a brief and concentrated period ... an explosive pandemic which swept through the final months of 1918'.[46] In September of his first year, he was transferred over 400 kilometres to the Military Hospital at Grenoble suffering from Spanish flu.

Why did he travel so far?

The influenza pandemic travelled to Europe with American troops early in 1918.[47] It acquired its signature as the 'Spanish flu' during an early excursion in the Iberian Peninsula in May. Two further waves affected most of the areas concerned for a period of a few weeks in the autumn and winter of 1918, the latter reaching into 1919. It was the second phase, when Gerth was infected, that was the 'most virulent and most deadly'. About 90 per cent of all flu deaths occurred between August and November 1918. It was the 'emotional and judgemental juxtaposition of the epidemic with the ending of the war' which excited major immediate comment.[48] The disease struck most and in the millions in Asia, with China and India to the forefront, but the 'historians were westerners and the awfulness of the flu was partly hidden as an addendum of the war'.

It is also contrasted awkwardly with the proven leaps in medical practice brought about through dealing with war wounded. The allies frequently claimed that the epidemic's source was among the Germans, perhaps as

---

45   *ICRC*, P 44693, 9/9/1918.
46   Rasmussen, 'Spanish Flu', in Winter, *First World War*, Vol. III, pp. 334-57. See, also, Hartesveldt, *1918-1919 Pandemic of Influenza*, 1992; Mickels, *Die spanische Grippe 1918/19*, 2010, pp. 1-33.
47   Chickering, *Urban Life*, pp. 564-65.
48   Vaughan, *Doctor's Memories*, pp. 428-29.

the latest version of poisoned wells, corrupted milk and air deliberately contaminated with microbes. 'A new sickness is raging among the Germans: it is the oedema of the war. It begins with a general weakening ... caused by a lack of dietary fats.'[49] 'The dreadful hygiene conditions in prison camps supposedly added to this, allowing the flu into prisoners' home countries when they were repatriated.'[50]

The effect of the blockade on weakening German civilians and soldiers alike was little discussed by the Allies. It is likely that Gerth was not long at Grenoble, incubation was brief and 'people fell seriously ill in a few hours'. Victims experienced a variety of symptoms: high fever, headaches, intense pain in the muscles and bones, inflammation of the pharynx and throat, a state of prostration, and perhaps coughs, intestinal pain, nausea, rash nerve pains and depressive states.[51]

Approximations of deaths varied widely, but grew through various studies over the years. Jordan in 1927 suggested 21.6 million, a little more than one per cent of the world's population.[52] In 1991, Patterson and Pyle estimated 30-40 million deaths, around two per cent.[53] By 2002, Johnson and Müller proposed between 50-100 million deaths, between one in twenty and one in forty of everyone across the world who survived the war.[54]

Prisoners' rations in France deteriorated in 1918, not due to shortages 'but rather to the impact of Franco-German negotiations'.[55]

In April 1918, two extraordinary international conferences took place in Berne which brought together all agencies for humanitarian aid for prisoners.[56] These conferences resulted in two accords, signed between France and Germany in March and April, that recognised agreed standards for prisoner rations, punishments, working hours and working conditions.[57] Ironically, this actually meant a cut in bread rations for the average German prisoner in France.

---

49 Lucien-Graux, *Les fausses nouvelles de la Grand Guerre*, Vol. V, p. 265.
50 Rasmussen, 'Spanish Flu', p. 339.
51 Rasmussen, 'Spanish Flu', p. 345.
52 Jordan, *Epidemic Influenza*.
53 Patterson & Pyle, 'Geography and Mortality'.
54 Johnson and Müller, 'Updating the Accounts'.
55 Jones, *Violence*, p. 239.
56 Becker, *Oubliés de la Grande Guerre*, pp. 255-66.
57 MA-BA, Freiburg, RM 20/505, 'Berner Bereinbarungen', 26/4/1918.

The April accord covered forty pages and was printed in two columns, German and French. Article 26 of the April Accord set rations of 2,000 calories for non-working prisoners, 2,500 for ordinary workers and 2,850 for workers engaged on heavy manual labour. Article 30 precluded bread from being sent to individual prisons, only cake and gateaux. Article 36 specified that no punishment should last longer than thirty days unless there was a break of a week between punishments. Additionally, it was 'formally forbidden to confiscate personal papers from POWs, but the State had the right to take copies'. A general had the right to his own batman, high ranking officers had to share one between four. Generals and high-ranking officers also had the right to two pillows. Officers were limited to five candles each.

Under Clause 10 of the Armistice Treaty, Germany was obliged to release all Allied prisoners immediately whereas the release date of German prisoners in Allied hands remained indefinite. The clause called for the ...

> ... *immediate repatriation without reciprocity, according to detailed conditions which shall be fixed, of all allied and United States prisoners of war, including persons under trial or convicted. The allied powers and the United States shall be able to dispose of them as they wish ... However, the repatriation of German prisoners of war interned in Holland and in Switzerland shall continue as before. The repatriation of German prisoners of war shall be regulated at the conclusion of the preliminaries of peace.*
>
> *In addition, Clause 18 called for repatriation, without reciprocity, within a maximum period of one month ... of all interned civilians, including hostages under trial or convicted, belonging to the Allied or associated powers.*

Of particular interest to Georg Gerth, perhaps, Clause 21 stated that 'all naval and mercantile marine prisoners of the allied and associated powers in German hands to be returned without reciprocity'.

The end of the war did not mean the end of captivity. An enormous gap, a further war crime to many minds, developed between French and German views of prisoner repatriation.

The end of the war offered immediate liberty to the prisoners of the conquerors, 'those of the conquered found themselves hostages, unregulated by the suspended Berne Accords'. The optimism of Berne conferences quickly deteriorated following the end of the fighting.[58] The Armistice agreement did not authorize the return of German POWs before a definitive peace agreement. The fifteen months maximum foreseen in April 1918 for the repatriation of the last prisoners became the minimum for the German prisoners.

'If during the war the prisoners had had a terrible outcome on both sides of the front line, for the German prisoners the defeat was going to be paid for twice.'

> *While Allied prisoners returned from Germany rapidly in late 1918, released under the terms of the Armistice, German prisoners remained in British and American captivity until mid 1919 and in French captivity until 1920, retained by France as human reparations.*[59]

Marshal Ferdinand Foch proposed retaining German prisoners to compensate losses, to put the country back together again and reconstruct those regions which had been devastated and occupied. When it was pointed out to him that this measure would be contrary to the engagements undertaken by France, he replied that the situation did not allow such 'elegances'.

The Allies agreed that German prisoners would not be repatriated until after the ratification of the Treaty of Versailles by Germany and by three of the other powers involved.[60] About 100,000 POWs were transferred into the French 'liberated zones' and formed working parties for departments like Nord-Pas-de-Calais, Champagne-Ardennes and Lorraine which had been at the front line.[61]

Under the authority of General Antoine de Mitry, 700 camps, each averaging 400 men, took part in the reclamation of the region in the North and North East.[62] Men were sent from camps all across the country to reconstruct the war-ravaged regions. From January 1919 to January 1920, between 270,000 and 310,000 German prisoners worked under French command, and some 200,000 under the British, in atrocious conditions clearing ordnance and debris

---

58   Becker, *Oubliés de la Grande Guerre*, pp. 255-66.
59   Dufour, 'Prisonniers du guerre', p. 23. Jones, 'Prisoners of War', p. 289.
60   Willis, 'Hoover and the Blockade', p. 291. Jones, *Violence*, pp. 300-2.
61   Dufour, 'Prisonniers du guerre', p. 9.
62   Delpal, 'Prisonniers de guerre', p. 155.

from fields, trenches and canals.[63] 'This had the added advantage of removing prisoners from jobs to which demobilised French soldiers were returning.'

Forced and dangerous labour became a lengthy and deliberate policy of the French Government. Captain T Hage, a Danish visitor, noted that if this work was extremely dangerous it was equally so for the French military and for the recently liberated prisoners from German camps.[64]

Britain and France regarded German prisoners as a 'bargaining tool and saw their labour as a form of living war reparation'.[65] The great disparity fuelled resentment in the camps and in Germany. In the tense atmosphere awaiting liberation, which was always being delayed, on 1 May 1919 there were 'seditious' demonstrations with red flags and posters hostile to France' at the camp at Île Longue.[66] Captain Hage conducted a study in the liberated regions of northern France, from Calais to Switzerland in 1918 and 1919. He made a connection between the number of escapes, punishments and 'serious incidents' in the camps between Armistice and the final application on 15 January 1920 of the clause of the Treat of Versailles which allowed the freeing of all prisoners.[67]

Initially, the German negotiators viewed the delay as a temporary stay on German prisoner repatriation which would be remedied as soon as all Allied prisoners reached home. The French viewed the situation rather differently. 'Thus, even after the fighting, the need for forced labour drove an escalatory dynamic leading to deterioration in prisoner welfare ... For France, in the immediate post-war period, German prisoners were dangerous perpetrators to be punished, not victims; they derived no compassion.'[68]

German prisoners represented security, ensuring German compliance with French demands. They also represented a sizable army of military men to whom Germany had no access. As early as April 1918, the French believed that Germany wanted its prisoners back 'because she wishes to get back the military instructors of which she had need'. This mentality continued to govern French perceptions after the Armistice;

---

63 Kramer, *Prisoners*, p. 86.
64 Delpal, 'Prisonniers de guerre', p. 153.
65 Jones, *Violence*, pp. 260, 296.
66 Dufour, 'Prisonniers du guerre', p. 15.
67 Delpal, 'Prisonniers de guerre', p. 153.
68 Jones, *Violence*, pp. 258-59.

an emasculated France, which had lost so many men in the war, would be more vulnerable once German prisoners returned home.[69]

The French decision to continue to use German prison labour caused immense and mounting anger in Germany and was seen in Germany as an irrational and cruel act 'motivated purely by a vindictive victor's desire for revenge'. A massive public relations campaign was launched to bring the prisoners home including a *People's Union for the Protection of German War and Civil Prisoners* and the *German Women's League for the Repatriation of Prisoners of War*. The latter sent a petition to Mary, wife of King George, Queen of the United Kingdom (and also Princess of Teck in the Kingdom of Württemberg) in 1919.[70]

Your Majesty
The blood-stained weapons have been laid down. A merciless death has laid one and a half millions of our children in foreign soil. An ocean of tears has flown on their account, and thousands of German hearts have been broken and died. The misery is not yet over. By the Armistice, Germany handed back all her millions of prisoners, but 800,000 German prisoners have been left in the hands of the conquerors to an uncertain fate, our poor sons, husbands, brothers. Now these prisoners, some of whom have been separated for four years from the bosoms of their families, find themselves condemned to hard perilous labour in restoring the ruins of France. The hearts of millions of German women are again torn. We know the great physical and spiritual longings of our dear ones. We know how in utter despair they stretch out their hands to us, their mothers and their children. Their cry for help rings hourly in our ears. Their tear-stained eyes follow us day and night, but we can do nothing to help them.

Author Gerhard Rose was commissioned by the *People's Union for the Protection of the German War and Civilian Prisoners* to write a book detailing the efforts made to seek repatriation. It was published in Berlin in 1920 during the first French repatriations and makes detailed and harrowing reading.[71]

The book explained that, in the fourteen months before the end of the war was legally validated by the Peace Treaty, German citizens who were in the hands of the Allies as war or civilian prisoners suffered under the same,

---

69   Rose, *Krieg nach dem Kriege*, pp. 170-184.
70   *TNA*, FO 608/136, pp. 6-8, 22/2/1919.
71   Rose, *Krieg nach dem Kriege. Der Kampf des deutschen Volkes um die Heimkehr seiner Kriegsgefangenen.*

or even worse, conditions than during the previous fifty-one months of war. The situation was 'adverse to all human feeling and sensible consideration; the desperation, disappointment and bitterness about the delay of the POW's return caused the families to doubt the government and their own elected leaders and accuse them of being partly to blame for the lack of success'. The prisoners were under the impression that 'incompetence and lack of determination of their own people and its leaders had a share in their hard fate'. This opinion was strengthened by enemy propaganda.[72]

Some brief excerpts from the book demonstrate the strength of feeling in Germany:

> *'During these despotic times, each nation would show their true character in the way they treated foreign prisoners of war' – French 'sadism' became apparent ... The expectations raised by the negotiations at Berne and in The Hague regarding prisoner exchange were completely disappointing. 'Mainly the French government was to blame for this as they had only reluctantly agreed to ratification of the treaty having been pressurised by the influential French Association des familles des prisonniers de guerre.' According to the treaty regulations, in the first five months, 60,000, or in the worst case at least 50,000 prisoners should have been released on each side but the actual figure was only 4,000 ... The actions after the Armistice showed that the 'principle of brutal exploitation of power over the prisoners was the key to their treatment'. Germany's enemies use POWs as 'human bargaining chips'. 'Hard and firm was the will of the enemy to commit the rape [of the German prisoners] and the German government and people were powerless to affect that will' ... The enemy wanted to 'satisfy their hate by retaining the prisoners'.*[73]

Protestors in Holland on 25 May 1919 demanded the immediate return of German POWs and the suspension of the hunger blockade, a demonstration which had a particular impact on public opinion in England.

On 24 July, the liberal press in Britain began to call for the repatriation of German prisoners. At the end of July 1919, Churchill explained in the House of Commons that 20,000 German POWs were needed for England's agriculture, the rest in France for reconstruction work.

---

72 Rose, *Krieg nach dem Kriege*, pp. 9-13.
73 Rose, *Krieg nach dem Kriege*, pp. 14-21, pp. 56-57.

Rear Admiral von Reuter, late of Scapa Flow and now interned at Donington Hall, the most senior representative of the German forces in England, passed a petition to Prime Minister Lloyd George through the Swiss Legation in London in August.[74] 'The uncompromising attitude of the British Government shows that it is not fully informed about the psychology of prisoners or war ... Unjust and inhuman ... Every day longer in captivity lowers their vitality and lessens their opportunity in life.'

The International Red Cross issued a formal protest letter, but Clemenceau refused to compromise, asking Britain and America to give France their German prisoners instead of repatriating them to Germany. The Swiss failed to get permission to return the German prisoners interned in their country.

'Indignation, shock and despair turned into a storm first aimed against the behaviour of the enemy, the broken promises of the Entente, but was then directed against the German government.'[75] Politicians were called traitors. At a protest meeting at the *Berlin Philharmonie*, 10,000 women demanded the resignation of the government. By August, the public mood started to worsen, even in France.

Once the Versailles treaty was signed, British and American attitudes changed. They were now keen to return their German charges. Despite French reluctance, the British and Americans went ahead. The British began repatriation with one thousand healthy prisoners on 1 September 1919 and completed on 1 November 1919. Not least of the British concerns was that 5,000 British troops were employed on guard duty at a cost of £30,000 a day.[76] The trains that brought British prisoners home were no longer returned empty to Germany.

Switzerland quickly released its interned German prisoners. In August, 150,000 prisoners returned from the western front, the largest part from English hands. Hearing the news, Clemenceau again demanded the transfer of British-held German POWs to France for reconstruction purposes.

In November, General Neill Malcolm, chief of the British Military Mission to Berlin, telegrammed London asking whether it was possible to do anything to get prisoners returned from France. 'Their retention is causing very bitter feeling and is weakening the position of the Government which is accused of

---

74 *TNA*, FO 608/136, pp. 68-71, 18/8/1919.
75 Rose, *Krieg nach dem Kriege*, pp. 129, 152-53, 164-67.
76 *TNA*, FO 608/136, pp. 26, 36.

criminal indifference by all parties.' Across Germany, there was the 'deepest indignation and bitterness about the French barbarism'.

> *Despite the public opinion of the neutral world, France condemned German prisoners to captivity, indeed slavery, blackmail and exploitation ... It was an outrage against all principles of international law; a stigma France will never be able to wash off.*[77]

Clemenceau remained obdurate into 1920, even in the face of a majority of the French army and of the chairman of the Peace Commission. The Germans called him 'brutal'.[78]

> *If the repatriation of prisoners by our Allies began in September it is because the French government was unable to oppose it. None of our Allies was as badly injured in its emotions and its interests as the population of the north of France was. How can this population wandering in the ruins of their homes ... accept to see the German prisoners, employed upon work of the utmost urgency ... leave France before the time appointed by the Treaty of Versailles, which fixed the end of their captivity on the definitive ratification – the entry into force of the treaty?*[79]

The denigration of the French was endorsed by leading German politicians.[80] Walther Rathenau, shortly to become foreign minister in the Weimar Republic and, in 1922, assassinated in Berlin by the right-wing terrorist group *Organisation Consul*, wrote, 'It is outrageous ... that our prisoner fellow citizens do not return home'. He described the situation as 'slavery'. Philipp Scheidermann, who proclaimed Germany a republic during the revolution and, later, became the second head of government of the Republic, stated, 'I believe the whole world must join with us in crying out against this last insult to humanity.'

It was not until 21 January 1920 that France finally began to repatriate her German prisoners of war. Karl Raabe died two days later. Georg Gerth arrived home on 1 March.

---

77 Plassmann, *German prisoners of war in France*, wintersonnenwende.com, accessed 1/5/2017.
78 Rose, *Krieg nach dem Kriege*, p. 120.
79 Becker, *Le retour des prisonniers*, p. 73. *NA*, FO 608/136, von Lersner to Clemenceau, pp. 113-15, 7/11/1919.
80 Jones, PhD dissertation, 'The Enemy Disarmed', p. 366.

17
AMIDST THE RUINS

[RAF] Bomber Command's offensive against Germany in the Second World War was one of the most remarkable passage of arms in history. It began when Winston Churchill could see no other road to victory, as England stood alone in 1940. It was undertaken with almost messianic fervour by a generation of senior airmen determined to prove that strategic air power could make a unique and decisive contribution to war. It ended in a controversy, moral and strategic, which has been raging ever since. The cost was very high, 55,573 aircrew, almost all officers and NCOs [Non-Commissioned Officers], among the finest and most highly trained material in the British Empire, were killed ... The sacrifice was greater than the British Army's total loss of officers in the First World War.[1]

In March 1920, Gerth got off his train in the German capital after almost three years in a French prison camp. Georg found Berlin and his older brother Erich much changed.

There was death and hunger in the streets; he needed to see if his mother was safe and well. His sworn-leader, the Kaiser, was replaced by a shaky republican government run, hardly to be believed, by socialists, most of whom were in hiding.

Erich, now a socialite and party-goer, had married a rich, widow and ex-countess. He had acquired powerful new friends to go with his old shipmate from naval training, Wilhelm Canaris. They were right-wing extremists like

---

1   Hastings, *Bomber Command*, p. xi. Bomber Command's aircrew losses in WW2 were about ten times higher that the German u-boat crew losses in WW1.

ex-Minister of State Friedrich Wilhelm von Loebell, Walther Rathenau, head of the electrical giant AEG, Heinrich Pabst and Erich Ludendorff, leader of the Imperial Army when Georg was last in Germany.

Erich's father-in-law, Salomon Marx, was of Jewish background, ran one of the country's most successful private banks, and had fingers in many commercial pies. With his widespread and determined network, now shared with Erich, Marx was trying to undermine the Versailles peace treaty.

Georg's arrival coincided with the week of the quickly abortive Kapp-Lüttwitz Putsch. The previous May, leading figures involved in the Putsch met at Marx's Brückenallee address to discuss plans to depose the government. The *Reichsbürgerrat*, a pressure group headed by Marx, published a pamphlet calling for the revision of the Versailles Treaty because its demands could not be met and were, in any event, wrong and unfair.

The war was now long over. After his u-boat service and his escape attempt from Boyardville, Georg's active life had been dull and repetitive. His martial commitment was dulled by three years of imprisonment. His head, however, was full of Hesse, Kant, Nietzsche and Rilke, the philosophical studies of his internment. He had no immediate future other than that which the Admiralty determined. The humiliating Treaty was signed leaving few fighting ships; every submarine was gone.

To cap it all, brother Erich was working covertly with Georg's old boss from Flanders, Karl Bartenbach, and with Admiral von Trotha and Wilhelm Canaris, to provide u-boats for the next war.

How long was it before Erich shared the new realities with his younger brother?

For Georg, this would all take some getting used to.

On a positive note, Georg Gerth found that a court of enquiry, held the previous month in Bremen, had already interviewed his engineer Johannes Giese on the reasons for the stranding of *UC 61* at Wissant in 1917.[2]

Giese had also just returned from captivity. His short verbal account was counter-signed by a Leutnant zur See Scharper, holding the lowest officer rank in the German Navy, so this was no high-powered tribunal. By chance, Giese and Gerth were both from Charlottenburg so one could imagine that the two men met in Berlin to discuss the circumstances and atmosphere at Giese's

---

2 9/2/1920 (KTB, *UC 61*, addendum, V4), pp. 35-39, Cuxhaven.

hearing. Gerth was not asked to travel to Bremen and, instead, hand-wrote his version of events over four sheets of paper, leaving the left hand side free for official comments. There were a lot of notations and initialled signatures. That it seems was the end of the matter.

Georg Gerth said a few years later that he took a position in the International Law Department on the admiralty staff for nine months until he resigned in December.[3] In fact, he joined the navy team contributing to the Peace Commission negotiations. Files for his period in office were not found at the naval archives in Freiburg, but enough general material exists to build a satisfactory picture.[4]

There is an immediate surprise: the commissary to the four-man team of noble officer sailors who headed the delegation was Leutnant z.S. Sharper who questioned Giese at Bremen. Apart from the necessary formality of interviewing the commander of a lost ship, perhaps that whole episode was mostly to see if Gerth was available for a role in the Commission? Perhaps Erich was in the background pulling strings?

Admiral Adolf von Trotha, the Admiralty chief, specified the sort of men he wanted. 'Fluent in at least one of the main languages (English or French), eloquent, confident, experienced travellers with extensive knowledge of the organisation of the navy and skilled in radio telegraphy and coding messages, cool, professional and discrete behaviour, observing the correct formalities at all times.'[5]

This was a precise description of 'Raven' Gerth's skills, given that 'correct formalities' was a euphemism for 'loyal to the officer corps'.[6]

The main issue for Trotha was 'unfair unilateral obligations for Germany as outlined in the peace treaty regarding disarmament, surrender and destruction of German naval vessels, reduction of naval staff, impossibly short time limits'. He felt that the peace conditions had 'no basis in international law, put an extraordinary economic strain on Germany [and were] unacceptable for economic and financial reasons'.

---

3 Curriculum vitae, Würzburg University, 5/1923.
4 *Freiburg*, RM 20/525, Reichs-Marine-Amt 11/1918-3./1919, and RM 21/1-2, Archiv der Marine, Vols. 1-2, 11/1918-1/1920, 2/1920-3/1920.
5 Letter, Trotha, Berlin, 22/10/1919 (RM 21/1, Vol. 1, 11/1918-1/1920).
6 *Cuxhaven*, Obituary, biographical profile, Georg Gerth, *Marine Offizier Vereinigung*, 'Navy Officers' Association', 11/2016.

There were six sub-sections of the naval peace delegation which mainly concentrated on the trade war, the naval air force and mine field clearance and, of course, Gerth could have been employed in any of them. However, it seems likely that he was used in the either of the units covering 'Transition to Peace Time', especially in its dealings with naval PoWs, although this work was largely concluded, or in the section for 'Submarines and Submarine War' whose responsibilities, said Trotha, covered:

German submarines delivered to the Allies and USA, memoranda on the justification of the submarine war (4/2/1915) as well as the unrestricted submarine war (31/1/1917), list of vessels sunk or damaged by German submarines/naval forces/fighter planes, collection of material dealing with the accusations made against our submarines regarding cruel treatment of crews of sunk ships, materials about the Baralong case and similar cases, collection of news about submarine traps, Q-boats etc. especially with regard to the cruelties committed by the enemies in their warfare against our submarines.[7]

Gerth's short stay at the Admiralty suggests his mind had already turned to a future away from the military. His work may have taken him to the French border town of Saarbrücken almost 500 miles away from the bustle and intrigue of Berlin.

In 1920, Saarbrücken became the capital of the Saar territory administered by the League of Nations. Under Articles 47 and 48 of the Treaty of Versailles, the Saar coal mines were made the exclusive property of France for fifteen years as compensation for the destruction of French mines during the war.[8] Gerth resigned from the Peace Commission and immediately at the start of 1921 took a post in the Transport and Customs Department of the Saarbrücken

---

7   Coles, *Slaughter at Sea, The Truth Behind a Naval War Crime*. Cole's book is a detailed indictment of British conduct by the Baralong's captain and crew. For original material, *HMSO*, London, 'Memorandum of the German Government in regard to Incidents Alleged to have Attended the Destruction of a German Submarine and its Crew … and Reply of His Majesty's Government', Cd. 8144, 7/1916. Also, for alterative views: Newbolt, *Naval History*, p. 94; and Chatterton, *Q-ships*, pp. 20-23.

8   There is a useful view of the Saar Territory in Reichstag discussions reported in Kessler, *Rathenau*, pp. 372-74. The Versailles Treaty also provided for a plebiscite at the end of the fifteen-year period to determine the territory's future status. In 1935, more than 90 per cent of the electorate voted for reunification with Germany, while only 0.8 per cent voted for unification with France. The remainder wanted to rejoin Germany, but not while the Nazis were in power (wikipedia).

Chamber of Commerce where smuggling was a primary concern.[9] His command of French and English would have been of great use in what must have been a chaotic period. Gerth noted that 'in addition to my official job, I managed the Association of the Distilleries of the Saar Territory' with a great emphasis on brandy and gin production.[10]

Within a few months, he began studies at the University of Würzburg and, from the spring, worked for the Employers' Association at Trier.

The city of Trier, another Saar region border town, this time with Luxembourg, was the birthplace of Karl Marx, the philosopher and revolutionary socialist. It is worth a small diversion for Trier is closely connected with this general story. It was in Trier in 1919 that John Maynard Keynes, the British financial representative on the Supreme Economic Council, twice met German delegates to try to alleviate the famine in Germany. It was also in Trier that Smiley Blanton, a medical officer with the American Army of Occupation's Department of Sanitation and Public Health, conducted his ground-breaking study into the damage caused to young German children by malnutrition brought about by the English blockade. Blanton wrote in his report, printed in 1919,

> *The city of Trier is situated on the Moselle River and is the centre of the wine industry for the Moselle Valley. It has about 55,000 inhabitants, the majority of whom are small shopkeepers, artisans and officials. There are several thousand factory workers in about thirty factories which include leather and tobacco factories and iron foundries. The rich people are chiefly wine merchants, many of whom have grown quite rich during the war. Before the war, there was much wine drinking among the poorer classes and much hard liquor was consumed as well. The people have large families and among the poor people malnutrition was common before the war. On the whole, I believe that we are justified in saying that the people of Trier are not so well developed physically and not so well off economically as the people in the neighbouring cities of Cologne, Bonn and Coblenz.*[11]

---

9   Records of the Saarbrücken Chamber of Commerce before 1944 were destroyed by WW2 bombing (private email, Oliver Groll, 4/4/2016).
10 Curriculum vitae, Würzburg University, 5/1923. Cuxhaven, biographical profile.
11 Blanton, *Mental and Nervous Change*, p. 7.

There is some determination and planning evident in the moves to Saarbrücken, Trier and Würzburg, all within a year of Gerth's return to Germany. The triangle formed by the three cities has a longest commuting distance of under 200 miles. Support for this conjecture comes from an unusual direction, a study of Gerth's signature which was conducted in London in 2017 without any knowledge of Gerth's history.[12]

If this analysis meets with some surprise, it is not new investigative ground. James Joll of Oxford University and professor at the London School of Economics wrote that the 'historian must seek his explanations where he can find them, even in unorthodox or unprofessional places. After all, even [Sir Lewis Bernstein] Namier [an historian of the British parliament with a legendary hatred of Germany] was not ashamed to use the services of a graphologist in reconstructing the character of the writer of manuscript documents'.[13]

> *The writer [Gerth] had a strong personality having lasting emotional energy and staying power. A man with a strong sense of purpose and conscientious attitude to all his endeavours. Gerth had a good analytical intellect and would seek his own answers for any projects rather than just accepting any information. Fairly outgoing but quick to react and could be defensive, impatient and subject to mood swings. A man with good coordination and manual dexterity and confident in his ability to succeed. He was able to inspire others with his ideas and take control demonstrating strong leadership qualities. An assertive individual with a strong desire to acquire which could be glory as well as to obtain and possess material objects. Highly competitive, willing to carry the fight, somewhat ruthless, with the desire to push forward and challenge. A man with great initiative, high goals, ambition and enduring determination.*

The glue to this new life was surely Gerth's second cousin, Maria Leinecker, whom he was to marry on 8 September 1921 in her home town of Würzburg. It is likely, therefore, that the couple were romantically linked from Gerth's return to Berlin or even from before the war.

Maria's mother, Anna Maria (her preferred Christian name) Helene, was also a Gerth, a convert to Catholicism on marriage; her father and Georg's

---

12 Ruth Myers, handwriting consultant, London, 3/2017.
13 Joll, *Unspoken Assumptions*, p. 9.

father were brothers who lived in Berlin.[14] So, Georg Gerth's mother-in-law was also his first cousin.

Maria was just a few days short of her twenty-first birthday at marriage; Gerth was twelve years her senior. Memories of lost family photographs describe her as 'very pretty'. Georg stood 1m 80, had blond hair, clear, blue eyes and bad hearing, a notorious affliction of early submariners. He spoke German like someone from Berlin, English with an Oxford accent, and had good French.[15] He was always a student of philosophy rather than either the military man that he had been and was to be again, or a businessman that he was to become in order to earn his living. He learned Sanskrit, the liturgical language of Hinduism, in order to trace the path of Buddhism across south east Asia and, particularly, its translation into Zen or Japanese Buddhism. His other love was landscape painting.

It was a life-lasting love match, but also a good match for Georg as the Catholic Leinecker family were rich, their wealth founded on a coffee, sugar and wine wholesale business, well-known in Würzburg. The family coffee firm was founded by Joseph Leinicker in 1815.[16] The Leinecker family home in Würzburg for some generations was a substantial detached house at Sanderring 22, Riemenschneiderstraße 1, and this eventually passed to Georg and Maria Gerth.[17]

A combination of income from Saarbrücken and Trier, a pension from the navy and, presumably, accommodation and some Leinecker funds, saw Gerth through his doctorate at the Faculty of Law and Political Science at the Bavarian Julius-Maximilian-University, Würzburg. In 1922, he studied

---

14   Anna Maria's parents were Heinrich Carl Wilhelm Emil Georg Ernst Gerth, brother to Ernst, Georg's father, and Friederike Wilhelmine Emilie Leben, married 18/7/1861 in Brandenburg (ancestry.com).
15   Interview, Christa-Maria Gerth, 15/11/2106. Berlin's citizens are well known in Germany for their fast, quick-witted, loud-mouthed, slightly vulgar, over-confident bordering on arrogant, way of speaking. This is summed up in the term *Berliner Schnauze*, 'Berlin snout/gob'. The most comparable British dialect would be the Cockney dialect of Londoners. The chatty cabbies of both cities are similar in this respect. The German stage version of the musical *My Fair Lady*, which celebrated London and Cockney speech, was set in Berlin and used Berlin dialect.
16   Joseph Nikolaus Leinicker (with a middle 'i'), born 8/10/1789, Würzburg, merchant, died 20/10/1843, Würzburg, Maria's great-grandfather. The foundation date of the firm is found on company promotional literature celebrating 150 years of business in 1965.
17   Maria Leinecker's father was Oberstleutnant z.D. Josef Richard (preferred Christian name) Leinecker, a career soldier, who on 4/8/1914 was *Kommandant der Ersatzabteilung*, commander of the reserve, 11 Field Artillery Regiment, Royal Bavarian Army.

National Economics, Economic Statistics and, in 1922/23, added the Versailles Treaty, Population Statistics, and a Comparison of National and State Law. His 142-page dissertation, successfully submitted in May 1923, was titled 'The Brandy Industry of the Saar Territory since Application of the Versailles Peace Treaty'. He became a Doctor of Political Science, 'Dr. rer. pol'.

No doubt the degree was part-time and Gerth's attendance was balanced with his employments, particularly at Saarbrücken. The document itself is mostly typed, but the appendices, tables and many corrections are handwritten.[18] Georg used freely information, data, business contacts, legal knowledge and personal experience that he gained during his employment. This insider knowledge of the brandy and spirits industry, current legislation, customs duties, taxes, commodity prices, main competitors, would eventually come in useful for an anticipated position as a manager in the Leinecker family business.

Georg's lack of academic credentials, apart from his school matriculation, would not normally allow him to undertake post-graduate studies. The explanation is probably that, after WW1, universities made allowance for a generation of young men who had missed further education because they had fought in the war, and fast tracked their subsequent academic careers. The same leniency occurred in many countries after WW2. It is unusual, however, to have such a practical subject for PhD study with its links to most recent current affairs, including the politically sensitive German-French relations after the ratification of the Versailles Treaty. As such, the dissertation is more of an up-to-date report than an in-depth piece of analytical study based on academic research and reflection.

The brandy and coffee industries, particularly among the many food infrastructures all but destroyed during the war, were struggling to get back to some kind of normality. As an example, in 1916, the German government issued five decrees which affected seriously the rights of the merchants.[19] The first two laid down strictures about the importation of tea and coffee, the next two regulated the sale of these, and the last dealt with substitutes for coffee. In future, the importation of both tea and coffee lay in the hands of the 'War Committee for Tea, Coffee, and their substitutes'. Merchants with

---

18   University of Würzburg archive, 1923, 10582.
19   *TNA*, FO 371/2679, 16/5/1916, p. 49.

stocks of 10kg of raw coffee and 5kg of tea or more 'must report these to the committee and must deliver them immediately when ordered to do so'. The committee settled the price to be paid as compensation. Chicory roots were a preferred substitute and could not be used as animal fodder. Only 350,000 sacks of uncommandered coffee remained in Germany, enough for six weeks' civilian consumption. However, the Army and Navy had sufficient supplies for six months.

The scarcity of coffee led many dealers to refuse to sell either coffee or its substitutes to their customers. The authorities forbade this, but a customer could not get more than 1lb at a time. Some merchants were fined five marks and sentenced to one day's imprisonment for selling roasted barley prepared to resemble coffee. The Reichstag then ordered the creation of a Board to control the sale of strong brandy. Spirits could no longer be used for lighting or cooking.

Gerth concluded that after a pre-war busy exchange of goods with Germany and France, the Saar territory in 1920 hardly imported or exported any brandy.

> *French imports which dominated the Saar territory have been increasingly reduced and German imports have ceased almost completely. The local industry now provides the Saar territory with spirits, liqueurs and, partly, distilled wines, but there is little demand ... At the end of 1922, the brandy industry of the Saar is a predominantly stand-alone, self-contained economic unit. Because of the political breakdown of the German empire after the armistice, Germany was unable to protect its borders in the West against foreign trade. As a result the occupied territories were flooded with banned foreign goods. The German economy was hugely damaged by the duty free import of luxury foods, drinks and tobacco, toiletries and perfumes and especially spirits, brandy and liqueurs of French origin. Because of its geographical location, Saarbrücken became the hub of unlicensed trade. As for all of the occupied territories this time of effortless profit came to an end after the coming into force of the Versailles Treaty when the Saar territory joined the French customs area and all exports of goods to Germany had to follow German customs regulations.*[20]

After his doctorate, Gerth immediately found employment as head of finance for the Richard Kahn Group of mainly automotive companies, founded in

---

20 Dissertation, 5/1923, University of Würzburg.

1921. This important first commercial job meant a move back to Berlin where he stayed until 1925. While in Berlin, Gerth enrolled for one semester during the winter of 1923 at the Philosophical Faculty of the Friedrich-Wilhelms-Universität where he studied psychology.[21] He moved with Maria into his mother's apartment at Keithstraße 22. Maria often 'spoke enthusiastically' to her children about this time in the capital as 'she enjoyed taking part in big city life'.[22]

In September 1923, just before Georg and Maria arrived in Berlin, Georg's mother, Hedwig, was found dead at the Keithstraße apartment.[23]

Hedwig was 61-years-old and died from gas poisoning, *Gasvergiftung*, presumably at the apartment because the time of her death was recorded as seven in the morning. There is no indication on the official forms or in the newspapers of whether it was an accident or suicide, a case of accidental overnight gas escape or a deliberate ending of a life. Perhaps of significance was that the record was signed by the *Oberstaatsanwalt*, the Senior Public Prosecutor, at the Landgericht II District Court. Eighteen printed words were firmly deleted from the death record. The funeral at the Protestant Kaiser-Wilhelm-Gedächtniskirche, the Kaiser Wilhelm Memorial Church, was conducted with the 'assistance' of a cleric with the initial 'G'.[24] A church service was not at all normal for a declared suicide. Perhaps her remembered depression, her 'melancholia', her twenty-five year widowhood, her loneliness during the war, some ailment, all became too much.

On the other side, Christa-Maria Gerth, who never met her grandmother, remembers particularly that her own father, Georg, was 'very fond of his mother, more than Erich', and shared with her a tendency to depression. This

---

21 Matriculation No. 1861/114R, 6/11/1923 to 24/1/1924 (University email, Auste Wolff, 29/5/2017).
22 Personal email, Christa-Maria Gerth, 18/3/2017.
23 Hedwig Gerth, née Boch, born Aken, district of Calbe on the River Saale, 19/5/1862, died 12/9/1923 (Civil Registry Office Berlin III, Berlin-Tiergarten, 1923: No. 775), buried 15/9/1923 (Parish of the Kaiser-Wilhelm-Gedächtniskirche, Berlin-Charlottenburg).
24 The church was built in the 1890s and was badly damaged in a bombing raid in 1943. The present building, which consists of a church with a foyer and a separate belfry with a chapel, was built between 1959 and 1963. The damaged spire of the old church has been retained and its ground floor has been made into a blue-glass-walled memorial hall. The Church today is a famous landmark of western Berlin, nicknamed *Der hohle Zahn*, 'the hollow tooth' (wikipedia).

insight makes matters the more sad because Hedwig died knowing that Georg was coming to live in Berlin for at least a few years.[25]

Georg, practical experience gained at Kahn's, returned in 1925 to Würzburg as a manager in the Leinecker family firm, his career for the rest of his business life. Relations with his brother Erich remained close even with the physical distance that separated them. During the early years of the second world war, they did manage to meet up at least twice. Erich made a loan to the Leinecker company and this was repaid by his wife at a crucial time after the war.

Georg and Maria had four children who arrived later in life, the last, Christa-Maria in 1939.[26] Georg developed his love of landscape painting, but his first passion remained philosophy. Maria had her own coffee shop in Würzburg, was celebrated locally as a painter and an artist, and was wealthy. None of Maria's three brothers married and Georg was destined to assume control of the company as the founding family died out or lost interest. The Leinecker family home in Würzburg, Sanderring 22, became the Gerth family home.

Georg, in the naval reserve as war approached, was appointed to the senior rank of Korvettenkapitän.[27] Membership of the Nazi party was a requirement for all German officers and Gerth signed up. He was called into the navy on 1 January 1940, six weeks after Christa-Maria's birth. Records of his war service are sketchy and the following relies on personnel records and various war diaries.[28]

Gerth was sent first as a *Marine-Nachrichten-Offizier*, 'naval intelligence officer', for a few months to Memel, now Klaipeda in Lithuania, on the Baltic coast, reporting to Base Commander Captain von Bredow. He arrived on 1 April in freezing conditions, warships needed the help of ice breakers.[29] Hundreds of recruits for various training courses in radio and gunnery poured in. On 11 May, the first units of the 1st and 2nd u-boat training flotilla were moved to Memel, sailing in around lunch time and taking their moorings in the southern

---

25   Christa-Maria Gerth, email 183/2017.
26   Ernst Richard, born 25/9/1926 (no children), died 8/6/1995; Ilse Marie (married Nikolaos Paparafiu, no children) 24/8/1934, died 2016; Hedwig-Therese (married Alfred Kremheller, no children) 24/7/1936, died 27/1/2016; Christa-Maria 14/11/1939 (two sons).
27   Equivalent to Lieutenant Commander in the Royal Navy; Major in the British Army.
28   Georg Gerth's service during WW2 has been found in *Freiburg*, RM 17, Navy Personnel Office – officer staff records.
29   RM 17/65: Document by the Memel Base Commander, Captain von Bredow, dated 29/3/1940. RM 45 I/83, KTB of the Base Commander, 1-6/1940.

part of the winter harbour. On 15 June, Memel's coastal monitoring station reported that the Russians were invading Lithuania. All leave was cancelled. Memel was ordered to repel any crossing of the borders between Germany and Lithuania.

Gerth was next sent to Sandnessjöen on the island of Alsta in occupied north Norway, a town with just a few thousand inhabitants. He arrived on 1 October 1940, where he continued as naval intelligence officer, second-in-command to Kapitän Johannes Bachmann.[30] Bachmann, who commanded the light cruiser *Emden* before the war, was killed fighting the Americans in Willebadessen in 1945.

The invasion of Norway from April to June 1940 took sixty-two days, the longest any country apart from the Soviets held out against the Nazis. The records immediately before Gerth's arrival show that military consolidation was the main activity: the preparation of a naval radio station at Bodø, the sighting of a surfaced submarine near Trondheim, six English fighter planes dropping mines, and the escape and recapture of downed English fighter plane crews from the island of Leka. Reinforcements arrived regularly, including the 10th Company, Infantry Regiment 263, one officer and sixty-nine men, and the promise of a fourth trained battery crew.

One of Gerth's first tasks was to take over the writing of the daily war diary for his commanding officer, a most personal task during his u-boat commands twenty-five years before. However, this time, Gerth's entries were of a different nature. On 10-12 October, popular concerts and social events were recorded: the *Regimentsmusik*, the musical band of the Infantry Regiment, played for German soldiers and the Norwegian population at a teacher training college, at a hospital, at an officer's home with tea, string music and the mayor as special guest of honour.

On 14 October, the Admiral of the Norwegian north cost, Captain August Thiele visited to inspect the naval constructions and emplacements. Thiele was a recent hero who received the Knight's Cross of the Iron Cross for his command of the pocket battleship *Lützow* and his leadership of *Kampfgruppe V*, '5th battle group', during the invasion of Oslo. Thiele took command of the

---

30 RM 17/75: Document by Commander Sea Defence Sandnessjöen, dated 27/9/1940. RM 45 III/190 KTB, of the Commander, Sea Defence, 17/7/1940-31/12/1941, extract 1/7-31/10/1940.

battle group after the sinking of the heavy cruiser, SMS *Blücher*, Konteradmiral Oskar Kummetz's flagship, in Oslo Fjord, after close fire from shore batteries.

From Trondheim on 26 October, Thiele criticised Bachmann and Gerth on three grounds. The war diary for 1 October, Gerth's first day, reported the emergency landing of a seaplane and stated that 'the commander did not initiate anything as a secret messaging connection did not exist with Brønnøysund so the harbour master could not be contacted'. Thiele explained that, for notification of sea emergencies, a secret messaging connection was not required. Thiele then moved onto 'reports about promenade concerts, social evenings and tea invitations' which did not belong in a war diary 'even if they serve to entertain the members of the armed forces and help contact with the Norwegian civilians'. Finally, Thiele insisted that the war diary was to be signed personally each day by the local commander. There were no more signatory duties for Gerth.

On 23 October, Gerth reported a message in Morse from the harbour master at Bodø regarding the stranding of a German steamer which, it turned out was the Norwegian steamer *Princess Ragnhild*, hit and sunk by an English mine. Seventy-one German soldiers were rescued alive, fourteen dead. Thiele later criticised the Bodø harbour master for the delay in rescue.

After an eventful two months in Sandnessjöen, Gerth moved to Warnemünde, near the city of Rostock on the Baltic, to take up duties as intelligence officer on 1 January 1941.[31] Gerth's duties here are not described, but he moved yet again after another few months to join Coastal Command, Western Baltic, at Kiel, on 1 October 1941. 'Dr Gerth' was appointed first Adjutant, third in line after the commander, Vice Admiral Werner Grassmann, killed in Berlin in 1943, who was a fellow sea cadet in Gerth's Crew of '07, and the Chief of Staff Captain Grattenauer.[32]

On 1 April 1942, Gerth took on additional responsibilities as *Personalreferent*, 'Personnel Officer' and on 1 July added *Offizierpersonalreferent*, Officer's Personnel Officer, but now number four in line after the Assistant to the Chief of Staff, Willy Quaatz. With all of these quite rapid changes in appointment, there is a suspicion that the local admiralty staff did not know quite what to do with their fifty-four-year-old ex-u-boat commander, a philosopher with a doctorate,

---

31   RM 17/54: Document, Warnemünde, 30/12/1940, repeated in documents 19/3, 1/4 and 20/6/1941.
32   RM 17/54-5: Document, Kiel 7/4/1942.

who was used to running his own successful brand-name business in peacetime. Perhaps his demeanour was insufficiently war-like? Perhaps, also, while a stout defender of Germany, the fate of his brother, reported elsewhere, gave him second thoughts about his commitment to the Third Reich?[33] Perhaps, even, his old classmate Grassmann rescued him?

At least Kiel was an eighteen-month appointment. On 1 January 1943, Gerth moved finally to the Torpedoversuchsanstalt, 'Torpedo Research Centre', at Eckernförde, as 'Head of Division' and stayed for almost two years.[34] Here, Gerth was finally dealing with a subject of which he had hands-on experience. It was while Gerth was serving in Eckernförde that his brother, Erich, died, probably killed by the Gestapo in Rome.[35]

Georg Gerth retired from the navy for a second time on 1 November 1944, aged fifty-seven, less than a year later. Georg returned to the coffee and wine business of Leinecker in Würzburg and to tragedy. He never saw combat and was seemingly of limited use to the Third Reich in its final months.

On the night of 16 March 1945, RAF High Command in High Wycombe, England, decided to firebomb Würzburg using the half-timbered and cramped buildings of the old city as a tinder box.

Cities like Würzburg were primarily selected because they were easy for the bombers to find and destroy. Because they had a medieval centre, they were expected to be particularly vulnerable to fire attack.[36]

Leading the attack was the same air group, using eleven Mosquito twin-engine bombers and 225 Lancaster heavy bombers, which the month before had burned Dresden. Proportional to the size of Dresden, Würzburg experienced an even higher rate of death and destruction.

The Mosquitoes first marked the target with green flares, called 'Christmas Trees' by the Germans, as a marker for the main bombers. As a result of meticulous planning, each bomber was over the target for less than one minute.

---

33   Erich Gerth's story is told in Heal, *Saints & Sinners*.
34   RM 17/45: Document, Eckernförde, 21/12/1942 listing officer staff at the *Torpedoversuchsanstalt*, 1/1/1943.
35   Heal, *Saints & Sinners*.
36   Siebert, 'British Bombing Strategy in World War Two' (bbc.co.uk/history/worldwars/wwtwo/area-bombing_04.shtml), p. 4, 1/8/2001.

Then, Würzburg's roofs and windows were destroyed with 256 heavy bombs and aerial mines and, finally, 300,000 incendiary bombs rained down. A single area-wide fire storm saw temperatures reaching 2,000 degrees Centigrade. Returning bombers could see the flames from 240 kilometres away. Just one bomber was shot down by a German night fighter; five others were lost during or after the attack.

The population had minimum warning and little protection from the heat. Many tried to reach the banks of the Main river on the edge of the town. An estimated 5,000 people were killed, only 3,000 were identified, and almost 89 per cent of the buildings in the historic town, 68 per cent in the suburbs, were obliterated in a raid that lasted seventeen minutes. This was a war-time record on several counts.[37]

Specifically, this meant 21,062 homes and thirty-five churches destroyed. From June 1944 to March 1945, Würzburg suffered ten other air attacks, together killing over 500 people. Hildesheim was half-destroyed six days after the main Würzburg raid, Paderborn in another five days, and half of Plauen on 10 April.

'The final catalogue of air attacks could not be restrained even by Churchill.' Seventy German cities were area bombed by the RAF alone between 1942 and 1945 in 365 raids.[38]

> *It is right to say that the shockwave triggered by Dresden swept away what was left of the will to resist, as the Germans now feared that such a catastrophe could be repeated daily. Awareness of the inevitable defeat increased and the belief in miracles disappeared but, above all, here was the growing realisation that it would be better if the end came soon ... better to have a terrible end than endless terror.*[39]

Officially, Würzburg was targeted as a traffic hub, but every large town is a crossroads. It was known that Würzburg's main war duty was as a hospital town, there were over forty hospitals in the centre at the time of the attack. On 14 February 1942, the Area Bombing directive was issued to Bomber

---

37 Overy, *Bombing War*, p. 397.
38 Hastings, *Bomber Command*, Appendix E, pp. 482-87.
39 Bergander, *Dresden im Luftkreig*, p. 349, cited in Probert, *Bomber Harris*, p. 321.

Command. Bombing was to be 'focussed on the morale of the enemy civilian population and, in particular, of the industrial workers'.[40]

Although never officially admitted at the time, the British were to carry out 'unrestricted area bombing' on a scale which dwarfed the 'unrestricted submarine warfare' of the first war and over which the British had used such demonic language. The over-riding drive behind the RAF raid on Würzburg was the determination of Air Marshall Arthur 'Bomber' Harris, to break the will of the German people by hitting unprotected civilian populations. The policy was much debated internally with leaders like Churchill frequently vacillating because of the horror of success.[41]

Would it not be preferable to attack strategic targets like steel production, rail networks and oil supply?

The ultimate aim of an attack on a town area is to break the morale of the population which occupies it. To ensure this, we must achieve two things: first, we must make the town physically uninhabitable and secondly, we must make the people conscious of constant personal danger. The immediate aim is, therefore, twofold, namely to produce destruction and fear of death.[42]

Christa-Maria Gerth remembers that nobody expected an attack this late in the war, especially as Würzburg was a hospital city.[43] The three sisters had been sent to the countryside for safety several months previously, but on this night all were back home again. Her brother had been conscripted into the navy and was serving in Denmark. During previous alarms, the family went with local residents into the low basement, the vaulted wine cellar, of their house in Sanderring 21, which survived this attack although the house did not. The Gerths were not in the cellar that evening.

I do remember that in the late afternoon we walked towards Altertheim, about twenty kilometres from Würzburg. My parents knew the forest ranger in Irrtenberg. When

---

40 Probert, *Bomber Harris*, pp. 132-33.
41 Hastings, *Bomber Command*, Chapter 7, 'Protest and Policy'; Overy, *Bombing War*, pp. 410-12, Chapter 10, 'Balance Sheet of Bombing'; Probert, *Bomber Harris*, pp. 147, 316-22; and much else throughout these books and others.
42 British Air Staff paper, 23/9/1941 in Harris, *Despatches on War Operations*, p.7.
43 Christa-Maria Gerth was four-years-old at the time so any discrepancies in memory and chronology can be readily forgiven.

we arrived, many other people had already come to this place so that we couldn't find accommodation in the forester's house. We went to a barn which was laid out with layers of straw. In the distance we saw the red light of fire. Würzburg was ablaze, but nobody moaned. Everyone present had escaped the fire storm alive – the only important thing.

Sanitary facilities were missing completely. A tree trunk was placed above a dug-out pit and you had to balance on it when going to the toilet, the so-called 'thunder beam'. After a short while, we moved into the forester's house with many other people. The ranger housed as many people as he could. I can't remember his face, only that he and his wife were helpful and kind. Years later we would regularly go on a trip to Irrtenberg in the summer and visit them. We were not hungry.

We were under strict orders to lie down flat on the ground as soon as we heard a low-flying plane approaching. We played outside on the meadow and nobody was hurt.

Then the Americans came. A few 'clever' villagers placed some tree trunks on the roads as barriers – a ridiculous idea as they were no obstacle for the tanks! In addition, it was completely unnecessary. The Americans were friendly to us, especially the children. They gave us chocolate and chewing gum and the first oranges of our life.

In the day time, my parents were, I assume, in Würzburg and we had every freedom until they returned in the evening. This included smoking cigarillos in the ditch by the road until we were feeling sick.

Back in Würzburg, the Gerths were allocated two rooms in an undamaged house. 'This was the end of our freedom. The owners behaved in a hideous way and we had to creep on tiptoes through the house'. Brother Ernst returned, 'fortunately uninjured'. Then aunt Eva, Erich Gerth's widow, with her four children came from Rome.[44]

We suffered great hardship which I as a five-year-old could not fully comprehend, but sensed nevertheless. Würzburg presented a ghostly vision. Streets lined with ruins, mountains of rubble wherever you looked. There was a lack of water due to damaged water pipes. Fetching water in buckets and canisters from a public water pipe at restricted times became part of a daily ritual. Whingeing was not allowed!

Ernst went to Nürnberg, the first intact university in Franconia/Bavaria having completed the so-called Notabitur, 'Emergency A-levels', during the war. Both

---

44 These are memories of a long time ago. It is possible that Eva Gerth's visit to Wurzburg was some time after the war ended.

Christa-Maria's sisters attended the boarding school of the 'Angelic Young Ladies' in Bad Kissingen.

Life went on somehow. Everything was 'passed on' – shoes, dresses, coats, all second-hand. Then food tokens were introduced. We were never starving, but a roll, warmed up in the oven for breakfast on a Sunday was a rare highlight. And black marketing was flourishing. Even I noticed that. Women of Würzburg were standing on mountains of rubble and chipping bricks for re-use. These were the legendary Trümmerfrauen, 'Rubble Women', wearing aprons and head scarves.

Much of the family conversation concerned regaining their wealth. Georg was not allowed to work initially because, as a naval officer, his membership of the Nazi Party had been required. His process of de-Nazification took several months.

Entnazifizierung, 'De-Nazification', was an Allied initiative to rid German and Austrian society, culture, press, economy, judiciary, and politics of any remnants of the National Socialist ideology. Nazi Party members were removed from positions of power and influence. The Allies and the United States in particular [which controlled Würzburg] began to lose interest in the programme, and it was carried out in an increasingly lenient and lukewarm way until being officially abolished in 1951. The American government soon came to view the program as ineffective and counterproductive. Additionally, the program was hugely unpopular in Germany and was opposed by the new West German government.[45]

However, Maria could work and she restarted the wine wholesale business immediately in adverse circumstances on the plot of the Old University. Of course, Georg did work, quietly, for his wife. During this 'grey' period, Christa-Maria went everywhere with her almost unknown father and, as a six-year-old, gradually developed a close relationship with him. For three months, they walked the woods, told stories, read books, which included a personal present of a poetry book into which favourite poems were copied. The Gerths were given the chance to extend a barn in the *Josefshof*, 'Joseph's Court', on the outskirts of Würzburg as their home. They were surrounded by fields, cattle, and many German refugees who had come from the east.

---

45   wikipedia.

We all went to school, three quarters of an hour one way, past the American barracks. On Fridays, when they got alcohol, I was sometimes a bit afraid as I had to walk alone for the last bit of my school route. I often ran rather than walked. Because there were only a few intact schools, teaching was organised in shifts, sometimes in the morning, sometimes in the afternoon, and the teachers, who were mostly of the older generation, demanded strict discipline. By hitting my fingers with the ruler, they forced me who was originally left-handed to use my right hand for writing.

Georg was eventually allowed to work again. He managed the Leinecker wholesale food business. Slowly things improved everywhere. Blocks of flats were built replacing the ruins. Social housing became the order of the day for many years.

I also remember the currency reform. The newly allocated money was spread out on the big dining table, the D-Mark. We could get cream and fruit and rolls! Pure paradise. Many things had also been lost irretrievably in the war, but my family was fortunate that no family member had been killed.

Georg and Maria steadily rebuilt their life and business. All Gerth's landscape paintings with almost all of the family belongings were lost in the bombing. Gerth rekindled his interest in philosophy and Zen Buddhism. He read extensively; many of his books are still on Christa-Maria's shelves. He enjoyed ice cream, loved a cigar, a glass of red wine, had a Meerschaum pipe, and, perhaps harking back to his u-boat days, a caged canary. The Leinecker business prospered, eventually owning four wholesale premises, two in Würzburg, and one each in Dortmund and Hildesheim, one of them managed briefly by a swindler.

Georg gradually cut back on work in the 1950s; he had the first touches of cancer. He kept in touch with his shipmates, especially from Crew '07. Their old comrades association worked hard to organise annual meetings and to send out regular newsletters many of which survive in the admiralty records at Freiburg.[46] In 1953, Gerth wrote from Würzburg that his health was 'not quite up to scratch any more'. His wife worked from early to late in her own business. His son, Ernst supported Georg at Leinecker's. His three daughters all still attended school, the oldest about to do her *Abitur*.

---

46   Freiburg, MSG 2/18640, Crew 1907, Notes (1909-1978).

'Georg is very happy about every visit he receives from ex-crew visitors. He will try to visit 'Braune' in late autumn in Flensburg, take part in a crew meeting in Hamburg and afterwards be taken to Lüneburg.'[47]

Next year, Gerth was critically ill with several operations and 'endless stays in hospital'.[48] Flensburg was 'off'. His 'enjoyment of life had been dampened for years by the illness within him, but after his convalescence he hoped to return stronger than before'. In 1957, he pulled out of the 50th Crewfest.[49] Two years later, Gerth wrote that he was feeling better again, but that he wanted to finally retire.[50] In 1962, he announced the wedding of his son Ernst with Miss Winni Ritter in Braunschweig.[51] Messages through the 1960s spoke increasingly and briefly about the effects of illness.[52] He lived at home 'like a hermit'.[53]

Maria died three months before Georg, but he was not told. For the last three years, he did not speak and lived in total silence, slept on a mattress on the floor kept in by side supports; suffered from dementia and held his newspaper upside down. He was helpless and needed intimate care.

Death has reaped a rich harvest among our crew: On 19 June 1970, our crew sister Frau Maria Gerth died in Würzburg, aged 70. For many years she had cared for her husband who soon after WW2 often suffered from bad health, especially in the last five years in which he was bound to his bed and arm chair.[54] *Suffering become harder year to year for 'Raven Gerth' who died on 13 September, aged 82.*

According to naval custom, the senior living member of each annual Crew wrote the obituary.[55] In Gerth's case, this was the legendary Werner 'Fips'Fürbringer, who died aged ninety-one in 1982 in Brunswick, one of the most successful WW1 u-boat commanders, sinking 102 ships.[56]

---

47 Message sheet No. 10, p. 2, 8/8/1953.
48 Message sheet No. 12, p. 1, 24/6/1954.
49 Message sheet No. 19, p. 1, 15/4/1957.
50 Message sheet No. 25, p. 2, 6/10/1959.
51 Message sheet No. 31, p. 2, 14/5/1962.
52 Message sheets No. 34, p. 3, 25/8/1963; No. 38, p. 3, 2/9/1965; No. 40, p. 2, 8/11/1966; No. 44, p. 2, 20/4/1968.
53 Interview, Christa-Maria Gerth, 15/11/2106.
54 Message sheet No. 51, p. 1, 3/12/1970.
55 Wegener, *Naval Strategy*, p. li.
56 *Cuxhaven*, Obituary, 11/2016.

Fürbringer was in command of *UB 110* in the Flanders Flotilla at the same time as Gerth's service. On 19 July 1918 off the coast of Scarborough his u-boat was damaged by depth charges, forced to surface, and rammed by the destroyer HMS *Garry*. Fips was captured. Fürbringer alleged that, after the sinking, HMS *Garry* hove to and opened fire with revolvers and machine guns on the unarmed survivors. During the ensuing massacre, Fürbringer watched the skull of an 18-year-old member of his crew being split open by a lump of coal hurled by a Royal Navy sailor. The shooting only ceased when the convoy the destroyer had been escorting, and which contained many neutral-flagged ships, arrived on the scene.

Fürbringer later recalled, 'As if by magic the British now let down some life boats into the water.'[57] Twenty-three members of the crew died during the sinking and the alleged ensuing massacre. Lieutenant Commander Charles Lightoller, who was the most senior officer to survive the sinking of the *Titanic*, was awarded a bar to his Distinguished Service Cross for the sinking of *UB 110*. During the next war, Lightoller took his 'little ship', a small motor yacht, to the Dunkirk evacuation and brought back over 120 British servicemen.

Fürbringer wrote of Gerth, 'always the burning cigar between his fingers and the red wine in the background ... he spread a special atmosphere of comfort and was always open for any humour ... Gerth was reliable with high intellectual abilities, unshakable calm, and his personal style nominated him as a high-quality person and an outstanding officer ... he was highly popular and commanded maximum respect among his companions ... Way too early, his heavy suffering captured him. Only rarely, when you visited him at the end, did the memories light up his eyes'.

---

57   Fürbringer, *Legendary*, pp. 118-21.

18
LONG ARM OF THE WAR

1917: Insulting the cavalry

Cavalry officers can be sensitive. After the crew of *UC 61* were successfully escorted to the Calais Citadel on 26 July 1917 that might have been the end of their involvement, another small job concluded in four years of war.

However, imagination was fired; elements of the Belgian Press were anxious to gain renown for their fighting forces. What had been a simple support role rapidly turned into something much more significant. Within a few weeks, the 5th Regiment of Lancers had actually brought the crew ashore. From there it was only a small step to a story that spread around the world of how a u-boat had been captured by the Belgian cavalry: 'Quand la Cavalerie belge captura un sous-marin allemande'.[1]

There was already considerable antipathy among infantry regiments to the cavalry of all of the Allies. Originally intended to wait behind the front lines until the infantry achieved a bloody breakthrough, the plan at the start of the war was for the fast-moving horsemen to pour through the gap, fight gloriously with sword and lance, and cause havoc in the enemy's rear. The trouble was that there were few gaps and, in any event, when there was one it could not be charged by horses because of the mud, shell holes, trenches and barbed wire.

---

1   1914-1918.be/insolite_sous_marin.php.

The reputation of the cavalry was made worse in several ways. The cavalry, always the senior regiment and, perhaps with a certain arrogance, rode everywhere. Their units demanded precedence on the road, often leaving badly-needed foot soldier reinforcements waiting their turn at crossroads.

Forage was the largest item by weight shipped from England to France, exceeding 'even ammunition' and it probably took 'more shipping space than was lost to German submarines'.[2] During the war, channel transports carried 5,916,104 tons of oats and hay, cavalry fodder by no means accounting for the total, while the amount of ammunition was 5,296,302 tons. By 1917 and the stranding of *UC 61*, many cavalry regiments on both sides of the front line were reduced to providing mounted infantry to plug gaps that were desperate and dangerous rather than to charge through them. Ludendorff declared that by 1916 'trench warfare offered no scope for cavalry'.[3]

Cavalry regiments, like the Belgian lancers, invariably took their rest and recreation far away from the front at a safer and more relaxed seaside, especially where there were wide beaches to exercise the horses. So it was for the 5th Regiment at Wissant.

Quickly, after the arrival of *UC 61*, all the lancer units of the Belgian cavalry were given the life-time soubriquet, 'Submarines'.[4]

In October 1917, infantrymen of a company of the 11th Regiment of the Line treated a squadron of the 3rd Lancers, innocent parties all, with ironic comments, perceived as insults, 'se plaignant des injures', as they paused on the road giving way to the cavalrymen. The commander of the lancers complained to his opposite number, General Jules Marie Alphonse Jacques, 1st Baron Jacques de Dixmuide.[5] General Jacques founded Albertville in the Congo in 1894 and was one of those whose colonial behaviour was questioned by the British. From early in 1917, Jacques commanded the 3rd Belgian Army division and was credited by the Belgian government with preventing Dixmuide from falling to the Germans for which feat he was elevated to Baron.[6]

---

2 *Statistical Abstract of Information*, Imperial War Museum, 1919, quoted in Marquis of Anglesey, *History of the British Cavalry*, Vol. 8, pp. 286-87. See also Liddell Hart, *First World War*, pp. 61-62.
3 Ludendorff, *Own Story*, Vol. 1, p. 457.
4 *Royal Museum of the Armed Forces and of Military History*, Brussels, AU 9089/2, p. 108. See also 4th Regiment HQ correspondence (Box 308, 26/7/1917).
5 Letter 31/10/1917, Baecken, *Historique du 5° régiment*, p. 131.
6 Compare the achievements of Frenchman Pierre Ronarc'h in the same battle.

On hearing of the 'insults' to the lancers, Jacques 'immediately ordered a strict investigation' to find the culprits. 'Express orders' were given to 'avoid the repeat of similar events which I myself, as much as yourself, regret and which can affect the good relations between brothers-in-arms'.

The investigation found that an infantry soldier had shouted 'Submarines' at the passing lancers. He claimed it was a 'simple joke' and was not meant to be 'offensive to the cavalry'. If the soldier had realised that he might be misunderstood he would have shouted, 'Here are the conquerors of submarines.' However, the lancers needed greater appeasement. The soldier was placed in solitary confinement for four days and deducted twelve days of war pay supplement. The lieutenant in command of the infantry company was given six days of simple arrest for 'not immediately suppressing the discourteous act and for not reporting it to his senior officers'. A punishment of eight days' confinement to the camp area was given to the adjutant 'as commander of a platoon exercising on a road, leaving his troops at rest while a squadron of cavalry passed, and when one of his men was discourteous to this detachment did not find out the name of the culprit so as to inform his company commander'.

1920: Salvaging the scrap

War over, the pieces of *UC 61* settled slowly into the Wissant sand and became a minor tourist attraction. Children played on and around the wreck. The serious matter of responsibility for the scrap needed to be decided. In 1920, M. R. Mazerat for the Navy Ministry wrote to the Vice Admiral, Commander in Chief of the Maritime Prefecture at Cherbourg, explaining the position:

> *Following the various notes you have sent concerning the German submarine UC 61 grounded at Wissant, I bring to your attention [the fact that] this vessel is strictly speaking neither a wreck nor the spoils of war; it is military equipment abandoned by the enemy. All the same, given the little value that remains in the hull of UC 61 as all the useful parts have already been taken off by the Navy, I consider that it is advisable to pass it to the Administrator of the Maritime Area in Calais who will take charge of it as a wreck and will dispose of it as necessary.*[7]

---

7   Letter 22/5/1920, Bundle 70-75 (*SHD*, Cherbourg, Box MV SS Gr 43), p. 70.

Disposal began in the form of M. Charlemagne Honvault, citizen of Wissant, who, it may be remembered, was on duty on the morning of July 1917 at the nearest semaphore and customs post to where *UC 61* stranded. It was Honvault, national hero Coastguard 2nd class Stanislas Pierre Louis Serin, and the unnamed shrimp girl who first spotted the submarine, who combined to alert the authorities. The wreck remained since stranding in the same place on the beach and was quickly auctioned off in 1920 under the auspices of the *Inscription Maritime*, the 'Naval Register'. It was bought for 1,500 francs by Honvault who accepted the task of removal.[8]

In truth, Honvault's intent was not so much removal, but the collection of 'large quantities' of bronze and copper. He intended to use *Melinite* explosive to expose *UC 61*'s interior.[9]

Honvault was an hotelier, restaurateur and seller of timber salvaged from wrecks. He died in 1920, the same year as his purchase of *UC 61*. Honvault's son, Maurice Charlemagne Honvault managed the demolition in 1928.[10] In 2006, local diver Alain Richard tracked down Charlemagne's grandson, Lucien, still living in Wissant, and confirmed details of the story with Lucien's wife, Léone.[11] Honvault apparently recovered a significant amount of worthwhile metal from the wreck although there do not seem to be any figures. The family still operates a restaurant in Rue Gambetta in Wissant in 2017. Perhaps, the establishment might be renamed, or a least sub-titled, *Restaurant UC 61* in recognition of the u-boat's possible contribution to its development.

There was a surprise in store for Maurice and his workforce when they began their investigation of the wreck. They found a bronze torpedo launcher containing a self propelled torpedo, four metres long and 'weighing around 500-600 kilos'. It was live.[12]

---

8   Chatelle, *Calais Pendant La Guerre*, pp. 163-65.
9   Picric acid was the first high explosive nitrated organic compound widely considered suitable to withstand the shock of firing in conventional artillery. In 1885, based on research by Hermann Sprengel, a French chemist, Eugène Turpin patented the use of pressed and cast picric acid in blasting charges and artillery shells. In 1887, the French government adopted a mixture of picric acid and guncotton under the name *Melinite*. In 1888, Britain started manufacturing a similar mixture in Lydd, Kent, under the name *Lyddite* (wikipedia).
10   Richard, Coulon and Lowrey, 'L'odyesée de 5 sous marins allemands', *Sucellus*, pp. 61-85.
11   Conversation with Alain Richard at Wissant, 18/7/2016.
12   *Le Miroir*, 'On découvre une torpille dans l'épave du sous-marin allemand échoué à Wissant', 'A torpedo discovered in the wreck of the German submarine beached at Wissant', 30/6/1928 (*SHD*, Cherbourg, Box MV SS Gr 43).

UC 61 carried eighteen mines and five self propelled torpedoes. Two of the torpedoes were fired by commander Georg Gerth in his attempt to lighten the submarine and were later collected from the sea. Two more were salvaged from the wreck by the French military. The last torpedo, together with ten of the mines in buckled shafts, was left on board because a two-day storm sank *UC 61* one and a half metres into the sand and made removal impossible. After an experimental Belgian mortar produced a 'huge explosion', the wreck was raised in the air and turned. Everyone present believed that the remaining munitions had been destroyed.

Another French hero entered centre stage to save the day. An 'honourable fellow citizen', M. Carton, a retired head Artificer, offered to defuse the torpedo 'on a voluntary basis'. During the war, Artificer Carton of Calais trained and educated military teams in the defusing of bombs, torpedoes, shells and mines. In 1928, he still travelled to areas outside Calais and Boulogne to carry out his 'painstaking and dangerous work for love of his trade'.

The newspaper, *Le Miroir*, continues the story,

> *The torpedo was removed from the tube and it was decided to destroy it. To carry out this dangerous operation, it was necessary to move the lethal bomb to the foot of the cliffs at Blanc Nez. However, this was a most difficult operation. In effect, nobody wanted to lend a hand. Only a sailor from Wissant, M. Pourre, known as Mont Blanc, was prepared to help. M. Cousin from Sangatte offered his wagon. But it still needed a driver. This was how M. Leon Fournier, a man of private means living at rue de l'Amiral-Courbet, Calais, agreed to stand-in. Accompanied by these two men, Carton took the torpedo to the foot of the cliff and proceeded to destroy it. Thanks to his technical knowledge and dexterity, this operation was carried out in an excellent manner.*

According to Carton, says the newspaper, there were still two unexploded torpedoes in the wreck of the submarine. This theory was clearly laid to rest as Honvault continued to work with his *Melinite*.

> *This new exploit pays tribute to our courageous fellow citizen who, during the war, proceeded to defuse all the aerial bombs falling on the town and submarine mines gathered up off Calais. We heartily congratulate M. Carton for this new exploit, which adds to the already long and extensive list of similar exploits, in hoping that*

one day the Government will be able to reward as it suits them the selfless devotion of this brave servant of the pyrotechnic art.

1920 onwards: Tourist attraction

In the following years, the u-boat appeared as the focus of souvenir items sold in Wissant's tourist shops.[13] It was mentioned in war books and articles and became popular on the internet because of its 'capture' by the Belgian cavalry. A wash painting of *UC 61* on the beach featured in a 1920 book, *La Guerre Navale Racontée par Nos Amiraux*. In 1996, Robert Chaussois, in an edition of the regional newspaper *La Voix du Nord*, summarised the history of the u-boat comparing it to a North Korean submarine stranded on a South Korean beach.[14] The end of *UC 61* is cited by Gallois (1984), Gonsseaume (1988) and Dufossé (2002, 2014).[15]

1958: Exhibiting a compressor head

In 1958, there was another *UC 61* surprise, when a 'compressor head' from the submarine mounted on a wooden frame was presented by a M. Pierre de Hauteclocque to the Belgian 4th Lancers.[16] The presentation prompted some small mysteries.

Was the piece really a 'compressor head'? Its function remains uncertain. It stands about 350cm high and is heavy enough to need two hands to carry it. It is stamped to work with pressures between 160 and 225 atmospheres and therefore needed to be robust. It is seriously crumpled which was likely caused by an explosion and this makes its lettering difficult to read. There is a letter 'M' with a crown on top [Imperial navy = Marine?]; the part word 'SAUER' [probably *sauerstoff*, oxygen]; and the maker's name, the Maschinenfabrik

---

13   A souvenir low-value envelope knife was recently found at the home of the Honvault family. It carries the legend, 'Souvenir du sous-marin Allemande échoué à Wissant 26 juillet 1917'.
14   Chaussois, 'Le cigare naviguait trop près de la cote', *La Voix du Nord*, 6-7/10/1996.
15   Philippe Gallois, 'Le Wissant d'hier et ses environs', *SI de Wissant – site des 2 Caps* (Print Forum, Lille 1984), p. 153. Christian Gonsseaume, Naufrages et fortunes de mer, Book 2 (Amis du Musée de la Marine d'Étaples, 1988), p. 285. Franck Dufossé, *Wissant, des origines aux années 1930* (AMA, 2002), p. 203; *Wissant 1914-1918* (Art et Histoire de Wissant, Mairie de Wissant 2014).
16   Guido Mathieu, custodian, Museum Cabour WOII & 2/4 Lansiers, Moeresteenweg 141, 8660 Adinkerke, Belgium.

Ges. [*Gesellschaft*, Company) Gelsenkirchen. The Berlin Sauerstoff Company merged with Gelsenkirchener Maschinenfabrik in 1905 and became known as Westfalia Maschinenfabrik. Westfalia produced oxygen rescue apparatus and regenerators for submarines during WW1.

David Townsend, the submarine technical export who contributed earlier to the review of *UC 61*'s stranding, commented, 'I have not been able to find an equivalent in allied boats other than the possibilities of a compressed air reservoir for a pressurised water system, an internal blowing tank to pressurise a compartment in event of flooding, or, if pure oxygen, a reserve breathing apparatus.' Commander Chris Phillips suspected that 'as it specifically mentions *sauerstoff*, it could be for adding oxygen to the atmosphere in the boat to allow for longer periods dived'.

There is some confusion about the origin of the exhibit. One report says that it was recovered from the beach in 1917 on the day of stranding and was blown out when the Germans set off their bombs which ruptured and set fire to their craft.

Another story suggests it was a remnant from the Belgian mortar experiments of a few months after stranding and which sent a cloud of material thirty metres into the air.

Yet another thought is that is was found by Honvault during his salvage. One imagines, however, that if it was found by Honvault it would have been sold for scrap value.

Another tale is that Hauteclocque, a Frenchman and 'owner' of the exhibit, was serving in Africa in the 1950s alongside a detachment of 4th Lancers when he found out the background to the lancers' 'Submarines' name, and decided to make a gift of the memento. A version of this latter explanation seems most likely. Pierre de Hauteclocque was a member of the French Foreign Legion and a cousin of the celebrated WW2 French military leader Maréchal Leclerc de Hauteclocque.[17] Pierre de Hauteclocque saw service in Norway, England with Charles de Gaulle, battles at Dakar, Koufra, El Alamein and in Syria. He also served in Madagascar, Morocco and Indo-China, ending his career in, again, Morocco. He left the army as a lieutenant-colonel in 1958, the year he donated the 'compressor' to the Belgian lancers.[18]

---

17 wikipedia.
18 Pierre de Hauteclocque married Nicole de Saint-Denis, an important member of the French resistance in WW2, receiving the Croix de Guerre, and later a prominent politician in Paris.

The 'compressor' is now on display at a small, but excellent, *Museum Cabour WOII & 2/4 Lansiers* in De Panne, Adinkirke, in Belgium where Guido Mathieu is a most helpful and knowledgeable custodian.[19] The museum is also home for the trophies of the now combined 2/4th Lancers.[20] As the *UC 61* crew was escorted by the 5th Lancers, the exhibit's plaque is wrongly attributed and is also wrong in its commemoration of a u-boat capture as, according to the French Naval Ministry, *UC 61* was not captured, but rather abandoned. The exhibit is a cuckoo in the museum's nest, although a most interesting one.

1991 and 2008: English memorabilia

About 1991, Tomas Termote, the underwater archaeologist quoted throughout this book, was pursuing his hobby of metal detecting through the magazine *Treasure Hunting*. He read an article from a detectorist in Devon or Cornwall in England: 'I cannot exactly remember where.' The detectorist sought more information on a low-quality copper ring he had found in a field which carried the inscription 'U-61 Wissant August 1917'.[21] The ring is now with Termote.[22]

The u-boat number is wrong, but there can be no doubt it refers to *UC 61*. It seems likely that the ring was made from a piece of copper pipe taken from the wreck during an August visit. This rules out one of the crew as its maker because the month is later than the crew's capture, the identifier is wrong, and the crew left the site immediately in July. Most probably it was made by a British seaman who visited the wreckage on the beach and picked out a souvenir piece of piping, made the ring and it was subsequently lost it when taken to England.

The English West Country connection continues. In 2008, at a local flea market in Somerset, Geoff Pringle bought a carved wooden lifeboat plaque from the SS *Broomhill*.[23] The *Broomhill*, a 1,700-ton collier bound from Penarth to Sheerness, was sunk on 9 May 1917 by *UC 61*.[24] Two brothers from Caernarvonshire were killed. The eighteen surviving crew rowed to Weymouth

---

19 www.depanne.be/product/1083/museum-cabour-wo-ii-en-24-lansiers.
20 Museum Cabour WOII & 2/4 Lansiers, Moeresteenweg 141, 8660 Adinkerke; +32 58 42 97 53.
21 Email, Termote, 17/8/2016.
22 Termote, *Krieg Unter Wasser*, p. 318.
23 Emails, Pringle, 29/2/2016.
24 *TNA*: ADM 137/1296; ADM 137/2692; ADM 137/4114.

in their single lifeboat. The nameplate was likely a memory piece for a safe return. Pringle's business, oldnautibits, sold the item quickly.²⁵

> *Sadly, it came with no history so I really can't add anything to the research I did at the time. Looking at the paintwork and ageing to the varnish, etc, I am sure it is as we have described and a period item. Seeing the Broomhill was lost in Lyme Bay, it is reasonable to assume the rescued crew members were landed after their ordeal in the West Country. It looks as though it may have had a paper label on the back at some stage which might well have confirmed the provenance but sadly nothing to read when we bought it.*

2014: Safeguarding surfers

The wreck of *UC 61* disappeared as the Wissant sands were moved around by fast tides and channel storms. However, local diver Alain Richard knew there was always the likelihood that it would reappear some day. 'We have seen the remains of the English trawler *Lord Grey* which was wrecked the same year as *UC 61* and which are still visible at the bottom of the foreshore to the southwest of the beach of Wissant, at Châtelet.'²⁶

A survey conducted by SHOM in 1977 found that the wreck of *UC 61* was buried under the sand northeast of Wissant beach, towards Strouanne, to the right of Herlen Creek. The wreck site was deleted in 1985 following a general revision of SHOM charts.²⁷ After storms at the beginning of 2014 and high tides that March, wrecks reappeared along this stretch of coast including SS *Socotra*, south of Le Touquet, and the remains of the *UC 61*.²⁸

Mme. Laurette Maquignon was alerted of the reappearance by beach walkers. She reported its rediscovery and notified DRASSM, the *Département*

---

25   Item 4377, oldnautibits.com.
26   *Lord Grey*, trawler, lost 2 December 1917 (www.naval-history.net/WW1LossesBrRNA-L.htm, accessed April 2016). SHOM reference 21601059.
27   SHOM is the *Service d'Hydrologie et d'Océanographie de la Marine* – the French Navy Hydrology and Oceanography Service which edits all French sea charts. It is also responsible for the management of wrecks. SHOM wreck record 21601056, coordinates 50° 53'614 N - 1° 39'865 E (Euro 50) was invalidated in 1985.
28   On 26 November 1915, the British steamer SS *Socotra* ran aground off Le Touquet, France, while en route from Brisbane to London with general cargo (wrecksite.eu/wreck.aspx?2911), accessed 8/4/2016.

des Recherches Archéologiques Subaquatiques et Sous-Marins, and the GPD, a divers' clearance group. Maquignon also discovered on the beach some 'Rommel Piles' that presented explosion hazards.[29]

Alain Richard was appointed by DRASSM to investigate the wreck as it was a possible danger to surfers who practised at Wissant. He was also to pinpoint and to measure the site and to make safety recommendations. He found *UC 61* in two parts within a few metres of each other at the limit of the supervised beach swimming areas.[30]

After the survey, four buoys were installed to warn the surfers. Then the wreck disappeared again. The author with co-researcher and interpreter Jacqui Squire visited the site under the direction of Richard at low water on an ice-cream and shorts evening in July 2016 to find, against predictions, that *UC 61* had resurfaced.[31] The visit therefore allowed assessments to be made of the u-boat's original position on wrecking using contemporary photographs and also assessed probable firing angles to the hole in *UC 61*'s conning tower. *UC 61* stranded parallel to the dunes and facing Cap Gris Nez. Site measurements confirmed that the cannon had been fired from the sea and, therefore, while *UC 61* was at sea.

2016: Parisien watering hole

In 2016 in Paris, a new cocktail bar opened in the Rue de l'Arc de Triomphe.[32] Its grey, always locked front door is in an uninspiring street setting. Access is gained by ringing a bell, but requires a combination of inquisitiveness and determination. Inside is unobtrusive and welcoming. The bar is long and

---

29   Underwater constructions to prevent landing craft gaining a French beach during an invasion by the Allies in WW2.
30   One section measured 4.35m by 2.55m with a height of 0.70m, lying to the northeast in the direction of Blanc-Nez at a point 50° 53'557 N - 1° 39'793 E. It is not far from the wreck point cancelled by SHOM 21601056. The co-ordinates on a Euro 50 tracking device processed on WGS 84 gave 50° 53'564 N - 1° 39'785 E. The second section lies towards Wissant and extends for 11.60m; the largest width is at the centre, 3.60m, while at each end the width is no more than 2,70m. In WGS 84 points, the average position is 50° 53'551 N - 1° 39'780 E (DRASSM report OA 2533, No, 2014-105).
31   18/7/2016.
32   uc-61.com.

narrow, the rough size and shape of the interior of a WWI submarine. The cocktails are good.[33]

> *UC-61 is the new venue by the guys behind 'La Conserverie'.*[34] *This tiny bar boasts a slightly quirky German submarine theme with various nautical bits and pieces, even a 'captain's quarters'. It's an easy place to miss. Hidden away on a quiet street with virtually no external signage and a buzzer you'll need to ring to gain entry. You could walk right past it. But that would be a mistake. It's a hip yet relaxed place with some great cocktails. The prices are on the high side, but they are reflected in the quality and the bar attracts slightly more savvy and sophisticated people who know their cocktails and value good service. The atmosphere reflects this, convivial yet elegant, the kind of place you can have a conversation while savouring your drinks and these are drinks to savour.*[35]

But why chose the name '*UC-61*'? Here is the email response of the founder, Eric Bulteau, who specialises in restaurant and cocktail bar start-ups:

> *Apart from memories of a small boy who played on the remains of UC 61, we have no direct links with this boat. Its unusual story inspired us and the bar space has implicitly guided the choice of name. We have no intent to develop a 'museum' effect. The illusion is sufficient. Customers are ready to play the game and to try to find out what is hiding behind this enigmatic symbol 'UC-61' on the outside door. So, it is possible to combine 'history' and 'a good drink'. Who would have thought it!*[36]

2016: Würzburger Torte

Georg and Maria Gerth's son, Ernst, became a professor of economics, published several books, and emigrated to California. His last address in 1995 was thirty minutes drive from his aunt Eva Gerth's last address in the same county.[37] There were many contacts and get togethers between Ernst and Eva, and also her four children.

---

33   Visit 12/10/2016.
34   The bar '*La Conserverie*' has now been relaunched as '*Le Fou*'.
35   worldsbestbars.com/bar/paris/champs-elysees/uc-61.
36   Private email, Eric Bulteau, 17/8/2106.
37   US Social Security Applications and Claims Index (ancestry.com).

Georg and Maria's two eldest daughters, Ilse and Hedwig, lived together in Kiel after widowhood and both died in 2016. Christa-Maria stayed with her family until the Leinecker wholesale shops were sold. Later, it was her 'duty' to work in the family coffee shop. After her parents died and she was freed from their care, Christa-Maria made a remarkable life as a sculptress, potter, translator, historian, and developed a renowned *Kaffe und Kuchen* shop, where her *Würzburger Torte* was held in high regard. She has two sons who live nearby. Her most treasured possession are the books on philosophy left by her father; his most precious gift is her commitment to Buddhism.

2016: Annoying young mothers

Back on Wissant beach, two young mothers shepherd their children away from the small pieces of wreck of *UC 61*. Their annoyance is briefly overheard,

> *Whoever put that dangerous metal there on a beach for toddlers? Who would have thought anyone could be so selfish? What on earth were they thinking of?*

2017: Une lecture erronée[38]

> *When we were on the beach on 26 July, I had noticed that the presumed location of the wreck seemed to me to be a lot further than previously!! In fact, my GPS was giving a faulty reading with an error of 200/1000 minutes on the latitudinal coordinates: it was this that led us about 300 metres beyond the estimated position of the wreck!*
>
> *Since then I have done another re-positioning with a new GPS, which conforms closely to the previous data. The rear of the wreck (much less visible) towards Cap Blanc Nez is at 50° 53' 556N - 1° 39' 794E. The central point, corresponding to the starboard side of the submarine is at 50° 53' 551N 1° 39' 782E. The far ends towards Cap Blanc Nez are at 50° 53' 552N - 1° 39' 785E, the other end towards the south is at 50° 53' 550N - 1° 39' 778E.*
> *Alain Richard*

---

[38] Private email, Alain Richard, 6/9/2017.

2017: Centenary thank-you

On 26 July 2017, some twenty archivists, historians, translators, enthusiasts and family members who had helped piece together the Gerths' story were invited to attend a day-long centenary event at Wissant where Georg Gerth stranded *UC 61* one hundred years before. Attendees, vicarious u-boat travellers all, came from Belgium, France, Germany and the UK.

Pride of place went to Frau Christa-Maria Gerth, the last-surviving child of Georg Gerth, and her two sons, Franz and Frédéric who travelled from Bavaria for their first visit to the area. Other important guests were Alain Richard, diver and u-boat wreck historian and writer, who produced the 1977 wreck report on *UC 61* for the Service d'Hydrologie et d'Océanographie de la Marine, and his wife Ingrid, who was then curating the travelling exhibition 'La Grande Guerre sous La Mer', which dealt with wrecks of the first world war, many of them u-boats, on the Opal Coast.

The *UC 61* commemorative party met in the morning inside Wissant Town Hall where to the hour one hundred years before, the crew were stripped of the personal documents (but allowed to keep their bread and sausage) and received their first cursory interrogations. These documents were recently found in Paris and photographs of them were shared with the party.

Everyone then walked along the beach to the wreck site which was found using GPS and a metal detector. The wreck rises and falls within its covering of tidal sand. It was visible last autumn, but on this anniversary visit was under 1.5 metres of sand. Here, on the exact spot, in the sunshine, the circumstances of the grounding were discussed. Two weeks later, like a good submarine, *UC 61* had risen again.

The group then had lunch in a nearby restaurant when they were joined by town dignitaries and historians. About 100 pictures associated with the crew and the stranding were played on a looped slide show as a wall background. Commemorative t-shirts were distributed. Some of the party then drove the twenty kilometres from Wissant to Calais Citadel, mostly following the route walked by the crew under its guard of Belgian lancers. At the Citadel, the main interrogations and first imprisonment occurred. Details of the interrogations were shared from original documents found recently in Cherbourg.

That evening, the *Art and History Society of Wissant* managed a conference, 'La mission inachevée de l'UC-61', which was attended by almost 200 people.[39]

Christa-Maria Gerth was introduced by the society's president, M. Jean-Marie Ball, to a round of applause. Lieutenant-Colonel Henri Lesoin outlined the course of the naval war in the North Sea and the Channel with emphasis on the submarine war. Dr Chris Heal was then invited to give a presentation, with live interpretation by Jacqui Squire, on four points: a description of the last voyage, theories on the reason for the stranding with emphasis on the cannon hole found in the conning tower; the secrets of the wreck; and the fate of the crew, three of whom died during imprisonment, while the rest were held until March 1920.

At the end, local historian, M. Gallois, introduced some documents and photographs about the final life of the wreck which were discovered only the week before.

At the lunch, Christa-Maria Gerth, as a survivor with her father of the loss of their home to WW2 carpet bombing, gave a short, poignant and impromptu speech, interpreted by her eldest son Franz:

Thank you for allowing me to say a few personal words. This hadn't been planned at all, but then I never thought that this event here would touch me so much!

My father - like most men - never talked about the war, neither the first nor the second. I was only affected by the aftermath of WW2 as a child and could talk about this experience. But now here, 100 years later – a lump of iron in the sand, I see a vision of my father in front of me thanks to the research of you all and the photos that have emerged.

A young man, just like his older brother Erich, two years his senior, who joined the Imperial Navy straight after leaving school and then did his service for Kaiser and fatherland. Nobody knows if this was his lifetime dream; personally, I suspect it wasn't for he was a thoroughly philosophical and religious man. He also used the time of his captivity to study the works of the German philosopher Immanuel Kant. He was thirty years old when he stranded here in his submarine and became a French prisoner of war. Thirty strikes me as incredibly young when I look at my son Frédéric who is even six years older than that. My father was treated fairly during captivity – he told me so himself and you have found out that he was also fair in his dealings

---

39 *Memoire d'Opale*, Alain Richard, 'Quatre Épaves', No. 9, 2017, pp. 47-67.

with his crew and his enemies. I'm very glad about this as this is how I knew him in his civil life.

By your work, I have got to know my 'unknown' father. I am grateful for this; unfortunately, so late in my life. My father has been dead for more than thirty years, but you can still have conversations with the dead, this I now know.

I could finish here. But time went on and soon after WW1 followed WW2 - as devastating and cruel as the first one. I remember many things: hastily getting up in the middle of the night and taking refuge in the air raid shelter. Later heaps of rubble, queuing at a public standpipe, housing shortages, playing in the ruins. My home town, Würzburg, one of the most beautiful German cities, was literally reduced to rubble by the English – I'm sorry to say. But there was one of them, an Englishman – I've forgotten his name – who said, 'Stop!' and prevented our Residenz [the Palace of the Prince Bishops] from being totally destroyed. It is now a world heritage site.[40] His courage and his appreciation of values is praised every year on the anniversary of the date of destruction, 16 March 1945.

I cannot comment on the question of guilt. But I know what it means that we have had peace for many years now and I also know how threatened this peace is in our time. I would like to end quoting the words of British Prime Minister Theresa May - 'Enough is enough' - even if she used them in a different context.

Yes, it has been enough, but the fact that we can sit together as friends and talk about the war is a reason to celebrate.

Thank you.

---

40 Frau Gerth can be forgiven a small lapse in memory which confused the 'Englishman' with an American, part of the occupying forces in the area of Würzburg at the end of the war. This unnamed American recognised that while the roof of the *Residenz* was destroyed, the precious wall and ceiling works below were mostly undamaged. He arranged quickly for extensive tarpaulins to be used to act as a makeshift roof and thereby saved the internal structure and its paintings from further damage (Private conversation with Dr Jarl Kremeier, *Die Hofkirche der Würzburger Residenz*, 1999, 1/9/2107).

Appendix 1
CREW OF UC 61 (26 JULY 1917)[1]

Officers

Gerth, Georg Carl, 29, Kapitänleutnant, Active, born 3/3/1888 Berlin
3/4/1907 cadet entry; 10/1915 u-boat school; Bremen 12/1916; Commander *UB 12*, joined *UC 61* 12/1916; POW, released 3/1920. Court of enquiry Bremen 9/2/1920. Left naval service 31/1/1921. Died 13/9/1970
POW camps: Montoire 5/5/1917, Boyardville, Carcassonne

Dancker, Karl Otto Hermann, 27, Leutnant, Reserve, born 2/9/1890 Wolfhagen
Officer Hamburg Amerika Linie; in New York, returned on Norwegian ship 1/1915; adjutant *Kaiser Freidrick*: Wetting; submarine school 2/1916; *UC 24* two months. Joined *UC 61* 12/1916
POW camp: Montoire 5/5/1917

Giese, Johannes Waldemar, Ingenieur Leutnant, Active, born 8/3/1891 Berlin
UA 10/1915; Libau 1/1916; seven months on *UB 6*, Flanders Flotilla, left before ran aground 12/3/1917 Maas River, crew interned; *UC 74*; joined *UC 61* at Kiel 11/1916. Gave evidence at court of enquiry 9/2/1920
POW camps: Montoire 5/5/1917, 84

---

1 *Freiburg, Gefangenenkompanie*, 'POW company'; Kp. 150518; RM 20/504 31/3/1919; RM 86/18: RMA 10139, 15.5/1918; Gef. Kp. 100718; ancesrry.com; grandeguerre.icrc.org/en/List/480150/897/24302. Some of the writing on these archival documents is very poor; best efforts have been made.

Deck personnel

Eggers, Max, 21, Seaman, III Marineinfanterieregiment, Active, born 3/1/1896 Grömitz
Next of kin: Heinrich Eggers, Wicheldorfstraße Grömitz, Neustadt Holstein
Seebatallion, Wilhelmshaven 12/1915; Battalion in Bruges 6/1916-5/1917; reserve one month. Joined UC 61 6/1917. First voyage
POW camps: 90, 80B

Ihn, Paul Otto Franz, 22, Seaman, Active, 1/1/1896 Pyritz
Next of kin: Franz Ihn, Rohrsdorf bei Bahn, Pomeranie
Fisherman; Kiel Matrose Division 10/1915-4/1916; *Augusta* to 9/1916; ten weeks signal school, Kiel; ten weeks *Veneta*; *UB 24*; Flanders Flotilla 1/1917. Joined UC 61 28/3/1917; third class passage Hamburg to Winslow via New York, Hamburg-Amerika Line, on *Westphalia*, 6/12/1923
POW camps: 90, 80B.

Koch, Kurt Richard, 19, Seaman, Active, born 26/3/1898 Berlin
Next of kin: Lonia Koch, Kleiststraße, Glasow Kreis, Brandenburg; mother Emilie Alwine Koch
Landsturm-Infanterie-Bataillone, Würzburg II/B/7, joined 6/1915; u-boat volunteer; nine months Lubeck; Freiwilly to 4/1916; Kiel 1st Matrose six months; Freiwilly; UA to 8/1916; Flanders Flotilla reserve. Joined UC 61 3/1917
POW camps: 90, 80B

Lengs, Hubert Gaspar, 30, Steuermann, Reserve, born 16/10/1896 Dortmund
Next of kin: Elisa Lengs, Stirperstraße, Lippstadt
UA 1/1915; Libau; returned winter 1915/16; 2/1916 to Flanders; Kiel training ship *Hertha*; training *Acheron* three months; Flanders Flotilla; ship to Bremen. Joined UC 61 7/1917; first voyage. On watch on stranding, sounding route. Suspected spy with Boulogne currency. Spoke French well
POW camps: Arrived 15/8/1917, 84, 90, Croisset to St Aubin-Epinay 3/9/1917, Serres-Carpentras 30/9/1917

Nagal, Andreas Peter Klaus, 29, Bootsmannsmaat, Active, born 3/2/1888, Krautsand S/Elbe
Next of kin: Wilhelm Nagel, Krautsand S/Elbe, Hanover

Libau 1915, *Kaiser Vilhelm II* to 3/1915, *Kaiser Friedrich III* to 7/1915; 9-12/1916 Wilhelmshaven; Kiel *U11*; *UC 17* to 4/1917, commander Ralph Wenniger sick; reserve personnel to 6/1917. Joined *UC 61* 6/1917
POW camps: 90, 80B, Rouen-Lev
Neumann, Adalbert (Albert), 23, Seaman, Cook, Active, born 22/8/1894 Tolkemit
Next of kin: Albert Neumann, Tolkemit, Prusse Occ
Matrose Division, Kiel, 12/1915-12/1916; *Furst Bismarck* nineteen weeks, UA, *Veneta*, cooking seven weeks, Flanders Flotilla 10/1916; reserve; *UB 40*; UAK Bremen 23/12196-3/1917; three trips to Biscay. Joined *UC 61* 12/1916
POW camps: 90, 80B, 12 (Orval, Ribecourt, Equipes de battage (Oise)
Neumann, Willy, 23, Seaman, Active, born 18/8/94 Soltemin bei Vollin
Next of kin: Albert Neumann, Soltemin bei Vollin
Matrose Division, Wilhelmshaven 8/1915-1/1916; 4/1916 Flanders Flotilla reserve for *UB 12*; joined *UC 61* 12/1916. Died in French captivity 17/10/1917
POW camps: None found
Pucknus, Richars Max, Oberbootsmannsmaat, Loan, born 14/6/1889 Tilsit
Next of kin: Fritz Pucknus, Frischstraße 26, Brunsbüttel (Koog Schleswig Holstein)
Supplement to crew. Month loan from battleship *Schleswig Holstein*. Joined *UC 61* 7/1917
POW camps: 86 to 90 1/3/1917, 84 to 90 15/8/1917, 90 to 13 22/8/1917, Zône to Rouen-Croisset 8/10/1917, Croisset to Dieppe 17/11/1917
Sänger, Willy Hans, 22, Seaman, Active, born 23/4/1896, Graudenz
Next of kin: Frau Z Sänger, Speicherstaße 32, Graudenz
Matrose Division, Kiel, 7/1915, one year, infantry; *UC 11*, Kiel, training ship 7-12/1916; training ship *UB 25*; *U 1* training ship; *U 9*. Joined *UC 61* Bremen 12/16, two months; re-joined 2/1917; two voyages: Biscay, Spain, and 6/1917; two weeks' leave
POW camps: 84, 24
Zäbisch, Franz Karl, 22, Bootsmannsmaat, Active, born 1/11/1895, Gippe (Kisterberg)
Next of kin: Heinrich Zäbisch, Cippe near Kisterberg, Saxony
Joined 1911, Flensburg Training School; 4/1912 *Hertha*; 4/1913 Flensburg; 11/1913 Torpedo Division, Wilhelmshaven; 1/1916 *V106* training ship, Kiel; then *V105*, *V108* to 5/1916. Promoted from Boy. UA 3/1916; 5/1916 *Vineta*;

three trips *UB 11, UC 11*; one trip *UB 10*; *U 38* to Hamburg. Joined *UC 61* at Bremen 11/1916
POW camps: 90, Bureau de renseingnements, Paris

Engine room

Barthold, Paul, 29, PO Second Class, Machinist mate, Reserve, born 12/10/89 Berlin
Next of kin: Mle Inge Balzerson, Flensburg Teichstraße 5, Schleswig Holstein
Volunteer. Braunschweig, one year; Torpedo School, Flensburg, eighteen months; Flanders Flotilla reserve from Kiel 5/1916. In charge electrical apparatus and services engines. Fitting-out party *UC 61* 6/1917
POW camp: 13 (Bellinglise, Coupe-Gueule, St Leger-aux-Bois, Choisy Aux Bac)

Becker, Friedrich, 22, First stoker, Active, born 1/6/1895 Ludwigshafen
1st Werft Division, 1/10/1915, eight months; UA Kiel, three months; training *UB 11, UB 5*; *Acheron*; Ostend Flanders Flotilla reserve 10/1916. Joined *UC 61* Bremen, 12/916. *UC 61* in shelter during Ostend bombardment
POW camp: 84

Bock, Otto, 22, Telegrapher, Ob. Gst, Active, born 4/2/1895, Hoisbüttel
Next of kin: Augusta Bock, Schmalem-becker, Hamburg Staras 18
2nd Werft Division, 1/10/1915, Wilhelmshaven; FelsburgFunk (radio) training school 16/1/1916; UA, 3/8/1916; *UB 12* to 11/1916; reserve to end 2/1917; joined *UC 61* 3/1917
POW camps: Zône des armées 84, Mouy-Bury, SA2

Bodrich, Fritz, 24, PO Second Class, Machinist mate, Active, born 6/12/1892, Seepothen
Next of kin: Frau Rebut, Siegelscheinstaße 3, Elbing, Prusse Occ
1st Werft Division Hesse, 1912; 10/1913 divisional training school six months' theory; *Lotharingen*, four weeks, 10/1914; UA Bremen to 1/1915; *U 3*, three months to 4/1915; Hamburg *UC 7*, eight weeks; Kiel; 8/1915-2/1916 to Flanders Flotilla; B&V shipyard, Hamburg; *UB 39*. Last two u-boats sunk after leaving. Fitting-out party *UC 61*, 11/1916
POW camp: 84

Carstensen, Christian, 23, Stoker, Active, born 27/11/1894, Flensburg
Next of kin: Karl Bostorf, Schloßstraße 44, Flensburg, Schl. Hols.

Kiel, 12/1915; *Furst Bismarck*, stokers' school, 10/1916; UA; Flanders Flotilla; training, *UC 26*, two voyages; Kiel, joined *UC 61* 12/1916. Three notes from Oran found in wallet
POW camp: 84
Gerigk, George, 24, PO Second Class, Machinist mate, Active, born 30/7/1893 Prohlow
Next of kin: Frau Gerigk, Mickelsdorf, Prusse Occ
Torpedo division 1/10/1913, six weeks; one year Werft Division, Kiel; under officer school for torpedoes 1/4-9/1915, Kiel, six weeks. On 'Y' 1915 to 9/1916. Training ships *U1*, *U 2*, *UB 25*, *UB 28*, reserve 10/1916-1/1917; four-five cruises. Fitting-out party, *UC 61*, Kiel 10/1916. No more voyages. Returned 8/7/1917. Gerth 'not best commander'. In charge mines & torpedoes
POW camps: 90, 80B, Pont-Sainte-Maxence, SE5
Goosmann, Franz, 19, Stoker, Machinist trainee, Active, born 3/6/1898 Düsseldorf
Next of kin: Hermann Goosmann, Behrenstraße, Düsseldorf
Freiwilly, volunteer, 3/4/1916; 2nd Werft Division, six months' exercises; UA Kiel end 8/1916, *Acheron*; training school, Flanders Flotilla, 9/1916, *UB 38*; joined *UC 61* Bremen 12/1916. Refused questions
POW camps: 90, 80B
Kleinsorg, Peter, 24, PO I, First machinist mate, Active, born 8/2/1893 Frechen
Next of kin: Bertel Kleinsorg, Frechen
Kiel, 1911, first trip *Wettin*; UA three months training ship *UC 11*; training ship *UC 1*. Fitting-out party, Bremen, *UC 61*, 11/1916. First under officer, Obermaschinemat. Complained of different mechanisms to other UC boats
POW camps: 90, 80B
Naumann, Alfred Ernst Hermann, 23, PO 2, Machinist mate, Active, 15/11/1894 Alt-Neudöbern
Next of kin: Hermann Naumann, Neu Petersheim, Brandenburg
1st Werft Division, Freiwilly, machinenschlosser, 5/1914; 21 months' infantry; SMS *Hessen* 7/1914; Norway; *Grosser Kurfurst*, one year; Mechanics School, Kiel, six months, 1915; 3/1916 UA; course on practical techniques; worked on u-boats at Vulcan yard. UAK, four weeks, *Acheron*; Flanders Flotilla reserve 3 weeks, 6/1916; *UC 6*; *UC 1*, six weeks; Bremen 9/1916. Fitting-out party *UC 61* 12/1916

POW camps: 90, 116 (Villeneuve-s-Fere, Roncheres, Fere-en-Tardenois)
Petersen: No details: Suspect, only found on initial crew interrogation
Raabe, Karl, 21, Stoker, Active, born 8/10/1896 Essen
Next of kin: Wittor Raabe, W Buttmanstraße 34, Essen
Born, 3/10/1896; 1st Werft Division, 1/10/1916-1/1917, eight weeks, infantry course; joined *UC 61*, Kiel, 1/1917. Died in French captivity 23/1/1920
POW camps: 90, 80B
Schindler, Paul Emil, 22 Stoker, Active, Grosse Schlocher, born 9/2/1896 Leipzig
Next of kin: Gustav Schindler, Wiegandstraße 34, Leipzig
Born 9/2/1895; unmarried son of Gustav & Mary Schindler; 1st Werft Division, 1/10/1915-8/1916; reserve Flanders Flotilla; *UB 29*; Bremen; joined *UC 61* 11/96. Died in internment in Davos, 26/7/1918
POW camps: 90 to 25 (Roye Cote, Tilloloy, Rosieres, near to Crépy-en-Valois) 26/8/1917; Seaman's Hospital, Arsenal, Brest (bronchitis) 2/5/1918; Davos-Wiesen, Switzerland
Starke, Wilhelm, 24, Lead stoker, First stoker, Active, born 26/9/1893 Dortmund
Next of kin: Johann. Starke, Silbenstraße 9, Dortmund
2nd Werft Division, 1/10/1914, eight months; UA Kiel, training six weeks, 5-6/1915; *Acheron*; workshop to 12/1915; then Flanders Flotilla; training, *UB 19*, one trip; reserve to 11/1916. Joined *UC 61* 12/1916
POW camp: 84
Weidner, Michael, Stoker, born 3/8/1895 Neustadt
Next of kin: Johann Weidner, Gasfabrikstraße 50, Weiden, Bavaria
1/10/1916; UA 1916; *UB 25*; *UB 16*, Flanders Flotilla, 1916; joined *UC 61* 1/1917
POW camps: 90, 80B

Appendix 2
ABBREVIATIONS & COMMON GERMAN WORDS

Abitur	A set of examinations taken in the final year of secondary school
ASDIC	Allied Submarine Detection Investigation Committee
BIR	Board of Investigation and Research, Royal Navy
BRT	Gross registered tonnage
CID	Committee for Imperial Defence
DRASSM	Le Département des Recherches Archéologiques Subaquatiques et Sous-Marines, Department of Underwater Archaeological Research
Ecpad	Etablissement de Communication et de Production Audiovisuelle de la Défense
Fähnrich	Midshipman
Freicorps	Post-World War 1 German para-military unit
Great War	World War 1, 1914-1918
GPS	Global positioning system
HVB	Handelsverkehrsbuch
HMS	His Majesty's Ship
ICRC	International Committee of the Red Cross
Kaiser	Kaiser Wilhelm II, 1890-1919
Kaiserliche Marine	The Imperial German Navy, 1871-1919

Kriegsmarine	Navy of Nazi Germany, 1935-1945
KTB	Kriegstagebuch, War Diary
KRA	German War Materials Department
MA-BA	Bundesarchiv-Militär Archiv, Federal Military Archives, Freiburg, Germany
NARA	National Archives and Records Administration, Washington, DC
NID	Naval Intelligence Division, Royal Navy
NMM	National Maritime Museum, Greenwich, London
OHL	Oberste Heeresleitung, Supreme Army Command, Germany
PGL	Pan-German League
Reichsmark	German currency before the Deutschmark
Seeoffiziere	Naval executive officer
SHD	Service historique de la Défense, Historical Defence Service, headquarters Vincennes, France
SHOM	Service d'Hydrologie et d'Océanographie de la Marine – the French Navy Hydrology and Oceanography Service
SKN	Signalbuch der Kaiserliche Marine, German navy signal book
SMS	Seiner Majestät Schiff, His Majesty's Ship
SPD	Sozialdemokratische Partei Deutschlands, Social Democratic Party
TNA	The National Archives, Kew, London
VB code	Verkehrsbuch Weimar German Republic, 1919-1933
Weltpolitik	German expansionist overseas foreign policy, 1890-1919
ZAN	Zone des Armées du Nord
Zur See	Naval executive officer

Bibliography

Abel, Theodore, *Why Hitler Came into Power* (1938, reprint Harvard University Press, 1966)

Adler, Selig, 'The War-Guilt Question and American Disillusionment, 1918-1928', *The Journal of Modern History*, Vol. 23, No. 1, 1951, pp. 1-28

Afflerbach, Holger, Falkenhayn: Politisches Denken Und Handeln Im Kaiserreich, Beitrage Zur Militargeschichte (Oldenbourg Wissensch, 1994)

Albertini, Luigi, trans. Masset, Isabella *The Origins of the War of 1914* (1952; Enigma Books, New York 2005), 3 Vols.

Anonymous

La Guerre Navale Racontée Par Nos Amiraux (Librairie Schwartz, Paris, undated)

The Starving of Germany, Papers read at Extraordinary Meeting of United Medical Societies held at headquarters of Berlin Medical Society, Berlin, 18 December 1918 (Berlin, 1919)

Arnold-Forster, W, *The Blockade 1914-1919, Before the Armistice – and After* (Oxford Pamphlets on World Affairs, No 17, Clarendon Press 1939)

Ascherson, Neal, *The King Incorporated, Leopold II in the Age of Trusts* (Allen & Unwin, London 1963)

Aspinall-Oglander, Cecil, *Roger Keyes, Being the Biography of Admiral of the Fleet Lord Keyes of Zeebrugge and Dover* (Hogarth Press, London 1951)

Asprey, Robert B, *The German High Command at War, Hindenburg and Ludendorff and the First World War* (William Morrow, New York 1991)

Bacon, Admiral Sir Reginald H

The Dover Patrol, 1915-1917, Vols. 1&2 (Hutchinson, London 1919)

The Concise Story of the Dover Patrol (Hutchinson, London 1932)

Baecken, Charles, *L'Historique du 5th Régiment de Lanciers* (Maréchal de Logis, undated)

Bane, Suda Lorena, and Lutz, Ralph Haswell, *The Blockade of Germany After the Armistice, 1918-1919; Selected Documents of the Supreme Economic Council, Superior Blockade Council, American Relief Administration, and Other Wartime Organizations* (Stanford University Press, 1942; Howard Fertig, New York 1972)

Banks, Arthur, *A Military Atlas of the First World War* (Leo Cooper, Barnsley 1997)

Barnett, L Margaret, *British Food Policy During The First World War* (Allen & Unwin, Winchester, Mass., 1985)

Barrett, Michael B, *Operation Albion, The German Conquest of the Baltic Islands* (Indiana University Press, 2009)

Bauer, Hermann, *Als Führer der U-Boote im Weltkriege* (Koehler & Amelang, Leipzig 1941)

Beesley, Patrick, *Room 40: British Naval Intelligence 1914-1918* (Hamish Hamilton, London 1992)

Becker, Annette, *Oubliés de la Grande Guerre, Humanitaire et culture de guerre 1914-1918, Populations occupées, déportés civils, prisonniers de guerre* (Pluriel 2012)

Bell, A C, *A History of the Blockade of Germany and of the countries associated with her in the Great War: Austria-Hungary, Bulgaria, and Turkey 1914-1918* (HMSO, London 1937)

Bell, Christopher M

'Sir John Fisher's Naval Revolution Reconsidered: Winston Churchill at the Admiralty, 1911-1914', *War in History*, 18(3), 2011, pp. 333-56

'On Standards and Scholarship: A Response to Nicholas Lambert', *War in History*, 20(3), 2013, pp. 381-409

Churchill and Sea Power (Oxford University Press, 2013)

Bendert, Harald

Die UB-Boote der Kaiserlichen Marine 1914-1918. Einsätze, Erfolge, Schicksal (E S Mittler, Hamburg 2000)

Die UC-Boote der Kaiserlichen Marine 1914-1918, Minenkreig mit U-Booten (E S Mittler, Hamburg 2001)

Birnbaum, Karl E, *Peace Moves and U-Boat Warfare: A Study of Imperial Germany's Policy towards the United States April 18, 1916 – January 9, 1917* (Almqvist & Wiksell, Stockholm 1958)

Blahut, Fred, 'The Allied Attempt to Starve Germany in 1919', *The Barnes Review*, April 1996, pp. 11-14

Blanton, Smiley, *Mental and Nervous Changes in the Children of the Volksschulen of Trier, Germany, Caused by Malnutrition* (The National Committee for Mental Hygiene, New York 1919); reprint from *Mental Hygiene*, July 1919, No. 3, pp. 343-386

Bloch, Ivan Stanislavovich, *Is War Now Impossible?: Being an Abridgment of 'The War of the Future in Its Technical, Economic & Political Relations'* (Grant Richards, London 1899; eprint War College Series 2017)

Blond, Georges, *The Marne, The Battle that Saved Paris and Changed the Course of the First World War* (Prion, London 2002)

Blücher, von Wahlstatt, Evelyn M, *An English Wife in Berlin: A Private Memoir of Events, Politics and Daily Life in Germany Throughout the War and the Social Revolution of 1918* (Constable, London 1920)

Blum, Matthias, 'Government Decisions Before and During the First World War and the Living Standards in Germany During a Drastic Natural Experiment', *Explorations in Economic History*, Vol. 48, Issue 4, Dec 2011

Boemeke, Manfred F; Feldman, Gerald D; and Glaser, Elisabeth, eds., *The Treaty of Versailles, A Reassessment after 75 Years* (The German Historical Institute, Washington, DC; Cambridge University Press 1998)

Bouton, S Miles, *And The Kaiser Abdicates, The German Revolution November 1918-August 1919* (Yale University Press 1920; reprint Wildside Press 2016)

Bowles, Thomas Gibson, *The Declaration of Paris of 1856: being an account of the maritime rights of Great Britain; a consideration of their importance; a history of their surrender by the signature of the Declaration of Paris; and an argument for their resumption by the denunciation and repudiation of that declaration* (Low, Marston, London 1900; Relnk Books, Delhi, India 2017)

Bown, Stephen R, *A Most Damnable Invention, Dynamite, Nitrates, and the Making of the Modern World* (Thomas Dunne, New York 2005)

Boyle, David, *Before Enigma, The Room 40 codebreakers of the First World War* (Real Press, 2016)

Brandt, Karl, *Management of Agriculture and Food in the German-Occupied and Other Areas of Fortress Europe, A Study in Military Government*; Germany's Agricultural and Food Policies in *World War II*, Vol. 2 (Stanford University Press, Bridgland, Tony, *Outrage at Sea, Naval Atrocities in the First World War* (Leo Cooper, Barnsley 2002)

Bridgman, Jon M, *The Revolt of the Hereros, Perspectives on Southern Africa* (California University Press, 1992)

Bruntz, George G, *Allied Propaganda and the Collapse of the German Empire in 1918* (Stanford University Press 1938; SN Books reprint, India 2017)

Canini, Gerard, 'L'utilisation des prisonniers de guerre comme main-d'oeuvre 1914-1916, *Les Fronts invisible, nourrier, fournir, soigner'* (Pressue universitaire de Nancy, 1984), pp. 247-262

Carter, Geoffrey, *The Royal Navy at Portland Since 1845* (Maritime Books, Liskeard 1987)

Carpenter, Captain Alfred F B, *The Blocking of Zeebrugge* (Herbert Jenkins, London 1922)

Chambers, Frank P, *The War Behind The War 1914-1918, A History of the Political and Civilian Fronts* (Faber and Faber, London 1939)

Chatelle, A, and Le Bon, E, *Boulogne et sa marine pendant la guerre 1914-1918* (Imprimeries réunies, Boulogne-sur-Mer 1921)

Chatelle, Albert, and Tison, G, *Calais Pendant La Guerre 1914-1918* (Librairie Aristide Quillet, Paris 1927)

Chatelle, Albert, *La Base Navale du Havre et La Guerre Sous-Marine Secrète en Manche 1914-1918* (Les Éditions Médicis, Paris 1949)

Chatterton, E Keble
  Q-ships and their story (Sidgwick and Jackson, London 1922; facsimile reprint 2016)
  The Big Blockade (Hurst & Blackett, London 1932)

Chickering, Roger
  We Men Who Feel Most German, A Cultural Study of the Pan-German League, 1886-1914 (George Allen & Unwin, Boston, USA 1984)
  The Great War and Urban Life in Germany, Freiburg, 1914-1918 (Cambridge University Press, 2007)

Churchill, Winston S
  The World Crisis 1911-1918 (1930, reprint Four Square, London 1964);
  The World Crisis 1915 (Thornton Butterworth, London 1923)

Clark, Christopher
  Iron Kingdom (Penguin, London 2006)
  Kaiser Wilhelm II (Penguin, London 2009)
  The Sleepwalkers, How Europe went to War in 1914 (Penguin, London 2013)

Clausewitz, von Carl, trans. Graham, J J, *On War* (Wordsworth Classics, Ware 1997)

Cobb, Stephen, *Preparing for Blockade 1885-1914, Naval Contingency for Economic Warfare* (Ashgate, Farnham 2013)
Coles, Alan, *Slaughter at Sea, The Truth Behind a Naval War Crime* (Robert Hale, London 1986)
Compton-Hall, Richard, *Submarines at War 1914-1918* (1991, reprint Periscope Publishing, Penzance 2004)
Connolly, James B, & Schenk, Karl von, *U-Boat War 1914-1918: Two Contrasting Accounts from Both Sides of the Conflict at Sea During the Great War: The U-Boat Hunters; The Diary of a U-Boat Commander* (Leonaur, 2008)
Consett, Rear Admiral M W W P, *The Triumph of Unarmed Forces (1914-1918): An account of the transactions by which Germany during the Great War was able to obtain supplies prior to her collapse under the pressure of economic forces* (Williams and Norgate, London 1923; electronic reprint 2016)
Coogan, John W, *The End of Neutrality, The United States, Britain, and Maritime Rights 1899-1915* (Cornell University Press, 1981)
Cooper, Caroline Ethel (the Letters of), *Behind the Lines, One Woman's War 1914-18*, ed. Denholm, Decie (Norman & Hobhouse, London 1982)
Corbett, Sir Julian, *Some Principles of Maritime Strategy* (1911; Conway, London 1972)
Corbett, Sir Julian S, and Newbolt, Henry, *History of the Great War, Naval Operations*, (Longmans Green, London 1920-31), 5 Vols
Cox, Frederick J, 'The French Peace Plans, 1918-1919: The Germ of the Conflict Between Ferdinand Foch and Georges Clemenceau' in Cox et al, eds., *Studies in Modern European History in Honor of Franklin Charles Palm* (Bookman, New York, USA, 1956), pp. 81-104
Cravioto, Joaquin, 'Application of New Knowledge of Nutrition on Physical and Mental Growth and Development', *American Journal of Public Health*, No. 53, 1963, pp. 1803-9
Cron, Hermann, trans. Colton, C F, *Imperial German Army 1914-18: Organisation, Structure, Orders of Battle* (*Geshichte des Deutschen Heeres im Weltkrieg 1914-1918*, Berlin 1937; reprint Helion, Solihull 2002)
Cruttwell, C R M F, *A History of the Great War 1914-1918* (Granada, St Albans 1936)
David, Patrick and Serge, *14-18 La Guerre Maritime en Manche et en mer du Nord* (Du Bout du Monde, undated)

Davis, Belinda J, *Food Politics, and Everyday Life in World War I Berlin: Home Fires Burning* (University of North Carolina Press, 2000)

de Chair, Admiral Sir Dudley, *The Sea is Strong* (Harrap, London 1961)

Delanoy, Gilbert, *Guerre 1914-18, Citations à L'Ordre de L'Armée des Formations and des Bâtiments de la Marine Française*

Delpal, Bernard, 'Prisonniers de guerre en France, 1914-1920', pp. 145-159, in Gueslin, André; Kalifa, Dominique; *Les Exclus en Europe, 1830-1930* (Ouvrières, L'Atelier, Paris 1999)

Devlin, Patrick, *Too Proud to Fight, Woodrow Wilson's neutrality* (Oxford University Press, 1971)

Ditte, Général, *Calais (1914-1918)* (Militaire Universelle, Fournier, Paris, undated)

Docherty, Gerry, and Macgregor, Jim, *Hidden History: The Secret Origins of the First World War* (Mainstream Publishing, Edinburgh 2013)

Doenitz, Grand Admiral Karl, *Memoirs: Ten Years and Twenty Days* (1958; Frontline Books, Barnsley 2015)

Dorling, Taprell (Taffrail), *Swept Channels being an Account of the Work of the Minesweepers in the Great War* (Hodder and Stoughton, London 1935)

Dorpalen, Andreas, *Heinrich von Treitschke* (Kennikat, New York 1973)

Doty, Madelaine Zabriskie, *Short Rations: An American Woman in Germany 1915-1916* (Century, New York 1917)

Doyle, Arthur Conan, 'Danger! Being the Log of Captain John Sirius', pp. 7-31, also 'Preface', pp. 5-6, in *Danger! and Other Stories* (1912; Serenity, Rockville, Maryland 2011)

Dufeil, Yves, *Kaiserliche Marine U-Boote 1914-1918, Dictionnaire Biographique des Commandants de la Marine Imperiale Allemande* (Histomar, 2016)

Dufossé, Franck
Histoire de Wissant, des origines aux années 1930 (Éditions AMA, Paris 2002)
Wissant 1914-1918 (Art et Histoire de Wissant, Mairie de Wissant 2014)

Dufour, Pierre, 'Les prisonniers du guerre allemands', *14-18: Le magazine de la Grande Guerre*, August/September/October 2016, pp. 8-23

Dyson, Will, *Kultur Cartoons* (Stanley Paul, London 1915)

Edmonds, James E, *Military operations: France and Belgium, 1914*, Vol. 1: 'Mons, the Retreat to the Seine, the Marne and the Aisne, August-October 1914' (Official History: Imperial War Museum, London 1992)

Ehrenrangliste Der Deutschen Marine 1914-1918, CD (Deutsches Wehrkundearchiv, Helion)

Eley, Geoff, 'Reshaping the Right: Radical Nationalism and the German Navy League, 1898-1908', *The Historical Journal*, Vol. 21, No. 2, June 1978, pp. 327-354

Emmerson, Charles, *1913, The World Before the Great War* (Vintage, London 2013)

Erbe, Günter, Das Vornehme Berlin, Fürstin Marie Radziwill und die grossen Damen der Gesellschaft 1871-1918 (Böhlau Verlag, Köln 2015)

Essen, Léon van der, *The Invasion & The War in Belgium from Liège to the Yser with a Sketch of the Diplomatic Negotiations Preceding the Conflict* (Fisher Unwin, London 1917)

Ewart, John S, *The Roots and Causes of the Wars (1914-1918)*, Vols. 1&2 (George Doran, New York 1925)

Fayle, C Ernest, *Official History of the Great War: Seaborne Trade*, Vol. 2, 'Submarine Campaign', Vol. 3, 'The Period of Unrestricted Submarine Warfare' (1920-4; Imperial War Museum, London 1997)

Feldman, Gerald D
 Army, Industry and Labor in Germany 1914-1918 (Berg, Providence, Rhode Island 1966)
 The Great Disorder: Politics, Economics, and Society in the German Inflation, 1914-1924 (Oxford University Press, 1997)
 Die Deutsche Inflation / The German Inflation Reconsidered: Eine Zwischenbilanz / A Preliminary Balance (Gruyter online, 2011)

Ferguson, Niall
 The Pity of War (Penguin, London 1999)
 The House of Rothschild, The World's Banker 1849-1999 (Penguin, New York 2000)

Fischer, Fritz, *Germany's Aims in the First World War* (Chatto & Windus, London 1977)

Flemming, Jens, *Landwirtschaftliche Interessen und Demokratie, Ländliche Gesellschaft, Agrarverbände und Staat 1890-1925* (Verlag Neue Gesellschaft, Bonn 1978)

Fletcher, R A, *In the Days of the Tall Ships* (Brentano's, London 1928)

Forstnerr, Georg-Gunther von, König, Paul, Peckelsheim, Baron Spiegel von Und Zu, *U-Boat War 1914-1918:* Vol. 2 - *Three accounts of German submarines* during the Great War: The Journal of Submarine Commander von Forstnerr, The Voyage of the "Deutschland" & The Adventures of the U-202 (Leonaur, 2010)

Forstner, Georg-Gunther von, *The Journal of Submarine Commander von Forstner* (1916, abridged; USA 2016)

Frey, Marc, 'Bullying the Neutrals, The case of the Netherlands', in Chickering, Roger, Förster, Stig, eds., *Great War, Total War: Combat and Mobilization of the Western Front, 1914-1918* (German Historical Institute and Cambridge University Press, 2000), pp. 227-244

Friedman, Norman, introduction, *German Warships of World War I: The Royal Navy's Official Guide to the Capital Ships, Cruisers, Destroyers, Submarines and Small Craft, 1914-1918* (1918, reprint Greenhill Books, London, 1992)

Friedrich, Otto, *Blood and Iron, From Bismarck to Hitler the von Moltke's Family's Impact on German History* (Harper Collins, New York 1995)

Fuehr, Alexander, *The Neutrality of Belgium* (Funk and Wagnall, London 1915)

Fürbringer, Werner, *FIPS: Legendary U-boat Commander 1915-1918*, trans. & ed., Brooks, Geoffrey (1933; Leo Cooper, Barnsley 1999)

Gayer, Captain Albert, *General Survey of the History of the Submarine Warfare in all Theatres of War, 1914-18* (Stencilled and printed, Naval War College, Newport RI, 1930)

Geyer, Michael, 'Insurrectionary Warfare: The German Debate about Levée en Masse in October 1918', *Journal of Modern History*, Vol. 73, No. 3, 2001, pp. 459-527

Gibson, Hugh, *A Journal from Our Legation in Belgium* (Doubleday, Page, New York 1918)

Gibson, R H, and Prendergast, Maurice, *The German Submarine War 1914-1918* (John Constable, London 1931; reprint Periscope Publishing, Penzance 2002)

Glaeser, Ernst, *Class 1902* (1928; University of South Carolina, 2008)

Goffic, Charles le, trans. Simmonds, Florence, *Dixmude: The Epic of the French Marines (October 7-November 10 1914)* (1916; CreateSpace, USA 2014)

Grainger, John D, ed., *The Maritime Blockade of Germany in the Great War: The Northern Patrol, 1914-1918* (Ashgate, Navy Records Society 2003)

Graham, G G, 'Growth during Recovery from Infantile Malnutrition', *Journal of the American Medical Women's Association*, No. 21, 1966, pp. 740 onwards

Grant, Robert M
U-Boats Destroyed: The Effect of Anti-Submarine Warfare 1914-18 (1964, Periscope Publishing, Penzance 2002)
U-Boat Intelligence, Admiralty Intelligence Division and the Defeat of the U-boats 1914-1918 (1969, Periscope Publishing, Penzance 2002)
U-Boat Hunters: Code Breakers, Divers and the Defeat of the U-Boats, 1914-1918 (Written unpublished 1971; Periscope Publishing, Penzance 2003)

Gray, Edwyn A
The Killing Time: The German U-boats 1914-18 (Seeley, Service 1972)
British Submarines at War 1914 – 1918 (reprint Pen & Sword Maritime, Barnsley 2016), first published as *A Damned Un-English Weapon* (Charles Scribner's Sons, 1973)

Grelling, Richard, ('A German'), translated Gray, Alexander, *J'Accuse* (Hodder and Stoughton, London 1915)

Greenhill, Basil
The Mariner's Mirror, 'The Rise and Fall of the British Coastal Steamer', Vol. 27, Issue 3, 1941, pp 243-259
The Merchant Schooners, Vol. II (David & Charles, Newton Abbot 1968)

Grimes, Shawn T, *Strategy and War Planning in the British Navy, 1887-1918* (Boydell Press, Woodbridge 2012)

Gröner, Erich, *German Warships 1815-1945*
Vol. 1: Major Surface Vessels (1983; Conway, London 1990)
Vol. 2: U-Boats and Mine Warfare Vessels (1968; revised and expanded by Jung, Dieter, and Maass, Martin, 1983; translated by Thomas, Keith, and Magowan, Rachel, Conway Maritime Press, London 1991)

Guichard, Louis
Au Large (1914-1918) (La Renaissance du Livre, Paris 1919)
Bleu Marine (Société d'éditions géographiques, maritimes et coloniales, 1927)
Les Guerres des Enseignes (La Renaissance du Livre, Paris 1929)
The Naval Blockade 1914-1918, trans. & ed. Turner, Christopher R, (Phillip Allen, London 1930)

Fouqueray, Charles, *La Guerre Navale Racontée par Nos Amiraux* (Librairie Schwarz, Paris 1920)

Hadley, Michael L, *Count Not the Dead, The Popular Image of the German Submarine* (Mc-Gill-Queen's University Press, Montreal 1995)

Hankey, Lord, *The Supreme Command 1914-1918*, Vols. 1&2 (George Allen & Unwin, London 1961)

Hashagen, Ernst, *The Log of a U-boat Commander or U-boats Westward - 1914-1918* (Unwin, London 1931)

Hampshire, A Cecil, *The Blockaders* (William Kimber, London 1980)

Haws, Duncan, *Merchant Fleets – Britain's Railway Steamers – Eastern and North-Western Companies + Zeeland and Stena* (TCL Publications, Hereford 1993)

Heal, Chris
  Sound of Hunger (Unicorn, London 2018)
  Saints & Sinners (Chattaway and Spottiswood, Hampshire, UK 2023)

Heal, Chris, and Lesoin, Henri, *La dernière patrouille de l'UC 61* (Art et Histoire de Wissant, 2023)

Heimburg, Heino von, *U-Boot gegen U-Boot (Scherl, Berlin 1917)*

Herwig, Holger H
  'Admirals versus Generals: The War Aims of the Imperial German Navy, 1914-1918', *Central European History*, Vol. 5, No. 3 (September 1972), pp. 208-233
  The German Naval Officer Corps, A Social and Political History, 1890-1918 (Clarendon Press, Oxford 1973)
  The First World War: Germany and Austria-Hungary 1914-1918 (Arnold, London 1997)
  'The Dynamics of Uncertainty: German Military Policy during The First World War' in Millett, Allan R, and Murray, Williamson, eds., *Military Effectiveness*, Vol. 1, *The First World War* (Allen & Unwin, Winchester, Mass., USA 1988), pp. 80-115
  'Total Rhetoric, Limited War: Germany's U-Boat Campaign 1917-1918', *Journal of Military and Strategic Studies*, Vol. 1, issue 1, May 1998, and in Chickering, Roger, Förster, Stig, eds., *Great War, Total War: Combat and Mobilization of the Western Front, 1914-1918* (German Historical Institute and Cambridge University Press, 2000), pp. 169-188
  The Marne, 1914, The Opening of World War 1 and the Battle That Changed the World (Random House, New York, 2011)
  'Luxury' Fleet: The Imperial German Navy 1888-1918 (George Allen & Unwin, London 1980; reprint Routledge, Abingdon 2014)

Herzog, Bodo, *Deutsche U-Boote 1906-1966* (Pawlak, Koblenz 1990)

Hezlet, Vice Admiral Sir Arthur

The Submarine and Sea Power (Peter Davis, London 1967)
Electronics and Sea Power (Stein and Day, New York 1975)
Hinchcliffe, John & Vicki, *Dive Dorset: A Diver Guide* (Underwater World Publications, Teddington 1999)
Hobhouse, Emily
'Report to the Committee of the Distress Fund for South African Women and Children of a Visit to the Camps of Women and Children in the Cape and Orange River Colonies' (Friars, London 1901)
The Brunt Of The War And Where It Fell (1902; reprint Read Books, 2013)
Hobson, Rolf, *Imperialism at Sea, Naval Strategic Thought, the Ideology of Sea Power and the Tirpitz Plan, 1875-1914* (Brill, Boston 2002)
Hochschild, Adam, *King Leopold's Ghost, A Story of Greed, Terror and Heroism in Colonial Africa* (Pan, London 2006)
Hollweg, Konteradmiral Karl, *Unser Recht Auf Den U-Bootskrieg* (1917; Nabu reprint, USA 2016)
Hollweg, Theobald von Bethmann, trans. Young, George, *Reflections on the World War, Vol. 1* (Butterworth, London 1920; digital reprint Forgotten Books, 2015)
Horn, Daniel, *Mutiny on the High Seas, The Imperial German Naval Mutinies of World War One* (Leslie Freewin, London 1973)
Horne, John and Kramer, Alan, 'War Between Soldiers and Enemy Civilians, 1914-1915', in Chickering, Roger, Förster, Stig, eds., *Great War, Total War: Combat and Mobilization of the Western Front, 1914-1918* (German Historical Institute and Cambridge University Press, 2000), pp. 153-168
Howard, Keble (Bell, J Keble), *The Zeebrugge Affair* (George H Doran, New York, 1918)
Howard, N P
'Men against Fire: Expectations of War in 1914', *International Security*, Vol. 9, No. 1 (Summer, 1984), pp. 41-57
'The Social and Political Consequences of the Allied Food Blockade of Germany, 1918–19', *German History*, Vol. 11, No. 2 (June 1993), pp. 161-188
Hull, Isabel V
The Entourage of Kaiser Wilhelm II, 1988-1918 (Cambridge University Press 1982)
Absolute Destruction, Military Culture and the Practices of War in Imperial Germany (Cornell University Press 2005)

A Scrap of Paper, Breaking and Making International Law during the Great War (Cornell University Press 2014)

Humphreys, Roy, *The Dover Patrol 1914-18* (Sutton Publishing, Stroud 1988)

James, Admiral Sir William, *The Code Breakers of Room Forty* (St Martin's Press, New York 1956; reprint Literary Licensing, 2016)

Jamieson, Alan G, 'Martyr or Pirate? The Case of Captain Fryatt in the Great War', *The Mariner's Mirror*, Vol. 85, No. 2, 1999, pp. 196-202

Jane's Fighting Ships of World War I (1919; reprint Studio Editions, London 1990)

Janicki, D A, 'The British Blockade During World War 1: The Weapon of Deprivation', *Student Pulse, 6(06), 2014*

Jasper, Willi, trans. Spencer, Stewart, *Lusitania: The Cultural History of a Catastrophe* (Yale University Press 2016)

Jellicoe, Admiral of the Fleet, The Right Hon. The Earl, *The Submarine Peril: The Admiralty Policy in 1917* (Cassell, London 1934)

Johnson, Niall, and Müller, Jürgen, 'Updating the Accounts', *Bulletin of the History of Medicine*, 2002, pp. 105-15.

Joll, James, *1914: The Unspoken Assumptions* (Weidenfeld and Nicholson, London School of Economics and Political Science 1968)

Joll, James, and Martel, Gordon, *The Origins of the First World War* (Pearson, Harlow 2007)

Jones, Heather,
Violence against Prisoners of War in the First World War: Britain, France and Germany, 1914-1920 (Cambridge University Press, 2011)
'The Enemy Disarmed: Prisoners of War and the Violence of Wartime: Britain, France and Germany 1914-1918', PhD dissertation (Trinity College, University of Dublin, December 2005)

Jung, Hans, 'The New Berlin Horse Railway Company', *Traffic History Sheets*, Berlin, Issue 4, 1960, pp. 17-18

Karau, Mark D, *The Naval Flank of the Western Front, The German MarineKorps Flandern 1914-1918* (Seaforth Publishing, Barnsley 2003)

Keyser, Carl de, and Reybrouck, David van, *The First World War, Unseen Glass Plate Photographs of the Western Front* (University of Chicago 2015)

Kelly, Patrick J, *Tirpitz and the Imperial German Navy* (Indiana University Press, 2011)

Kemp, Paul, *U-Boats Destroyed, German Submarine Losses in the World Wars* (Arms & Armour, London 1997)

Kennedy, Greg
  'Intelligence and the Blockade, 1914-1917: A Study in Administration, Friction and Command', *Intelligence and National Security*, No 5, October 2007
  'The North Atlantic Triangle and the blockade, 1914–1915', *Journal of Transatlantic Studies*, Vol. 6, No 1, 2008
Kennedy, Paul
  The War Plans of the Great Powers 1880-1914, edited (Allen &Unwin, London 1979)
  'Britain in the First World War', in Millett, Allan R, and Murray, Williamson, eds., *Military Effectiveness*, Vol. 1, *The First World War* (Allen & Unwin, Winchester, Mass., USA 1988), pp. 31-79
Keyes, Sir Roger, *The Naval Memoires of Admiral of the Fleet, Scapa Flow to the Dover Straits 1916-1918* (Thornton Butterworth, London 1935)
Keynes, J M, *Two Memoirs, Dr Melchior: A Defeated Enemy and My Early Beliefs* (Hart-Davis, London 1949)
King, M S, Woodrow *Wilson: Warmonger, A Brief Analysis of How America was Deceived Into World War I* (Author, USA 2016)
King-Hall, Sir William Stephen Richard, *The Diary of a U-boat Commander* (Amazon reprint)
Kitchen, Martin, *The Silent Dictatorship, The politics of the German High Command under Hindenburg and Ludendorff, 1916-1918* (Croom Helm, London 1976)
Kloot, William van der, 'Ernest Starling's Analysis of the Energy Balance of the German People During the Blockade 1914-1919', *Notes and Records of the Royal Society of London*, Vol 57, No 2, May 2003
Koebner, Richard, and Schmidt, Helmut Dan, *Imperialism, The Story and Significance of a Political World, 1840-1960* (Cambridge University Press, 1965)
Koerver, Hans Joachim
  German Submarine Warfare 1914-1918 in the Eyes of British Intelligence (LIS Reinisch, Steinbach 2012)
  War of Numbers 1914-1916, The Kaiser's Navy Gone Rogue (LIS Reinisch, Steinbach 2016)
Kramer, Alan R, 'Prisoners in the First World War', Chap. 4, in Scheipers, Sibylle, ed, *Prisoners in War* (Oxford University Press, 2010)
Kühnis, Beni, 'Deutsche Kriegsinternierte in Davos während des 1. Weltkrieges' (Extended A-level Project Essay, 2014)

Kutz, Martin, 'Kriegserfahrung und Kriegsvorbereitung. Die agrarwirtschaftliche Vorbereitung des Zweiten Weltkrieges in Deutscheland vor dem Hintergrund de Weltkrieg I – Erfahtung', *Zeitschrift für Agrargeschichte und Agrarsoziologie*, No. 32, 1984, pp. 59-82, 135-163

Langmaid, Captain Kenneth, *The Approaches are Mined!* (Jarrolds, London 1965)

Lambert, Nicholas A
   Sir John Fisher's Naval Revolution (University of South Carolina Press 1999)
   'On Standards: A Reply to Christopher Bell', *War in History*, 2012, 19(2), pp. 217-240
   Planning Armageddon: British Economic Warfare and the First World War (Harvard University Press, London 2012)

Langsdorff, von Werner, *U-Boote am Feind, 45 deutsche U-Boot-Führer erzählen* (Bertelsmann, Gütersloh 1937)

Larn, Richard & Bridget, *Shipwreck Index of the British Isles: Isles of Scilly, Cornwall, Devon, Dorset* (Lloyd's Register of Shipping, London 1995)

Laurens, Alphonse
   Le Blocus et la Guerre sous-marine, 1914-1918 (Libraire Armand Colin, Paris 1924)
   Histoire de la Guerre Sous-Marine Allemande, 1914-1918 (Société d'Éditions, Paris 1930)

Leith, Captain Lockhart, *The History of British Minefields 1914-1918 (Admiralty private use, 1920, charts added 1932, Library of the Royal Naval Museums, Portsmouth)*

Liddell Hart, B H, *History of the First World War* (1930; Cassell, London 1973)

Lindsay, Samuel McCune, Swiss Commission in the United States, edited, *Bulletin of Social Legislation on the Henry Bergh Foundation for the Promotion of Humane Education, No. 5, Swiss Internment of Prisoners of War, An Experiment in International Humane Legislation and Administration* (Columbia University Press, New York 1917)

Lipkes, Jeff, *Rehearsals: The German Army in Belgium, August 1914* (Leuven University Press 2007)

Low, Professor A M, *Mine and Countermine* (Hutchinson, London 1940)

Lowenthal, David, *The Past is a Foreign Country* (Cambridge University Press, 1986)

Lubbock, Basil, *Last of the Windjammers*, Vol. 1 (Brown, Son & Ferguson, Glasgow 1927)

Ludendorff, Erich von
  Ludendorff's Own Story: August 1914-November 1918, Vol. I (1919, Harper; reprint Kessinger Legacy, USA 2016)
  My War Memories, 1914-1918, Vol. II (Hutchinson, London 1919)
Lutz, Ralph Haswell, *The Causes of the German Collapse in 1918: Sections of the officially authorized report of the Commission of the German Constituent Assembly and of the German Reichstag, 1919-1928, the selection and the translation officially approved by the commission* (1934; Archon, USA 1969)
McCartney, Innes
  Lost Patrols: Submarine Wrecks of the English Channel (Periscope Publishing, Penzance 2003)
  British Submarines of Word War I (Osprey, Oxford 2008)
  The Maritime Archaeology of a Modern Conflict: Comparing the Archaeology of German Submarine Wrecks to the Historical Text (Routledge, Abingdon 2015)
  'The *Tin Openers* Myth and Reality: Intelligence from U-boat Wrecks During WW1', *Proceedings of the Twenty-Fourth Annual Historical Diving Conference*, Poole, November 2014, www.researchgate.net/publication/275957885
  'The Historical Archaeology of World War I U-boats and the Compilation of Admiralty History: The Case of (UC79)', *UNESCO Conference, Bruges*, 26 June 2014, chapter July 2015, researchgate.net/publication/280925727
  'Paying the Prize for the German Submarine War: U-boats destroyed and the Admiralty Prize Fund, 1919-1932', *The Mariner's Mirror*, Vol. 104:1, February 2018, pp. 40-57
McDermott, John, 'Trading with the Enemy: British Business and the Law During the First World War', *Canadian Journal of History / Annales Canadiennes d'Histoire*, XXXII, No 2, Aug 1997
McDowell, Duncan, *Steel at the Sault* (University of Toronto Press, 1988)
Macintyre, Captain Donald, *Jutland* (Evans Brothers, London 1957)
Mahan, Captain Alfred Thayer
  The Influence of Sea Power upon History 1660-1805 (1890, Bison, London 1980)
  The Influence of Sea Power upon the French Revolution and Empire 1793-1812, Vol. II (Sampson, Low, Marston, London 1896)
Manning, T D, *The British Destroyer (Putnam, London 1961)*
March, Edgar J, *British Destroyers, A History of Development 1892-1953* (Seeley Service, London 1966)

Marder, Arthur J

   Portrait of an Admiral; the life and papers of Sir Herbert Richmond (Harvard University Press, 1952)

   From the Dreadnought to Scapa Flow, The Royal Navy in the Fisher Era 1904 – 1919,

   Vol. I: *The Road to War: 1904-1914* (Oxford University Press, London 1961)

   Vol. II: *The War Years: To the Eve of Jutland 1914-1916* (1965; Seaforth Publishing, Barnsley 2013)

   Vol. IV: *1917: Year of Crisis* (1969; Seaforth Publishing, Barnsley 2014)

   Vol. V: *Victory and Aftermath January 1918-June 1919* (Oxford University Press 1970)

Marreo, Javier Ponce, 'Logistics for Commerce War in the Atlantic during the First World War: The German *Etappe* System in Action', *The Mariner's Mirror*, Vol. 92, No. 4, November 2006, pp. 455-64

Martel, Gordon, *The Origins of the First World War* (1987; Longman, London 1996)

Massie, Robert K

   Dreadnought: Britain, Germany, and the Coming of the Great War (1991; Vintage, London 2007)

   Castles of Steel: Britain, Germany and the Winning of the Great War at Sea (Vintage, London 2007)

Mayer, Arno J, *The Persistence of the Old Regime, Europe to the Great War* (Croom Helm, London 1981)

Mead, Margaret, 'The Changing Significance of Food', *American Scientist*, No. 58, 1970, pp. 176 onwards

Messimer, Dwight R

   The Merchant U-boat: Adventures of the 'Deutschland', 1916-18 (Naval Institute Press, Maryland, USA 1988)

   Find and Destroy: Antisubmarine Warfare in World War I (Naval Institute Press, Maryland, USA 2001)

   Verschollen: World War I U-Boat Losses (Naval Institute Press, Maryland, USA 2002)

Messinger, Gary S, *British Propaganda and the State in the First World War* (Manchester University Press 1992)

Molodowsky, N, 'German Foreign Trade in 1899-1913', *The Quarterly Journal of Economics*, Vol. 41, No 4, Aug 1927

Mommsen, Wolfgang J, 'The Debate of German War Aims', *Journal of Contemporary History*, Vol. 1, No. 3, July 1966, pp. 47-72

Morel, Edmund D

The Congo Slave State, A Protest against the new African Slavery; and an Appeal to the Public of Great Britain, of the United States, and of the Continent of Europe (Richardson, Liverpool 1903)

The Fruits of Victory. Have our Statesmen Won the Peace our Soldiers Fought For? (Union of Democratic Control, London 1919)

Military Preparation for the Great War, Fact versus Fiction (Labour Publishing, London 1922)

The Secret History of a Great Betrayal (Owen, Washington 1924)

Mueller, Michael, trans. Brooks, Geoffrey, *Canaris, The Life and Death of Hitler's Spymaster* (Greenhill, Barnsley 2017)

Munro, Dana C, Sellery, George C & Krey, August C, *German Treatment of Conquered Territory being Part II of 'German War Practices'* (The Committee of Public Information, Washington DC, USA, 1918; reprint Kessinger Publishing, 2016)

Mulligan, Timothy P, *Neither Sharks Nor Wolves* (Chatham, London 1999)

Murray, H Robertson, *Krupp's and the International Armaments Ring, The Scandal of Modern Civilisation* (Holden & Hardingham, London 1915)

Murray, Stewart Lygon, *The Reality of War, a Companion to 'Clausewitz'* (Hodder and Stoughton, London 1914)

Neureuther, Karl, and Bergen, Claus, eds., *U-Boat Stories. Narratives of German U-boat sailors (Wir leben noch!, 1931;* reprint The Naval & Military Press, Uckfield 2005)

Newbold, J T Walton

The War Trust Exposed (National Labour Trust, Manchester 1913)

How Asquith Helped the Armaments Ring (National Labour Trust, undated pamphlet)

How Europe Armed for War 1871-1914 (1916; reprint Isha, New Delhi 2013)

Newbolt, Henry

A Note of the History of the Submarine War (George Doran, New York 1917)

Submarine and Anti-Submarine, The Allied Under-Sea Conflict During the First World War (Leonaur, 2013 reprint)

*A Naval History of the War, 1914-1918 (*Hodder and Stoughton, London 1919-20)

Niemöller, Martin, *From U-boat to Concentration Camp: The Autobiography of Martin Niemöller* (William Hodge, London 1939)

O'Brien, Patrick, 'The Economic Effects of the Great War,' *History Today*, Vol. 44, Issue 12, Dec 1994

Offer, Avner
  'The Working Classes, British Naval Plans and the Coming of the Great War', *Past and Present*, no. 107 (May 1985), pp. 204-226
  'Morality and Admiralty: 'Jacky Fisher', Economic Warfare and the Laws of War', *Journal of Contemporary History*, Vol. 23 (Jan 1988), pp. 99-118
  The First World War: An Agrarian Interpretation (Clarendon Press, Oxford 1989)
  'Bounded Rationality in Action: The German submarine campaign, 1915-18' in Gerrard, Bill, ed., *The Economics of Rationality (Routledge, London 1993), pp. 179-202*
  'The Blockade of Germany and the Strategy of Starvation, 1914-1918', in Chickering, Roger, Förster, Stig, eds., *Great War, Total War: Combat and Mobilization of the Western Front, 1914-1918* (German Historical Institute and Cambridge University Press, 2000), pp. 169-188

Ogden, C K, *Sailing Directions of the North Coast of France*, Part 1 (Imray, Norie & Wilson, London 1908)

Olusoga, David, and Erichsen, Casper W, *The Kaiser's Holocaust, Germany's Forgotten Genocide and the Colonial Roots of Nazism* (Faber and Faber, London 2010)

Osborne, Eric W, *Britain's Economic Blockade of Germany 1914-1919* (Routledge, Abingdon 2013)

Pakenham, Thomas
  The Boer War (Abacus, London 1991)
  The Scramble for Africa 1876-1912 (Weidenfeld and Nicolson, London 1997)

Paddock, Troy R E, ed., *A Call to Arms: Propaganda, Public Opinion, and Newspapers in the Great War* (Praeger, Westport, CT, 2004)

Parmelee, Maurice, *Blockade and Sea Power: The Blockade, 1914-1919, and its Significance for a World State* (Hutchinson, London 1924)

Patterson, A Temple, *Jellicoe: A Biography* (Macmillan, London 1969)

Patterson, David, & Pyle, Gerald, 'Geography and Mortality', *Bulletin of the History of Medicine*, 1991, pp. 4-21.

Peterson, H C, *Propaganda for War: The Campaign Against American Neutrality, 1914-17* (University of Oklahoma Press, 1939)

Pitt, Barrie, *Zeebrugge* (Ballantine Books, New York 1959)
Phillips, Ethel, 'American Participation in Belligerent Commercial Controls 1914-1917', *The American Journal of International Law*, Vol. 27, No 4, Oct 1933
Poolman, Kenneth, *Armed Merchant Cruisers* (Leo Cooper, London 1985)
Porch, Douglas, 'The French Army in the First World War' in Millett, Allan R, and Murray, Williamson, eds., *Military Effectiveness*, Vol. 1, *The First World War* (Allen & Unwin, Winchester, Mass., USA 1988), pp. 190-228
Quigley, Carroll, *Tragedy and Hope, A History of the World in Our Time* (Macmillan, New York, 1966)
Raico, Ralph
    Review, Vincent, *Politics of Hunger, Review of Austrian Economics*, Vol. 3, No. 1, 12/1989
    Great Wars and Great Leaders, A libertarian Rebuttal (Ludwig von Mises Institute, Auburn, Alabama 2010)
Ramsay, David, *'Blinker' Hall: Spymaster, The Man who Brought America into World War 1* (Spellmount, Stroud 2009)
Ranft, Bryan McL, ed
    '*The protection of British seaborne trade and the development of systematic planning for war, 1860-1906*' in *Technical Change and British Naval Policy 1860-1939* (Hodder and Stoughton, Sevenoaks 1977)
    The Beatty Papers 1902-1918, Vol. 1 (Scholar Press, Navy Records Society Aldershot 1989)
Read, James Morgan, *Atrocity Propaganda 1914-1919* (Yale University Press 1941)
Reader, W J, *'At Duty's Call', A Study in Obsolete Patriotism* (Manchester University Press 1988)
Reichs-Marine-Amt
    Vorschriften für die Ergänzung des Seeoffizierkorps nebst Ausführungsbestimmungen (Reichs-Marine-Amt, Berlin 1909)
    Vorschriften für die Ausbildung der Seekadetten auf den Schulschiffen (Reichs-Marine-Amt Berlin, 1910)
Reports of British Officers on the Economic Conditions Prevailing in German, December 1918 – March 1919; Cmd-52, Army (HMSO, London 1919)
Richard, Alain, and Coulon, Jef, 'La guerre sous-marin en 1914-1918 dans le Détroit du Pas-de-Calais: armes utilisées par les sous-marins allemands et

lutte anti-sous-marins des alliés', *Sucellus: Dossiers archéologiques, historiques et cultural du Nord-Pas de-Calais*, No. 56, 2005, pp. 41-58

Richard, Alain, Coulon, Jef, and Lowrey, Michael, 'L'odyssée de 5 sous marins allemands, mouilleurs de mines, coules en 1917-19 dans le Detroit du Pas-de-Calais UC26 – UC46 – UC61 – UC64 – UC79', *Sucellus*: No. 57, 2006, pp. 61-85

Richardson, Matthew, *The Hunger War, Food, Rations and Rationing 1914-1918* (Pen & Sword, Barnsley 2015)

Richter, Lina Speiss, *Family life in Germany under the blockade*, preface Shaw, Bernard (National Labour Press, London, 1919)

Ritter, Gerhard, *The Schlieffen Plan* (Oswald Wolff, London 1958)

Ronarc'h, Admiral Pierre-Alexis, Souvenirs De La Guerre, Vol. 1 (Payot, Paris 1921)

Rose, Gerhard, *Krieg nach dem Kriege. Der Kampf des deutschen Volkes um die Heimkehr seiner Kriegsgefangenen* (Dem Rockbound zum Schultze der deutschen Krieges- und Zivilgefangenen, Berlin 1920)

Rössler, Eberhard, trans. Erenberg, Harold, *The U-boat, The evolution and technical history of German submarines (*Arms & Armour Press, London 1981)

Roth, Joseph
  What I saw, Reports from Berlin 1920-33 (Granta, London 2013)
  Job, The Story of a Simple Man (1930; Granta, London 2013)

Rüger, Jan, *The Great Naval Game, Britain and Germany in the Age of Empire* (Cambridge University Press, New York 2007)

Russell, Bertrand, *Justice in War Time* (Spokesman, Nottingham 1917)

Ryheul, John, *Marinekorps Flandern 1914-1918* (E S Mittler, Hamburg 1997)

Saville, Allison Winthrop, 'The Development of the German U-boat Arm, 1919-1935' (PhD dissertation, University of Washington, USA, 1963)

Scheer, Reinhard, Admiral, *Germany's High Sea Fleet in the World War* (1919; Shilka Publishing, Truro 2013)

Schierbrand, Wolf von, *Kaiser's Speeches Forming A Character Portrait of Kaiser Wilhelm II* (Harper Brothers, New York 1903)

Schneider, William, *Operations Research Applications for Intelligence, Surveillance and Reconnaissance: Report of the Defense Science Board Advisory Group on Defense Intelligence* (Diane Publishing, Darby, PA, 2009)

Schoenermarck, A, ed., *Helden-Gedenkmappe des deutschen Adels* (Petri, Stuttgart 1921)

Schreiner, George Abel, *The Iron Ration: The Economic and Social Effects of the Allied Blockade on Germany and the German People* (John Murray, London 1918)

Schröder, Joachim, *Die U-Boote des Kaisers: Die Geschichte des deutschen U-Boot-Krieges Gegen Großbritannien im Ersten Weltkrieg* (Bernard & Graefe Verlag, Bonn 2003)

Sedrati, Mouncef, Anthony, Edward J, 'Confronting coastal morphodynamics with countererosion engineering: the emblematic case of Wissant Bay, Dover Strait', *Journal of Coastal Conservation*, Springer Verlag, 2014, 18 (5), pp. 483-494

Seligmann, Matthew, *Spies in Uniform, British Military and Naval Intelligence on the Eve of the First World War* (Oxford University Press 2006)

Seligmann, Matthew S, Nägler, Frank, and Epkenhans, Michael, eds., *The Naval Route to the Abyss, The Anglo-German Naval Race 1895-1914* (Ashgate, Naval History Society, Farnham 2015)

Sims, William Sowden, *The Victory at Sea, The Allied Campaign Against U-Boats During the First World War 1917-18* (1920, reprint USA, 2016)

Siney, Marion C, *The Allied Blockade of Germany 1914-1916* (University of Michigan Press 1957)

Spies, S B, *Methods of Barbarism? Roberts and Kitchener and Civilians in the Boer Republics, January 1900-May 1902* (Human and Rousseau, Cape Town 1977)

Spiess, Johannes, *Six Ans de Croisières en Sous-marin* (Payot, Paris 1927)

Spiegel, Edgar, Baron von und zu Pecklesheim, *The Adventures of the U-202, An Actual Narrative* (1917; Project Guttenberg EBook 2010)

Spindler, Arno

Der Krieg zur See 1914-1918: Der Handelskrieg mit U-Booten, Band 3, Oktober 1915 bis Januar 1917 (E S Mittler, Berlin, 1934)

Der Krieg zur See 1914-1918: Der Handelskrieg mit U-Booten, Band 4, Februar bis Dezember 1917 (E S Mittler, Berlin 1941; reprint 1964)

Starling, E H, 'The food supply of Germany during the war', *Journal of the Royal Statistical Society*, No. 83, pp. 225-254, 1920

Strachan, Hew, *The First World War* (Pocket Books, London 2006)

Sutherland, Jon, and Canwell, Diane, *U-Boats at World Wars I and II: Rare Photographs from Wartime Archives (Images of War)* (Pen & Sword Maritime, Barnsley 2009)

Steffen, Dirk, 'The Holtzendorff Memorandum of 22 December 1916 and Germany's Declaration of Unrestricted U-boat Warfare', *The Journal of Military History*, Vol. 68, No. 1, 1/2004, pp. 215-224

Stock, M B, and Smythe, P M, 'Does Nutrition during Infancy Inhibit Brain Growth and Subsequent Intellectual Development?', *Archives of Disease in Childhood*, No. 38, 1964

Stoker, Donald J, *Girding for Battle, The Arms Trade in a Global Perspective, 1815-1940* (edited with Grant, Jonathan A, Praeger, Westport, Connecticut 2003), Chapter 6, Forsén, Björn, and Forsén, Annette, 'German Submarine Exports, 1919-35', pp. 113-33.

Swetman, Deryck, 'The Flanders U-Boat Flotilla, A Nest of Vipers Spawned by Allied Intelligence?', MA Maritime Studies, *University of Portsmouth*, 2003/2004

Tarrant, V E, *The U-boat Offensive 1914-1945* (Cassell, London 1989)

Ten Cate, J H, 'Das U-Boot als geistige Exportware: Das Ingeniuerskantoor voor Scheepvaart N.V., 1919-1957' in Melville R, et all, ed., *Deutschland und Europa in der Neuzeit, Festschrift für Karl Otmar, Freiherr von Aretin, zum 65* (Stuttgart, 1988)

Tennent, A J, *British Merchant Ships Sunk by U boats in World Wars l and ll* (Pen & Sword Maritime, Barnsley 2009)

Termote, Tomas
 Krieg Unter Wasser: Unterseebootflottille Flandern 1915-1918 (E S Mittler, Hamburg 2015)
 War Beneath the Waves: U-boat Flotilla Flandern 1915-1918 (Uniform, London 2017)

Terraine, John
 Mons, The Retreat to Victory (Batsford, London 1960)
 Business in Great Waters, The U-Boat Wars, 1916-1945 (Leo Cooper, London 1989)
 The Smoke and the Fire (Leo Cooper, London 1992)

Terry, C Sanford, ed., *Ostend and Zeebrugge, April 23: May 10, 1918, The Dispatches of Vice-Admiral Sir Roger Keyes and other Narratives of the Operations* (Oxford University Press, 1919)

Thomas, Lowell, *Raiders of the Deep* (Garden City Publishing, New York 1932)

Thomazi, A, 'La Guerre Navale dans la Zone des Armées du Nord' (1924; Payot, Paris 1928)

Tooley, Hunt, *The Western Front, Battle Front and Home Front in the First World War* (Macmillan, Basingstoke 2003)
Trentmann, Frank, and Just, Flemming, editors, *Food and Conflict in Europe in the Age of the Two World Wars* (Macmillan, Basingstoke 2006)
Tuchman, Barbara W, *The Guns of August – August 1914* (Four Square, 1964)
Tucker, Spencer C, editor, *The European Powers in the First World War, An Encyclopedia* (Garland Publishing, New York 1999)
Turner, L C F, *Origins of the First World War* (Edward Arnold, London 1970)
Ullrich, Volker, trans. Beech, Timothy, *Bismarck* (1998; Haus Publishing, London 2015)
Vagts, Alfred, *A History of Militarism: Civilian and Military* (Revised edition; Free Press, New York 1967)
Vigness, Paul G, *The Neutrality of Norway in the World War* (Stanford University 1932; Kessinger Reprint, USA, 2016)
Vincent, C Paul, *Politics of Hunger: The Allied Blockade of Germany, 1915-19* (Ohio University Press, 1985)
Ward-Jackson, C H, *Stephens of Fowey, A Portrait of a Cornish Merchant Fleet 1867-1939* (National Maritime Museum, London, Maritime Monographs and Reports, No 43, 1980)
Warner, Philip, *The Zeebrugge Raid* (William Kimber, London 1978)
Wegener, Vice Admiral Wolfgang, trans. Herwig, Holger H, *The Naval Strategy of the World War* (1929; Naval Institute Press, Annapolis, Maryland 1989)
Weinreb, Alice, *Modern Hungers, Food and Power in Twentieth-Century Germany* (Oxford University Press 2017)
Weir, Gary E, *Building the Kaiser's Navy, The Imperial Naval Office and German Industry in the von Tirpitz Era, 1890-1919* (United States Naval Institute, Annapolis, Maryland 1992)
Williamson, Gordon, *U-boats of the Kaiser's Navy* (Osprey, Oxford 2002)
Willis, Edward F, 'Herbert Hoover and the Blockade of Germany, 1918-1919' in Cox et al, eds., *Studies in Modern European History in Honor of Franklin Charles Palm* (Bookman, New York, USA, 1956), pp. 81-104
Willmott, H P, *World War I* (Dorling Kindersley, London 2012)
Wilson, Keith, edited, *Forging the Collective Memory, Government and International Historians through Two World Wars* (Bergahn Books, Oxford 1996)
Wilson, Michael, *Baltic Assignment, British Submariners in Russia: 1914-1919* (Leo Cooper, London 1985)

Winick, Myron, and Noble, Adele, 'Cellular Response in Rats during Malnutrition at Various Ages', *Journal of Nutrition*, No. 89, 1966, pp. 300-6

Winter, Jay, ed, *The Cambridge History of First World War*, Vols. I-III (Cambridge University Press, 2014)

Winter, Jay, and Prost, Antoine, *The Great War in History: Debates and Controversies, 1914 to the Present* (Cambridge University Press 2005)

Winton, John, *Convoy: The Defence of Sea Trade 1890-1990* (Michael Joseph, London 1983)

Wislicenus, Georg, *Deutschlands Seemacht, sonst und jetzt* (1895; Grunow, Leipzig 1901)

Wodiczko, Krzysztof, *The Abolition of War* (Black Dog, London 2012)

Woodward, E L, *Great Britain and the German Navy* (Clarendon Press, Oxford 1935)

Yarnall, John, *Barbed Wire Disease, British and German Prisoners of War, 1914-1919* (History Press, Stroud 2011)

Zweig, Stefan, trans. Bell, Anthea, *The World of Yesterday* (1942; Pushkin, London 2009)

Zweiniger-Bargielowska, Ina, Duffett, Rachel, and Drouard, Alain, editors, *Food and War in Twentieth Century Europe* (Ashgate, Farnham 2011)

Chris Heal's books are available through selected Hampshire retailers and major internet booksellers. Find details at www.candspublishing.org.uk.

Saints & Sinners (2023) (*sister history to The War of The Raven*)
Between the world wars, three powerful men befriended and influenced the young u-boat captain, Erich Gerth, all vehemently anti-communist and on the far right of German politics: master spy Wilhelm Canaris, Admiral Adolf von Trotha who secretly planned the u-boat fleet for the next war and Salomon Marx a banker of considerable wealth who wielded much influence in Jewish, financial and political circles. This is the story of Gerth's career, backed by extensive research across European archives and supported by private interviews with his descendants, finally rediscovered in the USA.

Bad Moon Rising (2023)
Three novellas about despair: 'The Voice of Rage and Ruin, The End of Alton'; 'Bad Times Today, The Sad Life of Mary May'; 'Don't Go Round Tonight, Earth's Last Second'.
The line between cosy normality and disaster is thin. All it takes is a malign or uncaring person. Then your world collapses. And there's usually nothing you can do about it.

The Winchester Tales (2022) (*concluding part of the Ridge Trilogy*)
An Anglo-Norman love story set during the invasion of England after 1066.
Gilbert of Bayeux, orphan, linguist and administrator, is brought to Winchester by Bishop Odo in 1067 to mastermind the appropriation of the land of the Saxon thegns fallen at Hastings. For the next forty years in Hampshire, he treads a precarious path through the Norman occupation. His great love, Ailgifu, is an outspoken mead seller from Medstead. His servant, Lēofric, provides challenging and dangerous company.

Ropley's Legacy (2021) (*second part of the Ridge Trilogy*)
The Ridge Enclosures, 1709 to 1850: Chawton, Farringdon, Medstead, Newton Valence and Ropley and the birth of Four Marks.
The very first private parliamentary enclosure in England was in 1709 in Ropley. Driven by the less than saintly bishop of Winchester, it was a highly contested land grab seeking to make money by taking control of the common fields. Over 150 years, the government sanctioned theft spread to all the neighbouring ridge villages.

The Four Marks Murders (2020) (*updated second edition; first part of the Ridge Trilogy*)
In this true-life thriller, Chris Heal investigates deliberate and untimely deaths in what was thought to be one of the quiet backwaters of Hampshire. The twenty murders begin in Roman times with over half since 1900 and three within the last few years. They beg the question, 'Is Four Marks the murder capital of Southern England?

Reappearing (2020)
The semi-autobiographical sequel to Disappearing. If an elderly couple save you from a bad death in the Sahara, there's an honest debt to be paid. But this couple have conflicting plans. The only escape is down the River Niger where some unpleasant people await. The hunt is on for an elusive father who fought for the French across the globe in the dog days of empire.

Disappearing (2019)
A nomad with a violent past, infuriated by petty bureaucracy and the surveillance society, determines to live happily ever after, throwing off identity and leaving no trace. Things go awry: fighting for Biafran successionists, gun running in Morocco, murder in Brussels, terrorists in Nairobi and a deathly Saharan escape. Semi-autobiographical.

Sound of Hunger (2018)
The depth and breadth of this book is staggering. You would have to read a dozen others to get anywhere close to what's given you. The author wants you to know that WW1 was not won by the titanic slaughters, but by the slow starvation of the civilian populations of Germany and Austria. This is mature erudition from a man of three score and five who has produced a magnum opus to which I say, 'Bravo, Sir.' This is the kind of book I love because as soon as you finish it you start reading it again to see what you missed and enjoy it all over again.

Jack V Sturiano
This handsomely produced volume will be recognised as a distinctive and valuable contribution to the history of the First World War. Its author has been very careful in his research and shows both commendable levels of objectivity combined with real imaginative sympathy for his subjects. This is gripping stuff and should not disappoint its audiences. Four years into the publishing jamboree that is the War's centenary, here is a title that stands out and deserves its place on (and one hopes frequently off) the shelf.
Dr Richard Sheldon
A major contribution to WWI military history … excellent work … the author writes extremely well and his style is both lucid and engaging … such a scholarly source book is a welcome addition to my bookshelf … an objective, dispassionate foreigner's view of German history.
Col John Hughes-Wilson (retd.)

www.ingramcontent.com/pod-product-compliance
Lightning Source LLC
Chambersburg PA
CBHW041312110526
44591CB00022B/2886